P9-CKA-034

POETS OF SENSIBILITY
AND THE SUBLIME

Modern Critical Views

Henry Adams
Edward Albee
A. R. Ammons
Matthew Arnold
John Ashbery
W. H. Auden
Jane Austen
James Baldwin
Charles Baudelaire
Samuel Beckett
Saul Bellow
The Bible
Elizabeth Bishop
William Blake
Jorge Luis Borges
Elizabeth Bowen
Bertolt Brecht
The Brontës
Robert Browning
Anthony Burgess
George Gordon, Lord
    Byron
Thomas Carlyle
Lewis Carroll
Willa Cather
Cervantes
Geoffrey Chaucer
Kate Chopin
Samuel Taylor Coleridge
Joseph Conrad
Contemporary Poets
Hart Crane
Stephen Crane
Dante
Charles Dickens
Emily Dickinson
John Donne & the Seven-
    teenth-Century Meta-
    physical Poets
Elizabethan Dramatists
Theodore Dreiser
John Dryden
George Eliot
T. S. Eliot
Ralph Ellison
Ralph Waldo Emerson
William Faulkner
Henry Fielding
F. Scott Fitzgerald
Gustave Flaubert
E. M. Forster
Sigmund Freud
Robert Frost

Robert Graves
Graham Greene
Thomas Hardy
Nathaniel Hawthorne
William Hazlitt
Seamus Heaney
Ernest Hemingway
Geoffrey Hill
Friedrich Hölderlin
Homer
Gerard Manley Hopkins
William Dean Howells
Zora Neale Hurston
Henry James
Samuel Johnson and
    James Boswell
Ben Jonson
James Joyce
Franz Kafka
John Keats
Rudyard Kipling
D. H. Lawrence
John Le Carré
Ursula K. Le Guin
Doris Lessing
Sinclair Lewis
Robert Lowell
Norman Mailer
Bernard Malamud
Thomas Mann
Christopher Marlowe
Carson McCullers
Herman Melville
James Merrill
Arthur Miller
John Milton
Eugenio Montale
Marianne Moore
Iris Murdoch
Vladimir Nabokov
Joyce Carol Oates
Sean O'Casey
Flannery O'Connor
Eugene O'Neill
George Orwell
Cynthia Ozick
Walter Pater
Walker Percy
Harold Pinter
Plato
Edgar Allan Poe
Poets of Sensibility & the
    Sublime

Alexander Pope
Katherine Ann Porter
Ezra Pound
Pre-Raphaelite Poets
Marcel Proust
Thomas Pynchon
Arthur Rimbaud
Theodore Roethke
Philip Roth
John Ruskin
J. D. Salinger
Gershom Scholem
William Shakespeare
    (3 vols.)
    Histories & Poems
    Comedies
    Tragedies
George Bernard Shaw
Mary Wollstonecraft
    Shelley
Percy Bysshe Shelley
Edmund Spenser
Gertrude Stein
John Steinbeck
Laurence Sterne
Wallace Stevens
Tom Stoppard
Jonathan Swift
Alfred, Lord Tennyson
William Makepeace
    Thackeray
Henry David Thoreau
Leo Tolstoi
Anthony Trollope
Mark Twain
John Updike
Gore Vidal
Virgil
Robert Penn Warren
Evelyn Waugh
Eudora Welty
Nathanael West
Edith Wharton
Walt Whitman
Oscar Wilde
Tennessee Williams
William Carlos Williams
Thomas Wolfe
Virginia Woolf
William Wordsworth
Richard Wright
William Butler Yeats

These and other titles in preparation

Modern Critical Views

POETS OF SENSIBILITY
AND THE SUBLIME

Edited and with an introduction by

Harold Bloom
Sterling Professor of the Humanities
Yale University

CHELSEA HOUSE PUBLISHERS ◇ 1986
New York ◇ New Haven ◇ Philadelphia

© 1986 by Chelsea House Publishers, a division of Chelsea
House Educational Communications, Inc.
   133 Christopher Street, New York, NY 10014
   345 Whitney Avenue, New Haven, CT 06511
   5014 West Chester Pike, Edgemont, PA 19028

Introduction © 1986 by Harold Bloom. Part of this essay
originally appeared in *The Art of the Critic*   © 1985 by
Harold Bloom. Chelsea House, 1985.

Printed and bound in the United States of America

∞The paper used in this publication meets the minimum requirements of the American National Standard for Permanence
of Paper for Printed Library Materials, Z39.48–1984.

Library of Congress Cataloging-in-Publication Data
Poets of sensibility and the sublime.
   (Modern critical views)
   Bibliography: p.
   Includes index.
   Summary: A collection of critical essays on English poetry
during the Age of Sensibility and the Sublime, the half-century
between the death of Alexander Pope in 1744 and the death of
Robert Burns in 1796.
   1. English poetry—18th century—History and
criticism.   2. Sublime, The, in literature.
3. Sentimentalism in literature.   4. Emotions in
literature.   5. Romanticism—Great Britain.   [1. English
poetry—18th century—History and criticism]   I. Bloom,
Harold.   II. Series.
PR575.S77P64   1986   821'.6'09   86–8323
ISBN 0–87754–679–7 (alk. paper)

Contents

Editor's Note

This book gathers together the best criticism yet published upon the poetry of a crucial interval in British literature, the Age of Sensibility and the Sublime, which occupies roughly the half-century between the death of Alexander Pope in 1744 and the death of Robert Burns in 1796. Traditionally, this literary period has been called "Pre-Romantic," or even "Post-Enlightenment," but Northrop Frye's designation, "An Age of Sensibility," has proved useful, and I seek to add to it here only the other traditional term for a central concern of that era, "the Sublime."

The crucial poets of the Age of Sensibility and the Sublime were Edward Young, James Thomson, Thomas Gray, William Collins, Christopher Smart, William Cowper, and two remarkable "forgers," James Macpherson, who asserted he had rediscovered the Nordic Bard, "Ossian," of the third century, A.D., and the boy, Thomas Chatterton, who similarly invented "a Secular Priest of St. John's," one "Thomas Rowley," supposedly a fifteenth-century poet. To these poets and fascinating cranks, we need to add the Scottish national poet Robert Burns in his bardic aspect, and the greatest of all these figures, the young William Blake, whose first volume, *Poetical Sketches*, can be termed the apotheosis of the poetry of Sensibility and the Sublime.

This book begins with the editor's introduction, which defines the Sublime mode partly by way of the work of the late Thomas Weiskel and suggests something of the complexity of the concept of Sensibility. Two kinds of essays are then grouped, theoretical inquiries and discussions of the poets. The essays in theory, arranged chronologically in the order of their original publication, begin with Northrop Frye's brilliant attempt to name and define the literary period under discussion. Frye is followed by Geoffrey H. Hartman's discussion of the Enlightenment's program to purge the ground of romance tradition, and by Martin Price's powerful introduction to the Sublime poem as a genre.

vii

Two younger critics complete the essays in theory, with Steven Knapp analyzing Sublime personification, and Ken Frieden describing the complex introjection of genius and originality by the eighteenth century.

The essays on the poets begin with Martin Price's masterly account of the Sublime "Theatre of Mind" in Edward Young and James Thomson. Three essays are then given each to Thomas Gray and William Collins. Paul H. Fry gives a reading of Gray's odes, and Peter Sacks of the celebrated "Elegy," while Jean-Pierre Mileur sketches the sense in which Gray shared the Romantic dilemmas of Wordsworth. Collins's three major odes receive related exegeses by Thomas Weiskel (on the "Poetical Character"), Paul S. Sherwin ("To Evening"), and myself ("To Fear").

Christopher Smart's extraordinary *Jubilate Agno* is keenly analyzed by Geoffrey H. Hartman, whose emphases are akin to some of those displayed by Patricia Meyer Spacks in her study of William Cowper's mode of "heightened perception." The two grand forgers, Macpherson-Ossian and Chatterton-Rowley, are portrayed in the mythically oriented essays of John L. Greenway and Donald S. Taylor, respectively.

My essay on Blake's experiments in his boyish *Poetical Sketches* is followed by Carol McGuirk's strong reading of the songs of Burns as achieved representations of a bardic stance. With her deeply informed sense of the history of sentimentalism, McGuirk concludes this book by returning us to the introduction's Longinian intensities.

Introduction

I

Our classical definition of what it is that the literary Sublime asserts can be found in the opening sentences of Thomas Weiskel's *The Romantic Sublime:*

> The essential claim of the sublime is that man can, in feeling and in speech, transcend the human. What, if anything, lies beyond the human—God or the gods, the daemon or Nature—is matter for great disagreement. What, if anything, defines the range of the human is scarcely less sure.

A few sentences further on, Weiskel concludes his book's first paragraph with the fine apothegm: "A humanistic sublime is an oxymoron." Weiskel's power as a theorist of the Sublime is condensed in his implication that the Hebraic or Christian Sublime, the Homeric Sublime, the daemonic Sublime, the natural Sublime—all evade oxymoronic status. They may also evade precise definition, indeed may blend into one another, but none of them is so problematical and paradoxical as that seeming self-contradiction, a humanistic Sublime. Sublime poets who are crucially humanistic in some aspects—Milton, Blake, Wordsworth, Shelley, Keats, Whitman, Stevens— must forsake the Sublime when they emphasize humanistic concerns.

Weiskel, as a critic, ultimately was in the tradition of Longinus rather than of Aristotle, which is to say that Weiskel was not a formalist but was himself a Sublime critic. Transcendence of the human in speech, particularly in the utterance within a tradition of utterance that is poetry, necessarily relies upon the trope of hyperbole, the overthrowing (or overtaking, or overreaching) that is closer to simplification through intensity than it is to exaggeration. Transcendence of the human, in feeling, is a universal experience (or illusion) and itself transcends most modes of utterance. Shakespeare, Western tradition's strongest poet, is peculiarly triumphant at representing the Sublime of feeling, as in Cleopatra's magnificent lament for Antony:

1

> The crown o' th' earth doth melt. My lord!
> O, wither'd is the garland of the war,
> The soldier's pole is fall'n! Young boys and girls
> Are level now with men; the odds is gone,
> And there is nothing left remarkable
> Beneath the visiting moon.

The soldier's pole is the banner that serves as the standard of measurement, and since it is fallen, all distinction, all difference ("the odds") is gone. Cleopatra deftly cries out that the Sublime is gone with her Antony, while marvelously speaking in sublime accents, which tells us that she is all of the Sublime that is left. What determines the presence or absence of the Sublime is the standard of measurement, consisting initially in the Platonic Ideas, but later honed down by Plato to a pragmatic knowledge able to answer the questions: more? equal to? less than? I am following Hannah Arendt's Heideggerian reading of *The Republic* in her essay on authority in *Between Past and Future*. Cleopatra sublimely elegizes the passing of the Sublime, because everything that remains is less than the lost Antony. What Cleopatra knows is that the Sublime is agonistic, a knowledge crucial to theorists of the Sublime from Longinus to Weiskel.

II

Criticism, which found three separate beginnings in Aristophanes, Plato, and Aristotle, emerges fully as an art only with the writer whom tradition has chosen to call "Longinus." We know that the work usually called "Longinus on the Sublime" was composed no later than the third century of the Common Era, but it had no influence until the sixteenth century, when the first modern edition appeared. Boileau translated it into French in 1674, and from then until the High Romantic period of the early nineteenth century, no other work of ancient criticism had anything like its intellectual effect and its literary popularity. Indeed the European literary period that goes from the last quarter of the seventeenth century all through the eighteenth century and on into the first quarter of the nineteenth might well be called "the Age of the Sublime," for the Sublime may be the category that most unites the Enlightenment and Romanticism. But what then was and is "the Sublime"?

To Alexander Pope, Longinus was "himself the great sublime he draws," a judgment confirmed by the historian Gibbon and by many after him. Emerson spoke of "the reader's Sublime," another emphasis upon the Sublime not so much as an affective as opposed to a cognitive phenomenon, but rather as an experience in which cognitive limits appear to be surpassed. Strictly speaking, the Sublime, or *hypsos*, of the treatise's title should be translated as "greatness" or "the height of heights" or even "great writing" or, as I would say, "strong poetry." The English word "sublime," however inappropriate for *hypsos*, is now traditional, and can even be rendered useful if approached properly, under the guidance of Cohn and Miles in their remarkable article "The Sublime: In Alchemy, Aesthetics and Psychoanalysis" (*Modern Philology*, February 1977).

> . . . the modern meanings of *sublime* developed . . . from its more spiritual and metaphysical sense, as used in the seventeenth century. From the alchemical meanings of purification and from the idea, again from alchemy, of elevation, came religious and secular meanings of purity and loftiness . . . .
>
> Beyond the religious uses of the word and the general seventeenth century meaning of the lofty and the purified, we find in this period the first relation between *sublime* and the art of rhetoric: the expression of lofty ideas in an elevated manner. The *OED* cites the first rhetorical use of the word in 1586, the point at which *sublime* enters the realm of aesthetics in English. By the eighteenth century the uses of *sublime* in aesthetics revealed the same confusion that the theological applications had shown in the seventeenth. While the *sublime* resided first in the style in which elevated ideas were expressed, it eventually came to mean the elevated ideas themselves. The shift accomplished, it was not difficult to find the source of such loftiness not only in art but in nature. The most important alteration of meaning, however, occurs when the *sublime* is used by English critics in the Longinian sense to describe not the eternal cause of a particular aesthetic state in the beholder, but that state itself; the sublime has moved from the object to the subject.

That shift in meaning indeed is Longinian, but in a complex sense that seeks to overcome what Wallace Stevens termed "the dumbfoundering abyss" between subject and object. *Contra* W. K. Wimsatt, who consistently condemns Longinus for critical subjectivity, it can be affirmed of Longinus that he inaugurates the true agon of criticism with philosophy, of poetry with Plato and even with Aristotle. Aristotle, like all his descendants down to Wimsatt, wishes to convince himself that a poem possesses a structure intrinsic to it. Longinus knows better; he had the implicit realization, still

shocking to many scholars, that the true poem is the reader's mind, or as
Emerson once remarked, that the student had to take herself or himself for
text and then had to regard all received texts as commentaries upon the self.
I do not find it useful, though, to regard Longinus (or Emerson) as an
antiformalist or affectivist; more simply I would say that Longinus was the
very first *experiential* critic, the first critic to bring forward his own pathos
or personality. There is after all no truth of the poem apart from the actual
experience of reading it, and the reader's Sublime is therefore the only pragmatic Sublime, the only literary difference that can make a difference.

Longinus rightly begins by insisting that *hypsos* is an attribute only of
the very greatest writers, whether of poetry or prose. Paul Fry, certainly his
most sympathetic contemporary champion, finds this emphasis upon greatness the one weakness of Longinus, because "it authorizes the Superman at
certain moments." Yes, but the Longinian (or Nietzschean) Superman is
precisely the person without a superego, or rather that aesthetic aspect of a
person that can escape the sadistic sway of the superego. Freud's "above-I,"
or superego, demands that the ego surrender its aggressivity, and then goes
on tormenting the hapless ego even more for every sacrifice of aggressivity.
But Longinus, like the Greek poets, knows only the agon, which is the
aesthetic transformation of aggressivity. His call to greatness truly is a denial
of the superego, and so does call us to what Blake later was to term Intellectual
Warfare. The dismissal of the superego is at one with the dismissal of pity
and fear, affects that structure reading for Aristotle but that Longinus rightly
dismisses as being antithetical to sublimity or aesthetic greatness, the proper
transport or ecstasy of reading.

Homer, rather than Plato, is the hero of *On the Sublime*, the Homer of
the *Iliad*, which Longinus praises as being always on the heights of the bard's
power. Homer's noble mind echoes in the *Iliad*, and reading the poem,
Longinus comes to be filled with joy and pride, until he believes he has
created what he has heard, which is precisely what Plato most deprecated.
But this may be the point where Longinus manifests the first "modern" sort
of critical anxiety of influence, in regard to Plato. Aristotle's anxiety about
Plato, like that of Euripides towards Aeschylus, is authentic enough, but
neither relationship seems as central as the shadowing effect of Plato upon
Longinus or, say, that of Dante upon Petrarch in another time. As Paul Fry
accurately notes, Longinus has a far less impoverished view of literary allusion
than most scholars now enjoy. Allusion, Longinus says, causes a lustre to
bloom upon our words, as our minds are troped or colored by the power of
our precursors' language. Fry observes that Longinus "cannot praise his

literary ancestor Plato without some word of qualification," because the great style and the agonistic concepts of Plato pervade *On the Sublime.*

Is psychic ambivalence then not the center of the Longinian Sublime, and perhaps of every Romantic theory of criticism following it? The contemporary rhetorical school headed by Jacques Derrida and the late Paul de Man would argue otherwise, an argument that has been elaborated by Neil Hertz in the subtlest essay yet published upon Longinus. Hertz (in *The End of the Line*) associates Longinus with the modern critic Walter Benjamin and deconstructs the method of both critics as

> the more or less violent fragmentation of literary bodies into "quotations," in the interests of building up a discourse of one's own, a discourse which, in its turn, directs attention to passages that come to serve as emblems of the critic's most acute, least nostalgic sense of what he is about.

To Hertz, this figurative movement of disintegration and subsequent reconstitution is essentially a rhetorical problematic masking itself as psychic ambivalence or as cultural history. But the ambivalence towards Plato in Longinus seems clear, and is grounded in literary inheritance rather than in literary language alone. Longinus understood implicitly what Nietzsche taught us to know explicitly, which is the agonistic nature of the literary experience, and so of all literary interpretation also. To achieve the readers' Sublime is to gain power over a text through interpretation, and to know greatness the reader needs to confront greatness. Longinus prophesied all the great personalist critics, even the neoclassical Dr. Samuel Johnson, even the Christian Romantic Coleridge, but more particularly Longinus fathered the Oedipal line of critics that includes Hazlitt, Carlyle, Ruskin, Emerson, Pater, Oscar Wilde, and Kenneth Burke, as well as certain contemporary figures who emphasize Nietzschean and Freudian approaches to interpretation. It is from Longinus that we continue to learn a vision in which the Sublime and the agonistic merge into one.

III

Angus Fletcher, who seems to me Weiskel's authentic precursor in my own generation of critics, emphasized in his seminal book *Allegory* (1964) that "the sublime appears to provide a cosmology for the poet." Taking as his own the Longinian desire to free us from the slavery of pleasure, or of a mere dullness, Fletcher followed Shelley's Longinian *Defence of Poetry* in emphasizing that the function of the Sublime was to so work, by "difficult ornament" and by heightened ambivalences, as to make us share in its agon, its ceaseless struggle against the superficial. Weiskel's *The Romantic Sublime*, like Fletcher's *Allegory*, shares the deep design upon us of Longinus and Shelley. We are to be persuaded to yield up easier pleasures for more difficult pleasures, or as Weiskel phrases this, we are to move from the egotistical Sublime to the negative Sublime:

> The egotistical sublime culminates in an intense ambivalence. Memory and desire practice a cheat: They lead us to a bosom all right, but the cost of the regression and the solitude or desertion implicit in its object have made that object a hated thing. In terms of what Freud called the family romance, identity is regarded with all the unresolved ambivalence of an Oedipal crisis in which there is, strangely, no symbolic father to come to the rescue. Yet we cannot fail to note that the structure of the egotistical sublime ends precisely at the point of ambivalence in which we found the beginnings of the negative sublime.

All theorists of the Sublime confront certain masterpieces of emotional ambivalence: the Oedipal struggle, the taboo, transference are among them. Equal and opposed feelings, antithetical forces who are enemy brothers or sisters, appear to be the emotive basis for the Sublime. Yet ambivalence, increased to excess, becomes irony, which destroys the Sublime. Acutely aware of this danger, Weiskel chose to defend against it through the example of Wallace Stevens, who in one of his aspects or perpetual phases is a last strong version of the egotistical Sublime of Wordsworth and of Walt Whitman. As a regressive structure, Stevens's Sublime refuses to grow up, but what does growing up mean in and for a poem anyway, except the loss of power? Weiskel as a Sublime critic rather than a mere moralist, made his own allegiance movingly clear:

> Poets, however, are up to such risks, which in any case they have no choice about. It is not in the assumption of spiritual risks that the egotistical romantic pays for the hybris of his sublimation. Nothing is got for nothing. The cost is there, and it is paid in the text, not in extrinsic circumstance.

Neil Hertz, working in the deconstructive mode of Paul de Man's conceptual rhetoric and influenced also by French feminist revisions of Freud, both credited Weiskel for dwelling intensely on the anxieties of the pre-Oedipal or maternal Sublime, and yet criticized him for "the relief he seemed to have experienced as an interpreter in at last bringing it all home to the Father." Hertz, I think, chooses to forget that the Sublime takes place *between* origin and aim or end, and that the only Western trope that avoids both origin and end is the trope of the Father, which is only to say that we do not speak of "Father Nature." Weiskel indeed is closer to Freud than Lacan or Derrida are, because he does not read his Freud through Heidegger.

Throughout *The Romantic Sublime*, Weiskel works toward a difficult kind of literary criticism, at once moral or primary, and de-idealizing or antithetical. The kind may not be possible to attain; certainly I, for one, have failed to achieve it. In Wordsworth's criticism, it would reconcile Matthew Arnold and A. C. Bradley, M. H. Abrams and Geoffrey H. Hartman. Perhaps Wordsworth as poet of nature *and* as poet of the Sublime can accommodate such divergent critics, but they necessarily must fail to accommodate one another. But Weiskel's attempt is itself Sublime; it involves yielding up easier pleasures for more severe pleasures, and perhaps it will mark always one of the limits of twentieth-century criticism of the High Romantic poets. Immensely moved as I am by all of Weiskel's study, I am most touched to meditation by his bold effort to define the Wordsworthian imagination:

> What then is this "awful Power" which Wordsworth names "Imagination"? In the late version [of *The Prelude*], Woidsworth will tell us that the power is "so called / Through sad incompetence of human speech" (6.592–93), but the name is of course entirely right, for the power of sight does rise in intensity from memory through salience to the occlusion of the visible. The Imagination may be structurally defined as a power of resistance to the Word, and in this sense it coincides exactly with the psychological necessity of originality. But a structural definition merely locates an experience; as an experience or moment the Imagination is an extreme consciousness of self mounting in dialectical recoil from the extinguishing of the self which an imminent identification with the symbolic order enjoins. Hence the Imagination rises "Like an unfather'd vapour": it is at once the ego's need and its attempt to be *unfathered*, to originate itself and thereby refuse acknowledgment to a superior power. The Imagination is not an evasion of the oedipus complex but a rejection of it. From a certain perspective (such perspective, for example, as is implied by the history of poetic influence) that rejection is purely illusory, a fiction. To reject the oedipus complex is not, after all, to dispel

it. But the fiction is a necessary and saving one; it founds the self and secures the possibility—the chance for a self-conviction—of originality. And so Wordsworth can turn to his "conscious soul" (1850) and say, "I recognize thy glory."

A necessary and saving fiction is both a Stevensian trope, and a return to Weiskel's own yearning to establish a structure and a psychology for transcendence. The hope, as in Emerson and in Stevens, is a very American modification of the European Protestant ethos, and Weiskel takes his rightful place in that tradition, both choosing and being chosen by it.

IV

The sentimental, neither as a Victorian exaltation of middle-class morality nor as a modern celebration of proletarian, natural simplicity, is a crucial mode of thought and feeling in the middle and later eighteenth century. Martin Price, one of its foremost expositors, calls it: "a vehement, often defiant assertion of the value of man's feelings." This self-conscious, overtly dramatic manifestation, sincere despite its theatrical overtones, was taken as the demonstration of a receptive spirit, compassionate and humane, and then was named as "Sensibility." Its great exemplar was Rousseau, and its principal British representative was the uncanny novelist Laurence Sterne.

In a complex fusion, the passion for the Sublime mode, agonistic and transcendental, was able to reconcile itself with the milder responsiveness of Sensibility. This fusion informs the poets Young, Thomson, Gray, Collins, Smart, and Cowper, and appears also in the archaic impostures of Macpherson as Ossian and Chatterton as Rowley. In Robert Burns and the early Blake, the unstable union of Sensibility and the Sublime helped stimulate the only poets of the eighteenth century who could rival Dryden and Pope. The aura of the poets of Sensibility and the Sublime has pervaded Anglo-American poetry ever since, partly through its Romantic descendants, and partly because of a curious modernity that we apprehend in the perilous balance and frequently catastrophic fates of these doom-eager poets. William Cowper's magnificent lyric "The Castaway" ends with the perfect motto for the poetry of Sensibility and the Sublime, a borderline poetry that fears, yet courts madness:

> No voice divine the storm allayed,
> No light propitious shone,

When, snatched from all effectual aid,
　　We perished, each alone:
But I beneath a rougher sea,
　　And whelmed in deeper gulfs than he.

NORTHROP FRYE

Towards Defining an Age of Sensibility

The period of English literature which covers roughly the second half of the eighteenth century is one which has always suffered from not having a clear historical or functional label applied to it. I call it here the age of sensibility, which is not intended to be anything but a label. This period has the "Augustan" age on one side of it and the "Romantic" movement on the other, and it is usually approached transitionally, as a period of reaction against Pope and anticipation of Wordsworth. The chaos that results from treating this period, or any other, in terms of reaction has been well described by Professor Crane in a recent article in the *University of Toronto Quarterly*. What we do is to set up, as the logical expression of Augustanism, some impossibly pedantic view of following rules and repressing feelings, which nobody could ever have held, and then treat any symptom of freedom or emotion as a departure from this. Our students are thus graduated with a vague notion that the age of sensibility was the time when poetry moved from a reptilian Classicism, all cold and dry reason, to a mammalian Romanticism, all warm and wet feeling.

As for the term "pre-romantic," that, as a term for the age itself, has the peculiar demerit of committing us to anachronism before we start, and imposing a false teleology on everything we study. Not only did the "pre-romantics" not know that the Romantic movement was going to succeed them, but there has probably never been a case on record of a poet's having regarded a later poet's work as the fulfillment of his own. However, I do not care about terminology, only about appreciation for an extraordinarily

From *Fables of Identity*. © 1963 by Harcourt Brace Jovanovich, Inc.

interesting period of English literature, and the first stage in renewing that appreciation seems to me the gaining of a clear sense of what it is in itself.

Some languages use verb-tenses to express, not time, but the difference between completed and continuous action. And in the history of literature we become aware, not only of periods, but of a recurrent opposition of two views of literature. These two views are the Aristotelian and Longinian, the aesthetic and the psychological, the view of literature as a product and the view of literature as a process. In our day we have acquired a good deal of respect for literature as process, notably in prose fiction. The stream of consciousness gets careful treatment in our criticism, and when we compare Arnold Bennett and Virginia Woolf on the subject of Mrs. Brown we generally take the side of Virginia Woolf. So it seems that our age ought to feel a close kinship with the prose fiction of the age of sensibility, when the sense of literature as process was brought to a peculiarly exquisite perfection by Sterne, and in lesser degree by Richardson and Boswell.

All the great story-tellers, including the Augustan ones, have a strong sense of literature as a finished product. The suspense is thrown forward until it reaches the end, and is based on our confidence that the author knows what is coming next. A story-teller does not break his illusion by talking to the reader as Fielding does, because we know from the start that we are listening to Fielding telling a story—that is, Johnson's arguments about illusion in drama apply equally well to prose fiction of Fielding's kind. But when we turn to *Tristram Shandy* we not only read the book but watch the author at work writing it: at any moment the house of Walter Shandy may vanish and be replaced by the author's study. This does break the illusion, or would if there were any illusion to break, but here we are not being led into a story, but into the process of writing a story: we wonder, not what is coming next, but what the author will think of next.

Sterne is, of course, an unusually pure example of a process-writer, but even in Richardson we find many of the same characteristics. Johnson's well-known remark that if you read Richardson for the story you would hang yourself indicates that Richardson is not interested in a plot with a quick-march rhythm. Richardson does not throw the suspense forward, but keeps the emotion at a continuous present. Readers of *Pamela* have become so fascinated by watching the sheets of Pamela's manuscript spawning and secreting all over her master's house, even into the recesses of her clothes, as she fends off assault with one hand and writes about it with the other, that they sometimes overlook the reason for an apparently clumsy device. The reason is, of course, to give the impression of literature as process, as created on the spot out of the events it describes. And in the very beginning of *Boswell in London* we can see the boy of twenty-one already practising the art of writing as a continuous process from experience. When he writes of his adventures with Louisa he may be writing several days after the event, but he does not use his later knowledge.

In poetry the sense of literature as a finished product normally expresses itself in some kind of regularly recurring metre, the general pattern of which is established as soon as possible. In listening to Pope's couplets we have a sense of continually fulfilled expectation which is the opposite of obviousness: a sense that eighteenth-century music also often gives us. Such a technique demands a clear statement of what sound-patterns we may expect. We hear at once the full ring of the rhyming couplet, and all other sound-patterns are kept to a minimum. In such a line as:

And strains from hard-bound brains eight lines a year,

the extra assonance is a deliberate discord, expressing the difficulties of constipated genius. Similarly with the alliteration in:

Great Cibber's brazen, brainless brothers stand,

and the fact that these are deliberate discords used for parody indicates that they are normally not present. Johnson's disapproval of such devices in serious contexts is written all over the *Lives of the Poets*.

When we turn from Pope to the age of sensibility, we get something of the same kind of shock that we get when we turn from Tennyson or Matthew Arnold to Hopkins. Our ears are assaulted by unpredictable assonances, alliterations, interrhymings and echolalia:

Mie love ys dedde,
Gon to hys death-bedde

. . . .

With brede ethereal wove,
O'erhang his wavy bed

. . . .

The couthy cracks begin when supper's o'er,
The cheering bicker gars them glibly gash

. . . .

But a pebble of the brook
    Warbled out these metres meet.

In many of the best-known poems of the period, in Smart's *Song to David*, in Chatterton's elegies, in Burns's songs and Blake's lyrics, even in some of the Wesley hymns, we find a delight in refrain for refrain's sake. Sometimes, naturally, we can see the appropriate literary influences helping to shape the form, such as the incremental repetition of the ballad, or Old Norse alliteration in "The Fatal Sisters." And whatever may be thought of the poetic value of the Ossianic poems, most estimates of that value parrot Wordsworth, and Wordsworth's criticisms of Ossian's imagery are quite beside the point. The vague generalized imagery of Ossian, like the mysterious resonant names and the fixed epithets, are part of a deliberate and well unified scheme. *Fingal* and *Temora* are long poems for the same reason that *Clarissa* is a long novel: not because there is a complicated story to be told, as in *Tom Jones* or an epic of Southey, but because the emotion is being maintained at a continuous present by various devices of repetition.

The reason for these intensified sound-patterns is, once again, an interest in the poetic process as distinct from the product. In the composing of poetry, where rhyme is as important as reason, there is a primary stage in which words are linked by sound rather than sense. From the point of view of sense this stage is merely free or uncontrolled association, and in the way it operates it is very like the dream. Again like the dream, it has to meet a censor-principle, and shape itself into intelligible patterns. Where the emphasis is on the communicated product, the qualities of consciousness take the lead: a regular metre, clarity of syntax, epigram and wit, repetition of sense in antithesis and balance rather than of sound. Swift speaks with admiration of Pope's ability to get more "sense" into one couplet than he can into six: concentration of sense for him is clearly a major criterion of poetry. Where the emphasis is on the original process, the qualities of subconscious association take the lead, and the poetry becomes hypnotically repetitive, oracular, incantatory, dreamlike and in the original sense of the word charming. The response to it includes a subconscious factor, the surrendering to a spell. In Ossian, who carries this tendency further than anyone else, the aim is not concentration of sense but diffusion of sense, hence Johnson's remark that anybody could write like Ossian if he would abandon his mind to it. Literature as product may take a lyrical form, as it does in the sublime ode about which Professor Maclean has written so well, but it is also the conception of literature that makes the longer continuous poem possible. Literature as process, being based on an irregular and unpredictable coincidence of sound-patterns, tends to seek the brief or even the fragmentary utterance, in other words to centre itself on the lyric, which accounts for the feeling of a sudden emergence of a lyrical impulse in the age of sensibility.

The "pre-romantic" approach to his period sees it as developing a conception of the creative imagination, which became the basis of Romanticism. This is true, but the Romantics tended to see the poem as the *product* of the creative imagination, thus reverting in at least one respect to the Augustan attitude. For the Augustan, art is posterior to nature because nature is the art of God; for the Romantic, art is prior to nature because God is an artist; one deals in physical and the other in biological analogies, as Professor Abrams' *Mirror and the Lamp* has shown. But for the Romantic poet the poem is still an artefact: in Coleridge's terms, a secondary or productive imagination has been imposed on a primary imaginative process. So, different as it is from Augustan poetry, Romantic poetry is like it in being a conservative rhetoric, and in being founded on relatively regular metrical schemes. Poe's rejection of the continuous poem does not express anything very central in Romanticism itself, as nearly every major Romantic poet composed poems of considerable, sometimes immense, length. Poe's theory is closer to the practice of the age of sensibility before him and the *symbolistes* after him.

In the age of sensibility most of the long poems, of course, simply carry on with standard continuous metres, or exploit the greater degree of intensified recurrent sound afforded by stanzaic forms, notably the Spenserian. But sometimes the peculiar problems of making associative poetry continuous were faced in a more experimental way, experiments largely ignored by the Romantics. Oracular poetry in a long form often tends to become a series of utterances, irregular in rhythm but strongly marked off one from the other. We notice in Whitman, for instance, that the end of every line has a strong pause—for when the rhythm is variable there is no point in a run-on line. Sometimes this oracular rhythm takes on at least a typographical resemblance to prose, as it does in Rimbaud's *Saison en Enfer*, or, more frequently, to a discontinuous blend of prose and verse in which the sentence, the paragraph and the line are much the same unit. The chief literary influence for this rhythm has always been the translated Bible, which took on a new impetus in the age of sensibility; and if we study carefully the rhythm of Ossian, of Smart's *Jubilate Agno* and of the Blake Prophecies, we can see three very different but equally logical developments of the semi-Biblical rhythm.

Where there is a strong sense of literature as aesthetic product, there is also a sense of its detachment from the spectator. Aristotle's theory of catharsis describes how this works for tragedy: pity and fear are detached from the beholder by being directed towards objects. Where there is a sense of literature as process, pity and fear become states of mind without objects, moods which are common to the work of art and the reader, and which bind them together psychologically instead of separating them aesthetically.

Fear without an object, as a condition of mind prior to being afraid *of* anything, is called *Angst* or anxiety, a somewhat narrow term for what may be almost anything between pleasure and pain. In the general area of pleasure comes the eighteenth-century conception of the sublime, where qualities of austerity, gloom, grandeur, melancholy or even menace are a source of romantic or penseroso feelings. The appeal of Ossian to his time on this basis needs no comment. From here we move through the graveyard poets, the Gothic-horror novelists and the writers of tragic ballads to such *fleurs du mal* as Cowper's "Castaway" and Blake's Golden Chapel poem in the Rossetti MS.

Pity without an object has never to my knowledge been given a name, but it expresses itself as an imaginative animism, or treating everything in nature as though it had human feelings or qualities. At one end of its range is the apocalyptic exultation of all nature bursting into human life that we have in Smart's *Song to David* and the ninth Night of *The Four Zoas*. Next comes an imaginative sympathy with the kind of folklore that peoples the countryside with elemental spirits, such as we have in Collins, Fergusson, Burns and the Wartons. Next we have the curiously intense awareness of the animal world which (except for some poems of D. H. Lawrence) is unrivalled in this period, and is expressed in some of its best realized writing: in Burns's "To a Mouse," in Cowper's exquisite snail poem, in Smart's superb lines on his cat Jeoffry, in the famous starling and ass episodes in Sterne, in the opening of Blake's "Auguries of Innocence." Finally comes the sense of sympathy with man himself, the sense that no one can afford to be indifferent to the fate of anyone else, which underlies the protests against slavery and misery in Cowper, in Crabbe and in Blake's *Song of Experience*.

This concentration on the primitive process of writing is projected in two directions, into nature and into history. The appropriate natural setting for much of the poetry of sensibility is nature at one of the two poles of process, creation and decay. The poet is attracted by the ruinous and the mephitic, or by the primeval and "unspoiled"—a picturesque subtly but perceptibly different from the Romantic picturesque. The projection into history assumes that the psychological progress of the poet from lyrical through epic to dramatic presentations, discussed by Stephen at the end of Joyce's *Portrait*, must be the historical progress of literature as well. Even as late as the preface to Victor Hugo's *Cromwell* this assumption persists. The Ossian and Rowley poems are not simple hoaxes: they are pseudepigrapha, like the Book of Enoch, and like it they take what is psychologically primitive, the oracular process of composition, and project it as something historically primitive.

The poetry of process is oracular, and the medium of the oracle is often in an ecstatic or trance-like state: autonomous voices seem to speak through him, and as he is concerned to utter rather than to address, he is turned away from his listener, so to speak, in a state of rapt self-communion. The free association of words, in which sound is prior to sense, is often a literary way of representing insanity. In Rimbaud's terrifyingly accurate phrase, poetry of the associative or oracular type requires a "dérèglement de tous les sens." Hence the qualities that make a man an oracular poet are often the qualities that work against, and sometimes destroy, his social personality. Far more than the time of Rimbaud and Verlaine is this period of literature, a period of the *poéte maudit*. The list of poets over whom the shadows of mental breakdown fell is far too long to be coincidence. The much publicized death of Chatterton is certainly one of the personal tragedies of the age, but an easier one to take than the kind of agony which is expressed with an almost definitive poignancy by Smart in *Jubilate Ango*:

> For in my nature I quested for beauty, but God, God, hath sent
> me to sea for pearls.

It is characteristic of the age of sensibility that this personal or biographical aspect of it should be so closely connected with its central technical feature. The basis of poetic language is the metaphor, and the metaphor, in its radical form, is a statement of identity: "this is that." In all our ordinary experience the metaphor is non-literal: nobody but a savage or a lunatic can take metaphor literally. For Classical or Augustan critics the metaphor is a condensed simile: its real or common-sense basis is likeness, not identity, and when it obliterates the sense of likeness it becomes barbaric. In Johnson's strictures on the music and water metaphor of Gray's "Bard" we can see what intellectual abysses, for him, would open up if metaphors ever passed beyond the stage of resemblance. For the Romantic critic, the identification in the metaphor is ideal: two images are identified within the mind of the creating poet.

But what metaphor is conceived as part of an oracular and half-ecstatic process, there is a direct identification in which the poet himself is involved. To use another phrase of Rimbaud's, the poet feels not "je pense," but "on me pense." In the age of sensibility some of the identifications involving the poet seem manic, like Blake's with Druidic bards or Smart's with Hebrew prophets, or depressive, like Cowper's with a scapegoat figure, a stricken deer or castaway, or merely bizarre, like Macpherson's with Ossian or Chatterton's with Rowley. But it is in this psychological self-identification that the central "primitive" quality of this age really emerges. In Collins's "Ode on the Poetical Character," in Smart's *Jubilate Agno*, and in Blake's *Four Zoas*, it attains its greatest intensity and completeness.

In these three poems, especially the last two, God, the poet's soul and nature are brought into a white-hot fusion of identity, an imaginative fiery furnace in which the reader may, if he chooses, make a fourth. All three poems are of the greatest complexity, yet the emotion on which they are founded is of a simplicity and directness that English literature has rarely attained again. With the 1800 edition of *Lyrical Ballads*, secondary imagination and recollection in tranquility took over English poetry and dominated it until the end of the nineteenth century. The primitivism of Blake and Smart revived in France with Rimbaud and Gérard de Nerval, but even this development had become conservative by the time its influence reached England, and only in a few poems of Dylan Thomas, and those perhaps not his best, does the older tradition revive. But contemporary poetry is still deeply concerned with the problems and techniques of the age of sensibility, and while the latter's resemblance to our time is not a merit in it, it is a logical enough reason for re-examining it with fresh eyes.

GEOFFREY H. HARTMAN

False Themes and Gentle Minds

The writers of the Enlightenment want fiction and reason to kiss. They are inexhaustible on the subject. "Buskin'd bards henceforth shall wisely rage," Thomas Tickell announces, foreseeing a new Augustan age. "The radian æra dawns," writes Akenside, when the long separation of imagination and science shall be overcome, and wisdom shall once more "Imbrace the smiling family of arts." The anonymous French author of *Poésies philosophiques* (1758) admonishes the new school of poets to invent "believable marvels": "Sans marcher appuyé du mensonge et des fables / Venez nous étaler des merveilles croïables." Another explains more curiously his desire for chaster fictions. "Women of today," he writes, "are so sated with fine phrases that there is no way of succeeding with them except to appeal to their reason." The enthusiasm for reason—and reasoning—is so great that Crébillon fils, in *Le Sopha* (1740), a degraded and libertine version of the metamorphosis myth, puts his hero-narrator in jeopardy of having his head cut off should he be tempted to *reflect upon* rather than simply *tell* his story. "By my faith," says the Sultan, "I swear I shall kill the next man who dares to reflect in my presence." Even with this threat, the novel ends on a defeated note. How difficult it is to tell a good, rousing story in an Age of Reason. "Ah Grandmother," sighs the Sultan, thinking of Sheherezade, "that's not the way you used to tell stories!"

It does not prove easy to give up the sophisticated superstitions by which literature had always amused, shocked, or instructed. Writers become intensely conscious of the primitive nature of these beliefs but also ingenious in accommodating them to rationality. In William Collins's *Ode on the Popular*

From *Beyond Formalism*. © 1970 by Yale University. Yale University Press, 1970.

Superstitions of the Highlands of Scotland, the problem is honestly and movingly set forth. Collins feels that he must forbear those great local myths which now live only in the far north and which he encourages his friend Home to keep up:

> Nor need'st thou blush, that such false themes engage
> Thy gentle mind, of fairer stores possest;
> For not alone they touch the village breast,
> But fill'd in elder time th'historic page.
> There SHAKESPEARE'S self, with ev'ry garland crown'd,
> In musing hour, his wayward sisters found,
> And with their terrors drest the magic scene.

This dichotomy of "gentle mind" and "false themes" (where "false themes" means the materials of romance, popular or classical in origin) remains the starting point of the great majority of writers between the late Renaissance and Romanticism.

The story I wish to tell is how that dichotomy is faced and perhaps overcome. Many, of course, accepted the alienation of the literary mind from the "exploded beings" (the phase is Dr. Johnson's) of folklore or mythology. They knew too well that great literature was magic and that reason could only flee from it, as from an enchanter. But others dared to think that literature might become a rational enchantment. They toyed with forbidden fire (with the "Eastern Tale", the Gothic romance, the Sublime Ode) and called up the ghosts they wished to subdue. In this they followed the example of the great poets of the Renaissance, who had at once revived and purified romance tradition. I begin, therefore, with Milton, the last about whom Collins could have said, as of Tasso-his "undoubting mind / Believed the magic wonders which he sung."

Milton is already belated; and it is his problematic rather than naive relation to Romance which makes him significant. He somehow transcends the very dichotomy of "gentle mind" and "false theme" which appears early in his poetry. Thus he dismisses as a false surmise his vision of nature spirits lamenting for Lycidas without renouncing that machinery of spirits, that multiplication of persons and gods, which is the clearest feature of romantic art—romantic in the largest sense of the word. He accepts a principle of plenitude which belongs to the Romance imagination rather than to an epoch in Lovejoyean history and which sets all action within a conspiracy of spirits. The world is made new or strange by opening into another world: an overhead—or underground—of mediations, of direct, picturable relations between spirit-persons. In such a world the human actor is only one kind of being, and his mind—or whatever else makes him the king-piece—is the target of a host of contrary intelligences.

Keats, thinking about the Enlightenment (the "grand march of intellect"), said that in Milton's day Englishmen were only just emancipated from superstition. It is true: Milton's consciousness is always ambushed by pagan or Christian or poetical myths. He is important for Collins and the Romantics because he shows the enlightened mind still emerging, and even constructing itself, out of its involvement with Romance. He marks the beginning of modern Romanticism, of a romantic struggle with Romance; and it is as a stage in the growth of the English poetic mind that I now want to present his poetry's earliest magic, the "Allegro"-"Penseroso" sequence.

You know how each poem opens, with a ritual exordium banning the undesired mood. In the first poem melancholy is dismissed; the second poem, like a recantation, hails melancholy and banishes joy. Milton, it has been argued, wished merely to picture the right king of joy and a purified melancholy. Yet the dramatic aspect of each poem is the stylistic breach as the speaker turns from anathema to invitation. It is like going from an older world creaking with morality plays and heavy emblems to a brave new world in which man is the master of his mood and his spirit machinery correspondingly fluent. The poet seems as interested in purifying an older style as in purging a humor. The poems are Milton's notes toward a gentler fiction.

If mythology old-style showed the mind at the mercy of humors or stars or heavy abstractions, these personifications of easy virtue, which constitute a mythology new-style, reflect a freer attitude of the mind toward the fictions it entertains. The change from

> Hence loathed Melancholy
> > Of *Cerberus*, and blackest midnight born,
> In *Stygian* Cave forlorn
> > 'Mongst horrid shapes, and shrieks, and sights unholy

to

> > Come pensive Nun, devout and pure,
> > Sober, stedfast, and demure

recapitulates the entire Renaissance movement toward a *dolce stil nuovo*. It recalls the great change in men's attitudes toward the ancient superstitions, which in the century preceding Milton allowed that freer use of Romance associated with (among others) Ariosto and Spenser.

In Milton's double feature it is not the character contrast of the two personae (melancholy and mirth) which is important, but this newer and emancipated kind of myth-making. Milton uses no less than three sorts of mythical persons: established divinities (Venus, Mab, Aurora); personified abstractions (Melancholy, Tragedy, Mirth); and spirits of place (the "Mountain Nymph, sweet Liberty"). He does not encourage us to discriminate these kindred spirits; in fact, by mixing them with a fine promiscuity, he produces the sense of a middle region in which everything is numinous or semidivine. This in no respect demythologizes his poetry but suggests that man lives in easy rather than fearful, and daily rather than extraordinary, intercourse with an ambient spiritworld. He walks in a feather-dense atmosphere among "the unseen Genius of the Wood," strange music, "dewey-feathered sleep," and the phantasms of his own imagination. It is an atmosphere that works against sharp moral or ontological distinctions; when the merry man is said to view

> Such sights as youthfull Poets dream
> On Summer eeves by haunted stream

there is delicate ambiguity, because the sights could be public performances ("mask, and antique Pageantry"), dream thoughts, or a real vision. And when Shakespeare is called "fancy's child," the cliché has power, in this context, to suggest once more an intermingling of gods and men—that numinous half-essence which bathes every feature of these landscapes.

What is the reason for this promiscuous and light-hearted divinization? Milton has created a new and sweeter style, but also one that is peculiarly English. Most of his early poetry moves programmatically beyond the erudite pastoralism of the Italians and toward the fresher pastures of an English lyricism. Yet in "L'Allegro" and "Il Penseroso" Milton does more than state his program. He seems to have found the right kind of spirit, or spirits, for English landscape. He has taken the exotic machinery of the classical gods and the ponderous abstractions of moral allegory and treated them all as, basically, local spirits. In Britain they must be temperate like the British, so that extremes of mirth and melancholy, and even of divinity itself, are exorcized. The genius loci suits the religio loci: Milton's romantic machinery is grounded in the reasonableness of a specific national temperament.

That this reasonableness, this pride in a via media, may be a national myth does not concern us: although it will concern Blake, who rejects Milton's compromise and engages on a radical confrontation of the poetic genius with the English genius. Milton himself takes the issue onto a higher level in *Paradise Lost*, where the old and sublimer mode of myth-making is reasserted. From that post-bellum height, "L'Allegro" and "Il Penseroso" appear like exercises in the minor mode of pastoral romance. Even as only that—as an accommodation of Romance to the English mind—they remain a significant attempt to have this kind of fiction survive an increasingly enlightened climate.

That "L'Allegro" and "Il Penseroso" are a special type of romance appears as soon as we go from the nature of the personifications to that of the persona or presiding consciousness. Who is the speaker here if not a magus, dismissing some spirits and invoking others? If we do not have an actual romance, at least we have a romancer: the poems are thoroughly ritualistic, with their exordium, invocation, and ceremonial tone. But the imperatives ("Tow'red Cities please us then," "There let *Hymen* oft appear") are really optatives, while the tone is lightened by Milton's easy, peripatetic rhythm. His style of address intimates a new power of self-determination vis-à-vis the spiritual environment in which we live and move and have our being. Though that environment remains demonic, the magus is clearly in control: the most formal sign of control is, in fact, the conceit governing his invitations, which reverses the oldest religious formula known to us, to *do ut des*—I give, so that you give. In "L'Allegro" and "Il Penseroso" the poet is not petitioning but propositioning his goddess: you give me these pleasures, and I will be yours. He lays down his conditions and enjoys them in advance. It is his pleasure or option to do these things, to be merry or melancholy—a pleasure of the human imagination.

Thus psyche emerges from the spooky larvae of masques and moralities like a free-ranging butterfly. Though still in contact with a world of spirits, it is no longer coerced or compelled. The spiritual drama is, as always in Milton, seduction rather than compulsion. The poet begins to invite his soul and opens the way to an authentic nature poetry. A similar development takes place on the Continent with Théophile de Viau and Saint-Amant, imitators of the lighter Pléiade strain, and who may have influenced Marvell. Their nature poems are little romances, adventures of the liberated and—as the case may be—libertine spirit.

Our mention of psyche may be more than a figure of speech. According to traditional speculation on genius or ingenium, each person was accompanied by two genii, a good and a bad, a protector and a deceiver. These are important figures in many morality plays and still appear in Marlowe's *Faustus*. Could Milton have changed this feature of popular demonology into his humors or states of mind, which are competing spiritual options? If so, he has adjusted an axiom of demonic religion to a more temperate zone and brought us an essential step closer to the modern idea of genius. By tempering the genii's astral nature, he has made them into attendants of the creative mind.

With Milton the spirit of Romance begins to simplify itself. It becomes the creative spirit and frees itself from the great mass of medieval and post-medieval romances in the same way as the Spirit of Protestantism frees itself from the formalism of temples. "L'Allegro" and "Il Penseroso" are not romances but romantic monologues. They show a mind moving from one position to another and projecting an image of its freedom against a darker, demonic ground. Poetry, like religion, purifies that ground: it cannot leave it. The newborn allegoric persons retain, therefore, something of the character of demonic agents even while being transformed into pleasures of the imagination. Indeed, the poems' rigidly stylized form reminds us that the imaginative man must join some god's party: the either/or situation remains; he cannot but assume a persona. Personification is still derived from the persona instead of the latter being freely inferred, as it is in modern poetry, from the projection of living thoughts.

If Romance is an eternal rather than archaic portion of the human mind, and poetry its purification, then every poem will be an act of resistance, of negative creation—a flight from one enchantment into another. The farewell to the impure gods becomes part of a nativity ode welcoming the new god. New personifications are born from old in "L'Allegro" and "Il Penseroso"; and *Lycidas* purges the genii loci of Italian pastoral only to hail a new "genius of the shore." This romantic purification of Romance is endless; it is the true and unceasing spiritual combat. At the conclusion of the first book of *Paradise Lost*, Milton transforms the Satanic thousands into fairies of Albion. Their moony music charms the ear of a belated peasant. It is, surely, a similar conversion of the demons which helps to animate the landscapes of "L'Allegro" and "Il Penseroso." The haunted ground of Romance is aestheticized; the gods become diminutive, picturesque, charming—in a word, neoclassical. But is this change perhaps a Mephistophelian deceit, a modern seduction? The gentle mind thinks it is free of demons, but they sit "far within / And in their own dimensions like themselves" (*Paradise Lost* 1. 792–93).

It is as if Milton had foreseen the triumph and trivialization of the descriptive-allegorical style. "L'Allegro" and "Il Penseroso" become the pattern for eighteenth-century topographical fancies with their personification mania. His nature-spirits are summoned at the will of every would-be magus. Romance loses its shadow, its genuine darkness: nothing remains of the drama of liberation whereby ingenium is born from genius, psyche from persona, and the spirit of poetry from the grave clothes of Romance. By the end of the eighteenth century poets must begin once more where Milton began, though fortified by his example. They must "in the romantic element immerse" and not be deceived by the neoclassical psyche flitting with faded innocence through gaudy landscapes. Keats's imitation of Milton leads from those superficial bowers to the face of Moneta, dark (like Melancholy's) with excessive bright, from pleasures of the imagination to the burdens of a prophetic spirit. This is the path inaugurated by Collins, who uses the formula of "L'Allegro" and "Il Penseroso" in invite a creative Fear—stronger even in Shakespeare than in Milton—back to his breast:

> O Thou whose Spirit most possest
> The sacred Seat of *Shakespear's* Breast!
>
> .   .   .   .
>
> Teach me but once like Him to feel:
> His Cypress Wreath my Meed decree;
> And I, O *Fear*, will dwell with *Thee*!

The theories accompanying the revival of Romance in the second half of the eighteenth century have often been studied. Van Tieghem's chapter on "La Notion de la vraie poésie" in *Le Préromantisme* contains in suggestive outline what needs to be known. But a fine essay by Emil Staiger on that strange confectioner of supernatural ballads, the German poet Bürger, takes us beyond theory to the inner development of romantic poetry.

Gottfried August Bürger was a witting cause of the ballad revival in Germany and an unwitting influence on Wordsworth and Coleridge. His ballads, first collected in 1778, sent shudders through the sophisticated literary circles of Europe. Their influence reached England in the 1790s: Scott became a ballad writer because of him, and Anna Seward describes how people petitioned her to read them Bürger's most famous work, the "Lenore": "There was scarce a morning in which a knot of eight or ten did not flock to my apartments, to be poetically frightened: Mr. Erskine, Mr. Wilberforce— everything that was everything, and everything that was nothing, flocked to Leonora . . . . Its terrible graces grapple minds and tastes of every complexion." Bürger is like the country boy in the fairy tale who finally taught the princess to have goosepimples by putting a frog in her bed. Yet, like almost every poet of the period, his first treatment of supernatural themes was jocose. Staiger shows that what began as a literary flirtation led suddenly to genuine "terrific" ballads. The sorcerer's apprentice is overpowered by spirits he had playfully evoked.

What interests us here is Bürger's literary situation and its difference from that of the English poets. Collins and later writers of the Age of Sensibility were also making mouths at the invisible event. When Gray, Percy, Mallet, Mason, Macpherson, and Blake were not redoing old romances, they inflated the neoclassical "godkins and godesslings" as giant epiphanic forms— pop art addressing a spiritualistic society. They could risk this because they knew the Enlightenment had gone too far for the old superstitions really to come back. Collins's visionary cry

> Ah *Fear*! Ah frantic *Fear*!
> I see, I see Thee near

invokes an emotion which is truly frantic: it wants to get at the poet, who wishes to be got at, but a historical fatality—the gentle mind, polite society— keeps them apart.

Now Bürger's situation is both more hopeful and more difficult. German poetry had had no golden age, no Renaissance. Hence there was no one between the poet and Romance tradition—no one, like Milton, to guide his steps, but also no one to demonstrate the difficulty and belatedness of such an enterprise. Where are *our* Chaucer, Spenser, Shakespeare, and Milton, Herder asks in an essay of 1777, which commends Bürger. English Renaissance poetry, according to Herder, was reared on the old songs and romances which originally belonged just as much to German poetry, because of a common Nordic heritage and because the spirit of Romance is everywhere the same: "In allen Länder Europas hat der Rittergeist nur ein Wörterbuch." But this heritage not having been mediated by poets like Shakespeare and Milton, the modern German writer has no living tradition of older poetry through which he might renew himself and grow as if on the very stem of national life. With us Germans, laments Herder, everything is supposed to grow a priori ("Bei uns wächst alles a priori").

Thus Bürger must somehow raise the Romance tradition by his own arts. What he knows of that tradition is limited: mainly popular songs and superstitions, copied (so he claims) from songs picked up in city or village streets at evening, in the awareness that the poems of Homer, Ariosto, Spenser, and Ossian were also once "ballads, romances, and folksongs." He is like a Faust who does not need the devil because the *Erdgeist* has agreed to be his spirit.

Among the most famous of Bürger's ballads is *The Wild Huntsman (Der Wilde Jäger)*. It depicts the rising blood-lust of a Sunday morning's hunt, and its tempo is wild from the start:

Der Wild- und Rheingraf stiess ins Horn:
"Hallo, Hallo, zu Fuss und Ross!"
Sein Hengst erhob sich wiehernd vorn;
Laut rasselnd stürzt ihm nach der Tross;
Laut klifft' und klafft' es, frei vom Koppel,
Durch Korn und Dorn, durch Heid und Stoppel.

This breakneck pace augments: two horsemen enter to accompany the earl; the right-hand one counsels him to respect the sabbath and turn back, the left-hand one spurs him on. The hunter overrides every objection; the pack rampages on, over a poor farmer's property, over the very bodies of a cowherd and his cattle; finally the earl pursues the beast into a hermit's sanctuary, violating it and blaspheming God. All at once—the transition takes place within one stanza—the clamor of the chase is gone, everything is vanished except the earl, and a deathly silence reigns. He blows his horn, it makes no sound; he halloos, no sound; he cracks his whip, no sound. He spurs his courser: it is rooted in the ground, stock-still. The silence is that of the grave; into it comes, from above, a voice of thunder condemning the hunter to be, until the Last Judgment, the prey of an eternal and hellish hunt.

The poem is totally steeped in myth and superstition: there is the motif of the blasphemy immediately answered (call the devil, etc.); that of the ride ending in the grave, perhaps indebted to the Nordic myth of Odin, who rides in the sky with his troops of dead souls; and, above all, the theme of the hunter lured by his prey beyond nature into visionary experience. Bürger wants to pack as much Romance as possible into each poem, as if to make up for Germany's lost time. He even classifies the ballad as a lyric kind of epic, not so much to stress that it must tell a story as to emphasize its ambition. The ballad is an epic in brief, a romance in brief. It sums up a life, a destiny, a whole ancient culture.

Yet behind these ballads is a pressure not explained by this ambition, which shows itself in their precipitous "Würfe und Sprünge," the speed of action (gesagt, getan"), the heroes' reckless *amor jati*, and everything else that tends to minimize the reflective moment. Here there is no shadow between the conception and the act, or even between this life and afterlife. No sooner has the earl blasphemed than he reaps his blasphemy; and Lenore's bitter yet innocent deathwish is rewarded in the same gross way. The mind is not given enough natural time in which to reflect.

Indeed, time in Bürger is intrinsically demonic. Although the supernatural erupts only at the climax of the action, it is there from the outset. One cannot speak of development: the earl is a hunted man from the first lines, a fated part of horse and pack and spurring sound; and the fearful symmetry, whereby hunter and hunted are reversed in the second part, appears like a natural rather than supernatural consequence. The first open hint of the supernatural is, of course, the appearance of the right and left horsemen, whose intrusion is so easy because in a sense they have been there all along. They are clearly the good and evil genii; and we see how externally, even superficially, the theme of reflection is introduced. There is only token retardation: the action consists of incidents arranged in climactic order with time moving irreversibly to the point of retribution. Having reached that point, the nature of time does not change: the hunter has simply run into himself. After a moment of absolute silence, which is like entering the looking glass, the reversed image appears and time continues its avenging course. There is no reflection and no true temporality: only this eschatological self-encounter.

Thus Bürger's ballads are ghostly in the deepest sense. But are they romantic? Are they not gothic—or, if you will, gothic romances? They belong to the world of that *Totentanz* explicitly evoked in "Lenore" and not absent from the mad and macabre ride of the earl. Death marries the bride, Death leads the hunt. This is not the world of the romances, not chivalry, and not *Rittergeist*. There is little of genial digressiveness, courtesy, or natural magic. Instead, the classical unities of action, time, and place become the strait and narrow road leading to a single, surreal, pietistic confrontation. The space for reflection is tighter than in Poe's "The Pit and the Pendulum" and more stingily inauthentic than in Kafka. Bürger did create a new visionary form, but at a certain cost. The false theme triumphs at the expense of falsifying the mind, which has become a mere reflector of compulsions and spectator of fatalities.

To turn from *The Wild Huntsman* to Wordsworth's "Hartleap Well" (1800) is to know the rights of the mind—the pleasures and pains of ordinary consciousness—fully restored. No ballad could be more parallel, and more opposed. The first lines strike the keynote of difference:

> The Knight had ridden down from Wensley Moore
> With the slow motion of a summer's cloud.

We begin with the chase almost over; that dramatic accumulation of incident, so essential to Bürger's pace, is at one subordinated to what Wordsworth named "character," but which is more like a consistent weather of the mind. His first image therefore describes a mood as well as a motion and places both into encompassing nature. The stanzas that follow explicitly defuse Bürger's climax of incorporating it in the features of a natural scene:

But, though Sir Walter like a falcon flies,
There is a doleful silence in the air

But horse and man are vanished, one and all;
Such race, I think, was never run before.

Where is the throng, the tumult of the race?
The bugles that so joyfully were blown?
This chase it looks not like an earthly chase:
Sir Walter and the Hart are left alone.

The silence means only that Sir Walter has outdistanced his helpers; there is nothing supernatural in it. Yet it does lead to an unearthly moment of solitude and reflection. There is something mysterious in the staying power of the stricken animal and in the knight's joy which overflows in a vow to commemorate the hunt. His joy, even so, may be consonant with a chivalric ethos, while the strength of dying creatures is proverbial. A naturalistic perspective is maintained. What hidden significance there may be must await the second part of the ballad, which is purely reflective.

This part introduces no new incidents. The poet, speaking in his own person and not as a naive bard à la Bürger, reveals that the story just told was learned from a shepherd he met on the way from Hawes to Richmond while pondering in a desolate spot marked by ruins. The natural and the contemplative frame of the story come together as he and the shepherd exchange views in the very spot where Sir Walter was left alone with the Hart. If part one is action, part two is reflection; yet part one was already reflective in mood. Hunter, shepherd, poet: all are contemplatives.

Their contemplations, however, are of a deeply primitive kind. They center on a feeling of epiphany, of revelation associated with a particular place: here a revelation of nature as a sentient and powerful being. Sir Walter erects his pleasure-house on a spot where a natural power verging on the supernatural was manifested. The peasant thinks the spot is cursed because nature sympathized with the agony of the beast. The poet also thinks its death was mourned by "sympathy divine," by "The Being, that is in the clouds and air, / That is in the green leaves among the groves," but he refuses to go beyond what nature itself suggests, beyond the simple, imaginative feeling of desolation. He rejects the idea that there is a blood curse. Thus the poem is really a little progress of the imagination, which leads from one type of animism to another: from the martial type of the knight, to the pastoral type of the shepherd, and finally to that of the poet. And in this progress from primitive to sophisticated kinds of visionariness, poetic reflection is the refining principle: it keeps nature within nature and resists supernatural fancies.

Wordsworth's animism, his consciousness of a consciousness in nature, is the last noble superstition of a demythologized mind. All nature-spirits are dissolved by him except the spirit of Nature. His poetry quietly revives the figure of *Natura plangens*, one of the great visionary personae of both pastoral and cosmological poetry. This link of Wordsworth's Nature to the Goddess Natura makes the formal moral of "Hartleap Well" almost indistinguishable from that of Bürger's poem: the one turns on "the sorrow of the meanest thing that feels"; the other on "Das Ach und Weh der Kreatur." But while Bürger's demoniacal horseman parodies the chivalric spirit (the *Rittergeist*), Wordsworth accepts chivalry as a false yet imaginative and redeemable way of life. In Wordsworth the new and milder morality grows organically from the old: there is no apocalyptic or revolutionary change, just due process of time and nature.

Now this kind of continuity is the very pattern, according to Herder, of the English poetic mind, which builds on popular sources and so revitalizes them. By giving the ballad precedence over his more personal reflections and allowing the characters of knight and shepherd their own being. Wordsworth exemplifies a peculiarly English relation of new to old. The internal structure of his poem reflects a historical principle of canon formation. Even when, as in *The White Doe of Rylstone*, he begins with personal speculation rather than with an impersonally narrated ballad, the essential structure remains that of the reflective encirclement and progressive purification of symbols from Romance.

There are, in the Romantic period, many variations on this structure. The emergence of the gentle out of the haunted mind is not always so gradual and assured. Coleridge's *Ancient Mariner*, a "Dutch attempt at German sublimity" as Southey called it, follows the Bürgerian model. Yet it has, in addition, something of the meander of Romance and of that strange interplay of dream vision and actual vision found in Malory or Spenser. It is clear that Milton is not the only master for the English mind. But he is among those who assured the survival of Romance by the very quality of his resistance to it.

MARTIN PRICE

The Sublime Poem: Pictures and Powers

The sublime is no longer a term that commands much response. We wince at its casual use and recall the vast and turgid works that were created in its name. Yet, as Lionel Trilling has observed, the theory of the sublime "has much more bearing upon our own literature than modern critics have recognized." In discussing the eighteenth-century sublime poem, which few read today, I shall not try to deal directly with its modern counterpart, but I hope that the connections may suggest themselves.

The term had many uses for the eighteenth century. It could be applied to the natural landscape, to a state of mind, to a literary mode; it could evoke orthodox religious experience or pantheistic rapture, Gothic terror or Doric severity, the grandeur of Michelangelo's sculpture or the factitious pleasures of medievalized romance. The sublime found a new meaning, one is tempted to say, every time a critic framed a new contrast between the shapely and the tremendous, between the formally satisfying object and the overwhelming impression. The sublime tended to be a name for those experiences whose power seemed incommensurate with a human scale or with formal elegance. Because the experiences were of many kinds, yet all of them seeming to defy the limits of form, the term itself produced esthetic confusion. But confusion may be fruitful; it holds together those elements that, once we separate them out, we may wish we could find a way of fusing again.

The sublime was an experience of transcendence, a surpassing of conventions or reasonable limits, an attempt to come to terms with the unimaginable. The moment of the sublime was a transport of spirit, and at such

From *The Yale Review* 58, no. 2 (Winter 1969). © 1969 by Yale University.

a moment the visible object was eclipsed or dissolved. The dissolution of the image threw the mind back on itself; typically, the failure of the image was expressed in a figure which played upon words that no longer sufficed. Such moments were fascinating to an age that had lost many of the forms of traditional piety and had diffused the religious experience—the sense of the numinous—over the natural world and over the processes of feeling as well.

The sublime, because it threw the mind back upon itself, became an experience of the highest psychological interest, and the attempts to explain it show the principal interests of the psychology of the time. The boldest theories, like Edmund Burke's, are behavioristic, psychophysical. They explain the sublime by the stress of a simple emotion and characterize the perceptions that stimulate the emotion. For Burke the emotion is terror, but the full experience of the sublime includes the counterstress of self-preservation. As David Hume had put it earlier.

> any opposition which does not entirely discourage and intimidate us has rather a contrary effect, and inspires us with a more than ordinary grandeur and magnanimity. In collecting our force to overcome the opposition, we invigorate the soul, and give it an elevation with which otherwise it would never have been acquainted.

It would be fair to say that the emotions are in this case blind; they respond to a stress with an appropriate counterstress, and the elevation the soul feels arises from a sense of its own power rather than from the nature of what it encounters.

Such a theory was opposed on several scores. First, it had no moral content. For an earlier critic like Shaftesbury, the elevation of the spirit came about not through terror but through a persevering faith in cosmic order. The threat that Burke finds in the terror of grandeur or obscurity, Shaftesbury finds in the apparent meaninglessness or disorder of the world or, conversely, in the seductive attraction of its external beauties. The moment of transcendence comes as man penetrates the multifariousness or the sensuous charm of the external and recognizes an implicit order, an ordering process that is divine. Such a process gives back to man on a cosmic scale the internal order he himself achieves in moments of moral and spiritual self-mastery. For Shaftesbury, therefore, the sublime is a moment both of supreme self-realization and of rhapsodic oneness with a divine ordering power in the world at large. The emotions in this case are not blind; they are tied to an act of recognition.

Shaftesbury's emphasis was followed by such writers as Mark Akenside and Thomas Reid. Reid rejects Burke's stress upon terror and distinguishes between dread and admiration. "In dread," Reid writes, "there is nothing of that enthusiasm which naturally accompanies admiration, and is a chief ingredient of the emotion raised by what is truly grand or sublime." Reid is so anxious to protect the moral or religious content of the sublime that he does not admit, as Shaftesbury does, the threat of meaninglessness that a divine creation may present. There remains no counterpart of Burke's terror in Reid, and very little but degrees of intensity distinguish the sublime from the beautiful. In tying the emotions to moral and intellectual awareness, Reid cures their blindness, but he distinctly enfeebles them.

Archibald Alison saw himself as carrying on the Platonic tendencies in Shaftesbury and Reid; their Platonism claimed a prior authority in man's intuitions or innate dispositions that could confirm what he discovered through experience. His responses are not blind and passive; he seeks what his mind requires and finds congenial, and he actively shapes experience in the very process of perception. Alison draws upon the association of ideas, a doctrine which earlier had hardly stressed the mind's activity or authority. But Alison uses it to show that the esthetic response to nature builds at every point upon its implicit human meaning. Alison constantly denies that objects have inherent properties that affect us as sublime; these properties gain their efficacy from the suggestions they carry of danger, power, magnificence, or solemnity. We feel a sublime delight in Rome not simply because of its formal qualities but also because of its ancient glory. Without its history Rome would be seen with a far different emotion.

Another kind of criticism was brought against Burke by Richard Payne Knight. In stressing the way in which the sublime approached infinity, Burke had pointed out the inevitable loss of clear images and indeed the value of obscurity. Accordingly, Burke questioned altogether the efficacy of the visual image in poetry; words were as much conceptual as pictorial, and their most powerful effect was achieved by their dramatic appeal to sentiment. Poetry, Burke said, seeks "to display rather the effect of things on the mind of the speaker, or of others, than to present a clear idea of the things themselves." For, as he put it memorably, "we yield to sympathy what we refuse to description." Knight did not dispute the value of sympathy, but he questioned the vagueness in which Burke left the object of our sympathy. He sees in Burke's catalogue of terrible objects the source of pseudo-Gothic claptrap and in Burke's ill-defined sympathy the source of bombast or demagogic nonsense.

"Critics have been led into the notion that imagery is rendered sublime by being indistinct and obscure," Knight wrote, "by mistaking energies for images, and looking for *pictures* where *powers* only were meant to be expressed." Knight is attacking the effort to define the sublime object by negation. If obscurity produces a sublime effect, would not utter darkness be the supreme instance of the sublime? If words work without images and produce a mere contagion of sympathetic feeling, why should not utter nonsense suffice? Knight is trying, like the self-styled Platonic school of critics, to restore the meaningfulness of the sublime experience. "I may *know* an object to be terrible; that is, I may know it to possess the *power* of hurting or destroying: but this is *knowledge*, and not *feeling* or *sentiment*; and the *object* of that knowledge is *power*, and not *terror*; so that, if any sympathy results from it, it must be a sympathy with power only."

Knight transfers our sympathy from the mind of the sublime speaker to those "energies of mind" that are embodied in any sublime object. Buildings of great dimension or magnificence are felt not as immediate awe-inspiring perceptions; they are seen as works of man and as demonstrations of his powers of mind. Great storms display "prodigious exertions of energy and power," and it is this, not the terror they awaken, nor simply the words in which they may be described, that makes them sublime.

Knight recognizes that "energy, which is the fundamental principle and indispensable requisite of all sublimity of character, is more frequently and more manifestly displayed in bad than in good actions: and in the pernicious, than in the amiable qualities of mind." But it is the energy of the bad action rather than its badness we respond to, and the energy must be made as distinct and characterized as sharply as is consistent with its nature. "What is it, that makes the impassioned language of Achilles, Macbeth, and Othello so interesting, but the strong sense and energy of mind that beams through it?" In most general terms, Knight replies to Burke: "The passions can sympathize with no images that the imagination does not comprehend distinctly."

What Burke's critics reject is the blindness of the emotions involved. To his behavioristic account they oppose a phenomenological one. By one means or another they try to characterize an encounter with a force or presence. Burke's stress upon terror can then be taken up as an insistence upon the otherness of this presence.

Rudolf Otto in *The Idea of the Holy* presents an analysis of the *mysterium tremendum* into its elements of awefulness, of overpoweringness, and of energy or urgency. The element of awe he sees as a sacred dread, a "quite specific kind of emotional response, wholly distinct from that of being afraid, though it so far resembles it that the analogy of fear may be used to throw light upon its nature." The overpoweringness Otto traces to a "consciousness of the absolute superiority or supremacy of a power other than myself" with a consequent "self-depreciation," that is, "the estimation of the self, of the personal 'I,' as something not perfectly or essentially real, or even as mere nullity." Finally, the urgency or energy of the numinous object, as Otto observes, is clothed in such symbolic expressions as "vitality, passion, emotional temper, will, force, movement, excitement, activity, impetus." In our encounter with the numinous, we "come upon something inherently 'wholly other,' whose kind and character are incommensurable with our own, and before which we therefore recoil in a wonder that strikes us chill and numb."

Otto's conception of the numinous as "wholly other" accounts for the sense of terror that Burke demands and explains Burke's impatience with such lesser emotions as admiration, which Reid wished to reinstate as the sufficient cause of the sublime. What is involved in this esthetic quarrel, then, is something more fundamental. The critics in the Platonic tradition, notably Shaftesbury among the English, stress the oneness of the human and the divine. The numinous for them is not "wholly other," but rather the divine in man freed of all limits and therefore released into the infinite and eternal. The transcendence which the sublime reveals is that moment when man feels most accurately in himself the divine principle that governs the cosmos.

Transcendence is a relationship: the point of departure helps to define the goal. Typically, the sublime poet moves from one kind of place to another:

> To unfrequented meads, and pathless wilds,
> Lead me from gardens deck'd with art's vain pomps.

> Tempe, no more I court thy balmy breeze;
> Adieu, green vales! embroidered meads adieu!

> Tell me the path, sweet wanderer, tell,
> To thy unknown sequestered cell

> O, let me pierce thy secret cell,
> And in deep recesses dwell!

> Tis Fancy's land to which thou sett'st thy feet;
> Where still, 'tis said, the fairy people meet.

This is a movement into a sacred precinct, a movement to a realm where the powers of awareness are different, where vision is given and the familiar scene is dissipated. The precinct is sacred because it is inhabited by a power, and to be drawn into its realm is to be made one with that power. The poet has the capacity to imagine such a realm and to seek it; he often calls upon a greater power to descend and take him there. The passivity of the poet is an appeal to otherness. He asks to be taken or to be led, to be snatched up and to be initiated into the mysteries of a new worship.

The preparations for the visionary experience are as ritualistic as the hero's prayer to the gods or the donning of his armor before he moves into the field of battle. The realm he enters may be a dark recess, a mysterious eminence, a place of unfathomable depth or height. The sublime precinct is a place where the poet is released from the swarm of sensuous detail or the swarm of people of a daylight world. Joseph Warton addresses Solitude:

> Musing maid, to thee I come,
> Hating the tradeful city's hum:
> O let me calmly dwell with thee,
> From noisy mirth and bus'ness free,
> With meditation seek the skies,
> This folly-fetter'd world despise!

The precinct of Solitude is a gloomy cavern or a barren rock, a place of total withdrawal from the world and therefore a scene of potential transcendence. It is a place where the poet is at one with the presence and where he can absorb its powers. Most of all, it is a place where he is most fully what he wishes to become; he is freed of those demands and responses that fritter away the sense of self or draw it into the orbit of others. Here he withdraws into the full exercise of his deepest, most mysterious powers. The dark recess is the realm of those powers the daylight world suppresses, and the high place or the spectacle of the vast and unlimited is the immensity which feeds or releases the intensity within.

The movement to a new realm may also be a movement in time, either to a prophetic futurity or to a heroic and mythical past. Thomas Warton broods over Stonehenge and rehearses "many an ancient tale" that may account for its mysterious form. The specific nature of its "wondrous origins" hardly matters; in fact, the very plenitude of myths serves to mark the otherness and unapproachable mystery of the monument. The pastness of Stonehenge is of a profound sort; it is more mysterious and suggestive than that of a classical monument, and it is also more intimately related to the English present. This peculiar mixture of remoteness and nearness, of otherness and identity, is extremely important; for the evocation is not simply of a power that is wholly other, but the evocation of deep-lying powers within the poet.

So, too, with the prospect of futurity. Thomas Gray's Bard looks out of a mythical past into a remote future. What he sees is a confirmation of the divine power with which he is inspired and of the power within all poets who recover the Bard's energy in new works of "invention and visionary conception." So in Thomas Warton's sonnet, the Druid frame of Arthur's round table molders in time but is kept immortal in Spenser's "verse sublime."

Time and space become correlative terms. The movement of the sublime poem is often a passage to freedom from enslaving tyranny. The poet may turn away from the false and formal arts of France:

> Rich in her weeping country's spoils, Versailles
> May boast a thousand fountains, that can cast
> The tortured waters to the distant heavens.

He moves to realms of freedom, where a stream roars freely down from an "abrupt and shaggy" precipice or flows twinkling through scenes of natural, invisibly cultivated, fertility. He may banish Superstition from the "active freeborn British mind" to "slavish Rome." Here the poet does not move to a sacred precinct; he purges his nation in order to make it a sacred place, a place which the ancient and eternal light of Plato may irradiate. Or again a place may become the precinct of communion with the stoic Brutus, as in Mark Akenside's ode to Lord Hungtingdon.

The presences called up are often personifications—Solitude, Fancy, the Passions, the Poetical Character, Liberty. These are frankly states or faculties of the poet, and his evocation of them is a release of their power within himself. William Collins's ode on *The Passions* ends with a prayer to Music:

> Arise as in that elder time,
> Warm, energic, chaste, sublime
>
> . . . .
>
> O bid our vain endeavors cease;
> Revive the just designs of Greece.
> Return in all thy simple state.

The appeal for the revival of Grecian modes is also an invocation of the simple energy of naked, passions, unmixed, unrestrained, uncorrupted. So again Collins's vicarious movement to the Scottish Highlands opens up a realm of poetic freedom where, like the peasants, he can ignore the limits of "sober truth" and believe utterly in what he imagines. In fact, Collins invokes here as in his "Ode on the Poetical Character" that realm where the Eden which the poet imagines can become his substantial dwelling, where—in Blake's terms—a "spirit and a Vision are not, as the modern philosophy supposes, a cloudy vapour or a nothing" but are "organized and minutely articulated beyond all that the mortal and perishing nature can produce."

The note that is sounded again and again is the desire for expansion or
intensity of spirit.

> Yet shall he mount, and keep his distant way
> Beyond the limits of a vulgar fate
>
> .   .   .   .
>
> Teach me but once like him to feel
>
> .   .   .   .
>
> Till dawn, till morning, till the breaking of clouds,
>   and swelling of winds, and the universal voice;
> Till man raise his darken'd limbs out of the caves of
>   night: his eyes and his heart
> Expand.

One feels the energy of the thrust; the recognition of possibility is the beginning of power. These prayers are almost self-fulfilling. Their principal
efficacy is to give aspiration a voice and a form; once it is called into imaginative being, the aspiration can be honored, fostered, lived out.

The voice of feeling had never been so strong and unguarded in poetry
before the middle of the eighteenth century. Perhaps one should say that
the desire for pure feeling, regardless of object, had hardly been voiced before.
The feeling that relates man to God or to his mistress has always been familiar;
but here the object becomes less and less simply other, more and more clearly
a power within the self. The sense of otherness remains, of course, as do
the ritual of prayer or invocation and the myth of the sacred place. But the
otherness has been displaced into a vision of the *other self*, the self at last
controlled by powers that have been submerged by culture, the self either
mastering the familiar world or annihilating it. These powers once awakened
are strange and awesome, if only because they have led so attenuated and
subservient a life in the economy of man's spirit. Now man transcends his
conventional, quotidian, empirical self and sees it as no less external than
the world that surrounds it.

We can see here the rejection of Alexander Pope's "clear, unchanged,
and universal light" for flashes of brilliance or the asylum of darkness. The
powers that are released have turned away from the actual, and the darkness
that blots out the mundane is curiously like the darkness that we learn to
loathe in the light-centered worlds of Spenser, Milton, and Pope. Pope's
Cave of Spleen is a travesty of a sacred precinct, where the passions erupt
as monsters, and Pope's Dulness is swathed in fogs that keep her sublimely
oblivious of the world. His mock-sublime is used to elevate the Dunces to
the point where the fall is most dramatic: their goddess turns out to be the

insensibility of sluggish matter, a "self without a thought." Pope and Swift see the sublime as always inviting a fall. It "may branch upwards towards Heaven, but the Root is in the Earth. Too intense a Contemplation is not the Business of Flesh and Blood; it must by the necessary Course of Things, in a little Time, let go its Hold, and fall into Matter." Appropriately, then, the first major manifesto of the new sensibility, Warton's *Essay* on Pope, regrets that Pope was so bound down by good sense and judgment. Pope, Warton explains, did not lack imagination, but "his imagination was not his predominant talent, because he indulged it not, and because he gave not so many proofs of *this* talent as of the *other*." "Whatever poetical enthusiasm he actually possessed, he withheld and stifled."

One might ask in turn where the indulgence leads. In Pope's mock-sublime the liberation of powers achieved by the sublime and the otherness of the self that is released become a demonic force, and we can see a movement toward the demonic in many of the sublime poets. When Collins invokes Fear, or Gray, Adversity, each of them releases torment as well as energy. Each desires the benign aspect of his goddess but knows that this is only one aspect. Gray wishes away and condemns as a superstitious view the "Gorgon horrors," the "thundering voice, and threatening mien." Collins admits the terrors as well as their splendid sublimation.

> O Fear, I know thee by my throbbing heart;
>   Thy withering power inspired each mournful line:
> Though gentle Pity claimed her mournful part,
>   Yet all the thunders of the scene are thine!

More telling, in the youthful bravado of the Wartons there is a curious note of cruelty. We can understand the aloofness from the world that Warton's Enthusiast seeks, but the poem closes with a simile that makes the cost of aloofness a harsh one:

> So when rude whirlwinds rouse the roaring main,
> Beneath fair Thetis sits, in coral caves,
> Serenely gay; nor sinking sailors' cries
> Disturb her sportive Nymphs, who round her form
> The light fantastic dance.

One can see here the forerunner of that figure Frank Kermode has presented in *Romantic Image*: the dancer, cruelly aloof, absorbed in her own ecstatic performance, indifferent to suppliant admirers or to the world about her. It is an image of symbolist art itself that Kermode presents—of art seen, in

Yeats's words, as "the one passion which alone remains out of the passions of the world." On another level, the indulgence that Wharton speaks of can be sought in those more sinister encounters of the Gothic novel.

It is not my intention to trace the path from the sublime to the romantic agony. This is, clearly, one direction the sublime may take. When Blake rebels against the cant of moralists, he asserts

> the grandest Poetry is Immoral, the Grandest characters Wicked, Very Satan—Capaneus, Othello a murderer, Prometheus, Jupiter, Jehovah, Jesus a wine bibber. Cunning and Morality are not Poetry but Philosophy; the Poet is Independent and Wicked; the Philosopher is Dependent and Good.

And the cultivation of extreme states of feeling, the summoning up of titanic energies from their caves of suppression, may take the form of satanism. We can see this in a work like *The Monk*, where the vision of Lucifer is of a beautiful naked angel with crimson wings and fiercely sparkling eyes—at once divine vision and homosexual fantasy, all the sublime beauties colored by guilt and ambivalent desire.

More essential to the romantic tradition is the movement toward self-acceptance and a joyful harmony of being. Wordsworth places high value on guilt, pain, and fear; and he is ready to see the deepest impulse fusing with the highest aspiration. At the close of *The Prelude* the radiant moon is seen at the same moment as the vast roar of waters rises from a "fixed, abysmal, breathing place." We can see this self-acceptance in Blake as well, where *The Marriage of Heaven and Hell*—in one sense at least of that puzzling title—leads angel and devil to honor together the belief that exuberance is beauty and energy eternal delight. For Blake and Wordsworth intensity of feeling is greatest as the sense of oneness and harmony extends over the immensity of space and time, reclaiming the deepest and earliest impulses. The self-division of doubt and despair that disables feeling is the greatest enemy. For them, therefore, the act of transcendence is the winning through to harmony and a transparency of being, where nothing need be hidden or denied, where "Every thing that lives is holy."

In language, too, the sublime has always been regarded as a form of excess, a surpassing of limits. The limits it surpasses may be those of rational expectation, of reasonable argument, of logic itself. Abraham Cowley, in the notes to his Pindaric paraphrase of the thirty-fourth chapter of Isaiah, describes the language he is creating:

> The manner of the *Prophets* writing, especially of *Isaiah*, seems to me very like that of *Pindar*; they pass from one thing to another

with almost *Invisible connexions*, and are full of words and expressions of the highest and boldest flights of *Poetry*, as may be seen in this Chapter, where there are as extraordinary Figures as can be found in any *Poet* whatsoever; and the connexion is so difficult, that I am forced to adde a little, and leave out a great deal to make it seem *Sense* to us, who are not used to that elevated way of expression.

In Isaiah's text there is "no Transition from the *subject* to the *similitude*: for the old fashion of writing was like *Disputing* in *Enthymemes*, where half is left out to be supplyed by the Hearer; ours is like *Syllogisms*, where all that is meant is exprest." Cowley's is one of the earliest descriptions we have in English of a sublime style; its emphasis is useful in pointing to the logical and syntactical obscurity that Cowley finds in both Greek and Hebrew versions of the sublime.

The rapidity and violence of the language of the sublime have been traced, since Longinus, to the ardor of an elevated spirit. Perhaps the most famous phrase in Longinus is the "echo of a great soul." We do not have Longinus's account of the passions of such a soul, but we can gather what they must be. In the description of natural objects, Longinus recalls that nature "has from the start implanted in our souls an irresistible love of whatever is great and stands to us as the more divine to the less. Wherefore not even the whole of the universe suffices for man's contemplation or scope of thought." At the very close Longinus tries to account for the loss of greatness in the literature of his day. The elevated desires are here set in contrast to love of wealth and love of pleasure, both of them mean in their objects and slavish in their bearing. One finds, then, a conception of passion that transcends material objects, that moves through the sensible universe in search of its grandest forms and yet can never find outward grandeur adequate to its inherent vision and its capacities of devotion. The intensity of the soul's passions is measured by the immensity of its objects. The immensity is, at its extreme, quite literally a boundlessness, a surpassing of measurable extension.

The Platonic strain in Longinus seems to imply a transcendence of the realm of the senses and a return to the realm of ideas. The struggle to voice such aspiration is also found, as Cowley observes, in Biblical poetry, and Bishop Robert Lowth's account of the style of Scripture gives Cowley's description a ground in the sublime experience itself:

Here the mind seems to exert its utmost faculties in vain to grasp
an object, whose unparalleled magnitude mocks its feeble en-

deavors; and to this end it employs the grandest imagery that
universal nature can suggest, and yet this imagery, however great,
proves totally inadequate to the purpose.

Lowth cites the method of description by "continued negation," "when a
number of great and sublime ideas are collected, which, on comparison with
the object, are found infinitely inferior and inadequate. Thus the boundaries
are gradually extended on every side, are at length totally removed; the mind
is insensibly led on toward infinity, and is struck with inexpressible admiration, and pleasing awe, when it first finds itself expatiating in that immense
expanse."

Here, as one might expect, the emphasis is on the subject's struggle to
become adequate to its object. But if the divine object drops out, we find
the emphasis shifting to an impatience of the poet with all institutions or
modes or perception that hide or enslave his other self—the self that is being
brought into realization in the experience of the sublime. Blake sees all natural
objects as occasions for passivity of spirit: the seduction of Vala is simply to
offer herself as a reality outside man's imagination. And Wordsworth learns
that the outward spectacle will not serve the mind's highest offices, that only
when the light of sense goes out does the mind find its proper home, "with
infinitude, and only there." Characteristically we move from the mind's
struggle to become adequate to the divine to the mind's inherent divinity
shedding the objects that limit its powers. Lowth has a sentence which catches
the outward form of this process: "Here we behold the passions struggling
for vent, laboring with a copiousness of thought and a poverty of expression,
and on that very account the more expressly displayed." This other self finds
its strongest dramatic realization in opposition to human institutions or the
natural scene, but perhaps its final struggle is with the empirical self.

This struggle becomes a struggle of idiom. Transcendence demands not
only a special syntax, as Cowley observes, but a distinctive kind of image.
The sublime image, Longinus tells us, is meant to astonish and overwhelm;
it is not, like the proportional analogy of persuasion, an aid to comprehension.
The sublime "produces not persuasion but transport," and to do this it must
often dissolve the visual image or convert it into a figure. Longinus cites
Hyperides: "It was not the orator who moved that decree; it was the battle
at Chaeronea." We are moving from image to figure, from the picture to the
dislocation of words that indicates the inadequacy of any picture. Yet it will
not do to claim, as Burke does, that a voice filled with passions struggling
for vent achieves a contagious effect upon the listener. For the passions are
tied to thought, and the eclipse of the pictorial is still meaningful. The

sublimity of the battle's moving the decree is much the same that Lincoln achieved in the Gettysburg address, with its invocation of those energies of spirit that participate in and consecrate our decisions.

The clearest instance of passions finding their voice in figure is the poetry of Edward Young, as he celebrates man's divine possibilities:

> Who looks on That, and sees not in himself
> An awful Stranger, a Terrestrial God?
> . . . .
> I gaze, and, as I gaze, my mounting Soul
> Catches strange Fire, Eternity, at Thee;
> And drops the World—or rather, more enjoys:
> How chang'd the Face of Nature! how improv'd!
> What seem'd a Chaos, shines a glorious World,
> Oh, what a World, an Eden; heighten'd all!
> It is another Scene! another Self!

And a few lines later, the sublime poet remarks:

> Is this extravagant? Of Man we form
> Extravagant Conceptions to be just:
> Conception unconfin'd wants Wings to reach him.

We can see in Young's lines an impatient use of metaphors, each moving beyond the last. None is sustained for long; it proves inadequate and is passed over. All of this is set, moreover, in the framework of a visionary encounter, where the soul's fire attests to its sense of tremendous presence, while its language explodes in a series of interjections, each corresponding to a new state of awareness, a new depth of vision.

The drama of encounter is more fundamental than the figurative play of metaphor or paradox. The passion rises to meet some vision of its own perfected form, some vision of the self as totally given to this passion, and therefore as other. Here is a passage from James Thomson's *Autumn*:

> He comes! he comes! in every breeze the power
> Of philosophic Melancholy comes!
> His near approach the sudden-starting tear,
> The glowing cheek, the mild dejected air,
> The softened feature, and the beating heart
> Pierced deep with many a virtuous pang declare.

> O'er all the soul his sacred influence breathes,—
> Inflames imagination, through the breast
> Infuses every tenderness, and far
> Beyond dim earth exalts the swelling thought.
> Ten thousand thousand fleet ideas, such
> As never mingled with the vulgar dream,
> Crowd fast into the mind's creative eye.
> As fast the correspondent passions rise.

What is striking in the passage is the interplay of the correspondent passions with the mind's creative eye. Each seems to advance the other in a reciprocal movement, and the presence of Melancholy is both felt within and seen without.

At last Thomson moves to a climax of imagery:

> Oh! bear me then to vast embowering shades,
> To twilight groves and visionary vales,
> To weeping grottos and prophetic glooms,
> Where angel-forms athwart the solemn dusk
> Tremendous sweep, or seem to sweep, along,
> And voices more than human, through the void
> Deep-sounding, seize the enthusiastic ear.

We have all the indistinctness of Burke's sublimity here, but the external scene is never allowed to remain fully external. Such adjectives as "visionary" and "prophetic," such qualifications as "or seem to sweep," and, most of all, the dissolution of the visible in the audible are all devices for making the outward scene the climate of the exalted soul. There is a steady progression, from landscape to angel-forms, from actual motion to seeming motion, from actor to voice; and there is a corresponding progression in scale from embowering shades or weeping grottos to prophetic glooms, from "tremendous sweep" to the "voices more than human, through the void / Deep-sounding." This is an approach to infinity but, more important, it is a sacred precinct that is not simply seen as a spectacle but felt as an environment; its space, light, and sound surround the speaker and seem to penetrate him. The ambiguity of internal and external makes the place of encounter a medium more than a site. We can see this presentation of encounter as a medium again in those remarkable metaphors of D. H. Lawrence which make the relationship between people an electric field created by the currents of their influence upon each other.

Distinctively Thomson's is another kind of passage in *Autumn*, where the imagination traces with devout curiosity the creative processes of nature. There is an impressive section that begins:

> I see the rivers in their infant beds;
> Deep, deep I hear them, laboring to get free.

And Thomson traces the growth of the river from the rocky fissures that receive rainfall down to its welling out to the surface of the land. The images are precise enough as geology; they trace a process through its stages, and each stage is given some pictorial presentation. But the emphasis remains upon the process itself and the wonder of the imagination's power to retrace it. The image exists for the sake of the wonder, and its precision only catches the intensity of the poet's curiosity. This kind of image can often become preternaturally vivid, as the eye fixes in awe upon the detail which reveals a vast process within itself.

Christopher Smart is a master of this kind of imagery, briefly presented, intensely vivid, sometimes quaint in its inspired pedantry. In his early Seaton poem "On the Immensity of the Supreme Being," he finds God not only in the lordly oak but in the underwood:

> Yet Thou art there, yet God himself is there,
> Ev'n on the bush (tho' not as when to *Moses*
> He shone in burning Majesty reveal'd)
> Nathless conspicuous in the Linnet's throat
> Is his unbounded goodness—Thee her Maker,
> Thee her preserver chants she in her song.

From Smart's linnet one readily turns to a remarkable passage in Blake's *Milton*:

> The Lark sitting upon his earthly bed, just as the morn
> Appears, listens silent; then springing from the waving
>   Cornfield, loud
> He leads the Choir of Day: trill, trill, trill, trill,
> Mounting upon the wings of light into the Great Expanse,
> Reechoing against the lovely blue and shining heavenly Shell,
> His little throat labors with inspiration; every feather
> On throat and breast and wings vibrates with the effluence
>   Divine.

Such a passage as Blake's opens up another kind of sublime image—the closeness of attention that all but obliterates the outlines of the natural object in its familiar form, finding in it the effluence of vast powers and rising in wonder to a contemplation of those powers through the object.

From such an instance it is only a short movement to the sublime which restores the actual in a new sense. Near the close of *The Task* William Cowper rises to an apocalyptic vision:

> Rivers of gladness water all the earth,
> And clothe all climes with beauty; the reproach
> Of barrenness is past. The fruitful field
> Laughs with abundance.

This foretaste of Heaven becomes the sustaining power in the life of retirement:

>   bespeak him one
> Content indeed to sojourn while he must
> Below the skies, but having there his home.
> The world o'erlooks him in her busy search
> Of objects, more illustrious in her view;
> And occupied as earnestly as she,
> Though sublimely, he o'erlooks the world.

Here, like a Kierkegaardian knight of faith, the sublime spirit separates itself from the world with no outward show:

> Its warfare is within. There unfatigu'd
> His fervent spirit labors. There he fights,
> And there obtains fresh triumphs o'er himself.

The poet has transcended the world. He must struggle constantly to regain that transcendence, but he disdains any show of power. His unsuspected mildness is as much instinct with energy as the lark's song; it serves only to protect the other self within.

This version of the sublime swells into fullness with Wordsworth and is carried on by a writer like George Eliot. The greatest moment in *Middlemarch* comes as Dorothea Brooke reviews her discovery of Will Ladislaw with Rosamond. She comes at last to ask herself: "Was she alone in that scene? Was it her event only?" At this point her stretch of awareness takes the form of sublime image:

> It had taken long for her to come to that question, and there was
> light piercing into the room. She opened her curtains, and looked

out towards the bit of road that lay in view, with fields beyond, outside the entrance-gates. On the road there was a man with a bundle on his back and a woman carrying her baby; in the field she could see figures moving—perhaps the shepherd with his dog. Far off in the bending sky was the pearly light; and she felt the largeness of the world and the manifold wakings of men to labor and endurance. She was a part of that involuntary, palpitating life, and could neither look out on it from her luxurious shelter as a mere spectator, nor hide her eyes in selfish complaining.

Here we find once more vastness of space and number, surrounding and lending solemnity to the simple human figures in the foreground. Dorothea's vision becomes an encounter. She rises to a sense of the majesty and otherness of this spectacle of human life and at the same time to a new capacity for sympathy with it. The sublimity she has sought in heroic exertions of the ego gives way to a sublimity she finds at a new level of her own being as well as of the world's.

I would propose that we see in the sublime two principal phases: they may interact or succeed each other. One is the heroic ascent into transcendence—invariably an act of self-discovery; the otherness it encounters becomes some aspect of self that is released and given a new, sometimes frightening, existence. The process by which this moment of transcendence is reached involves some encounter with a presence, some taking into the self or release from within of powerful energies. The other phase is less dramatic; it belongs to a less heroic, more assured sense of the transcendental. For the ascent lies behind it, and it descends once more to the actual with those high expectations that Wordsworth gives to the child in the Immortality Ode. It becomes a radical kind of vision. It may be lived out inconspicuously in retirement like Cowper's or in a "home epic" like Dorothea Brooke's; or it may inform the outrage as well as sympathy that we find in the Blake of the *Songs of Experience* or in the Dickens of the last novels. Both phases have come increasingly in our own time to assume that manner which Thomas Mann found the striking feature of modern art:

it has ceased to recognize the categories of tragic and comic. . . .
It sees life as tragicomedy, with the result that the grotesque is
its most genuine style—to the extent, indeed, that today that is
the only guise in which the sublime may appear.

STEVEN KNAPP

Sublime Personification: Implications for Poetic Practice

Kant's ambivalence toward the idealization of self parallels the Enlightened ambivalence toward allegory. . . . Both Kant and the English critics admire the imagination's power to identify empirical consciousness with abstract ideality. But in both cases such admiration is thwarted by fear of the consequences for the empirical individual. Yet "fear" is too strong, too psychologically precise a term for what is at least partly an artificial danger. After his awakening, by Hume, from the "dogmatic slumber" of rationalism, Kant was in little danger of backsliding; his commitment to important elements of empiricism remained secure throughout his development of the critical philosophy. Kant's vision of fanaticism is itself an impossible satirical ideal, a product of the fictional logic of the sublime, as the excessive language of pathology ("an undermining disease") and of oxymoron ("rational raving") suggests. Similarly, in eighteenth-century responses to Renaissance allegory, from Addison onward, hints of genuine admiration or uneasiness are often matched by antiquarian complacency and condescension. This is only to say that the interest in fanaticism, as in archaic modes of thought, is as much literary and ideological as it is psychological. The point of fanaticism is to establish, by means of contrast, the Enlightenment's sense of itself. The fanatic, like the allegorical personification, expresses an Enlightened fantasy of pre-Enlightened agency. (How far such fantasies also anticipated or responded to what would emerge as real threats to Enlightened notions of

From *Personification and the Sublime: Milton to Coleridge.* © 1985 by The President and Fellows of Harvard College. Harvard University Press, 1985.

agency—threats from Rousseau, Fichte, Wordsworth, evangelicalism, and events in France—would be hard to measure in general terms.)

This paradoxical desire for safe participation in ideal or fixated modes of agency accounts for the special relation of personification to the sublime. Personification in general no doubt served the range of stylistic functions surveyed by Bronson, Wasserman, and Chapin. But sublime personifications uniquely balance the conflicting criteria of power and distance required by the Enlightened stance of urbane admiration. With its individuality utterly absorbed by the ideal it embodies, the personification is the perfect fanatic. It is both devoid of empirical consciousness and perfectly, formally conscious of itself. But the reassuring condition of such perfection is its sheer and obvious fictionality.

Perfect self-consciousness accounts for one of the strangest features of many personifications, their oddly stylized reflexiveness. This is the peculiarity Coleridge criticized, for example, in Spenser. In marginalia on Robert Anderson's *Poets of Great Britain* (1793–1807), Coleridge singles out the description of dissemblance during the masque of Cupid in Busyrane's castle (*Faerie Queene*, III.xii.14). The trouble with this figure—whose "bright browes were deckt with *borrowed* hair"—is that it confuses description with allegorical content: "Here, as too often in this great poem, that which is and may be known, but cannot *appear* from the given point of view, is confounded with the visible. It is no longer a mask-figure, but the character, of a Dissembler." The whole point of dissemblance, Coleridge suggests, is that one cannot tell the hair is borrowed. But this apparent confusion of descriptive with thematic information leads Coleridge to another and, for our purposes, more crucial example: "Another common fault in stanza xvi: Grief represents two incompatibles, the grieved and the aggriever." Editor T. M. Raysor supplies the following lines, as misprinted by Anderson:

> Grief all in sable sorrowfully clad,
> Downe hanging his dull head with heavy chere;
>
> . . . .
>
> A pair of pincers in his hand he had,
> With which he pinched many people to the hart.

"Indeed," Coleridge concludes, "this confusion of agent and patient occurs so frequently in his allegorical personages that Spenser seems to have deemed it within the laws and among the legitimate principles of allegory." As occurs often in Coleridge, prescriptive criticism turns into descriptive insight; there is a note of fascination, as well as impatience, in this discovery of the figure's double relation to its idea. His choice of example is thematically as well as stylistically right. Kant's account of fanaticism shows why a brooding, fixating passion warrants a figure turned against itself; one thinks of Spenser's Despair, Milton's Sin, the figures ranged before the jaws of Virgil's hell, and virtually all the personifications the eighteenth century called "sublime." Even the word "passion" captures the paradox of Coleridge's "agent and patient." Kant's fanatic suffers from "an undermining disease"; the passion's real object and final victim is itself. Although most personifications are, like Dissemblance, identified with themes they express to the point of descriptive absurdity, the personified passion is especially self-referential and self-enclosed. This trait again confirms the analogy with the fanatic; unlike the enthusiast, whose energies, owing to the negativity of the ideal, are perpetually extroverted, the fanatic totally identifies the ideal object with the empirical faculty that pursues it.

A brief example will suggest that attending to the reflexiveness of personification might revise our ways of reading sublime poetry. To support her claim that eighteenth-century horror-personifications derived their contemporary power and interest from "association with other manifestations of the supernatural," Patricia Meyer Spacks quotes the following lines from David Mallet's *The Excursion* (1728):

> Behind me rises huge a reverent pile
> Sole on his blasted heath, a place of tombs,
> Waste, desolate, where Ruin dreary dwells.
> Brooding o'er sightless sculls and crumbling bones,
> Ghastful he sits, and eyes with stedfast glare
> (Sad trophies of his power, where ivy twines
> Its fatal green around) the falling roof,
> The time-shook arch, the column grey with moss,
> The leaning wall, the sculptur'd stone defac'd,
>
> . . . .
>
> All is dread silence here, and undisturb'd,
> Save what the wind sighs, and the wailing owl
> Screams solitary to the mournful Moon,
> Glimmering her western ray through yonder isle,
> Where the sad spirit walks with shadowy foot
> His wonted round, or lingers o'er his grave.

Next she cites, from a letter to Mallet, the response of James Thomson (who, she notes, had apparently seen the lines "in a slightly different form"):

> You paint RUIN with a masterly Hand
>   Gastful He sits, and views, *with* stedfast Glare,

> The falling Bust, the COLUMN grey *with* Moss
> This is such an Attitude as I can never enough admire,
> and even be astonished at.
>> Save what the Wind sighs, and the WAILING OWL
>> Screams solitary—
> charmingly dreary!
>> Where the *sad* Spirit walks, with *shadowy* Foot,
>> His wonted Round, or lingers o'er his Grave.
> What dismal Simplicity reigns thro these two lines!
> They are equal to any ever Shakespear wrote on the
> Subject.

And Spacks comments:

> Even with due allowance made for friendship, the fact that Thom-
> son chose to single out these lines for high praise suggests that
> for a contemporary audience they exercised a peculiar potency.
> Although the description of Ruin is not at all developed, de-
> pending on one line, Thomson finds it both admirable and as-
> tonishing. He praises his friend because he paints Ruin with a
> masterly hand, yet the fact is that Mallet paints Ruin almost not
> at all. Somehow, though, the effect of vivid personification is
> conveyed.

For Spacks, the rhetorical power here depends on "details" and "associations," linking Ruin both to its actual effects in the world and to a surrounding
atmosphere of supernaturally tinted gloom. The figure's vividness

> is conveyed through specific details about the physical surround-
> ings, details appropriate because they deal with the effects of ruin
> in the world of actuality, thus giving the personification firm links
> with reality, but justified also merely by their "dismal Simplicity"
> and the "charmingly dreary" atmosphere they project. The drear-
> iness of the atmosphere, however, comes not primarily from its
> physical details, but from its associations: the scene is one in which
> ghosts might be expected to walk ... Thus the figure of Ruin
> comes to seem truly a supernatural personage ... because he has
> been firmly placed in a supernatural context.

No one familiar with Thomson's own poetry will doubt his enjoyment
of lurid atmosphere and conventional details, though one might question

whether the phase "charmingly dreary" bears out Spacks's claim for the "truly" supernatural impact of Mallet's lines. More questionable, perhaps, is the claim that skulls, ivy, arches, columns, and broken statues—the furniture of countless allegorical paintings, recreated in countless gardens—were meant to provide "firm links with reality." But the main question raised by Spacks's commentary is whether such effects account for an interest in the personification itself. In the one sentence specifically praising the personification, Thomson emphasizes not the setting but the "Attitude" of the figure. While attitude no doubt has primarily its pictorial sense of posture or arrangement—older, according to the *Oxford English Dictionary*, than the psychological implication that entered the language during exactly this period (ca. 1725)—Thomson's sense of the pictorial here clearly includes the affective implications of "ghastful" and "glare." The glare is "stedfast" because the personification is fixated on the effects of his own agency. The striking peculiarity of Mallet's scene is not its stock treatment of a meditative landscape but its principal figure, for the agent at the center of the ruins, instead of a poet, or saint, or philosopher, is the brooding personification of Ruin itself. Is "ghastful" Ruin here a ghost or aghast, agent or patient of his own fanatic power? How genuine is the threat from a demon who is self-enclosed in a conventional space, designed precisely to express and enclose him? Ruin shares some of the stylized impotence of the nearly comical "spirit" who sadly walks his wonted round and lingers over his own grave. For the Enlightened poet and reader, such a figure gets its charm by perfectly filling its alien and artificial space.

KEN FRIEDEN

The Eighteenth-Century
Introjection of Genius

"Genius" has a spectacular history, and eighteenth-century England is the scene of its most dramatic metamorphoses. In the writings of Anthony Shaftesbury, and until mid-century, "genius" runs roughly parallel to the German *Geist*, and retains traces of its Latin heritage; all individuals have a genius (spirit or mind) of some sort. Afterward, despite occasional efforts to recover classical meanings, a new range of signification takes control. While Joseph Addison anticipates this result as early as 1711, the eighteenth century fully appropriates Addison's use of the word only after Edward Young's conjectures of 1759. Beginning in the 1750s, a craze of theoretical writings urges that the inspired need not *have a genius*; instead an inspired author *has genius* or *is a genius*.

English usage has never shaken off this powerful introjection. The gods have fled, or we have buried them within ourselves by means of a verbal turn. The eighteenth century is both the meeting ground of genius and monologue and the scene of a decisive battle between the languages of theology and psychology. When Young writes of genius as "that god within," theological genius symbolically cedes to subjective monologue.

In retracing certain pathways in the eighteenth-century discussions of genius, this [essay] is suggestive rather than comprehensive, and the present context excludes all analysis of the related theories of wit and imagination. Lord Shaftesbury and Joseph Addison sketch the early model for modern genius. Henry Fielding, Alexander Gerard, Edward Young, and William

From *Genius and Monologue*. © 1985 by Cornell University. Cornell University Press, 1985.

Duff propose improvements, often in the form of elaborate scenarios. Immanuel Kant, by importing their invention, reveals limitations in the English product. Viewed collectively, these authors' expressions of "genius" exemplify ways in which verbal transformations predetermine intellectual history.

CHARACTERISTICS AND AUTHORS OF GENIUS

The modern turn to subjectivity and monologue is signaled by Shaftesbury's identification of Greek *daimōn* and Latin *genius* with soliloquy: the influence of an externalized guardian spirit becomes indistinguishable from effects of individual intelligence. In Shaftesbury's usage, "genius" is a vague term like the German *Geist* roughly equivalent to "spirit," "mind," or "intellect." If individuals have genius to varying degrees, Shaftesbury's "Miscellaneous Reflections" can refer without redundancy to "the free Spirits and forward Genius's of Mankind" (*Characteristicks of Men, Manners, Opinions, Times*. I have italicized words originally printed all in capital letters). As a spirit may be free, so a genius may be forward. Comfortable with applying the word "genius" to individuals, Shaftesbury writes of what modernity calls geniuses as "the better *Genius's*." Shaftesbury also refers to "*divine* Men of a transcending Genius." Because "genius" no longer names a transcendent being or power, certain men may be said to possess "a transcending Genius"; another may be only a "popular Genius." As an individual has a personality, so individuals are characterized by a certain kind of genius.

"Genius" does not refer only to the mind of men in general; it also denotes a special capacity. Shaftesbury anticipates Addison's discussion when he writes of authors "who have a *Genius* for *Writing*" (*Char.* III, 272). Like Addison after him, he censures authors who "wou'd be *all Genius*." Every man and woman has a genius of some kind, and only rare authors have genius of the forward variety; yet "genius" can also signify a particular quality of writing that should not be exaggerated.

In his "Soliloquy; or, Advice to an Author" (1710), Shaftesbury further revises the notion of genius. When Shaftesbury explicitly associates soliloquy with the notions of "Daemon, Genius, Angel or Guardian-Spirit," the transcendent genius vanishes and is replaced by monologue as a kind of internal dialogue. If such "beings" did in fact accompany us, their existence would support his argument, "for it wou'd be infallibly prov'd a kind of Sacrilege or Impiety to slight the Company of so Divine *a Guest*, and in a manner banish him our Breast, by refusing to enter with him into those secret Conferences by which alone he cou'd be enabled to become our *Adviser* and *Guide*." But Shaftesbury disputes the belief that these spirits were ever independent of men and prefers to read them figuratively. The ancient authors meant that, through soliloquy, "we could discover a certain *Duplicity* of Soul, and divide our-selves into *two Partys*." A genius is no supernatural agency but rather our "self-dissecting" partner in "this Home-*Dialect* of *Soliloquy*."

On September 2, 1711, a long and productive Sunday, "genius" was transformed. The printers rested from their labors on *The Spectator*, and readers were at leisure to contemplate the mysterious fiction of the day before. In Saturday's issue, number 159, Addison had pretended to translate the "first Vision" of an obscure "Oriental Manuscript" entitled *The Visions of Mirzah*. The narrator of this extended allegory approaches "the Haunt of a Genius": "I drew near with that Reverence which is due to a superior Nature; and as my Heart was entirely subdued by the captivating Strains I had heard, I fell down at his Feet and wept. The Genius smiled upon me with a Look of Compassion and Affability that familiarized him to my Imagination, and at once dispelled all the Fears and Apprehensions with which I approached him." This is both a fictional tale of encounter with a divine being and Addison's account of his own approach to the classical term *genius*. The narrator first approaches fearfully, but his reverence is soon replaced by familiarity. (In the following paper, Addison shows how familiar genius has become to his imagination.) Addison's narrator has apparently read Shaftes-bury's "Soliloquy," and thus his guide "lifted me from the Ground, and taking me by the Hand, *Mirzah*, said he, I have heard thee in thy Soliloquies, follow me." As the allegory proceeds, the Genius shows a vision of human life as a bridge and reveals islands of eternity reserved for men after death. "Despite the immense popularity of this Mirzah paper," a modern editor notes, "no others were published": the allegorical bridge stretches, not only from mundane life to eternity, but also from the classical to the modern genius. A Genius fades from view at the close of number 159, and when the following number appears on Monday, "genius" makes its debut under a new guise.

Addison's decisive statement on genius, in *The Spectator*, number 160, opens with an epigraph from Horace:

> —Cui mens divinior, atque os
> Magna sonaturum, des nominis hujus honorem.
> [*Satires* I. iv. 43–44]

> —Honor him with this name [of poet],
> Who has a divine mind and a great voice.

This citation from the *Satires* is aptly ambiguous, for the *mens divinior* signals both divine intervention and introjected divinity. But the *absence* of the opening words of the excerpted lines is especially suggestive. The passage from Horace reads: *Ingenium cui sit, cui mens divinior, atque os / Magna sonaturum, des nominis hujus honorem*, which may be translated: "To whom there is genius [*ingenium*], who has a divine mind and a great voice, / Honor him with this name [of poet]." Addison omits the crucial word *ingenium* from the passage he cites. He will discuss a form of genius that derives from nature and chooses not to acknowledge that Horace employs the difficult word *ingenium*, rather than the familiar *genius*. Addison's innovation depends on his simultaneous usurpation of both ranges of meaning and denial of their difference. Addison makes English "genius" signify as does the Latin *ingenium*, at the same time displacing the spiritual notion of a guardian genius. He conceals the Latin origins of "genius" and shifts the emphasis to mental capacity without acknowledging its separate origins in *ingenium*. The guardian spirit steals away in silence.

In the opening words of his article in *The Spectator*, number 160, Addison soberly maligns the genius of his contemporaries: "There is no Character more frequently given to a Writer, than that of being a Genius. I have heard many a little Sonneteer called a *fine Genius*. There is not an Heroick Scribler in the Nation, that has not his Admirers who think him a *great Genius*; and as for your Smatterers in Tragedy, there is scarce a Man among them who is not cried up by one or other for a *prodigious Genius*." By fusing two notions of genius, Addison innovates (with a French accent) and at the same time gives his invention the appearance of age. Genius is indeed ascribed to all people, in the sense that every individual has a mind or mental capacity; by means of an implicit synecdoche, Addison pretends that "genius" must mean "great Genius." Addison exerts control over linguistic development by shifting the application of "genius" while retaining the fact of its frequent, former usage. Shaftesbury repeatedly refers to diverse type of "genius"; Addison moves toward the modern sense of "genius" as an extraordinary mind. Yet Addison also writes of "great Genius's," which is not redundant if "genius" retains the older sense of mental faculty in general. In his discussion of "great natural Genius's," then, Addison both retains an established sense and innovates, along the lines of contemporary French *génie*.

Solomon, Homer, Pindar, and Shakespeare are Addison's examples of "great natural Genius's, that were never disciplined and broken by Rules of Art." A second class consists of "those that have formed themselves by Rules and submitted the Greatness of their natural Talents to the Corrections and Restraints of Art." Addison discerns a "great Danger in these latter kind of

Genius's," for they may "cramp their own Abilities too much by Imitation, and form themselves altogether upon Models, without giving full Play to their own natural Parts." According to Addison, genius is a natural gift; the forces of genius have precedence over the forces of art, so that a genius is endangered by following rules and models. Despite an explicit denial, in other words, Addison prefers geniuses of the first, natural class: "An imitation of the best Authors, is not to compare with a good Original; and I believe we may observe that very few Writers make an extraordinary Figure in the World, who have not something in their Way of thinking or expressing themselves that is peculiar to them and entirely their own." Addison's *Spectator* essay unveils a fully formed mythology of an "extraordinary Figure," the "original Genius." At the same time that he expresses hostility toward convention, Addison favors peculiarity in a manner that is decisive for later expositions.

Fielding revives Addison's "genius" and may have provoked Young's formulations. The narrator of *Tom Jones* mentions characters of "great Genius," of *a* "great Genius," and of "the greatest Genius." If it is still possible to refer to a person's "vast Strength of Genius" without redundancy, then "genius" does not yet carry its modern signification. To speak of a "great Genius" is like speaking of a great mind or, in German, like speaking of a *grossen Geist*.

Whereas Addison's narrator tacitly takes leave of the archaic and exotic Genius in *Visions of Mirzah*, Fielding explicitly renounces all spiritual guidance. He notes, "The *Arabians* and *Persians* had an equal Advantage in writing their Tales from the *Genii* and *Fairies*, which they believe in as an Article of their Faith," yet adds: "We have none of these Helps. To natural Means alone are we confined." Nevertheless, Fielding is not beyond referring to genius in mock epic invocation. In his skeptical age, Fielding asks for the assistance of "Genius; thou Gift of Heaven; without whose Aid, in vain we struggle against the Stream of Nature." Here genius is a gift and not a "Geist" of heaven, for heaven gives a mental capacity, not a mythical attendant. Thus genius requires an education: "And thou, O Learning, (for without thy Assistance nothing pure, nothing correct, can Genius produce) do thou guide my Pen." Although this passage is fraught with irony, Fielding apparently does believe that genius is a "Gift of Nature." His empirical definition of genius is a forerunner of Gerard's theories: "By Genius I would understand that Power, or rather those Powers of the Mind, which are capable of penetrating into all Things within our Reach and Knowledge, and of distinguishing their essential Differences. These are no other than Invention and Judgment; and they are both called by the collective Name of Genius, as they are of those Gifts of Nature which we bring with us into the World." Fielding disputes the notion that invention is "a creative Faculty," instead arguing that it involves "a quick and sagacious Penetration into the true Essence of all the Objects of our Contemplation." Consistently opposed to mystification, Fielding anticipates the cautious theoreticians of the following decades when he adds that invention "can rarely exist without the Concomitancy of Judgment." Hence Fielding follows Addison, although he does not support the trope that equates "genius" with "a great Genius." At the same time, Fielding disputes the less rationalistic hints contained in *The Spectator*, number 62. The discussion of genius in terms of invention and judgment recurs in the writings of Gerard and thus indirectly influences the entire tradition after Kant.

Following Addison's prodigious leap from September 1 to September 3, 1711, almost fifty years pass before expressions of the new genius advance further. By synecdoche, Addison writes "genius" and signifies "a great Genius." When this trope comes into its own, it captures the theoretical imagination of the 1760s.

Alexander Gerard's *Essay on Taste* appears in the same year as Edward Young's "Conjectures on Original Composition," and although they represent opposing traditions, both rely on elaborate images to represent the workings of genius. Gerard is especially indebted to the associationism of Locke, whereas Young's reputation is founded on his poem entitled *Night Thoughts*.

Gerard concurs with Fielding when he asserts that "the first and leading quality of genius is *invention*," but he conceives this as "a readiness of associating the remotest ideas that are any way related." Like a magnet, invention first collects materials and then "by its magical force ranges them into different species." Genius distinguishes itself by its design of "a regular and well-proportioned whole."

Gerard's characterization emphasizes classical order and makes genius into "the grand architect which not only chuses the materials, but disposes them into a regular structure." For the perfection of its structure, however, genius requires the assistance of taste. The greatest tragic poets combined genius and taste: "The vigour of their imaginations led them into unexplored tracks; and they had such light and discernment, as, without danger of error, directed their course in this untrodden wilderness." Landscape imagery reappears throughout the tradition, for genius is typically in danger of straying into forests of wild figuration and of eluding the rigorous systematization Gerard seeks.

Meanwhile, some "forward Genius's" attempt to impose order. Samuel Johnson's *Dictionary* (1755) provides the clearest summary of previous applications of the word "genius." Johnson lists five senses:

1. The protecting or ruling power of men, places, or things
2. A man endowed with superior faculties
3. Mental power or faculties
4. Disposition of nature by which any one is qualified for some peculiar employment
5. Nature; disposition.

The first sense corresponds roughly to the archaic usage (still present in Shakespeare's *Macbeth* III.i). The second sense derives from Addison's article of 1711. Senses 3, 4, and 5 chronologically precede Addison's usage and are the basis on which he can write of geniuses of diverse types. Johnson's *Dictionary* entry expresses the eighteenth-century tensions between theological and psychological interpretations; the writings of Young and Duff exemplify two distinct paths of speculation within the new humanistic traditions.

LANDSCAPES OF GENIUS

Edward Young's "Conjectures on Original Composition" (1759) and William Duff's *Essay on Original Genius* (1767) both emphasize the originality or peculiarity of genius. At the same time, they blur the origins of originality, for how can original genius originate in men? If Addison demonstrates that a genius is a man of great "natural Parts," does it follow that original genius is really original nature? Although Young explicitly discusses Addison, his essay conceals the link between their "original" conceptions.

The "Conjectures on Original Composition" are framed by an epistolary convention. Subtitled "a letter to the Author of Sir Charles Gradison," referring to the novel published by Samuel Richardson in 1753–54, Young's essay is initially concerned with age, and the tone is apologetic. Young's immediate concern is to *justify* the production of his text. Because he values original composition, Young fears that a writer who is old may have no justification for his activity of writing. An elderly author, Young implicitly writes his essay to explain how, by virtue of genius, his mind may "enjoy a perpetual Spring."

The predominant imagery of the "Conjectures" is that of landscape. After describing his letter as "miscellaneous" and "somewhat licentious in its conduct," he notes that he has "endeavoured to make some amends, by digressing into subjects more important." *Digression* takes on special significance, both in the progress of the essay and in the content of Young's aesthetic theory. Young compares the movement of his essay to an extended scenario:

"A serious thought standing single among many of a lighter nature, will sometimes strike the careless wanderer after amusement only, with useful awe: as monumental marbles scattered in a wide pleasure-garden (and such there are) will call to recollection those who would never have sought in a church-yard walk of mournful yews." The reader of Young's letter is, then, like a "careless wanderer after amusement only" who will be affected by "useful awe" in confrontation with scattered, serious thoughts. Landscapes are central to the figuration of the essay, and at this point the entire essay is figured as "a wide pleasure-garden" in which "monumental marbles" are scattered. Genius and originality, like monuments in a garden, are the more serious thoughts to which Young wanders. Young continues his landscape imagery when he describes the "Conjectures" as a kind of voyage leading to a "hidden lustre." This natural scene provides the ground for Young's essay; Addison is the luminary he uncovers, but in fact the true goal of the "Conjectures" is Young's own revision of Addison's "genius." In terms of genius and originality, the remainder of the essay considers the difference between compositions that shine brightly and those that are extinguished.

Young further develops his version of genius by means of a series of natural images. He connects problems of linguistic originality and genius with processes of natural aging, for example, when he states that "it is with thoughts as it is with words, and with both as with men; they may grow old, and die." In contrast to this process of decay, Young writes that "the mind of a man of genius is a fertile and pleasant field; pleasant as Elysium, and fertile as Tempe; it enjoys a perpetual spring." References to Elysium and Tempe gesture in the direction of an explicit paradise myth of genius, associated with a supernatural nature. Defying the processes of deterioration that would make him imaginatively old, Young finds a way to defeat time by positing that genius is endowed with "a perpetual spring." Two kinds of growth, originals and imitations, arise from that spring; if not all fruits of genius are originals, an aging man of genius may have reason to doubt the merits of his writing. This complication leads to a more aggressive turn in the figuration.

With a hint at the world of exploration, Young shifts from the figure of natural growth to that of territorial conquest: originals "are great benefactors: they extend the republic of letters, and add a new province to its dominion." Behind this presentation stands a powerful myth that writing can (dis)cover *new ground*. On the other hand, an imitator is ultimately weak because he always "builds on another's foundation." When genius appears as conqueror, the artist begins to stand at a distance from the art he masters. Young leaves ambiguous whether the original author *is* nature or only has special powers like those of nature. Insisting on natural imagery, Young conceives genius as a spontaneous growth: "an original may be said to be of a vegetable nature; it rises spontaneously from the vital root of genius; it grows, it is not made." "Genius" names the magical place of creation ex nihilo, or rather, "out of a barren waste."

This mystification does not long retain its full force. After all, even a "barren waste" may have to be wrested from previous settlers, and a "new province" is not so easily annexed. "Why are originals so few?" Young asks. According to the previous account, a dearth of originals should result from a lack of genius or of new terrain, but Young explains that in fact "illustrious examples engross, prejudice, and intimidate." Obstructive presences, not a scarcity of genius, impede the creation of originals. Poetic originality demands both the natural power called "genius" and an avoidance of excessive exposure to previous examples. Overwhelmed by prior authors, we are inclined to "bury our strength."

Before acknowledging that a more radical move is necessary, Young returns to a naturalistic solution in answer to the problem, "Must we then (you say) not imitate ancient authors?" He responds: "Imitate them, by all means, but imitate aright. He that imitates the divine Iliad, does not imitate Homer; but he who takes the same method which Homer took, for arriving at a capacity of accomplishing a work so great. Tread in his steps to the sole fountain of immortality; drink where he drank, at the true Helicon, that is, at the breast of nature." But it is not enough to insist that the original author must drink "at the breast of nature." Young supplements this natural myth by suggesting that an author must turn away from his predecessors: "As far as a regard to nature and sound sense will permit a departure from your great predecessors; so far, ambitiously, depart from them: the farther from them in similitude, the nearer are you to them in excellence: you rise by it into an original." At this crossroad, the departure from predecessors, rather than spontaneous growth, appears to constitute originality: "All eminence, and distinction, lyes out of the beaten road; excursion and deviation are necessary to find it, and the more remote your path from the highway, the more reputable." Deviation replaces natural growth as the determining mark of the original. Images of travel or errancy undo the initial, natural myth and necessitate deviation rather than straightforward growth.

After the publications of Young and others, William Duff's situation is far more difficult. Although he does not refer to contemporary writers, in an "Advertisement" to the *Essay on Original Genius*, Duff shows his awareness that the field is already crowded. Speaking of himself in the third person, Duff writes that "he is at the same time well aware, that in an *Essay on Original*

Genius, Originality of Sentiment will naturally, and may, no doubt, justly
be expected; and where this is altogether wanting, no other excellence can
supply the defect. Whereas Young displaces his fears to the problems associated with old age, Duff directly confronts the necessity of justifying his
text, recognizing that his *Essay on Original Genius* must itself proceed in the
manner of original genius. Duff is "not a little apprehensive of the issue of
a strict examination" when readers employ originality as their criterion of
merit.

Duff's landscapes resemble Young's figures for imaginative activity, although he dispenses with the "perpetual spring." Instead of conceiving original genius as a natural growth, Duff immediately identifies it as an errant
traveler. "To explore unbeaten tracks, and make new discoveries in the
regions of Science; to invent the designs, and perfect the productions of Art,
is the province of Genius alone." Again, "it is the peculiar character of original
Genius to strike out a path for itself whatever sphere it attempts to occupy."
In Duff's treatise, literary landscapes are the only sites of divergences and
divagations by genius. Later, however, Duff admits that precursors may
represent serious obstacles: "A Poet of real Genius, who lives in a distant
uncultivated age, possesses great and peculiar advantages for original composition." Like Young, Duff prefers new imaginative ground. The genius in
an "uncultivated age" is free to uncover treasures without restraint, "the
mines of Fancy not having been opened before his time."

Duff emphasizes that *deviation* characterizes original genius by noting
that imagination, left to itself, has a tendency to deviate: "*Imagination* . . . perpetually attempting to soar, is apt to deviate into the mazes of
error." As if to excuse the aberrations of genius, Duff carefully transforms
these deviations into positive effects: "The objects he has, or ought to have
in view, are, to bring into open light those truths that are wrapped in the
shades of obscurity, or involved in the mazes of error, and to apply them to
the purpose of promoting the happiness of mankind." Duff's subsequent turn
away from the errant conception of genius occurs by mediation of "mazes
of error": those mazes by which the genius was endangered become those
that genius illuminates for the benefit of all.

As Duff would have it, then, the brightness of original genius serves to
illuminate obscure paths. Yet he cannot fail to acknowledge that genius is at
times the source of confusions. Duff discusses imagery as a distinctive mark,
an elevated style that corresponds to the flights characteristic of genius.
Elevated above "ordinary modes of speech," a poet's language attains "a
peculiar dignity." Images, however, do not always shed light, or rather may
blind by shedding too much light at once: "An original Author indeed will

frequently be apt to exceed in the use of this ornament, by pouring forth such a blaze of imagery, as to dazzle and overpower the mental sight; the effect of which is, that his Writings become obscure, if not unintelligible to common Readers; just as the eye is for some time rendered incapable of distinguishing the objects that are presented to it, after having stedfastly [*sic*] contemplated the sun." As excessive light produces darkness, an excess of metaphor obscures. If writings of an original genius are too extreme in their figuration, they overpower readers' abilities and cause pseudoblindness. Duff prefers to close his eyes to the danger that must consequently attach to creations of original genius.

Both Young and Duff acknowledge that original genius is known, not simply for what it is, but for what it is not; the lights of genius shine in contrast to other lights, and flights of genius astound in contrast to the motions of those who crawl. When Young considers the subject of words old and new, he returns to the theme that opens the "Conjectures": "It is with thoughts as it is with words, and with both as with men, they may grow old, and die. Words tarnished, by passing through the mouths of the vulgar, are laid aside as inelegant and obsolete; so thoughts, when become too common, should lose their currency; and we should send new metal to the mint; that is, new meaning to the press." Genius must take care to select proper currency, for the original genius is known by its "new metal." Young does not wish to lose the ground of original composition by undermining its supposed origins in genius, yet the subsequent passage suggests a need for new schemes: "So few are originals, that, if all other books were to be burnt, the lettered world would resemble some metropolis in flames, where a few incombustible buildings, a fortress, temple, or tower, lift their heads, in melancholy grandeur, amid the mighty ruin." The ambitious author might perhaps wish for such a conflagration; the blaze of genius returns as a burning of previous authors' works. Is the success of an original genius akin to the "melancholy grandeur" of ruins amid a charred city? What is the temple Young imagines still standing after the destruction of a city?

GENIUS, INTROJECTED DIVINITY

Young and Duff elaborate myths of genius because, without this figure, originality could threaten to subvert all grounds. To justify and explain innovations, genius must supply the ground and the new harvest of literary creation: as Young writes, "an original may be said to be of a vegetable nature; it rises spontaneously from the vital root of genius; it grows, it is not made." Similarly, Duff conceives original genius as a power that frees an author from the need to imitate:

> A Poet endued with a truly original Genius, will however be under no necessity of drawing any of the materials of his composition from the Works of preceding Bards; since he has an unfailing resource in the exuberance of his own Imagination, which will furnish him with a redundance of all those materials, and particularly with an inexhaustible variety of new and splendid imagery, which must be regarded as one distinguishing mark of original poetic Genius.

"New and splendid imagery" is supposed to derive from genius, especially in happier, freer moments when there is no necessity to deviate. Duff strives to make original genius the ultimate ground, whereas Young draws from the Roman tradition to intimate divine origins of genius. Young and Duff rely on much of the same naturalistic figuration; their difference arises from Duff's suppression of the theological dimension.

Young interprets the origins of originality through a myth of divine inspiration. But this genius is not analogous to the *daimonion* of Socrates nor to any of the guardian spirits suggested by tradition. Instead, Young radically introjects the divine spark: "With regard to the moral world, conscience; with regard to the intellectual, genius, is that god within." Young's "genius" does not descend to man but rises with him; he advises the aspiring author: "let thy genius rise (if a genius thou hast) as the sun from chaos; and if I should then say, like an Indian, Worship it, (though too bold), yet should I say little more than my second rule enjoins, (*viz.*) Reverence thyself." Young thus proposes a secularized religion of self-realization. Unfortunately, our genius does not necessarily present itself directly: "Genius, in this view, is like a dear friend in our company under disguise; who, while we are lamenting his absence, drops his mask, striking us, at once, with equal surprise and joy." Originals are the products of divinity in man, but divine epiphany occurs in a peculiar scene of self-demasking. To recognize our own genius, we must wait for the moment when the disguise is dropped. Our disguise presumably consists of "figures" borrowed from previous authors, and which we in rare moments escape—unless the "dear friend" whose absence we lament turns out to be, not our own genius, but a feared precursor. The Christian exorcism of "daemons" is a figure for the pseudoreligious turn Young proffers, the passage from multiple precursors to an original persona.

The theological framework of Young's "Conjectures" becomes most explicit at its close. Raising the subject of Addison's genius, Young considers

Addison's final words that "taught us how to die." If "the mind of a man of genius" is like "a perpetual spring" that assures eternal life, these dying words that "spoke human nature not unrelated to the divine" perform a similar function.

Young's final three paragraphs return to the image drawn by the initial two. He prefaces his remarks by writing of a wish to reveal the "hidden lustre" concealed in some monument. Now he refers again to "the sacred deposit, which by Providence was lodged in my hand." At the same time that he reflects the Roman tradition of a *genius* that passes on a torch to man, Young passes on his revised conception of genius. Addison, a Christian man of genius, turns out to be the "sepulchral lamp" mentioned earlier; Young has led us to "the long hidden lustre of our accomplished countryman, who now rises, as from his tomb, to receive the regard so greatly due to the dignity of his death; a death to be distinguished by tears of joy; a death which angels beheld with delight." Why is Young so concerned to praise Addison? In his praise, of course, he chooses to ignore Addison as a forerunner in the theory of genius. While Young asserts his wish to restore Addison's reputation, he simultaneously proclaims his own mission, to eulogize Addison, a "sacred deposit, which by Providence was lodged in my hands." To pronounce Addison's genius is for Young to become a divine messenger, to mediate between heavens and earth, to transform the light of the sun into sparks of thought and the blaze of imagery: to write with genius, as genius.

One striking absence from Duff's account is the theological ground that Young retains for genius. Young's original composition appears to "rise from the vital root of genius," and genius, in turn, "is that god within." Duff curtails the theological dimension and implies, firmly within the empiricist tradition, that genius is an independent power of mind. Although Young's "genius" prevails in the poetic tradition of the nineteenth century, his rival Gerard, whose associationist theory in some ways parallels Duff's, finds double-edged expression in modern aesthetics.

Eighteenth-century aesthetics culminates in the writings of Immanuel Kant, whose *Kritik der Urteilskraft* (1790) and the *Anthropologie in pragmatischer Hinsicht* (1798) present central statements on genius (*Genie*) in the tradition begun by Shaftesbury. Both brief passages begin by conceiving genius in connection with a theory of talented artistic creation. Section 46 of the third *Kritik* and section 47 of the *Anthropologie* attempt unified expositions of genius following the associationism of Gerard, but hints of the theological conception destabilize Kant's definitions.

Kant explicitly links the German *Genie* with French *génie* rather than with Latin *genius*—because he discusses genius as an inborn capacity of the artist, that is, he traces the word to Latin *ingenium* and keeps the Latin *genius* at a distance. The genius of the artist is the product of nature, not of divine agency. In a parenthesis, however, Kant acknowledges the buried etymology of genius: "For presumably the word *Genie* is derived from *genius*, from the peculiar guiding, guardian spirit that is given to a person at his birth, and from whose inspiration these ideas were supposed to come forth." The recognition of a double etymology allows Kant (Like Addison) to emphasize the meaning of "Genie" as a mental capacity (*ingenium*) while retaining the mythological overtones suggested by the notion of a guardian *genius*. But Kant (again like Addison) does not acknowledge the difficulties associated with combining psychological and mythological conceptions. The discussion in the *Anthropologie* also becomes more complex when Kant seeks to explain the reason for using a "mystical" name, *Genie*, to mean "the exemplary originality of talent":

> But the reason why the exemplary originality of talent is called by this *mystical* name, is that the one who has it cannot explain its outbursts to himself; nor can he make comprehensible to himself how he comes upon an art, which he could not have learned. For *invisibility* (of the cause of an effect) is a collateral idea of a spirit [*Geist*] (a genius [*Genius*], which accompanied the talented already at his birth), whose inspiration, so to speak, it only follows.

At the close of a century of dispute between theological and psychological explanations, Kant observes the final similarity between the notion of talent and the idea that a spirit accompanies a man from the time of his birth. The "exemplary originality of talent" that creates beautiful art cannot be explained, even by its possessor.

According to Kant's later analysis, then, *Genie* derives from Latin *genius*, but this guiding spirit appears essentially in the capacity of Latin *ingenium*. Although Kant directly acknowledges the work of Alexander Gerard, his efforts to equate *genius* with *ingenium* ultimately ally him with Addison and Young. Yet the palimpsest of "genius" asserts itself when Kant finishes by recognizing its etymology: a slippage from *Genie (ingenium)* to *genius* occurs in both the *Kritik der Urteilskraft* and the *Anthropologie*.

Whereas Greek *daimōn* names a vague transcendent power, and Latin *genius* refers to transcendent being, modern English "genius" characteristically signifies an immanent, self-sufficient mental activity. As the eighteenth century opens, Shaftesbury casts "genius" in the role of "mind," or "human spirit." This genius is not transcendent, and thus Shaftesbury mentions unusual "*divine* Men of a transcending Genius." Soliloquy, in Shaftesbury's terminology, names the independence of human genius; yet theorists of genius never agree concerning the origins of originality. "Transcending (original) genius," or mind that steps beyond established paths, uneasily seeks to usurp the place of transcendent guidance. Addison gives a radical turn to English "genius" by means of the synecdoche that equates it with "great Genius." All genius comes to be great though nontranscendent. In the wake of Locke's associationism, Fielding understands genius as a power of mind, a gift of nature that must be combined with learning. Gerard similarly writes of genius as a natural faculty of mind, closest to invention.

When Young persists in ascribing divine origins to genius, he simultaneously creates an introjected divinity, "that god within." An unnamed friend is like the Christian emperors who "expelled daemons, and dedicated their temples to the living *God*." The new "genius" suggests a religion of the self that purges itself of precursor-demons. Yet the notion of originality displaces transcendent origins, for the pre-Romantic genius strives to become its own originator. In a complex natural scenario, however, self-origination appears as a necessary deviation from overtrodden paths.

Despite their search for a sound basis of originality, then, eighteenth-century English authors represent originality as a swerve away from origins. The poet, who can no longer claim a transcendent muse, relies on natural talents that permit him to explore new paths. Genius turns inward, transformed from the status of an externalized divine guide into the role of a mundane wanderer in aesthetic realms. The new humanistic genius fails to replace spiritual guidance by soliloquy, however, for new forms of transcendence emerge.

MARTIN PRICE

The Theatre of Mind:
Edward Young and James Thomson

EDWARD YOUNG

Perhaps the best place to observe the histrionic note of mid-century poetry is in what Boswell called "a mass of the grandest and richest poetry that human genius has ever produced"—Edward Young's *Night Thoughts* (1742–45). Young's method becomes clear if we compare him with Pope. First, the great passage that opens the second epistle of the *Essay on Man* (1733):

> Know then thyself, presume not God to scan;
> The proper study of mankind is man.
> Plac'd on this isthmus of a middle state,
> A being darkly wise, and rudely great:
> With too much knowledge for the sceptic side,
> With too much weakness for the stoic's pride,
> He hangs between; in doubt to act, or rest;
> In doubt to deem himself a God, or beast;
> In doubt his mind or body to prefer;
> Born but to die, and reasoning but to err;
> Alike in ignorance, his reason such,
> Whether he thinks too little, or too much:
> Chaos of thought and passion, all confused;
> Still by himself abus'd, or disabus'd;
> Created half to rise, and half to fall;

From *To the Palace of Wisdom*. © 1964 by Martin Price. Doubleday & Company, Inc., 1964. Originally entitled "The Theatre of Mind."

> Great lord of all things, yet a prey to all;
> Sole judge of truth, in endless error hurl'd:
> The glory, jest, and riddle of the world!

And a corresponding passage in Young:

> How poor, how rich, how abject, how august,
> How complicate, how wonderful, is man!
> How passing wonder He, who made him such!
> Who centred in our make such strange extremes!
> From diff'rent natures marvelously mix'd,
> Connexion exquisite of distant worlds!
> Distinguish'd link in being's endless chain!
> Midway from nothing to the Deity!
> A beam ethereal, sully'd, and absorpt!
> Tho' sully'd and dishonour'd, still divine!
> Dim miniature of greatness absolute!
> An heir of glory! A frail child of dust!
> Helpless immortal! Insect infinite!
> A worm! a God!—I tremble at myself,
> And in myself am lost! At home, a stranger,
> Thought wanders up and down, surpriz'd, aghast,
> And wond'ring at her own: How reason reels!
> O what a miracle to man is man,
> Triumphantly distress'd! what joy, what dread!
> Alternately transported, and alarm'd!
> What can preserve my life? or what destroy?
> An angel's arm can't snatch me from the grave,
> Legions of angels can't confine me there.

>   (I, 68–90)

Pope's lines, among his most brilliant, draw upon the paradoxes of Pascal's double infinity and fix the rivalry of orders in the antitheses of the heroic couplet. Young makes more violent use of paradox. The movement of lines 79–81 (beginning with "An heir of glory!") is toward sharper and more shocking juxtapositions, which contract from a full phrase to a single adjective and noun, and at last to the bare terms *worm* and *God*. At this point, Young breaks off. His rhetorical argument has gone as far as it can. Words fail, and he shifts—in a way that is most important—from generalized irony to the personal predicament. He writes out of his condition, as one immersed in it and struggling toward meaning. When he returns, at the close, to the large scheme of the cosmos, the verbs have become fiercely kinetic and the paradoxical self has become a center of titanic struggle.

Young's poem asks to be set beside Pope's. Perhaps because the anonymously published *Essay on Man* had once been attributed to him by many, he defends his own poem—in the first of its nine long "nights"—by opposition to Pope's:

> Man too he sung: *immortal* man I sing;
> Oft bursts my song beyond the bounds of life;
> What now but immortality can please?
> O had *he* press'd his theme, pursu'd the track
> Which opens out of darkness into day!
>
> (I, 453–57)

Pope's poem, in Young's view, dwells in mundane light. It deals with man's earthly happiness and does not confront man directly with the prospects of eternal reward and punishment. Young's interest is in the light of eternity; he withdraws into that night where man is alone beneath the spectacle of the firmament. He has turned away from the social world and rejected all human achievements as "childish toys." He will settle for nothing less than infinity. George Eliot (in her famous denunciation "Worldliness and Other-Worldliness: The Poet Young," 1857) is affronted by Young's "deficient human sympathy," his "impiety towards the present and visible." All that she admires in Cowper (or Wordsworth) finds its contrary in Young's effort to startle, to dazzle, and to terrify: he "knows no medium between the ecstatic and the sententious," and his poetry is "a Juggernaut made of gold and jewels, at once magnificent and repulsive." His religion she sums up as "egoism turned heavenward."

Against this we have Boswell's testimony that he "who does not feel his nerves shaken, and his heart pierced by many passages . . . must be of a hard and obstinate frame." Young's poem may have had special appeal for Boswell; it is addressed to a young "man of pleasure and the world" (named Lorenzo), and conceived in terms Boswell might well have applied to himself. Lorenzo is the embodiment of worldly grace and wit, but he must be brought to despise the world and venerate his soul. Young makes use of typically Pascalian themes—the two infinities (IX, 1573–86), the *deus absconditus* ("Triune, unutterable, unconceiv'd, / Absconding, yet demonstrable, great God!" IX, 2290–91), the rival orders. The vehemence of his conceits derives from his constant separation of orders. When he portrays a devout Christian ("A man on earth devoted to the skies"), Young rings all the changes:

> He sees with other eyes than theirs: where they
> Behold a sun, he spies a deity;
> What makes them only smile, makes him adore.
> Where they see mountains, he but atoms sees;
> An empire, in his balance weighs a grain.
>   (VIII, 1081, 1107–11)

It is this kind of wit that leads George Eliot to speak of Young's "radical insincerity as a poetic artist": "The grandiloquent man is never bent on saying what he feels or what he sees, but in producing a certain effect on his audience." In "proportion as morality is emotional, it will exhibit itself in direct sympathetic feeling and action. . . . A man who is perpetually thinking in monitory apothegms, who has an unintermittent flux of rebuke, can have little energy left for simple feeling."

One need not defend Young against George Eliot: her principles of judgment would lead her to condemn far better poets. What matters is the kind of poetry he is trying to create. It is endlessly hortatory and ejaculatory, and it suffers from the effort to sustain intensity too long ("So long on wing," as he puts it, "and in no middle climes"). The effort forces Young into all kinds of devices—Senecan pointedness; extended conceits ("Let burlesque go beyond him," Johnson remarked of these); an imagery of bursting, soaring, and plunging. "No poet," Marjorie Nicolson has written, "was ever more 'space intoxicated' than Edward Young, no did any other eighteenth-century poet or aesthetician equal him in his obsession with the 'psychology of infinity'—the effect of vastness and the vast upon the soul of man." "There dwells a noble pathos in the skies," Young wrote, "which warms our passions, proselytes our hearts" (IX, 1632–33). And his paradoxes begin from the ever-present awareness of death:

> This is the bud of being, the dim dawn,
> The twilight of our day, the vestibule. . . .
> Embryos we must be, till we burst the shell,
> Yon ambient azure shell, and spring to life.
>   (I, 123–24, 132–33)

The darkness of night becomes the possibility of new life. Others may adore the sun, Young writes:

> Darkness has more divinity for me;
> It strikes thought inward; it drives back the soul
> To settle on herself, our point supreme!
> There his own theatre! There sits the judge.

Darkness the curtain drops o'er life's dull scene.
                              (V, 128–32)

This kind of paradox can culminate in such a line as

The King of Terrors is the Prince of Peace,
                              (III, 534)

a line that permits Blake, in his illustration, the great pictorial irony we see in his illustrations to Job: the threatening figure of Death who has appeared with his dart through earlier plates assumes the benign countenance and gestures of the Christ.

Young emphasizes the emptiness of the life to which Lorenzo is committed—its chanciness, futility, constriction:

Shall sons of aether, shall the blood of heav'n,
Set up their hopes on earth, and stable *here*,
With brutal acquiescence in the mire?
                              (VII, 54–56)

Young is calling forth from Lorenzo his sense of his own divinity—"Man's misery declares him born for bliss; / His *anxious* heart asserts the truth I sing" (V, 60–61). The tone ranges from satire to rapture:

Or own the soul immortal, or invert
All order. Go, mock-majesty! go, man!
And bow to thy superiors of the stall;
Thro' ev'ry scene of *sense* superior far.
                              (V, 290–93)

Only the awareness of eternity and of the divine in man "restores bright order" and "re-inthrones us in supremacy / Of joy, ev'n here" (V, 316–18). And, typically, this becomes kinetic imagery: "Man must soar. / An obstinate activity within, / An insuppressive spring, will toss him up," for "souls immortal must for ever heave / At something great" (V, 389–91, 399–400).

Unlike Pope, who tries to show man reasonable aspiration within his present state, Young's aim is to launch the soul into flight: "The soul of man was made to walk the skies" (IX, 1016). All of Lorenzo's worldly ambitions must be translated into another order and converted to a desire for eternity. Young offers eternity as the fulfillment of the latent energy within man rather than as a more traditional death and rebirth; the movement of the poem is the bursting out of constrictions, expansion into infinite space, progress toward unreachable perfection. The images of the heavens yield an atmosphere in which the soul

Freely can respire, dilate, extend,
In full proportion let loose all her powers;
And, undeluded, grasp at something great.
Nor as a stranger, does she wander there,
But, wonderful herself, through wonder strays;
Contemplating their grandeur, finds her own.

(IX, 1020–25)

The heavens present an order in disorder. "'Tis comprehension's absolute defeat"; yet it is "Confusion unconfus'd"—"All on wing! / In motion,
all! yet what profound repose" (IX, 1105, 1115–17). We return to Milton's
great imagery of the cosmic dance—the "circles intricate" and "mystic maze"
(IX, 1130). This energetic order corresponds to the order within man. Young
sees man as always grasping, dilating, in some form or other moving: "The
mind that would be happy must be great" (IX, 1379).

The visible and present are for brutes,
A slender portion, and a narrow bound!
These reason, with an energy divine
O'erleaps; and claims the future and unseen!

(VI, 246–49)

One of the interesting consequences of Young's themes is his treatment
of vision. When he seeks to free Lorenzo from the world, he demonstrates
its poverty by showing what man brings to it. The powers within man
descend from a divine source and confer beauty on the visible world. The
senses

Take in, at once, the landscape of the world,
At a small inlet, which a grain might close,
And half create the wondrous world they see.
Our senses, as our reason, are divine.
But for the magic organ's powerful charm,
Earth were a rude, uncolor'd chaos, still.
Objects are but th' occasion; ours th' exploit

. . . .

Like Milton's Even, when gazing on the lake,
Man makes the matchless image man admires.

(VI, 425–31, 435–36)

This doctrine of creative perception clearly goes back to the same kind
of Neo-Platonic sources upon which Shaftesbury's draws. It is the moment

of transcendent vision, however, that concerns Young more; and this is involved with the compelling power of feeling. Here is the instance of man contemplating the Crucifixion:

> Who looks on that, and sees not in himself
> An awful stranger, a terrestrial god?
>
> . . . .
>
> I gaze, and, as I gaze, my mounting soul
> Catches strange fire, Eternity, at thee,
> And drops the world—or, rather, more enjoys:
> How chang'd the face of nature! how improv'd!
>   (IV, 494–95, 499–502)

In both these senses of vision, Young seems to have had some influence on his illustrator, Blake. The bursting of the "ambient azure shell" is an image we find again in Blake; another is the "self-fetter'd" soul (Blake's "mind-forg'd manacles"). And Blake's *The Gates of Paradise* recalls these lines:

> How, like a worm, was I wrapt round and round
> In silken thought, which reptile Fancy spun!
> Till darken'd Reason lay quite clouded o'er
> With soft conceit of endless comfort here,
> Nor yet put forth her wings to reach the skies!
>   (I, 133, 157, 158–62)

Young anticipates the image of natural man enclosed in a cavern as well as the image of the cocoon: "Through chinks, styl'd organs, dim life peeps at light" (III, 450). These "influences" are not important as such, but they serve (and Blake's illustrations serve even better) to show us how Young could be read in his own century. His gloom and melancholy are far less important than his insistence upon man's expansive grandeur of spirit and upon the dramatic experience of self-discovery. He builds on the doctrine of divine punishment and reward, but his ultimate emphasis is on the energy that sanctifies the passions—their "grandeur . . . speaks them rays of an eternal fire" (VII, 527–30)—and informs the order of charity.

JAMES THOMSON

Young emphasizes throughout the *Night Thoughts* that the infinity of space and the intensities of light are internal dimensions of man as well (like Milton's Heaven and Hell). The firmament is "the noble pasture of the mind,/ Which there expatiates, strengthens, and exults" (IX, 1037–38). In James

Thomson's *The Seasons* (1726–28, revised continuously until 1746), while the imagery is far more minutely accurate and concrete, it has much the same function. Thomson draws not only from nature itself, but from Scripture, from Virgil's *Georgics*, from the great account of creation in the seventh book of *Paradise Lost*—and from Shaftesbury's *Moralists*. One of his early poems is, in effect, an adaptation of Shaftesbury, and his interest in Newtonian science could readily be accommodated to Shaftesbury's doctrines of cosmic harmony. Just as Theocles takes his friend on a circuit of all the regions of the earth to show the range and complexity of nature's order, so Thomson writes four poems on the seasons which explore the Arctic north, the torrid equatorial zones, and all between.

In *Paradise Lost* Milton created a poetry of nature that drew its force from the whole cosmos of the poem. Even in those passages of free and intense phantasy where Milton catches the energies of creative goodness, the cosmic and moral themes of the dramatic action are involved:

> The grassy Clods now Calv'd, now half appear'd
> The Tawny Lion, pawing to get free
> His hinder parts, then springs as broke from Bonds,
> And Rampant shakes his Brinded mane; the Ounce,
> The Libbard, and the Tiger, as the Mole
> Rising, the crumbl'd Earth above them threw
> In Hillocks; the swift Stag from under ground
> Bore up his branching head.
>
> (VIII, 463–70)

These are images of creatures bursting into life, dragging themselves from the womb of earth, rising into light like branching trees, yet with a swiftness that confounds our conception of the slow growth of a tree. They are defiant and jubilant images. In the spirit of the sublime, they overwhelm our familiar conceptions and demand the reach of imagination that is appropriate to their great theme. Here more successfully than anywhere else Milton outweighs the energy of the fallen angels with its divine counterpart, and the power of destruction just seen in the war in Heaven—"Heav'n ruining from Heav'n"—with the energy of ascending life.

But the great epic action has disappeared from Thomson's *Seasons*, nor has it yet been replaced—as it was to be in Wordsworth's *Prelude*—by a single dramatic movement toward a consummation of man and nature. At the heart of Wordsworth's poem is the deep underpresence that waits to be perceived and recognized, to be brought to the surface of awareness, and to be created anew in the consciousness. In Thomson we have only the beginnings of such a theme. The subject of his poem is not the poet himself but the divine order within the created world. But, once the epic narrative has given way to a descriptive and meditative structure, the movement of the poem reflects the movement of the poet's mind. The very arbitrariness of design, the constant shift between observation and reflection, makes us aware of the associative mind at work. His subject, moreover, is the natural scene, and the muteness of landscape throws the poet back on himself. Thomson teases images that are only partly claimed by general meanings and have, as a result, a suggestiveness and openness that bring a new quality to poetry.

The design of *The Seasons* can best be seen in the *Hymn* that Thomson appended to the four poems. The seasons are the aspects of the "varied God"; beneath their changes lies the art of God, but it can be perceived only with subtle and reverent perception—"Deep felt" (22)—lest man fail to discriminate "Shade unperceiv'd so softening into shade, / And all so forming an harmonious whole." The Hymn evokes the choir of all created things (as in Book V of *Paradise Lost*)—each creature animating every other:

> Bleat out afresh, ye hills; ye mossy rocks,
> Retain the sound; the broad responsive low,
> Ye valleys, raise; for the Great Shepherd reigns,
> And his unsuffering kingdom yet will come.
> (72–75)

The poet, finally, withdraws into his own consciousness; the outwardness of a given scene is of secondary concern:

> Since God is ever present, ever felt,
> In the void waste as in the city full;
> And where He vital breathes there must be joy
>
> . . . .
>   I cannot go
> Where Universal Love not smiles around.
> (104–7, 111–12)

And at last there is the movement toward self-transcendence—or is it Shaftesbury's "rational ecstasy?"—and the silence of communion:

>   But I lose
> Myself in Him, in light ineffable!
> Come then, expressive silence, muse His praise.
> (116–18)

In the poems of *The Seasons* there is a double movement—the descent of God in plentitude and the ascent of man's mind in recognition of Order. Between the two stands the challenge that lies at the outward edge of plentitude before the ascent can begin: the threat of the ambiguous or the meaningless. Thomson presents this threat as the extreme of heat or cold, the predatory cruelty of wolf or serpent, the utterly inhuman or hostile—or the internal confusion and betrayal of passionate and jealous love, as in *Spring*. These are limiting cases that test man's faith in Order; once they are met and passed by, the movement of ascent (or, in another figure, the movement back to the One from the borders of emanation) can commence.

Thomson is, as his language shows, particularly concerned with number; plentitude always confounds our powers of measure, and few adjectives are so frequent in Thomson's poetry as "innumerous." Blake was to write, among his "Proverbs of Hell": "The roaring of lions, the howling of wolves, the raging of the stormy sea, and the destructive sword, are portions of eternity, too great for the eye of man." And Thomson, even more frequently, creates phrases to distinguish the eye that can look at eternity from the mere sensual eye. Newton is "All intellectual eye," "all-piercing sage," with "well purg'd penetrating eye / The mystic veil transpiercing," he "whose piercing mental eye diffusive saw / The finish'd university of things" (*A Poem Sacred to the Memory of Sir Isaac Newton*, 1727). *The Seasons* are full of phrases like "philosophic eye" (opposed to "the grosser eye of man"), the "skilful eye" or "watchful eye," the "exalting eye," the "raptur'd eye," the "mind's creative eye."

The opening lines of *Winter* were cited by the painter Constable "as a beautiful instance of the poet identifying his own feelings with external nature." They give us the external and the internal—"vapors and clouds and storms" that "exalt the soul to solemn thought / And heavenly musing." The glooms are "kindred," the horrors "cogenial"; and the interanimation that we find in Milton's "Proserpin gath'ring flow'rs / Herself a fairer Flow'r" recurs in Thomson's

> Pleas'd have I wander'd through your rough domain;
> Trod the pure virgin-snows, myself as pure.
>
> (10–11)

Winter is a force of both destruction and purification. The white desert of unrelieved snow is the denial of life; but the severe test of endurance creates the stern virtues of those who meet it. Winter includes the external threat of annihilation and the social threat of oppressive indifference; and its desolation may call up resistance and fortitude. The poem weaves back and forth between physical and moral, between external and internal.

Throughout *Winter* the outward scene dissolves into the responses it calls forth. The first storm awakens the "pleasing dread" of sublime emotion (109), the sudden calm that succeeds the second brings the serenity of contemplation:

> Let me shake off th' intrusive cares of day,
> And lay the meddling senses all aside.
>
> (207–8)

The pattern of ascent is prefigured here, in the freedom of the poet from the formlessness of a life committed to the world and from its round of futile repetition. He prays to be saved from "every low pursuit," to rise to

> Sacred, substantial, never-fading bliss!
>
> (222)

The bleakness of the snow which erases forms and destroys life gives way to the icy cruelty of the "gay licentious proud," and that in turn to the wolves who descend from the Alps, "Cruel as death, and hungry as the grave" (393). The "smothering ruin" of the avalanche that overwhelms the small societies of man (422–23) leads to the retreat of the poet to the study of those heroes who represent the tenacity of the human spirit. He holds

> high converse with the mighty dead—
> Sages of ancient time, as gods rever'd,
> As gods beneficent, who bless'd mankind
> With art and arms, and humaniz'd a world.
>
> (432–35)

The political heroes are lawgivers, defenders of liberty and martyrs to tyranny, men of "awful virtue," down to Hammond, the newly dead friend and patriot. And from these heroes Thomson ascends to the principles themselves which actuate such virtue:

> That portion of divinity, that ray
> Of purest heav'n, which lights the public soul
> Of patriots and of heroes.
>
> (595–97)

From the contemplative we move to the social—the "rural gambol" and the more sophisticated pleasure of the city—only to close in upon the figure of

Chesterfield, at once polite and virtuous, a man of wit and noble passion, the reincarnation of the classical heroes in a modern world.

In the last portion of the poem we confront the ambiguities of winter. It clarifies, purifies, invigorates: it produces the wholesome sports of Europe and the noble simplicity of the Goths and Scythians. But as we move farther north into the land of ice we see the frozen death of the merchant adventurer, and we descend to the "gross race" of rudest men who scarcely sustain life at all, "sunk in caves" (941). Still, the intrepidity of the explorer survives in the magnificence of Peter the Great, whose "active government" called a "huge neglected empire . . . from Gothic darkness" (950–54). Peter becomes the heir of ancient heroes; he animates the vast land and makes it "one scene of art, of arms, of rising trade." He represents the moral response to the challenge of winter, the moral power of vigorous action which its severity exacts.

In the picture of the thaw with which winter ends, Thomson brings back the threat of confusion. The terror of the icebergs is likened to the sinister threat of the whale in *Paradise Lost*, whose slumbering body the "Pilot of some small night-founder'd skiff" mistakes for an island, anchoring his vessel with deceptive security. Milton's whale is a figure for Satan, and Thomson is returning to the problem of evil at the close of his poem. In the earliest version he refers to "th' eternal scheme / The dark perplexity, that mystic maze, / Which sight could never trace nor heart conceive" (379–81). In the last version the optimism is firmer: "The great eternal scheme / Involving all, and in a perfect whole / Uniting, as the prospect wider spreads" (1046–48). Winter brings about the triumph of virtue and with it comes the promise of redemption:

> The glorious morn! the second birth
> Of heaven and earth! Awakening Nature hears
> The new-creating word, and starts to life
> In every heighten'd form, from pain and death
> For ever free.
>
> (1042–46)

The prospect of imperfect life on earth is widened to include the hope of heaven:

> The storms of wintry time will quickly pass,
> And one unbounded spring encircle all.
>
> (1068–69)

We are close to the conclusion of Pope's *Essay on Man*: in attaining virtue, man creates Eden anew and escapes the cycles of Time; the breadth of his vision (and, Pope would say, love) opens Eternity to him.

While this pattern is essential to our understanding of *The Seasons*, it does not entirely account for its successes. The pattern prepares us to sense each experience as implicitly moral in significance. In fact, the large structure might encourage one to look for little allegories or emblems in particular scenes, and Thomson occasionally confirms this view. But his landscape is more suggestive and elusive than this. He foreshadows Wordsworth in giving himself up to a scene, accepting its mysterious power over him, describing with the exactness of awed attention the least movement he sees. All his best landscapes involve tension and movement. It may be the tension of antici-pation, as all nature waits for the descent of rain or the breaking of a storm. It may be the movement into the deep recesses of shade and quiet. It may be the bursting force of a descending stream, roaring through a broken channel until it spreads over the valley below. What do these tensions and movements signify? It is hard to give them any simple moral import, or even a determinate psychological one. They accommodate meanings or feelings we bring to them. Like an abstract form—musical or pictorial—they artic-ulate patterns of tension that underlie or are embedded in much of our experience.

To some extent, Thomson is finding new vehicles for religious experi-ence and putting behind him the landscape of symbols we see in the Me-taphysical poets. He insists upon a scientific understanding of the operations of nature; and this attempt to see the splendor that streams through natural process makes for a minuteness of detail and at times a deliberate pursuit of the "unpoetic." Reynolds in his Eleventh Discourse (1782) warns the land-scape painter to content himself with "shewing the general effect" of what he himself knows anatomically: "for he applies himself to the imagination, not to the curiosity, and works not for the virtuoso or the naturalist, but for the common observer of life and nature." But Thomson, like Constable later, is filled with a natural piety that watches for the revelation that lies in the minute natural process. Constable, for example, praises a winter piece of Ruysdael that shows an exact knowledge of the atmospheric changes that "will produce a thaw before morning." "The occurrence of these circum-stances," Constable adds, "shows that Ruysdael *understood* what he was paint-ing." On the other hand, when Ruysdael paints *An Allegory of the Life of Man*, "there are ruins to indicate old age, a stream to signify the course of life, and rocks and precipices to shadow forth its dangers;—but how are we to discover all this?" (318–19).

This gritty fidelity to natural fact, which we find again in Wordsworth, underlies Thomson's ecstasies—just as Constable's studies of skies underlie his use of them as "the chief organ of sentiment" (85). Man, Constable said, "is the sole intellectual inhabitant of one vast natural landscape. His nature is congenial with the elements of the planet itself, and he cannot but sympathize with its features, its various aspects, and its phenomena in all its aspects" (329). Earlier he had written his wife of a visit to Suffolk: "Everything seems full of blossom of some kind and at every step I take, and on whatever object I turn my eyes, that sublime expression of the Scriptures 'I am the resurrection and the life,' seems as if uttered near me" (73). And of a painting of a "Boat Passing a Lock" he wrote to Fisher: "it is silvery, windy, and delicious; all health, and the absence of everything stagnant, and is wonderfully got together . . . " (141). This movement from close observation to intense feeling, and one might say *only* from close observation of the actual, is a distinctive contribution of Thomson, and it is his poetry that Constable cites more than once (as does Turner) in the catalogue entries for his exhibited paintings, and in the letterpress of *English Landscape*, the volume of engravings made of his work by Lucas.

But tracing the lineaments of design in nature or finding in it the vehicle of religious sentiment is too restricted an account of what Thomson does. Thomson has often been praised for his remarkable feeling for light, but one can say as much for his sense of space (in a passage Constable cites):

> As from the face of heaven the shattered clouds
> Tumultuous rove, the interminable sky
> Sublimer swells, and o'er the world expands
> A purer azure.
>
> (*Summer*, 1223–26)

Or, in the account of Hagley, we move with Lyttleton to a height,

>   from whose fair brow
> The bursting prospect spreads immense around:
> And snatched o'er hill and dale, and wood and lawn,
> And verdant field, and darkening heath between,
> And spiry towns by surging columns marked
> Of household smoke, your eye excursive roams—
> Widestretching from the hall
>
> . . . .
>
> To where the broken landscape, by degrees
> Ascending, roughens into rigid hills

> O'er which the Cambrian mountains, like far clouds
> That skirt the blue horizon, dusky rise.
>
> *(Spring*, 949–61)

What Thomson catches in these scenes is that curiously indefinable sense of
the "import" of space—the kind of sense the architect must try to articulate
in planning effects, different as they must be from these. In the first passage,
we are involved in breaking free of limits as we move above the violence of
the great clouds into the blue vacancy of endless space that "swells" and
"expands" with exaltation and freedom. In the second passage we break out
of the trees into the freedom of the prospect. We give ourselves to the motion
of freedom with "bursting prospect" and "spreads immense around"—words
that characterize not the scene so much as the experience of coming upon
it. The following lines emphasize the stretch of sight, the high view that
looks down upon hill and dale, wood and lawn, and (securely anchored to
the hospitable hall) looks over the slight traces of towns. And just as the "eye
excursive" pushes to the edges of the horizon, the scene composes with the
ascent of rough hills and the enclosing bowl of faint mountains. This second
landscape has something of pictorial composition, but what gives it peculiar
force is the motion contained and bounded by these last images. The passage
picks up suggestions from its context: we are following Lyttleton and his
Lucinda walking through grounds where

> Nature all
> Wears to the lover's eye a look of love;
> And all the tumult of a guilty world,
> Toss'd by ungenerous passions, sinks away.
> The tender heart is animated peace.
> . . . it pours its copious treasures forth
> In varied converse.
>
> *(Spring*, 936–42)

The landscape, at once extensive and peacefully protected, gives one the
spatial feel of this sentiment—its expansive "animated peace." The sentiment
finds definition in the landscape that embodies it.

Landscape can call emotion forth by offering a vehicle with its own
formal properties and its own power of suggestion. If man finds himself, in
Constable's terms, congenial with the elements of the planet itself, he can
lend himself imaginatively to those elements, filling out these movements
with the impulses of his own nature. His study of landscape becomes a
release of his own feelings into forms which will shape them; it allows him,

in other words, to project feelings that might otherwise have no mode of expression and to order them in ways that a moral system might not admit. This is important. We need not assume that there is a natural movement from Protestant individualism to sentimentalism to pantheism; these terms are too categorical to serve many particular instances. Thomson's sentimentalism is much greater in his narrative episodes than in his descriptive passages, and we need hardly infer from the sympathies with the phenomena of nature of which Constable speaks a doctrine of pantheism. What we have is something less systematic and more interesting: the discovery of a vehicle that opens up a range of feelings otherwise without expression and shapes them into a subtle unity which eludes any received canons of art.

One more example will illustrate the pattern we find in Thomson. In *Summer* there is a splendid passage on the "raging noon," when light has become a "dazzling deluge" that forces the eye to the ground, only to be met there by "hot ascending steams / And keen reflection pain." The heat is felt in the depth of the parched soil and the "throbbing temples" of the poet, who draws from it an "emblem" of a fevered world of vice. The "tempered mind serene and pure" of the virtuous man seeks its counterpart in the cool caverns of the forest-covered mountainside. Withdrawal into the shelter of "lofty pines" and "venerable oaks" brings new vigor: "The fresh expanded eye / And ear resume their watch." Below him the poet sees the meandering stream "scarcely moving" among reclining cattle and beside the sleeping herdsman—a nicely composed scene of indolent repose. Into this scene moves a flight of "angry gadflies" to disturb the cattle into bellowing motion. And this in turn admits the fierce motion of "the horse provoked":

> While his big sinews full of spirits swell,
> Trembling with vigor, in the heat of blood
> Springs the high fence; and, o'er the field effus'd,
> Darts on the gloomy flood with stedfast eye
> And heart estrang'd to fear: his nervous chest,
> Luxuriant and erect, the seat of strength,
> Bears down the opposing stream; quenchless his thirst,
> He takes the river at redoubl'd draughts;
> And with wide nostrils snorting skims the wave.
>
> *(Summer,* 507–15)

As the poet plunges once more into coolness and darkness, the intensity of the horse's motion evokes a contrary intensity of "awful listening gloom." The recess of meditation becomes a sacred place where "ancient bards" have had ecstatic visions in which angelic visitors descended.

> Deep-rous'd I feel
> A sacred terror, a severe delight,
> Creep through my mortal frame,
> (540–42)

and the voices speak of their gradual ascent through "stormy life" to "This holy calm, this harmony of mind" (550). The poet wakens from the "airy vision" to the sound of water. He traces the growth of a stream as it collects into "one impetuous torrent" that "thundering shoots" down the steep, dashing to foam on rocks below, sending up a "hoary mist," then roaring into separate channels until it spreads "Along the mazes of the quiet vale" (606).

The violent chiaroscuro of brilliance and blackness, the contrast of throbbing sunlight and gelid caverns, the fierce energy of the horse and the holy power of the visionary figures, the downward rush of the stream from the high recess through the turbulence of the waterfall to the quiet vale where the cattle browse—all of these form an indistinct but suggestive dialectical pattern. One feels that the force of outward energy that is caught in the heavy heat or in the frenzied motion has been absorbed into the seraphic vision, cleansed of its fever and raised to prophetic power. This absorption of the natural scene into man looks back to Addison's remark that "a spacious horizon is an image of liberty" and forward to Blake's "When thou seest an Eagle, thou seest a portion of Genius; lift up thy head!"

PAUL H. FRY

Thomas Gray's Feather'd Cincture:
The Odes

Selima, Horace Walpole's favorite cat, has no sense of distance: "Again
she stretched, again she bent, / Nor knew the gulf between." Unlike Gray's
more knowing creatures, she thinks that she has only to reach out in order
to possess "The genii of the stream." She thinks this partly because she is a
"nymph," and belongs, like Milton's tangled nymphs in their tangled thicket,
within the compass of the half-natural, half-figural object of her desire. The
comfortable wealth of Walpole's fish, their "golden gleam," discloses to her
classicist's eyes a familiar vestige of Apollo—of an Apollo in "armor" like
the more brilliant figure Gray elsewhere introduces for the use of many
future ode writers: Hyperion, with his "glittering shafts of war." But Walpole's fish only vouchsafe a last glitter; their scaly armor is defensive not
militant, and they are deeply overlaid by the japanning of civilized comfort.
Their living artifice recalls the morning-room atmosphere of natural illusion
in the opening lines of the poem: " 'Twas on a lofty vase's side, / Where
China's gayest art had dyed / The azure flowers that blow." This deftly
poised figure, with its evocation of the mixed hauteur and frivolity of Walpole
himself and its merger of death, breath, and blossoming, distills the culture
in which Gray finds himself trying to be a bard. Selima parodies Gray's
Bard in advance; she expresses her desire despite "the gulf between," and
plunges to a watery grave:

> Eight times emerging from the flood
> She mewed to every watery god,

From *The Poet's Calling in the English Ode*. © 1980 by Yale University. Yale University
Press, 1980. Originally entitled "Thomas Gray's Feather'd Cincture."

Some speedy aid to send.
No dolphin came.

(31–34)

Arion's power of music is no more, and the single remaining muse that is
not, cannot be, invoked by Selima's eight mews is Polyhymnia.

The gulf that Selima does not know until she fatally discovers it to be
the "slippery verge" of self-consciousness is the *"abîme infranchissable"* that
Count de Bonstetten (Gray's last Walpole) described as yawning steadily
between the poet and all his efforts to join the stream of life. Gray's irony
about his own alienation is reflected in his having devoted most of his rare
poetic attempts—for he neither "stretched" nor "bent" very often—to the
"vocal transports" ("Bard," 120) of the ode. That he took the term "ode"
seriously is most evident, as is usual with Gray, from his good-humored
disclaimers, as in this complaint about Walpole's indiscrimination of titles:
"You have talked to [Dodsley] of six *odes*, for so you are pleased to call
everything I write, though it be but a receipt for apple-dumplings. . . . I don't
know but a may send him very soon (by your hands) an ode to his own
tooth, a high Pindaric on stilts." Before "The Progress of Poesy," to which
he here refers, Gray had worked only with Horatian meters and tonalities,
but from the first, he had used the ode in one form or another to explore his
unvarying personal theme, which concerns the impossibility of narrowing
"the gulf between."

It is true that the speaker's isolation is pervasive not just in the odes but
also in the "Elegy," where the world of action is forfeited "to darkness and
to me." The speaker of the "Elegy," alienated from his locale by virtue of
his "Fair Science," remains anonymously mysterious in the eyes of his anonymous neighbors. But although the tone of the "Elegy" reverberates from
the speaker's solitude, the poem still differs significantly from any of Gray's
odes. Even the quality of solitude itself in the "Elegy" is different: it is
voluntary, a Penseroso choice intimately uniting the speaker with darkness
in a way that is suggested by the quiet zeugma of the fourth line. In the
ensuing lines, solitude in the *locus sanctus* becomes a jealously guarded tryst
between the melancholic and his gloom: "The moping owl does to the moon
complain / Of such as, wandering near her secret bower, / Molest her ancient
solitary reign." Solitude has become an identity, a mark of identification,
and results in what is rare in Gray until "The Bard," the charismatic visibility
of the speaking subject: " ' Oft have we seen him. . . . ' " He is alienated not
toward oblivion, then, but in order to become visible, and he can therefore
conclude with confidence that he has been seen by "his Father and his God."
Without touching upon the modulations of social sympathy in the "Elegy"

(which are also dutifully rehearsed in the odes), one can see that in that poem solitude is ultimately a triumph of communion, and that in this respect, again, the Elegy stands apart from the odes.

For Gray, the letter *o* (the vocative, the vowel of the ode) is most often an empty circle: "I have struck a medal on myself: the device is thus O, and the motto *Nihilissimo.*" This is an apt device for Gray's experiments with invocation. The slightest and least memorable of these, but in many ways also the most subtle, is the "Ode on the Spring."

Although there will be a great deal more to say about the metaphysics of seasonal poetry, for the moment it may suffice to suggest that seasonal odes (and topographies like Thomson's) occupied an increasingly prominent place in poetry at a time when subjectivism was also gaining ground, and when, therefore, it would become possible to question what it means for the conscious subject to be "present to" or determined by the changing weather, which seems, at first blush, virtually to constitute consciousness. The climatology of Montesquieu in Gray's "Alliance of Education and Government" looks forward in some ways to the rise of nationalism, but metaphyscially it is already a little archaic. Johnson's refusal to admit that we need be affected by the weather is a subjectivist's attitude that is quite inconsistent with his abhorrence of Berkeley and Hume, and that inconsistency betrays the unsettled ontological atmosphere of his period. (Johnson himself had written youthful odes to the seasons.)

Gray's "Ode on the Spring" is about alienation from the weather. The title of the poem was not his own, but Mason's instincts in choosing it were sound. It certainly is not an ode *to* the Spring. It was written in response to Richard West's "Ode to May," definitely an "ode to" that begins, "O join with mine thy tuneful lay / And invocate the tardy May." That is just what Gray cannot do, and his "ode on" should in fact be seen as a counter-ode.

Called "Noon-Tide. An Ode" in Gray's Commonplace Book, the poem evokes the idleness of the Hour of Pan, not as a condition of nature but as a state of mind. The Horatian moral of the poem wittily turns the speaker's contempt for the uselessness of human bustle against himself, since quietude, we are told, is just as useless. This peripety, which is what has caught the attention of most readers, fully parallels the more metaphysical peripety that I wish to stress: Gray is alienated from the weather because he wants to be, in hopes that a condition approaching solipsism will preserve him from time.

The opening sentence anticipates the course of the whole poem:

> Lo! where the rosy-bosomed Hours,
> Fair Venus' train, appear,

> Disclose the long-expecting flowers,
> And wake the purple year!

Time stands across the way, a stranger whose appearance in the distance seems to startle the poet, who enforces the reassuring safety of that distance through the echo of "where" in "Hours." Rosy-bosomed Time *is*, by the transference of an epithet, the pinkening of buds from within as well as the glow of sunshine. Not an agent in itself but an effect, Time is drawn into being by the Lucretian eroticism of *natura*. Gray has begun, then, waiving invocation, with an etiological myth: Venus begets Time, which begets the Year. But he keeps his myth veiled, distancing the myth itself as well as its content, behind a screen of epithets. His "poetic diction," here and everywhere in his poetry, is his way of indicating that he can "see, not feel" the force of nature that Wordsworth took to be wholly absent from his manner; and of indicating, furthermore, that he rather prefers distance to intimacy. Textuality in Gray, the dense layering of allusion and syntax, is a deliberately pronounced emblem of his isolation. The logic of poetic diction combined with allusion weaves a tissue of mediations. Every predication cancels the others, so that no one prosopopoeia can finally be held responsible for the presence of an atmosphere.

Since the "year" in the above passage is awakened by the hours (which in turn are led forward by Venus), the year itself cannot be a part of temporal existence. As indeed it is not: "purple" is no color at all in Gray but rather a sense of luxuriant brilliance, a linguistic sense that is brought into play by the sound of the Latin *purpureum*. Thus modified, the year is reduced to an occasional and intricately derivative text "on the spring" that is disunited from time's rosy blossoming. The violently transferred epithet "long-expecting," which modifies the flowers and the poet in different ways, marks this disunity while seeming to effect a fusion: either the flowers are purely rhetorical flowers that bloom prematurely in the poet's discourse or else, in the key of elegy, they are long expected but never come.

West had urged Gray to "invocate the tardy May." Both he and Gray would have felt that request as a prayer for the return of that "cool zephyr" ("Spring," 9), the health of the feverish West, whose coterie name was "Favonius." The most Gray can do, though, is to feign an invocation by planting specious imperatives in the midst of his predicative syntax: "appear, / Disclose." In fact, this speaker can command nothing, since Nature, the tutelary numen from which Gray is distanced by temperament and by having read too many odes to Spring, responds only within her own charmed circle:

> The Attic Warbler pours her throat,
> Responsive to the cuckoo's note,
> The untaught harmony of spring;

The poet is excluded from this exchange just as he will be excluded, in "The Progress of Poesy," from the intermingling of Greek melody with the native strain of "Nature's darling," Shakespeare. In the present passage Gray blends allusions of two kinds: first, to the elegiac mode of Propertius and Ovid that longs for the spontaneous voice of Spring, and second, to the world of Milton before the Fall—to the warbler of native woodnotes in *L'Allegro* and the " 'celestial voices' " that are still present in Eden (Adam reduplicates them by explaining them to Eve), " 'responsive to each other's note' " (*Paradise Lost* IV. 682–83).

The last stanza draws out as a moral what was implicit in the opening. Sitting apart "in rustic state" (an oxymoron that weakly reassociates the poet with the regality of the purple year and the enviable artlessness of the cuckoo), and sitting apart also from the rosy brilliance of the spring light, the poet in his "browner shade" has only slightly felt the breezes' synaesthetic dalliance with the unshaded world: "whispering pleasure as they fly, / Cool zephyrs through the clear blue sky / Their gathered fragrance fling." At the end of the poem his hearing is just as faint as his other senses have been: "Methinks I hear in accents low / The sportive kind reply." He must strain to hear himself admonished by characters from the world of Satire and the Moral Epistle because he has already told himself everything they can say in the more inward accents of thwarted invocation.

In part, then, Gray cannot be heard because he in his turn chooses not to hear. He typically reserves a clearer admission of what inhibits him as an odist for a comic moment, in the fragment called "Hymn to Ignorance": "Oh say—she hears me not, but, careless grown, / Lethargic nods upon her ebon throne." The poet apportions much of the blame to the goddess, whose name bespeaks the indifference toward human desire of all departed numina. But the poet is still confessedly at fault; he approaches the cloud of unknowing "with filial reverence," and his opening lines are, in fact, a specifically directed self-parody: the "antiquated towers, / Where rushy Camus' slowly-winding flood / Perpetual draws his humid train of mud" transfer to Cambridge the topography of Eton's "antique towers, / That crown the watery glade," in another and more famous poem of 1742 that ends: "Where ignorance is bliss, / 'Tis folly to be wise."

The keynote of the "Ode on a Distant Prospect of Eton College" is struck in the title and in the "distant spires" of the first line. Like the "Ode

on the Spring," this poem presents a lively scene that is far removed from
the poet's present outlook and opens a vast distance between the sportive
kind and the gloomy moralist. The second stanza apparently proffers the
claim that things were not always as they are now, and seems to anticipate
the Intimations Ode of Wordsworth in so doing:

> Ah, happy hills, ah, pleasing shade,
> Ah, fields beloved in vain,
> Where once my careless childhood strayed,
> A stranger yet to pain!
> I feel the gales, that from ye blow,
> A momentary bliss bestow,
> As waving fresh their gladsome wing
> My weary soul they seem to soothe,
> And, redolent of joy and youth,
> To breathe a second spring.

But in truth, as the poem at large and details even within this passage will
indicate, there was never even a first spring. Gray's "poetic diction" does
indeed mark the difference between him and Wordsworth, and does so very
tellingly. It was not the poet himself who was a happy child but rather,
more tautologically, his "careless childhood"—a personification taken from
countless Ages-of-Man allegories that underscores its own irrelevance to any
actual childhood. This device, together with the bold and un-Wordsworthian
prolepsis "in vain," reveals the private theme embedded in Gray's univer-
salizing diction: the childhood of the person who writes the speaker's lines
was, as far as he can realize it, empty and vain, and no more full of joy—
whether social or spiritual—than is the present.

Childhood itself is the etiological myth of the Eton College Ode, as of
the Intimations Ode, but Gray presents his myth self-consciously *as* a myth,
as a fiction of the soul's fair seed-time. If such a time ever existed, the poet
is too distant to recognize it. In this context, the premature present tense of
"all are men" is significant: taken at face value, as I believe Gray's diction
usually should be, the expression "all are men, / Condemned alike to groan,"
suggests that children themselves are not exempted from adulthood and its
misery. Gray's motto from Menander, "I am a man . . . ," contains no hint
of a prelapsarian myth and anticipates the calculated self-absorption of a
poem in which all conditions that are distant from the place and voice of the
speaker are known only as touchstones of homiletic discourse. The notorious
"chase the rolling circle's speed, / Or urge the flying ball" is overwrought to
warn the reader that the distant speaker knows nothing of the reality that

his phrasing buries; he is as ignorant of cricket as is the Latin language from which *urgo* is borrowed. The eighteenth century, which certain of its partisans are fond of calling "adult," does seem wanting in an authentic poetry of childhood. Gray's calculated distance is nothing to Shenstone's effusion in his "Ode to Memory": "Bring me the bells, the rattle bring, / And the hobby I bestrode."

Actuality, whether that of childhood or of any present that is not distant, is what cannot be invoked or evoked in Gray's odes, not only because of his temperamental aloofness, but also because he seems committed to the awareness that presentation in language can only be undertaken in blissful ignorance. It is best to assume this awareness, in any case, when one interprets the passage from Gray's *Correspondence* that is often cited by apologists for his diction as if it were transparently self-justifying and needed no explanation: "The language of the age is never the language of poetry." This gnomic utterance and the argument that follows are not in the least persuasive, and richly deserve to be ignored by all the polemicists for naturalistic diction from Wordsworth to Williams, unless the whole passage be reinterpreted as a critique of presentation. "The language of the age," in this case, would be language that spontaneously presumes contact with the actual. What I am suggesting is that the Eton College Ode, written six months later, requires no palinode in the unfinished "Hymn to Ignorance"; it is its own palinode, undermining the sententiousness of the gloomy moralist by denying that there ever was a world from which—and toward which—his prospect was not "distant."

The first five stanzas beguile the reader into thinking that the poet converses in the presence of beings of all kinds. Although nothing that is addressed ever answers, Gray's phantom invocations seem to build from the quiet of apostrophe to the strength of command: "Ye distant spires"; "Ah happy hills"; "Say, Father Thames." Having addressed the landscape without even telling it anything, much less being answered, the speaker then commands the river, a poor substitute for Mnemosyne borrowed from "Lycidas," to give him information, which "Father Thames," as Johnson said, "has no better means of knowing than himself." Being nearly as ruthless an opponent of "vicious" diction as Wordsworth, Johnson is nearly as little qualified to appreciate Gray. The artifice of Gray is the ornamentation of an empty circle, a private way of remarking that one chases the rolling circle's speed "in vain."

There is only one moment when the poem suspends its elegant variations on the device O, and that is the moment Wordsworth might well have acknowledged in his Preface as a hint for the transitional stage of his own childhood in "Tintern Abbey":

> Still as they run they look behind,
> They hear a voice in every wind,
> And snatch a fearful joy.

Here alone "voice" enters the poem as a point of contact with the human; more furtive and fruitless than for Wordsworth, and also perhaps more complacently distanced by the clink of oxymoron, the "joy" here imagined nevertheless opens the thought of the poem to a region of "vocal transport" (or transmission) that is not absolutely absent but absent only from the circle of the poet's neurotic defenses. His childhood still haunts him after all, but is it not the "careless childhood" he had wanted to describe. As a trace of guilt about the recollected pleasures of childhood surfaces in this passage, we again witness the revenge that an ode carries out from the depths against its author. Gray's ode has been disrupted by the forces of nature despite his poetics of distance: what he invokes will not come, but what he refuses to invoke is already present, writing his lines.

II

Childhood in the Eton College Ode races past with depressing speed. As soon as the punningly intended "sprightly race" appears, it speeds, flies, runs, snatches, and greets the morn fresh from the flying hence of "slumbers light." As soon as this race begins, however, a variety of retardations appear also. There are riverbanks and paths, the water is a solid that must be cloven in swimming, the captive linnet is enthralled (a capture of uninvoked voice that goes unremarked), and the little reign of the children has "limits." Most important, there are "graver hours, that bring constraint / [like this enjamb-ment] To sweeten liberty." Here Gray interjects the moral paradox that concludes his "Ode to Adversity," one that will persist in later odes until Keats's "Ode on Melancholy": the paradox governing the interdependency of oppression and freedom, pain and pleasure, sadness and joy. In having suggested that Gray's verbal artifice embroiders an empty circle, I mean that his mode of writing, in drawing interest to itself, gains opacity, density, and thus more effectively entraps meaning than does the naturalistic diction that allows meaning to slip through its transparency; even if it captures nothing, Gray's writing still has the happiness of being formal. In my remaining remarks on Gray, I shall trace his early figures of circularity forward to later figures of weaving and texture, suggesting finally that in the later odes an accommodation is brought about between vocality and the medium of writ-ing—an accommodation that results, as for the ode writers of the seventeenth century, in a fortunate loss.

In a letter written nine years after the "Ode to Adversity," Gray called the poem a "hymn," which designation appeared in the editions of his poems in the fifties and sixties. In 1768, Gray asked Dodsley to change the title back to "Ode." This Dodsley failed to do, but in the same year James Beattie saw to it that in the Glasgow edition Gray's wish would be honored. "Adversity" meanwhile had readily become a "hymn" in the minds of all concerned because of its apparently impersonal deference to moral norms and its close adherence to the structure of the classical cult hymn: invocation, myth, petition, and at least the hint of a *votum* in the closing lines. It may be conjectured that religious scruples led Gray to prefer the title "ode" late in life; they would be understandable, since the poem must be read allegorically if it is to be taken for a Christian prayer, and it retains the pantheistic atmosphere for which its structure is designed, however firmly demythologized into psychic attributes its pantheon may be. Gray knew that "Adversity" was the sort of poem that proponents of the "sacred ode" from John Dennis to Bishops Lowth and Hurd would characterize as a "secular ode."

It would seem at first that, barring its author's scruples, "Adversity" might well qualify as a hymn. It invokes a norm of moral restraint that matches its own formal limits, the "rigid lore" of Gray's moderately intricate Horatian stanza: *a b a b c c d d*. The Alexandrine is not directly indebted to Spenser, I believe, but to Milton's Nativity Ode stanza, in which, as Louis Martz has aptly said, the Alexandrine "draws his poem . . . into the larger area of this poet's predestined goals." For Gray, each stanza with its Alexandrine is an emblem in miniature of his poem's goal, namely, the increased latitude of Adversity's bondage and of the poet's sympathies. Gray's motto, from the famous chorus on suffering as the origin of wisdom in the *Oresteia*, gives the cue for these expansions by recalling the whole of the source text to mind, including the conversion of the Furies to Eumenides. Altered from nemesis to "form benign" by the end of Gray's poem, Adversity seems to affirm, by this change, the course of self-discipline that may revive "The generous spark extinct." Gray's etiological myth in the second stanza appears smoothly to bridge this conversion by assigning Adversity as governess to Virtue, whose reciprocal influence softens the "Stern rugged nurse" for the rest of the poem. Interpreted thus far and no farther, the poem indeed appears to resemble the sort of choral hymn that supplies its motto.

There are, however, a good many gaps in this pleasant reading, and when these are considered, the poem becomes an ode again. In the first place, it is clear that the "Ode to Adversity" attempts without success to repudiate the psychology of distance that governs the other odes of 1742. In Gray's myth, the role of Adversity is that of the "gloomy moralist" ("Spring"), whereas the role of Virtue, with "her infant mind," is that of the boys at Eton and the "untaught" birds of Spring. Governed by this contrast, Virtue is not far removed from "Folly's idle brood," and it may fairly be questioned how she will find the strength of character to put herself to school. Again owing to the predicative fracturing of personification, there is no "aspect" that can properly be called Virtue's own, not even the power of sympathy: taught to recognize "sorrow" by Adversity, "she learned [from her own woe] to melt at others' woe."

Despite the inessentiality of Virtue, it appears to be her, and not Adversity, whom the poem honors with its myth of origin. Invoked patronymically, Adversity becomes an older sister who seems to have no childhood. Like her cousins the Furies, she has always existed. Virtue, on the other hand, is one of the more lightly conceived off-spring of Jove's later years. One reconsiders these kinships as allegory only to reach strange conclusions about the psyche that the allegory shadows forth. Recapitulating the philogeny of cultural history, human consciousness is born to itself, comes to know itself, as a feeling of savage imprisonment, of self-laceration in chains. This condition crushes the "proud" and the "purple tyrants" who are rejected as parental models ordinarily at the height of a child's auto-genetic fantasies. Belated Virtue, herself empty of content, is the sublimation of precisely these tyrannical origins, while Adversity is the disruptive force that is not, in fact, external but is rather the firstborn of the psyche itself. Gray's poem shares with the early odes of Collins an Aristotelian theory of catharsis; but the coupling of Adversity's "frown terrific" with Pity's "sadly-pleasing tear" cannot purge the original tragedy, consisting as it does simply of having been born, that is somewhat more stoically acknowledged in the other odes of 1742. Having annotated the *Republic*, Gray was well aware of Plato's warning—evaded by Aristotle—that the deliciousness of pity weakens the psyche's defenses and results in self-pity.

The pressures that undermine this poem's attempted resolution and independence are reflected in Gray's having realigned the pantheon of the poem that Johnson was the first to name as its source, Horace's ode "To Fortuna." Not the scourge but the patroness of "purpurei . . . tyranni," Fortuna is not at all the same goddess as Adversity. Horace feels no need to rationalize the amorality of her power, and he finally petitions her, therefore, not to chasten him gently but to bring the Empire victory in an offensive war. The "iron scourge" of Gray's beginning is deliberately blunted during the course of his poem, whereas at the end of Horace's poem Fortuna is implored to resharpen the "retusum ferum" of Rome. As befits her ethical neutrality, Fortuna is flanked symmetrically by evil and benign forces. The wholly evil force, "saeva Necessitas, / clavos trabales et cuneos manu / gestans aëna," is none other than the scourge-wielding Adversity of Gray's invocation.

The logic that preconditions Gray's poem will not permit the Aeschylean conversion of Adversity; her coming first binds everything that follows within a deterministic chain. Gray struggled all his life to free himself from this chain. "That we are indeed mechanical and dependent beings, I need no other proof than my own feelings," he writes in 1758 and then gamely continues: "and from the same feelings I learn that we are not merely such." Unable to end complacently, however, he therefore adds, referring to the more skeptical *Philosophes*, "I can be wretched enough without them." For once, in the "Ode to Adversity," the gesture of invocation succeeds; Gray summons Nemesis and cannot make her go away. Having chosen "I am a man. That is reason enough to be miserable" for the motto of another poem in the same month, Gray now actually petitions Adversity (so helpless is he before her) to be taught how to "know myself a man." By allusion, perhaps, this ending is meant to recall the more redeemably bipolar Man of the *Essay on Man* and Young's *Night Thoughts* ("A worm! a god!" I, 81), but it remains closest to the Man of the Eton College Ode.

Horace's ode is a poem on an affair of state; Gray's has entirely to do with a state of mind. He seeks the protective coloring of Milton's Penseroso, whose patroness appears in Gray's poem as one of Adversity's mediators, "Melancholy, silent maid / With leaden eye that loves the ground." But the force of Gray's dilemma changes Milton's sense along with Horace's. Melancholy does not soothe and abet Gray, but grounds him like a leaden plummet and binds him to the influence of Adversity. Self-cloistering may paradoxically result in liberty for the melancholic—"leave us leisure to be good"—but the mere protection from evil could never have satisfied the Milton of, say, the *Areopagitica*. The urge to expand Gray's limited freedom is one motive of Wordsworth's "Ode to Duty," which may be considered here to complete the synchronic setting, bounded by Horace and Wordsworth, of which Gray's "Adversity" is most fully to be understood as the center.

Wordsworth's open reconciliation with Gray in the "Ode to Duty," which takes over Gray's stanza as well as an aspect of his theme, fittingly accompanies Wordsworth's own prolonged farewell to "unchartered freedom." The "Ode to Duty" is so full of self-restraint that it is easy to overlook the idea of freedom that is meant to lend it a compensatory dignity:

> Through no disturbance of my soul,
> Or strong compunction in me wrought,
> I supplicate for thy control;
> But in the quietness of thought:

Once duly registered, however, this passage then demands to be taken more seriously than it can be. Far more than in the case of Gray's "leisure to be good," the integrity of this moment depends on our believing that the Penseroso's chosen rigors precede the mere reflexivity of cloistered habits. Wordsworth seems to be on safe ground, since his Duty has the appearance of a volunteer, whereas Gray's Adversity comes before she is called. But Duty, according to Wordsworth's motto from Seneca (added in 1837), *is* "Habit," and the notion that habits can be taken up and left off at will exposes Wordsworth to a psychic anomaly that is as intractable as Gray's.

An example of the formalism that Wordsworth newly proposes to embrace and be embraced by is set forth in his invocation, which violates every tenet of his 1800 poetics in two lines. Wordsworth doubles the distance of Gray's invocation; whereas Adversity is the "Daughter of Jove," Duty is the daughter of "the Voice of God." (The increased importance of mediation for Wordsworth may be seen yet more clearly if one compares this phrasing with its closest source, *Paradise Lost* IX. 652–53.) She is twice removed, and it is rather difficult, in fact, to trace her descent from her mother, Voice, since she is not at all vocal, except perhaps as a permanent echo. The venerable *quocunque gaudes nomine* of the second line also out-Grays Gray and bespeaks a humble remove of such great distance from Voice that the numen is no longer audible as a name. Wordsworth's ode recommends a religion, and implicitly a poetry, of precept, and seems more plausibly entitled to the name of hymn than does Gray's ode. It is a High Church poem that turns against the inner voice of antinomianism.

However, there is one critical lapse from this intention:

> I, loving freedom, and untried;
> No sport of every random gust,
> Yet being to myself a guide,
> Too blindly have reposed my trust;
> And oft, when in my heart was heard
> Thy timely mandate, I deferred
> The task.

The nostalgia that lurks in this passage briefly confuses Wordsworth's new perspective and effects the disruption of his poem. Duty is here imagined in a former aspect, not as The Daughter of Voice but as Voice itself; resident in the heart without discipline, in those days she was scarcely to be distinguished from Conscience; or, for that matter, from consciousness and inspiration. This nostalgia offers a much more crucial challenge to the affirmative cast of the poem than the one presented by the rather impersonal recollection of glad animal movement in the second stanza. The Tom Joneses and Winander Boys of the world have not ceased to exist, but the vogue for benevolism has passed, and the hint of an etiological myth in the second stanza is prelapsarian without reason. Wordsworth's most important genealogy is contained in his invocation, and its divine origin is subtly and tellingly in conflict with the human past that is rejected in the fourth stanza. If the "mandates" of Duty have always been present in the heart, as who can doubt, what motivates their superfluous invocation at this moment?

The poem does not come upon Duty for the first time, but rather warms for the first time to what the eighteenth century would have called the Pleasures of Duty; pleasures, perhaps, that anaesthetize pain. Wordsworth's kerygmatic gesture gains him nothing, since nothing can be demythologized and replaced that has always existed in its present form. It is too late, in the fifth stanza, to repeat Gray's fleeting impression that self-restraint is less oppressive than "unchartered freedom" (37). The first word of this phrase is as puzzling as it is in Blake's "London," but its primary sense is probably "uncharted," a too long delayed figuration of the past as a formless chaos. One can observe how perfunctory Wordsworth's myth of the past has become by tracing palinodic echoes of the Intimations Ode in the next stanza:

> Flowers laugh before thee in their beds
> And fragrance in thy footing treads;
> Thou dost preserve the stars from wrong;
> And the most ancient heavens, through Thee, are fresh and
>   strong.

Duty universalized as natural repetition, as a beaten path for flower beds and astral orbits, here becomes a kind of Christian *Themis*. However profound this concept may be, it offers even less individual initiative than the diminished philosophic present of the Intimations Ode, when splendor is still in the grass and glory in the flower, when the heavens are not harmonized by custom but by "the primal sympathy / Which having been must ever be," and when "strength" comes not from duty but from a "timely utterance" of the poet's own voice that "again has made me strong." The "Ode to Duty" completes the inland journey of the earlier poem.

It is important to notice how clumsily the Alexandrines of the "Ode to Duty" are handled. The weariness of the first of them is a mild triumph of imitative form effected by its elegiac echoes of "Tintern Abbey" and Gray's "Elegy," but after that the Alexandrines are dull ("Yet seek thy firm support, according to their need"), and they seem compulsively to stutter: "*for a re*pose;" "through thee"—a phrase that forces duty upon the stars through the fence, as Homer would say, of their teeth. Wordsworth's "Adversity" stanza is averse to its own opening out, and refuses to miniaturize the thematic pull of the poem. Duty offers no latitude, and the last stanza recalls the insistent narrowing of the Nativity Ode, where an "order serviceable" harnesses the bright beginning of the last Alexandrine. Wordsworth's last Alexandrine is lit by Milton's "handmaid lamp," but "tru*th thy*" stutters between the light and its Bondman, signaling the implicit betrayal of Voice in every predication of freedom as bondage. Like the designed allusion to Pope and Young at the end of the "Ode to Adversity," the designed allusion at the end of Wordsworth's poem also misfires. We are meant to hear the close of *Il Penseroso:* "These pleasures, Melancholy, give, / And I with thee will choose to live." But instead we are reminded of the reluctantly hymnic closure of another ode, where pleasure has been "fixed" in an order that is no more than serviceable.

Both Wordsworth's and Gray's odes about discipline are corrupted by disclosures that make them odes rather than hymns: Wordsworth's by the inadvertent discovery that the past requires no new birth as a supplement, and Gray's by the discovery that a force supposedly from without is in fact a force from within. Gray's discovery could be said to be Wordsworth's also, since Wordsworth surprises Duty in his heart: but even in the "Ode to Duty" Wordsworth far surpasses Gray in his power of turning the "mandates" of psychic force to complex advantage. We now leave him with that advantage and return to witness Gray's struggle with his more "adamantine chain."

III

"nor seek from me a loudly resounding song. It is not for me to thunder; that is the business of Zeus." And indeed, when I first placed a writing tablet on my knees Lycian Apollo said to me: "poet, feed the victim to be as fat as possible; but my friend, keep the Muse slender."

—CALLIMACHUS, *Against the Telchines*

Roger Lonsdale has a persuasive theory about what may have happened to Gray after his "Elegy" made him famous: the rusticated poet in that poem was anonymous no more, and the "Long Story" recounts, not without anxiety, a comic invasion of his crippling but addictive distance from the madding crowd. Gray's next ode and first Pindaric, "The Progress of Poesy," was intended to estrange his new public. It has a motto in what Gray hoped was the unintelligible language of Pindar that means "Vocal [*phonanta*] to the Intelligent alone." Gray's later affectation of surprise at the witlessness of his readers extended to the circle of scholars to whom "Intelligent" presumably refers. "I converse with none but the dead," he once wrote half-flippantly, leading me to suspect that "the Intelligent" are the voices of dead poets, a fit audience though few toward whom his "distant way" (121) urges him. Reassured of his distance from present admirers, Gray sets out along new paths to lessen his distance from the well-springs of vocality.

There could be no more ironic purpose for a Progress Poem; Gray's Progress is written steadily under the shadow of that purpose, and of the related but more generalized irony that recent critical approaches to progress poetry from Gray to Keats have made familiar. For Gray, however, the problem of belatedness takes an unusual turn: in his writing, the burden of the past is an *audible* burden that he wishes not so much perhaps to carry forward as simply to hear. Even that modest wish will open a new and difficult distance that is not wholly conceded by its first admission in the "progress"—"But ah! 'tis heard no more" (111)—or even by the later admission, in "The Bard," that "distant warblings lessen on my ear" (133). It is unwise to assume that Gray wishes to add so much as a grace note to the vocal harmony of his precursors; what he does wish to do, as I shall attempt to show, is to "capture" them, as though they were the warbling linnets of an earlier poem, in the enthrallment of writing. This capture will result in an altogether surprising and atypical exaltation of the self.

The prevenient doom of Gray's Progress appears at line 4: "A thousand rills their mazy progress take." Both as periphrastic birthplaces for poets and as fonts of inspiration (if these are separable), rivers crisscross the "Progress" but not always with equal fluency. The departure of the Muses from an enervated Greece is foreknown by the landscape, "Where Maeander's amber waves / In lingering lab'riths creep" (69–70). The waters that flow from Helicon have thickened since the origin of poetry, but their pattern remains the same: it is not a fluency but a texture that captures the channeling of sound through time in a grid, and makes a stasis of progress. The maze of Helicon's thousand rills is an emblem of the hermeneutic palimpsest that Gray calls an ode.

The perfunctoriness of the invocation to Pindar's and the Psalmodist's lyre, which reminds one of "Hail, Muse, etc." in Byron's almost-epic, is appropriate for an almost-ode. Gray's metonymy ignores Pindar and calls down the *technique* of Pindar's odes—their triadic form, profusion of epithets, and dialectical progression. There is no sustained vocative energy in Gray's poem, nor is meant to be. His emphasis on lore rather than logos is the reverse of the purely vocative emphasis of Blake's Progress Poems, the five odes to the seasons and the evening star in *Poetical Sketches*, of which Geoffrey Hartman has written: "The primacy of the invocational-prophetic mode suggests that this progress is linked to the very energy of anticipation, to a poetry that can envision what it calls for." Nearly all of Gray's ode is what Scaliger would have labeled a "genealogical hymn," with Poesy the absent numen who is uninvoked but still traced philologically to her source.

The major turns of Gray's argument, unlike those of Jonson's Cary-Morison Ode, appear as skillful transitions between triads, with each triad therefore containing a more or less continuous block of composition. What syncopates the triadic form is the coming and going of confidence in Gray's argument. As the lassitude of his invocation shows, he is strangely unable to register excitement and unhappiness in the right places, and the most significant shape of his poem is created by this formally decentered ebb and flow of response. At the level of the stanza and also at the level of the triad, the highest pitches of confidence appear roughly at a midpoint, rising out of a blockage, lull, or note of absence carried over from the fall of preceding lines. As I shall now argue in detail, this stanzaic framing of sonority uncannily becomes a wordless commentary on the enthrallment of voice.

The brief invocation and the foretaste of "mazy progress" start the first strophe uneasily. Early songs then begin to resonate, building toward the confident, "Deep, majestic, smooth, and strong" at line 8, the tone of which gathers the "thousand rills" into a "rich stream of music" (7). But the strophe ends disturbingly by recalling the exlusionary communion of Nature with herself in the "Ode on the Spring": "The rocks and nodding groves rebellow to the roar." Early lyricists, in other words, the descriptive naturalization of whom culminates with Horace's image of Pindar as a mountain torrent (10–11), *are* Nature: they speak only to each other, and Gray's first attempt at capture closes him out of the net. The first antistrophe renews the invocation to the lyre, this time with more apparent enthusiasm; the trouble is, however, that an initial command has now been replaced by a purposeless apostrophe, no longer conative. This loss of command just when the river's momentum casts up the first epithet that is sonorous enough to be worth commanding amounts to a confession: by the end of the strophe the speaker has awakened voices that are engaged in speaking only to each other in a genial place and time.

The rest of the antistrophe reviews the Powers of Music, stressing only the power of music to *quell* the passions, in contrast with Dryden's emphasis in "Alexander's Feast." The antistrophe rises to its sonorous midpoint at the superb "On Thracia's hills the Lord of War / Has curbed the fury of his car": but this curbing begins to restrain the stanza. The continuation of textbook-sublime rhetoric contributes to the present theme, which is the anodynous effect of music, and as the speaker nods he suddenly blunders: "thy magic," he assures the enchanting shell, "lulls the feathered king." It is permissible for Pindar to say this, as he does in *Pythian* I, but when the present speaker says it the subdued bird becomes Pindar himself, the Theban Eagle. In the second antistrophe we shall find the "feathered king" transformed and redeemed in a rather remarkable way, but for the moment the epithet is a witty blunder: Gray has borrowed a progress of dulness or art of sinking from the *Dunciad*, and presented the false sublime in the act of reducing itself to the "dark clouds of slumber."

So much, then, for orotundity. The epode turns gratefully to the more spritely airs of "L'Allegro"; but if sublimity is dull, gaiety is trivial and touches nothing. The figure of "mazy progress" returns, again in reference to the more ephemeral modes of lyric: "Now pursuing, now retreating, / Now in circling troops they meet." These "Sports and Pleasures" attendant on their absent queen, Venus, are like children chasing the rolling circle's speed at Eton College. The very flirtatiousness of the elusive circle bespeaks absence, and the tone of the epode modulates richly, but also sadly, toward the Ionian mode, the "Slow melting strains" that prolong through the Alexandrine a figure of desire: "O'er her warm cheek and rising bosom move / the bloom of young desire and purple light of love." The movement of each stanza in this triad has been repeated in the triad as a whole; random and indistinct voices swell toward a sound that stupefies itself, giving way to fairy measures that fail to encircle the object of desire. The triad concludes its summary of the lyric modes in a state of restlessness, then, having captured none of them.

Still in the grip of this frustration, the second strophe begins bitterly, rehearsing Gray's usual litany of evils. Gray's 1768 note speaks of the "real and imaginary ills" in this passage, and in the poem he declares his intention of showing that poetry can cure the "fond complaint" of melancholia. He mounts as usual in mid-strophe to a peak of confidence, borrowed here from Milton and Pope, aligning his Progress with the Fortunate Fall in order to "justify the laws of Jove." We shall see in a moment the curious way in which this boast is modestly fulfilled. Meanwhile, though, a difficulty arises in this second strophe, the same difficulty that has closed the first strophe. Hyperion is introduced to purge the black bile of "Man's feeble race," but he fails to do so, as we see from the series of horror-gothic images that darkens nearly all the rest of the stanza and completes the hypochondriac catalog of the first lines. The too long delayed coming of Hyperion is magnificent but troubling. Why not Apollo? Apollo is more civilized and westerly than his predecessor, who had come "down the eastern cliffs afar." Perhaps Apollo is not called upon because he verges on the effete, the hellenistic: an urbane god, like Walpole's fish, he is made too much in the image of a feeble race to cure its ills. Therefore, the supplanted Hyperion is invoked, but he also fails. There is too much distance between the ailment and any possible figure of cure: Hyperion is, in fact, a figure of desire, not cure, confined by myth to the energetic cultural dawning of the first strophe. The second strophe therefore ends just where the first one did, and also where the first triad ended. There has been no progress—but the rayed phalanx of Hyperion's arrival fixes itself for future use as a new labyrinth.

We come now to the midpoint of the poem, the second antistrophe. Here the dilemma of belatedness is stated in the most extreme terms, yet this statement in itself supplies the trace of a solution. First, the inaccessible primitivism of Hyperion is taken a step further, "beyond the solar road," and the speaker reviews the extremes of climate and savagery where poetry and liberty, according to tradition, always appear together. The stanza is initially expansive, warming to the theme of boundlessness: "beyond the solar road," "The Muse [like Hyperion] has broke the twilight-gloom," not of melancholia in this case but of bestiality; in "Chile's boundless forests," "loose numbers wildly sweet" are repeated in the "savage youth" of culture and poetry graces "the unconquerable Mind and Freedom's holy flame." But the stanza is only partly committed to the praise of boundlessness. At this moment of maximum freedom, the imagery of the labyrinth begins to accumulate, and to constitute a progress of its own. Texturation begins hesitantly with "shaggy forms." The "native's dull abode" is certainly not promising, but the "odorous shade" of the forests begins to suggest a pleasure, not of wildness, but of repetition; the total experience of the youth's repetitions by rote is regular, bounded by the sameness that ensures the continuity of a culture.

What began "beyond the . . . road" is now reduced to a "track," and the binding image of this reduction, I think, is that of the "feather-cinctured chiefs," which has much the same central and operative effect as does the garland "planted" on Cary's head in the Cary-Morison Ode. In the first antistrophe, Pindar, the figure of voice, was a "feathered king." Now the bird is dead, but traces of its vocal existence engirt man, a covering zone of quills usable for writing that is linked synecdochically with vocal origins. Now, "feather-cinctured chiefs" is not, I confess, a very exciting epithet. The speaker fills out a line with it, giving it no more heed than he gives dozens of other epithets, and furthermore it is a Wartonian commonplace— not even distinctly identifiable as Wartonian, in fact, but simply a scrap of jargon cast upon by the fashion of noble savagery. No doubt this would be Gray's own view of the phrase I have not *yet* finished magnifying, except that he would know that the commonplace is not, distinctly not, Wartonian. The Indian is Wartonian, but not the epithet, which is taken from Milton's simile for the covering of nakedness after the Fall:

> O how unlike
> To that first naked glory. Such of late
> *Columbus* found th' *American* so girt
> With feather'd Cincture, naked else and wild
> Among the Trees on Isles and woody Shores.
> [*Paradise Lost* IX. 1114–18]

For the moment, in Milton, Adam and Eve have no solace; this simile encounters them precisely at their nadir. The feather-cinctured chief for Milton is man fallen but unredeemed; but for Gray, whose temperament was more timid and decorous than Milton's, even Adam and Even themselves, without their covering, would be "naked else, and wild," with no attendant glory, and hence a cincture of feathers would in itself go a long way toward redeeming Gray's Indian. As I have said, there is no seriously entertained prelapsarian myth in Gray. His cincture of feathers covers the savage body and transcends the savage mind because it bears traces of the vocal elegance of the Theban Eagle's writing, which is Gray's model for this poem. What is "commonplace," then, is not this epithet but rather—and perhaps deliberately so—the *rest* of the second antistrophe. It is hard to imagine the gloomy moralist and learned prosodist writing "She deigns to hear the savage youth repeat / In loose numbers wildly sweet" without pausing to consider that the savage youth cannot write. Perhaps it is true, as the poet might go on to tell himself, that his ultracivilized "joys no glittering female meets" ("Spring"), but he, at least, can write. Writing . . . is a screen, a displaced symptom of man's inner "nature," and in Gray's poetry the displacement of nature in writing (of the eagle in the quill) actually becomes a substitute for the forfeited "responsive notes" of sexuality. Writing is Gray's fortunate fall, an unquestionable loss and a binding, a labyrinthine sign of self-consciousness, but still an accomplishment. It is at this point only, and not before, that Gray's actual Progress of written poetry from Greece to England can begin.

Gray rushes through his Progress once he has launched it, arriving in England by the beginning of the third triad. His treatment of Greece and Rome mainly concerns the Muses' departures—fittingly enough, since originary inspiration has already been shown to have fled before the progress of writing begins. "Inspiration breathed around" can only be reported *after* sound has departed from the Maeander. The Pindaric indirection of diverting the sense of an argument into landscape figures that Gray has used as a sign of self-exclusion in the first strophe continues here, as the "boundless forests" of antipodal life are centralized in a bounded canopy of "Woods that wave o'er Delphi's steep." As it emerges from the state of nature, space is covered and partitioned. Nature becomes landscaping. "Maeander's amber waves / In lingering lab'rinths" intensify the artifice by alluding, as Roger Lonsdale points out, to Ovid's comparison of the Maeander to the labyrinth of Daedalus.

Artifice, then, which I am identifying with the artifice of writing, governs the Progress from the first. It is clear in retrospect that Gray's chosen voice for an ode always subtly jars against his chosen mythology: in the rather quietly measured "Ode to Adversity" the etiology led inadvertently to a savage beginning, whereas now, in Gray's more rapturous "high Pindaric," the etiology is decorously screened off at the origin of *techne*, which saved man from the Minotaur. Jonson's hippocentaur, the Infant of Saguntum in the Cary-Morison Ode, is a far more candidly encountered monstrous birth than anything that appears in the tidier Pindarics of Gray. It can be said with some precision that for Gray, art is sublimation. Not repression, however, since Gray is a paradigm of what Harold Bloom would call a "weak poet"; what Gray screens out in order to reformulate his psychic distance is not the consciousness of strong origins, but rather the threatening idea that originality is strength. I call this screening "sublimation" because it involves forgetting that there is any connection between writing and the disruptive force of nature—which the Victorian Pindarist Coventry Patmore called "the Unknown Eros."

Sublimation this extreme becomes a stern decorum that submits even the most hackneyed praises of spontaneous energy to its censorship. As the third triad begins, even Shakespeare, the little prattler of "L'Allegro," warbles his woodnotes rather too much like a "savage youth," and Gray ushers him in through an ominous darkness, "Far from the sun and summer-gale." But this unease is enclosed in new cinctures that represent the comfort of coming home from the Mediterranean to the "sea-encircled coast" of Albion and the even more reassuring "green lap" of England's inland. With these frames in place, there is no need for the river Avon to stop flowing and begin meandering, but it is still kept from flowing rapidly. It is inclined to "stray," like Shakespeare's irregularity, but its being "lucid" keeps it clearly in view. Shakespeare's originality is held further in check by Nature, who teaches him to paint the passions by numbers. Still, however artificial it may be, Gray's catalog of the passions recalls the persistent desires and ills that Hyperion could not banish. Shakespeare remains a troublesome figure by daedal standards, and the strophe repeats the emotional parabola of the earlier stanzas, rising from darkness to the sounding epiphany of Nature's "awful face" and sinking back to the faint thrill of vicarious passions.

The apotheosis of Milton in the third antistrophe is held in place to the front by the hesitant "Nor second he" and to the rear by the coming of Dryden's "less presumptuous car." Milton, like "th' *American*" borrowed from him for Gray's second antistrophe, passes "beyond the solar road": "He passed the flaming bounds of space and time." There is little apparent sense of psychic unease in this description. If we compare Milton's blinding "with excess of light" to an early passage in Gray's *Correspondence*, we can see that the "presumption" of Milton need have no personal reference at all: "Must I plunge into metaphysics? Alas, I cannot see in the dark. . . . Must I pore upon mathematics? Alas, I cannot see too much light; I am no eagle." Milton has ventured on truths as absolute as mathematics, and Gray has screened out that region so thoroughly that he retains—or so it appears for the moment —no urge to compete for it.

Dryden is the only poet in Gray's ode who is not named periphrastically, in part because without a proper name his characterization could fit Pope equally well. But Dryden's name appears also because it is the first *nomen* that carries no unruly excess of numen. Dryden's political verse is vocal, thundering and "long-resounding," but since his "Two coursers" are couplets, a visual harness constrains his heroic resonance. Dryden's odes for music (Gray's note shows that he has "Alexander's Feast" in mind) retain only the faintest echo of sound in "Thoughts that breathe." Such odes belong chiefly to the visual and tactile borders of Horace Walpole's fishbowl:

> Bright-eyed Fancy hovering o'er
> Scatters from her pictured urn
> Thoughts that breathe and words that burn.

If there is a funerary hint in Keats's urn, so here also. Even though in *pictura* the nymph tipping an urn is often a figure of inspiration (Fancy was painted in this posture, as were Naiads standing at the source of their brook), in print the coupling of "urn" and "burn" unfortunately suggests cremation, words that self-consume. Dryden's "lyre," in any case, is not vocal but pictorial, and not surprisingly " 'Tis heard no more."

The topic of Dryden has spanned two verse units, this being the first time any topic has done so, and it forces the final topic to be an unequal quantity. It is Gray's self-portrait, designedly shorter than the portraits of his predecessors but still surprisingly ample. After the matter-of-factness of "Dryden," the denomination of Gray is once more periphrastic. The numen has returned, just where we would not expect to find it, carrying with it the last surprise of this maddeningly difficult poem. The self-portrait describes the "distant way" of a poet who is not vocal but who captures voice, and it will be important to notice how little pride is lost through this diminishment. Gray's is the first ode I have paused over that curbs itself willingly, with no apparent daemonic resistance, yet it is also the first that ends with an upsurge of confidence, at the last minute breaking the pattern of terminal decline that has hitherto been the structural norm of this poem and also, with respect at least to endings, of the ode in general. Only the last Alexandrine of Milton falls; only the first in Wordsworth's "Ode to Duty" rises; only the last rises in Gray, for reasons that reward consideration.

At first the self-portrait seems as modest as we might expect it to be. The "lyre divine" is no longer Aeolian, and the speaker, who began by commanding it to "Wake," is reduced to asking who wakes it now. Clearly the vocal expectations of Gray's ode have been lowered. As the lines on himself begin, Gray does not have to admit outright that in his art he has confined himself to merely lapidary craftsmanship, since that admission is accomplished by the allusion of the whole concluding passage to the "ego parvus" of Horace, with whom Gray throughout his poem has spun variations on the oxymoron "operosa carmina fingo." Horace, then, only one of whose odes was written to be sung, appears to have silently supplanted Pindar as Gray's presiding lyrist. This substitution, supposing it to have taken place, is not without dignity: "Though he inherit / Nor the pride nor ample pinion, / That the Theban eagle bear," the present speaker still has a cincture of quills.

The course of the ode has prepared and pared the self-portrait, but the self-portrait also rewrites the course of the ode: each former crux reappears, measured this time according to its place in abstract autobiography, and then, having absorbed the periphrastic identity of each forerunner in turn, the self suddenly inflates and rises beyond any of them. Pindar has appeared and then apparently been abandoned, "Yet [Gray] shall mount . . . "; the babe Shakespeare has appeared and then disappeared under censure, "Yet oft before [Gray's] infant eyes would run / Such forms . . . "; Hyperion's "glittering shafts of war" on their eastern cliffs have dispelled no gloom, yet now "Such forms as glitter in [Gray's] Muse's ray / With orient hues, unborrowed of the sun"—*visionary* forms—exist within the poet's frame of experience; Milton, finally, who also surpassed Hyperion in passing beyond the solar road, has nevertheless been dismissed, blinded by hubris, yet now Gray himself shall "mount . . . / Beyond the limits." Here, then, is an extraordinary return of the dead to exalt the living; the artifice of sublimation effects a mediate decorum that allows even the most timorous psyche to witness the sublime. Through unresisting self-limitation, Gray uncannily soars beyond limits and writes the most boastful ending to be found in any major ode in English. I do not say "the strongest ending," since Gray's pinions are never his own; what I have taken to be the figural turning point of the poem was stolen nearly verbatim from Milton. But that theft, and the application of alien figures to the self in the final epode, exactly bear out the definition of the sublime that Gray knew best: "as if instinctively, our soul is uplifted by the true sublime; it takes a proud flight, and is filled with joy and vaunting, as though it had itself produced what it has heard" (Longinus, *On the Sublime* VII). It is Horace who is effaced at the last minute after all, and through Milton the voice of the braggart Pindar lives on record, as it were, captured by the glittering shafts of his own feathers.

The last line is supposed to lay the subject of poetry to rest in favor of the subject that the progress of poetry is everywhere said to promote, human virtue flourishing in a state of liberty. The structure of the line supports our readiness to assume that this transition does occur, since it is the only line in the ode that resembles the chiastic conceit of an Augustan moral essay. But the two subjects, poetry and virtue, *are* closely related; the thematic drift of a whole poem cannot be canceled in a single line, and the controlled, privileged referent of a trope cannot completely supplant the uncontrolled logic of the trope itself. It *must* be concluded, then, that the poet's assertion of his moral independence carries with it, willy-nilly, his surprised and surprising assertion of being "far above the Great" voices he has captured. What it would mean, in this context, to be "Beneath the good how far," has to do, once again, with the sorts of disorder that a presentational ode in itself and also the arrogance of undertaking an ode are apt to bring to the surface.

IV

The noble art to Cadmus owes its rise,
Of painting words, and speaking to the eyes;
He first in wondrous magic fetters bound
The airy voice,and stop'd the flying sound.
     —"On the Invention of Letters,"
     Dodsley's *Collection* (1756) IV.297

"The Progress of Poesy" demands cautious respect, but it is not a wholly likable or even readable poem. Popular taste and scholarly taste agree very closely about Gray. His most readable poems *are* the "Elegy," "Eton College," and the "Favorite Cat." But a serious approach to Gray does unearth certain anomalies about the relation between readable poetry, which may be defined in part as well-ordered poetry, and the balance or well-ordering of psychic forces, anomalies that popular taste may find uncomfortable. Running through Gray's most elegant poems there are delicate disturbances: a tryst with darkness to "snatch a fearful joy," "the gulf between," the return of the Furies. "The Progress of Poesy," which Johnson called a "cucumber," is a painfully overworked and in some ways grotesque poem, but its very intricacy begins to seem like an expedient cure that sublimates the Minotaur. Its philology is a coming of age that protects both civilization and the psyche from the "savage youth" of its origins. The therapy is writing, but in "The Progress," the real and imaginary ills of civilization taint the art of writing too deeply for its suppression of voice to be entirely happy. In 1755, with the writing of Gray's next ode, "The Bard," perhaps already under way, we find him still exercised about the difference between voice and writing: "setting aside the difficulties, methinks [the equivalence of meter in strophe and antistrophe] has little or no effect upon the *ear*, wch scarce perceives the regular return of metres at so great a distance from each other. To make it succeed, I am persuaded the stanza's must not consist of above 9 lines each at the most. Pindar has several such odes." Strophe and antistrophe in the "Progress" have twelve lines, in "The Bard" fourteen. Gray designedly gives up the vocal in his Pindarics, but in so doing he at first increases the strain of writing.

    The original and translated antiquarian odes release some of the strain by projecting writing backward onto the mantic vocality of the past. Now writing becomes a metaphor for speech itself. These odes take their cue from the runic metaphor for prophecy, "weaving a spell." "The Bard" and the Norse odes represent themselves as vocal texture, at once pro-phatic—in the presence of voice—and spellbinding. They are woven incantations. Johnson felt something peculiar in this fusion, and objected that "theft is always dangerous: Gray has made weavers of the slaughtered bards, by a fiction outrageous and incongruous." In "The Fatal Sisters," the imprinting or char-actering of voice is like the shuttling of space and time by the spears of warriors:

> Glittering lances are the loom,
> Where the dusky warp we strain
> Weaving many a soldier's doom,
> Orkney's woe, and Randver's bane.
>
> See the grisly texture grow,
> ('Tis of human entrails made,)
> And the weights that play below,
> Each a gasping warrior's head.

Death falls in a dense pattern; it writes history in advance and each new stroke expels a last breath.

This writing is not in fact designed to know the future. All of Gray's bardic odes, including the "versions," self-consciously follow the wholly literary precedent of Horace's "Prophecy of Nereus," of Virgil in Hell, and of Dante in Hell. Dante's Farinata explains the limits of infernal foresight on grounds that the author of the "Distant Prospect" must necessarily accept: " 'We see, like those with faulty vision, things at a distance from us,' he said, 'so much light the Sovereign Lord still grants us; when they draw near or are present our intellect is wholly at fault and unless others bring us word we know nothing of your human state. Thou canst understand, therefore, that all our knowledge will be dead from the moment the door of the future is closed' " (*Inf.* X. trans. John Sinclair). Gray's "grisly texture," then, is not prophetic but an infernal prospect. It is a mark of absence from the light that screens out and thus prevents the becoming and full presence of things, and yet literally *is* the end of things—a fatal prolepsis. Gray's antiquarian odes could have been published together under the title "The Loom of Hell" ("Fatal Sisters," 2). The ease gained from narrative and dramatic situation in these poems makes them more fluent than the mazy "Progress," but they are also far more extensively suffused with loss. The upsurge at the end of the "Progress" is countered in "The Bard" by a plunge "to endless night." "The Bard" can be read as an allegory of Gray's unceasing theme of distance as absence, and of his awareness that an ode is always its own palinode.

In "The Bard," the texturing of voice is a far more continuous process even than in the "Progress." The third antistrophe, for rexample, rearranges several figures from the first epode of the "Progress." In "The Bard," the triumphal march of the Tudor monarchs forms a circle around Queen Elizabeth, and these monarchs in turn are cinctured by their retainers, "Girt with many a baron bold." Inferior rank makes the outer circle secondary, but it easily surrounds its royal center. Within this inner circle of kings, secondary in their turn, the numen stands contained: "In the midst a form divine!" This Elizabeth, then, seems concertedly opposed to the elusive figure of "Cytherea" in the "Progress," where the "queen's approach" is closed off by the morris dance of her Graces: "Now in circling troops they meet." When this Venus, whose earlier giving way to her "train" of Hours in the "Ode on the Spring" heralds her absence from all of Gray's poetry, moves toward the center of the tableau in the "Progress," she is surrounded, not by the dance but by a sign of her absence, "The bloom of young desire." By contrast, Elizabeth in "The Bard" is surrounded from the instant of her appearance, in fact preceded, by the circle that contains her "form divine," and she is then surrounded latterly by a figure of voice as encirclement:

> What strains of vocal transport round her play!
>
> . . . .
>
> Bright Rapture calls and, soaring as she sings,
> Waves in the eye of heaven her many-coloured wings.

These wings are the wings of Longinian rhetoric, the iridescently woven "colors" of oratorical design.

Gray's "antiquarian enthusiasm" appears to have a rather surprising bias in his essays and in the extant fragments of his planned History of English Poetry. Repeatedly he praises the Welsh bards, not for their wildness, as one might expect, but for "that excellent prosodia . . . which is perhaps the finest that any language affords," and which is "admirably suited for assisting the memory." What plainly interests Gray about oral poetry is its mnemotechnics, its capacity for interlocking and preserving voice. Although he asserts that the Welsh were the first British race to use rhyme, when he sorts out the history of rhyme by dates in his "Observations on the Pseudo-Rhythmus," the Welsh in their third niche on the list seem strangely belated and post-urbane:

At Rome before the Introduction of Christianity	137
In the Latin Church	420
In Use among the Welch	590

When Gray proceeds to discuss the surviving texts of the Welsh bards, he begins with a hypothetical objection that is exactly the one leveled by criticism to this day against Gray's own poetry: "it may naturally be thought that their verse is clogged with so many rules, that it is impossible to write a poem of common sense in their language." By the time Gray's Bard appears on his rock, then, seven hundred years after his ancestors had begun to use rhyme, and howls into the void a language that Edward I cannot understand, he represents not the youthful vitality of culture but a cultural endpoint. His last words delay the disappearance of voice, like Gray's last words in the "Progress," by means of the intertexturing of memory.

"The Bard" narrates the death of the Last Poet. In the sequence of events as they occur in the text, though not in history, his death comes after the future poets whose coming he predicts, poets whose voices "lessen on" his ear. Even before his death there is a "gulf between" him and his auditors, who pass far below his rock, as well as between him and his poetic predecessors, whose ghosts sit "on yonder cliffs." He can only begin to prophesy when he joins the voices of these ghosts to his; they sing through him, just as dead poets sing through the speaker of the "Progress." The bards are no sooner joined in "dreadful harmony" than they weave and finally *print* the coming of death:

> Weave the warp and weave the woof,
> The winding-sheet of Edward's race.
> Give ample room and verge enough
> The characters of hell to trace.
> Mark the year and mark the night.
>
> (49–53)

Line 51 could be an instruction to the printer of irregular Pindaric stanzas, after which, as the image develops, death is dated and published.

When the fatal phase of the prophecy is over, the harmony ceases and the ghosts vanish. Left alone, the Bard is briefly inspired with happy independence, and sings in solitude the progress of the Tudors and their Bards. But, in fact, he is alone only in spirit; the Renaissance poets who are outlived by his power of hearing fill his voice with phrases from their poems (125–33). They are as much his ghostly inspiration as his mantic predecessors were, and when their voices cease to resound, he has no further voice of his own. He has soared on their wings, as Gray soars at the end of the "Progress." In the present poem, though, the dead do not return. They are woven too deeply into the past, into the textured winding-sheet that has drawn even "vocal transport" into its pattern. The only way the bard can join the circle he has created is to plunge into the silence of having finished fabricating speech, of *having been* a poet. It is well known that when Gray was asked what he felt when writing "The Bard," he replied, "Why I felt myself the Bard!" He may have meant this rejoinder more pointedly than has been realized; I have tried, in any case, to bring into relief a pattern in "The Bard" that shows it to be a deadly serious parody or sixth act of Gray's own apotheosis in "The Progress of Poesy."

V

After "Odikle"—Gray's unvarying name for "The Bard" in his letters to friends—Gray as a writer of odes very nearly maintained the silence of his last protagonist. The 1769 Installation Ode for the Duke of Grafton's Chancellorship at Cambridge was written to repay obligations, and it could be argued that Gray got himself through the task by alluding as often as possible to his Cambridge mock-ode, the "Hymn to Ignorance." When the parodies of the Installation Ode began to appear—"Hence, avaunt, ('tis venal ground)," and so forth—Gray was of course hurt, but he could take comfort in knowing himself to be the author of his own best parodies. All of his odes flirt with parody; one imagines that tipping his hard-won phrases over the edge must have afforded a steady recreation from becoming the poet unsympathetically described by Wordsworth as "more than any other man curiously elaborate in the structure of his poetic diction." I am persuaded, indeed, that there is a strain of internal parody in all of Gray's odes, visible to anyone who has accepted their constant concession that they are not "vocal."

Among considerable English poets, only Collins and Keats can be said to have conducted an experiment with the possibilities of ode writing that is as sustained and as dialectically alert as that of Gray. It has seemed proper in this place to take up Gray's odes for the most part in sequence as answers to, or at least as extensions of, questions raised in his own previous odes, and to consider each ode, furthermore, as a theoretical assessment of its own generic identity. (In this last respect, for the present study, Gray's odes are significant beyond his own concerns.) This emphasis has not been meant to show merely that Gray's odes are "about poetry," but to show, more specifically, that they are about being odes. From the outset, Gray appears to have approached the ode as a confrontation with compulsion neurosis; as evidence, that is, of the need to repeat constructively, and thereby for the nonce to mediate, the chronic sense of being cut off from the self and from others that was so obviously the ground of his personal anxiety. The ode is a good choice for meeting this need, because its conventions force the poet to "purple" his discourse beyond any possibility of presentational illusion. Such is the motive, I have argued, for Gray's "curious elaboration." We need not go to the extreme of asserting that Gray has "a distinct and human voice" (e.g., in the "Elegy" and certain early odes) that he juxtaposes with a cold "public" voice in order to believe that he was not merely a hapless victim of his diction; he was unquestionably, in my view, the deliberate master and obscurantist of a current mode that he found ready to hand. This is not to say, however, that he was master of his neurosis, or of all the random implications created by the dense local texture of his diction. But then, all odes, not just the odes of Gray, come at last to betray their design; no text can masquerade as voice without betraying, as does "The Bard," the very idea of vocality to oblivion.

Absence, neurosis, writing: fashionable themes. But these were also fashionable themes in the mid-eighteenth century. I refer not only to the Gothic revival, to the outpouring of nostalgic treatises on the origin of language, poetry, and metaphor, to the high incidence of the word "nervous" (partly meaning sinewy) in criticism, and to the longing for noble savagery and nature's simple plan; I refer also to the ontological paradoxes that the fashion for ode writing in itself brought to the fore. John Cunningham, an altogether representative weather vane, wrote an amorous ode "On the Late Absence of May," which fails to convince the unhappy reader that that oft-invoked genius has yet returned or will ever do so. Thomas Parnell's well-known "Hymn to Contentment" (Cunningham wrote one also) invokes that condition, calls it heaven-born and everlasting, and then describes its absence for the rest of the poem; *if* the poet could only find contentment, he would sing the "Source of Nature" like "the ancient prophets," but alas, *non beatus ille*, and his poem has no content. It is true that in *The Gift of Poetry*, Parnell is delighted to report, having invoked Time, that "my call is favour'd"; but since Time needs no calling, this success is simply a travesty of invocation from an opposite direction.

An extremely intelligent approach to these difficulties, and a tentative association of them with neurosis, can be found in Anne, Countess of Winchelsea's long poem in pseudo-Pindaric strophes called "The Spleen." Having first lamented man's absence from paradise and from the soul's "native sky," Lady Winchelsea then characterizes spleen as a downward pull upon the soul by the body, causing a "dullness" that subverts the flight of vocative poetry: "I feel my verse decay, and my cramp'd numbers fail. / Through the black jaundice, I all objects see." This poem is a satire against its own Pindarism, "cramp'd" in large part by its chosen form; and Lady Winchelsea's analysis of the megrims later suffered by Gray in his Pindaric "Progress" is more dispassionate, perhaps, than Gray's would ever be.

Aided further by Matthew Green's poem on the same subject, spleen became a popular complaint during Gray's age of "imaginary ills." Hobbes had long before blamed spleen for the apparition of ghosts, and in Gray's odes the ghosts have completely vanquished the living. Gray fools his ghosts, though, by merely pretending to invoke them, and then, just when they think they are free from his curiously elaborate calling (since being called is what absents them), he enthralls their distant voices in the very "winding-sheet" that proves them merely to be signs of the dead. I have called this enthrallment writing. "The origin of allegorical expression," wrote Collins's first editor, John Langhorne, "arose from the ashes of hieroglyphics," because, he argued, writing must at first have been as close as possible to picturing. The extravagant artificiality of Gray's and Collins's odes arguably had, then, a rather startling rationale: it is not naturalness but rather the trappings of poetic diction that bring writing as close to being coeval with voice—mediated only by hieroglyphic "natural signs"—as arbitrary signs can ever come. Thus close, though, was scarcely close enough; Gray did not write, nor would Collins have written, the lost poem that Edmund Gosse called "the suppositious *Ode on the Liberty of Genius.*"

PETER M. SACKS

Gray's "Elegy"

There is some question as to whether Gray's "Elegy Written in a Country Churchyard" in fact belongs to the kind of elegy [defined as] a poem of mourning occasioned by a specific death. Gray had originally entitled the poem "Stanzas Wrote in a Country Church Yard," and the later title was his friend William Mason's suggestion. Mason recognized the alternatingly rhymed iambic pentameter quatrains as the form used by such "elegists" as Hammond and Shenstone, poets who were reviving the license of a merely formal definition to write so-called elegies on subjects of love or philosophical reflection.

And yet, Gray's poem is, of course, a poem of mourning. Even if we unwisely discount the specificity of his residual grief for Richard West (who had died in 1742), the "Elegy" mourns a particular death over and above those of the obscure villagers. This individual death, albeit imaginary, is that of the poet himself. The preliminary description and mediation in the grave-yard is, in part, a presentation of the sensibility of that poet and a definition of the terms by which he should be mourned. It is carefully modulated so as to climax with a plea on behalf of any dying person's desire for remembrance. And this is accordingly followed by a projection of the poet's death, a projection that includes a local swain's account of the poet's life and burial (stanzas 24–29), together with a presentation of the epitaph written by the poet himself (stanzas 30–32). This entire two-part closing section (stanzas 24–32) has an effect that is reminiscent of the original ecologic forms of

From *The English Elegy: Studies in the Genre from Spenser to Yeats.* © 1985 by The Johns Hopkins University Press. Originally entitled "Johnson, Dryden, and Gray."

pastoral elegy, in which one expression of mourning or memorializing supersedes another.

This very issue of supersession lies at the heart of the poem. It reflects Gray's need to develop a language for the "voice of Nature" crying from the tomb. He has to create a language that seems to supersede both his own living speech and the speech of the swain. And so urgently does the poet need the assurance that his final, posthumous language (the epitaph) will continue to assert itself beyond his death that he contrives an action *within* the poem in which that epitaph seems actually to be read. It is a superb accomplishment, all the more effective for the discretion of its managerial design.

As is well known, the figure of the poet in the opening scene derives from the Miltonic Penseroso, a melancholic solitary courting prophetic vision. Gray's deliberate cultivation of this figure is of course part of the mid-eighteenth-century revaluation of melancholy, a movement pursued by such contemporaries as Shenstone and the Wartons. But in view of what follows, the particularity of Gray's association with Milton will have to be stressed.

The introduction not only sets a scene but introduces several interrelated aspects of an attitude toward the dead, an attitude that the poet hopes will eventually be accorded to himself. The attitude includes piety, compassion, respect, and attentiveness—the kind of attentiveness we owe the mute. In fact, throughout, there is a fascinating preoccupation with the theme of muteness as opposed to sound, or eventually, of an epitaphic script as opposed to a living voice. The preoccupation is complex, since, as we may expect, Gray comes to favor the silence of his final script, despite his own desire for voice.

In the opening description there is, therefore, a specific attentiveness given to sounds that emerge from a predominating silence. Their emergence is usually one of near-redemptive exception, the ability to be "saved," quite literally, from the hold of "solemn stillness." In the context of a churchyard at nightfall, these are like the haunting sounds that escape or survive death—positive tokens, even models, we may suppose, for any elegist. But Gray seems already to be aware that any posthumous *human* language will be unvoiced, dependent on the quiet mediation of an epitaphic script. And he begins to woo not only our attention to, but also our respect for, quietude. Hence the contemptuous lines referring to varieties of useless sound:

> Nor you, ye proud, impute to these the fault,
>   If Memory o'er their tomb no trophies raise,

> Where through the long-drawn aisle and fretted vault
>   The pealing anthem swells the note of praise.
>
> Can storied urn or animated bust
>   Back to its mansion call the fleeting breath?
> Can Honor's voice provoke the silent dust,
>   Or Flattery soothe the dull, cold ear of Death?
>   (37–44)

The silent dust and cold ear are quite impervious to the provocations of voice or music. Hence, too, Gray elicits respect for "some mute, inglorious Milton," in a position of curious strength, now, relative to any vocalizer whom Death will silence. Having already suggested the unavoidable muteness of the dead, Gray uses that muteness as a perhaps illegitimate means to qualify the vocal strength even of such as Milton. In other words, by aligning himself with muteness as the only condition, if any, of a posthumous existence, Gray assuages his melancholy fear of being a mute inglorious Milton himself.

Similarly, Gray marshals a defense of obscurity at large by juxtaposing it against examples of fatuous and cruel "greatness" and revealing it as the necessary condition of the dead. His praise seems to extend, therefore, to those who live in such a way—obscure and silent—as to suffer the least alteration by death. Hence, too, "they kept the noiseless tenor of their way."

But a countervailing protest is rising beneath the burden of this repression, and in the final stanzas of the introduction (20–23) Gray expresses his desire for a saving power of voice. Admittedly, he begins with images of various scripts, but the eloquent plea for remembrance mounts to the following climax:

> On some fond breast the parting soul relies,
>   Some pious drops the closing eye requires;
> E'en from the tomb the voice of Nature cries,
>   E'en in our ashes live their wonted fires.
>   (89–92)

Here, then, recklessly overcoming the sober arguments for silence, is the urge for voice, albeit one displaced somewhat onto Nature. This is the most freely energetic moment in the poem. (Incidentally, no other stanza has verbs at the ends of as many as three lines.) But Gray has risen to the expression of a wish, not a truth. The first two lines are literally credible, for the supposed person is in the process of dying. But the last lines are different, and Gray cannot win us by sheer momentum. The sudden boldness of his figuration itself betrays him, striving as he is to believe that a vigorously crying voice or a fiery glow can outlast death.

With this crystallization of his desire for remembrance after death, the poet turns directly to the task of guaranteeing that remembrance. But predictably, the argument carries him away from the desire for vocal immortality and leads him instead to recognize his inevitable dependence on written words. Indeed, the transition is harsh, and as he turns to address himself ("For thee who, mindful of the unhonored dead"), we switch abruptly from the cry of voice to an explicit reference to the very lines of this poem ("Dost in these lines their artless tale relate").

And yet, the sound of a voice, even if no longer strictly the poet's, *does* continue, in the person of the "hoary-headed swain," who tells some possible "kindred spirit" about the poet. Here is a possible strategy, a form of posthumous ventriloquism, Gray putting his words into the mouth of a survivor. But this does not suffice, for several reasons. A measure of intimacy is lost; no swain can do justice to this poet, particularly considering the latter's obscurity and isolation; the swain himself is mortal, and his spoken account must fall mute when his breath, too, is extinguished.

So it is that the poet turns finally to the only form of language that can assure him of its, and therefore of his, posthumous identity. Despite the swain's rather touching use of the word *lay*, the transition from the oral narration to the silent script of the epitaph could hardly be more emphatic: "Approach and read (for thou canst read) the lay, / Graved on the stone beneath yon aged thorn." The repetition of *read* and the almost cruel distance between the illiterate swain and the literate "spirit" are jolting. (The choice of the word *spirit* suggests that now, finally, the poet's language is about to find an undying reader.) One cannot miss the heavily and irregularly accented *Graved*, a pun suggesting the relation between epitaphic writing and burial. Relentlessly, the detailed placement of the "graved" stone "beneath yon aged thorn" implies that the language of the epitaph will itself be communicating from within its own entombment.

When the swain stops speaking, the poem seems to fall silent. The reader falls into an uncanny solitude. There is no longer a voice to interpose between himself and the epitaph. Indeed, the poem has been about the dying of a voice. The reader must cross, now, from the alleged utterance of the living to the engraved script of the dead. And there he must attend even more intently than the poet, earlier, among the minute sounds of the churchyard, had invited him to do.

Regarding the figure of the elegized poet, as presented both by the swain and by the epitaph, many of his attributes should be familiar to us. Gray has blended the traits of the Penseroso with those of Lycidas and his elegist (compare "Oft have we seen him at the peep of dawn / Brushing with hasty steps the dews away, / To meet the sun upon the upland lawn" with "To- gether both, ere the high Lawns appeared / Under the opening eyelids of the morn, / We drove afield . . . "), as well as with those of that self-mourning elegist, Colin Clout (compare "Now drooping, woeful-wan, like one for- lorn, / Or crazed with care, or crossed in hopeless love" with "For pale and wanne he was, [alas the while,] / May seem he lovd, or els some care he tooke").

As we hear and then read of him, the poet himself thus seems to recede and merge into the generalized figures of elegy. Beyond them we recognize an archaic vegetation deity returning to the common mother ("Here rests his head upon the lap of earth, /A youth . . . "). It is from the distant repose of this carefully fictionalized existence, as much as from the bosom of his God, that the poet would not be disturbed, either by those who would disclose his merits or by those who would draw out his frailties. Despite his bid for remembrance, he has finally asked us to remember him as enshrined in a highly literary, even divine, obscurity.

JEAN-PIERRE MILEUR

Thomas Gray

Completed in 1750 when Gray was thirty-four, "Elegy Written in a Country Churchyard" became one of the best-known poems of the later eighteenth century and, as such, made Gray an influence to be reckoned with for the first-generation Romantics. As we will see, this is especially true for Wordsworth, who singles Gray out for criticism in his famous preface to the Lyrical Ballads and whose "Intimations" ode is perhaps most profitably seen as a revisionary response to the "Elegy."

Gray's poem begins in that imaginative space ably defined by Geoffrey Hartman in his essay "Evening Star and Evening Land"—the liminal state, separating the full light of day from the coming darkness, so admirably suited to convey the sense of diminished poetic possibility appropriate to the final stages of a declining poetic tradition:

> The Curfew tolls the knell of parting day,
> The lowing herd wind slowly o'er the lea,
> The plowman homeward plods his weary way,
> And leaves the world to darkness and to me.
>
> (1–4)

Here, the twilight state, as it is epitomized by William Collins's "Ode to Evening" (1747), is even further condensed as Gray crowds right up against the moment when darkness finally blots out sense—"Now fades the glim-

---

From *Literary Revisionism and the Burden of Modernity*. © 1985 by The Regents of the University of California. University of California Press, 1985.

mering landscape on the sight" (5)—and does entirely without the Hesperidean promise of the Collins poem.

Throughout the "Elegy," Gray displays an intense formal self-consciousness, manifested in a remorseless process of reduction. An entire tradition of temporal poetry, dealing with the cycle of the seasons and the times of day, shrinks into the form of the evening poem, which is itself further reduced to this moment on the edge of darkness. Similarly, the shaded and secluded bower, privileged for poetry since the beginnings of pastoral, is first transformed into the churchyard and then further reduced to the grassy grave plots with their epitaphs: "Where heaves the turf in many a mould'ring heap, / Each in his narrow cell for ever laid, / The rude Forefathers of the hamlet sleep" (14–16). Finally, all poetry written in the twilight of the tradition is necessarily elegiac—the form appropriate to the penultimate or evening stage of poetic progress, just as the epitaph with which the poem ends is appropriate to its ultimate, purely nostalgic night.

As the locus peculiar to poetry in his own age, Gray presents the churchyard as a place in which the poet confronts the future he shares with all men and becomes a part of the tradition, himself a "Forefather" to someone. Death is especially privileged in this vision as the intersection of the poet's personal fate and the fate of poetry in the imminent future. The result is a kind of compensation granted to the later poets as the proximity of encompassing death eases the burden of past greatness and the giants of the tradition are similarly chastened by their new vulnerability as the "rude Forefathers" of the poetic hamlet. For this reason, the tone of the poem is more melancholy than sad, which is to say that there is a pleasurable element of new freedom mixed into the sadness—the freedom accompanying a defeat for which one cannot be blamed and against which no amount of genius can prevail.

On a somewhat more superficial level, the poem proceeds with the poet appealing to his audience to appreciate the humble virtues of these good rural farmers and laborers and not to diminish them by inappropriate comparisons with the greatness associated with opportunities they never had. The increasing eloquence and urgency of the poet's appeal reveals an identification beyond mere sympathy, which is, of course, based on his own wish to be judged in terms of the diminished poetic possibilities available to him. His too are the virtues of the good workman, making the most of his limited station:

> Oft did the harvest to their sickle yield,
> Their furrow oft the stubborn glebe has broke;

How jocund did they drive their team afield!
How bow'd the woods beneath their sturdy stroke!

Let not ambition mock their useful toil,
Their homely joys, and destiny obscure;
Nor grandeur hear with a disdainful smile,
The short and simple annals of the poor.

The boast of heraldry, the pomp of pow'r,
And all that beauty, all that wealth e'er gave,
Awaits alike th' inevitable hour.
The paths of glory lead but to the grave.

Nor you, ye Proud, impute to These the fault,
If Mem'ry o'er their Tomb no Trophies raise,
Where thro' the long-drawn isle and fretted vault
The pealing anthem swells the note of praise.

Can storied urn or animated bust
Back to its mansion call the fleeting breath?
Can Honour's voice provoke the silent dust?
Or Flatt'ry sooth the dull cold ear of Death?

                                                    (25–44)

Since all, including the greatest, are ultimately reduced to dust, death becomes the poet's most effective defense, however pyrrhic, against the crushing greatness of the tradition. But the poetic *tu quoque* defends the modern poet by reviving in lines 41–44 the very dangerous question also addressed by Milton in "Lycidas": what good is poetry in the face of death? In that poem, Milton grants poetry's detractors their most damaging premise, characterizing it, in essence, as a dallying with "false surmise." In a brilliant reversal, he goes on to argue that it is the very artificiality, the unreality of poetry that makes it the language of faith, which is, after all, "the substance of things hoped for, the evidence of things not seen" (Heb. 11:1).

What is so pyrrhic in Gray's way of stating the problem is that in attacking the pretensions of greatness in the face of death, he calls into question poetry's most fundamental compensatory myth. In effect, Gray is challenging the notion prevalent since Homer and (probably) before of the value of poetic fame—that poetic greatness somehow provides an immortality in the minds of men that trancends the limits of mortal existence. Gray, despite his later insistence on the saving value of commemoration, raises the possibility that poetry itself and hence poetic fame are also mortal.

Clearly, Gray's is the fear that there will be no one to perform for him and the others of his generation the acts of commemoration that he performs for those before. He is struggling to preserve a faith in posterity sufficient to ensure that even if he can no longer have the fame of a Milton, he can at least anticipate some modest existence in the poetic memory after death.

Yet this desire to believe in a poetic posterity is belied by the use of death as a leveling defense against the accusation represented by past greatness. If "the paths of glory lead but to the grave," then the very notion of fame is undercut, and the pretensions of any poetic fame whatever could scarcely be more absurd.

As a defense, the universality of death is a dangerous failure, calling into question the myth of fame on which all poets depend in order to express the desire that makes them poets; it is also a failure necessary to the freedom peculiar to the poet late in the tradition. In order to understand this, we must look a bit more closely at the nature of defense. Repression, for example, is not known in and of itself but through the consequences of its failure—a failure that suddenly transforms the literality of behavior into something interpretable. Indeed, it is precisely the failure of defense that makes possible the interpretive activity of psychoanalysis. To put it another way, the existence of such an interpretation requires both that there be something like defenses and that they fail. From the point of view of literary criticism, whether carried out implicitly by poets or explicitly by critics, what this suggests is that there is a paradoxical interpretive relationship between failure and the will to power.

The damage done to the myth of fame by the power Gray grants to death opens up a new area of poetic endeavor: to make up for the loss of faith in fame by redefining poetry in order to give it different goals and to identify it with new bases of value and authority. In this sense, the stance of lateness or minority is clearly a way of making space, although we have yet to determine if the cost is not too high.

From this point, Gray speculates:

> Perhaps in this neglected spot is laid
> Some heart once pregnant with celestial fire;
> Hands, that the rod of empire might have sway'd,
> Or wak'd to extasy the living lyre.
>
> But knowledge to their eyes her ample page
> Rich with the spoils of time did ne'r unroll;
> Chill Penury repress'd their noble rage,
> And froze the genial current of the soul.

Full many a gem of purest ray serene,
The dark unfathom'd cares of ocean bear:
Full many a flower is born to blush unseen,
And waste its sweetness on the desert air.

Some village-Hampden, that with dauntless breast
The little Tyrant of his fields withstood;
Some mute inglorious Milton here may rest,
Some Cromwell guiltless of his country's blood.

(45–60)

We are tempted to respond immediately that a "mute inglorious Milton" is
not a Milton at all, yet here Gray prepares the way for the Wordsworth of
the Preface in arguing that one is not a poet by virtue of actually having
written poetry but by virtue of an essential disposition of the self. Such a
view is an important compensatory complement of a fundamentally impersonal and deterministic view of history. In the lines above, Gray emphasizes
that impersonal circumstances of birth, time, and place are sufficient to
overpower even genius. Clearly, it would be intolerable if the individual were
held responsible for the limits imposed by history. On the other hand, to
remove the identity of the poet from its objective manifestation in having
written is also to move away from a visible canon as the shape and source
of literary authority toward an altogether vaguer, internal standard.

However, the poem continues: if circumstance kept these villagers from
recognizing their own potential greatness, it also prevented them from in-
dulging in the excesses of greatness (61–76). Recognizing the essential violence
of greatness, Gray goes on to suggest a connection between that excess and
a revolt against death:

Yet ev'n, these bones from insult to protect
Some frail memorial still erected nigh,
With uncouth rhimes and shapeless sculpture deck'd,
Implores the passing tribute of a sigh.

Their name, their years, spelt by th' unletter'd muse,
The place of fame and elegy supply:
And many a text around she strews
That teach the rustic moralist to die.

(77–84)

The alternative recommended by Gray is a poetry of acceptance, a
poetry freed by its final defeat at the hands of death and history. But this

reduction of poetry to elegy deprives poetry of its due seasons—gone are the stages of growth (pastoral, georgic, epic) with their unique concerns corresponding to the times of life. In the twilight of the tradition, all poetry is aimed at being reconciled to its fate:

> For who to dumb Forgetfulness a prey,
> This pleasing anxious being e'er resigned,
> Left to the warm precincts of the chearful day,
> Nor cast one longing ling'ring look behind?
>
> On some fond breast the parting soul relies,
> Some pious drops the closing eye requires;
> Ev'n, from the tomb the voice of Nature cries,
> Ev'n in our Ashes live their wonted Fires.
>
> (85–92)

Here Gray returns to a much muted version of the myth of fame, in which poetry is no longer seen as striving against mortality but as easing our acceptance of death by assuring that someone cares. Poetry becomes the privileged language of this anxiety/caring because it too is in decline toward death.

Begun the year after the publication of "Elegy" and completed in 1754, Gray's long Pindaric ode "The Progress of Poesy" makes explicit the idea of poetic history underlying the melancholy of the earlier poem. It traces the westward progress of the focus of poetic greatness from Greece, to Rome, to England and, after extolling the virtues of Shakespeare, Milton, and Dryden, concludes:

> Oh! lyre divine, what daring Spirit
> Wakes thee now? Tho' he inherit
> Nor the pride, nor ample pinion,
> That the Theban Eagle bear.
> Sailing with supreme dominion
> Thro' the azure deep of air:
> Yet oft before his infant eye would run
> Such forms, as glitter in the Muse's ray
> With orient hues, unborrow'd of the Sun:
> Yet shall he mount, and keep his distant way
> Beyond the limits of the vulgar fate,
> Beneath the Good how far—but far above the Great.
>
> (112–23)

The convoluted syntax of that last line very nearly succeeds in obscuring Gray's conviction that the progress of poesy represents for moderns a permanent decline in greatness. This new Pindar anticipated by Gray, though soaring far above the merely good, is nevertheless doomed to remain far below the truly great. Indeed, although he does not slight Shakespeare and Milton by saying so, Gray manages to suggest that the power and spontaneity of the Greeks was never recaptured in later poetry, for all its virtues.

Before launching into his account of the actual progress, Gray devotes his first sixty-five lines to rehearsing the original, undiminished powers of poetry, including the power to alleviate care, control passion and distract from violence, and give voice to love and desire. Once, he even suggests, poetry was a sufficient answer to death itself:

> Man's feeble race what Ills await,
> Labour, and Penury, the racks of Pain,
> Disease, and Sorrow's weeping train,
> And Death, sad refuge from the storms of Fate!
> The fond complaint, my Song, disprove,
> And justify the laws of Jove.
> Say, has he giv'n in vain the heav'nly muse?
> Night, and all her sickly dews,
> Her spectres wan, and birds of boding cry,
> He gives to range the dreary sky:
> Till down the eastern cliffs afar
> Hyperion's march they spy, and glitt'ring shafts of war.
>
> (42–53)

The translation of Milton's intention, expressed in the famous invocation of Paradise lost, to "justify the ways of God to Man" into the gratuitous and sadly self-conscious classicism of "And justify the laws of Jove" suggests not only the poetic weakness of Gray's classicism but also the pedantic rather than imaginative foundations of much of his verse.

The decision to add in the 1768 edition notes to "The Progress" and its companion ode, "The Bard," serves only to emphasize the way in which the poems are, in a sense, already footnoted, if not partially reduced to footnotes themselves, by the many echoes of previous poems, unrelated in meaning to their immediate context, which they contain—echoes clearly designed to be recognized as evidence of an erudition shared by reader and poet as the basis of their relationship.

Not only does this indicate the need for new poetic myths to give imaginative life to Gray's subject matter; it also suggests that a poem, whatever its ostensible subject, will inevitably become a poem about its own status as poetry. And what are we to make of the "Advertisement," also added in 1768?

> When the author first published this and the following Ode, he was advised, even by his Friends, to subjoin some few explanatory Notes; but had too much respect for the understanding of his Readers to take that liberty.

We can only assume that between 1757 and 1768 Gray was persuaded that his faith was misplaced and the distance between himself and his audience somewhat greater than he had imagined. We do know that his nonoccasional poetry after 1754 is dominated by a search for extracanonical and nonclassical sources in various northern traditions. The first and most important of these efforts, "The Bard," was completed in 1757 and published along with "The Progress of Poesy." "The Bard" was followed in 1761 by "The Fatal Sisters," "The Descent of Odin," and "The Welsh Odes."

"The Bard" is particularly interesting for our purposes because it promises to redefine the tradition outside the deterministic history and overburdened self-consciousness of "The Progress," but it ultimately fails to seize the opportunity and ends up reinforcing and extending the pessimism implicit in the earlier poems.

In his "Advertisement" Gray tells us:

> The Following Ode is founded on a Tradition current in Wales, that Edward the First, when he compleated the conquest of that country, ordered all the Bards, that fell into his hands, to be put to death.

As the poem begins, the last of the Welsh bards curses the king with a prophetic vision of the disasters to befall his line before it dies out to be replaced by the new promise of the Tudors. The contrast between Edward and Elizabeth is a contrast between poetry at odds and allied with temporal power and the forces of history. But it is difficult to know what conclusions we are to draw. On the one hand, the story seems to suggest a compensatory principle at work in history, with present memories to be replaced by future glories; on the other hand, since Gray's "history" stops with Shakespeare, "The Bard" is a kind of complement to rather than replacement for the view expressed in "The Progress of Poesy," especially since it makes the canonical Shakespeare the fulfillment of the bard's hopes.

There also seem to be certain parallels between Gray's vision and that of Collins at the end of "Ode to Evening" and in "The Manners" (1746). In the final lines of the former poem, Collins associates the new, muted poetic of evening with the social virtues of "Fancy, Friendship, Science, smiling Peace" (50). In "The Manners," he begins by bidding farewell to the self-involvement of larger intellectual and imaginative ambitions and turns outward to cultivate a harmony, antithetical to the aggressivity of greatness, of the natural and social worlds:

> Youth of the quick uncheated sight,
> Thy Walks, Observance, more invite!
> O Thou, who lov'st that ampler Range,
> Where Life's wide Prospects round thee change,
> And with her mingling Sons ally'd,
> Throws't the prattling page aside:
> To me in Converse sweet impart,
> To read in Man the native Heart,
> To learn, where Science sure is found.
> From nature as she lives around:
> And gazing oft her Mirror true,
> By turns each shifting Image view!
> Till meddling Art's officious Lore,
> Reverse the Lessons taught before,
> Alluring from a safer Rule,
> To dream in her enchanted School:
> Tho' Heav'n, whate'r of Great we boast,
> Has blest this social Science most.
>
> (19–36)

Gray draws a distinction between the old bards' powers and those of Spenser, Shakespeare, Milton, and those who follow them. Before the massacre of the old bards, there was "Cadwallo's tongue, / That hush'd the stormy main" (29–30) and "Modred, whose magic song / Made huge Plinlimmon bow his cloud-top'd head" (33–34). The great revival of poetry ushered in by Elizabeth promises:

> The verse adorn again
> Fierce War, and faithful Love,
> And Truth severe, by fairy Fiction drest.
> In buskin'd measures move
> Pale Grief, and pleasing Pain,
> With Horrour, Tyrant of the throbbing Breast.
> A Voice, as of the Cherub-choir,

Gales from blooming Eden bear;
And distant warblings lessen on my ear,
That lost in long futurity expire.

(125–34)

In light of "The Progress of Poesy," this line may seem a trifle ominous
since the five hundred years between the thirteenth and eighteenth centuries
seem sufficient to qualify as a "long futurity." But the bard's song, his
prophetic curse, is itself the best example of the gap separating the earlier
greatness from the later. If those who could actually bend nature to their
wills by song are gone, the lone survivor can speak a prophecy of five hundred
years' duration and bring disaster down on his enemy's line. It is this sense
of poetry as power that is missing from Gray's account of the more modern
greats.

The difference seems to suggest that poetic power of the prophetic kind
is intimately linked with disaster. A prophecy like this requires an occasion,
and it is difficult to imagine a suitable occasion that could be anticipated
with any pleasure. Thus, the conditions of poetic power seem completely at
odds with the natural and social harmony envisaged in "The Manners."

Much in this poem hinges on the necessity of the bard's suicide:

Enough for me: With joy I see
The different doom our Fates assign.
Be thine despair, and scept'red Care,
To triumph and to die, are mine.
He spoke, and headlong from the mountain's height
Deep in the roaring tide he plung'd to endless night.

(139–44)

The truth of the prophecy and efficacy of the curse, the sheer poetic power,
is not enough to give the bard any vision of his own future or even to allow
him to contemplate his own survival. He knows that his poetic identity, his
fellowship with the poets of power, binds him to the past by excluding him
from a future in which he can have no part except by becoming another kind
of poet entirely. And, finally, it is not the evident truth of the prophecy or
power of its utterance that validates it, but the death of the poet—the ultimate
evidence of sincerity.

Defeated by history, yet seeking a literal validation of poetic power
outside poetry itself, the bard can prove this power only by his willingness
to die—a gesture that mortgages the poetic future by committing it in advance
to eulogize him, even as Gray is now doing. There is no sublimation of death

here, no metaphorical drive to be elsewhere, and hence nothing to compete with the reality of death. "The Bard" rejoins the vision of "Elegy Written in a Country Churchyard" in conceiving poetry as the means by which, like Huck and Tom, we contrive to be spectators at our own funerals. This helps to explain our peculiar position in this poem as those who bear witness and, in doing so, recognize that we are the living fulfillment of the bard's prophecy. In this view, history is prophecy fulfilled, beyond revision or, to put it another way, history is death.

All of this, especially the sense of history as death, encourages us to see in "The Bard" a dark allegory of originality as disaster. Indeed, the bard's originality is inseparable from the disaster that befalls his tradition and leaves him trapped in a past whose obsolescence he is even now declaring but without which his prophetic vision could not be. Tied to that origin defining his originality, he is powerless to join the future he envisions. The bard's is the trap of all prophecy: realized, it ceases to be prophetic and becomes history, and, hence, the original poet is a Moses who cannot enter his promised land.

Thus, the link between the ideal of originality and the ineffability of the ideal self becomes apparent. The heroism of the defeated bard is internalized, and this internalized heroism, founded in a despair of the present, is originality, which eternally finds its ultimate triumph somewhere just beyond its reach and so seeks to postpone indefinitely its final defeat. Such an internalization, stripping heroism of its external supports, its points of reference in a living community, cuts off the avenues of externalization, the opportunities for the adequate gesture, and leaves the hero of origins alone with death, at once the end of ambivalence and the threshold of a desired future. Here, in germinal form, we have the origin of Wordsworth's effort to redeem originality by sublimation—an evasion implicitly confirming the connection or originality with death—and of Shelley's attempt to overcome Gray and Wordsworth both by severing this connection.

From the point of view of the Romantics who follow, Gray represents an exhausted orthodoxy. He makes no attempt to subvert the reality of death by rendering it a figure of itself, nor does he strive to keep alive in any vital form the poetic ambition to surpass death, either by sublimating it (in order to forestall disappointment) or by rejecting sublimation altogether (in order to seek an alternative reality). Nevertheless, as Bate points out, Gray's poetic is very much a part of the secular revisionism of the eighteenth century, which the Romantics both extend and define themselves against.

Wordsworth's conservative revisionism is based on sublimation just as Shelley's radicalism is based on the rejection of sublimation. . . . [Harold]

Bloom's rejection of sublimation as the doctrine of the second chance marks his as an extreme Gnostic revisionism and seems to set him apart from the tradition of sublimation dominating literary humanism after Wordsworth. For all of this, Shelley through Wordsworth and Bloom through Shelley remain powerfully bound to Gray's reformulation for secular poetry of the revisionist problematic of gain-through-loss.

THOMAS WEISKEL

William Collins's "Ode on the Poetical Character"

Collins's most ambitious poem, the "Ode on the Poetical Character," presents notorious difficulties, but they are conceptual rather than psychological.
Perhaps the psychological themes—sexuality, the imagined relation between
the parents, the expulsion from a blissful commerce with them—are too
much on the surface of the poem to have attracted commentary. Surely
Collins's theory of the creative imagination, which looks now traditional
(Neoplatonic) and now revolutionary (Romantic), is but a small part of his
claim for a serious reading. What will concern us here—no doubt too exclu-
sively, but we are redressing a balance—is the status of the poetical character
with respect to anxiety, Romance, and the sense of historical possibility.
Throughout the poem the sense of an "I" is muted, and the arena of mental
conflict is displaced to the welcome indirection of mythopoeic statement.

The strophe consists of an expanded simile in which the poet's election
by the muse Fancy is paralleled to a competition at one of Spenser's
tournaments:

> As once, if not with light regard
> I read aright that gifted bard,
> (Him whose school above the rest
> His loveliest Elfin Queen has blessed)
> One, only one, unrivalled fair
> Might hope the magic girdle wear,

From *The Romantic Sublime: Studies in the Structure and Psychology of Transcendence.*
© 1976 by The Johns Hopkins University Press. Originally entitled "The Sublime
as Romance: Two Texts from Collins."

At solemn tourney hung on high,
The wish of each love-darting eye;
Lo! to each other nymph in turn applied,
    As if, in air unseen, some hovering hand,
Some chaste and angel-friend to virgin-fame,
    With whispered spell had burst the starting band,
It left unblest her loathed, dishonoured side;
    Happier hopeless fair, if never
    Her baffled hand with vain endeavour
Had touched that fatal zone to her denied!
Young Fancy thus, to me divinest name,
    To whom, prepared and bathed in heaven,
    The cest of amplest power is given,
    To few the godlike gift assigns
    To gird their blest prophetic loins,
And gaze her visions wild, and feel unmixed her flame!

                                                        (1–22)

The terms of this loose simile look egregiously disproportionate. "Young Fancy" has no evident parallel at the tourney, the "angel-friend" seems to have wandered in from *Comus*, and the disparity between "One, only one" (which looks forward to Milton's exclusive claim in the antistrophe) and "few" (which suggests a more generously conceived elite) places two versions of election in competition. Suppose these matters are conceded to the expansive privilege of epic simile; still we must wonder about the heart of the comparison: how are the prophetic poets like the nymphs of this beauty contest? What they evidently have in common is a kind of sexual test in which only the chaste are blessed with success. The unchaste are exposed, left "unblest . . . loathed, dishonoured." To aspire to the "cest of amplest power" is not only to risk failure but to risk shame.

    In Spenser the girdle has the power to give "the vertue of chast love," and "to bind lascivious desire, / And loose affections streightly to restrain." But this magic works only with the already chaste, for "whosoever contrarie doth prove, / Might not the same about her middle weare, / But it would loose, or else a sunder teare" (4.5.3–4). The girdle has the talismanic ambiguity common in allegorical imagery; it is at once emblem and cause. If Collins's simile is to be taken at face value, poetic election is a crisis in the course of sexuality where those whose desire is impure are separated from those few who feel Fancy's flame "unmixed." The latter are rewarded with "amplest power" and invited to what seems, oddly enough, a quasi-sexual communion with Fancy. "And gaze her visions wild, and feel unmixed her flame!" is delicately ambiguous, and not free of scopophilia—which should not surprise us in a poem about the origins of the poetic imagination. Two kinds of sexuality are contrasted: the one is secretly unchaste and then leads to shame and impotence; the other is chaste, rewarded with amplest potency, and leads to an elite participation in the desire of the divine muse Fancy.

In broad outline, the burden of Collins's conceit is conventional, and it evokes not only the chastity theme of the earlier Milton but also a range of doctrine on sublimation from the biblical to the Platonic and even to *amour courtois*. The notion that the higher love is also the more intense resolves into the fiction of Innocence, which always has it both ways. Desire is chaste yet fulfilled: sublimation has no cost—or better, since an economic view already presupposes the Fall, sublimation is unnecessary, since desire has not yet encountered opposition in a reality principle or an experience of shame. Collins is unmistakably invoking a prelapsarian state of mind as the essential condition of poetic election. Milton had insisted upon a full and shameless sexuality before the Fall, and no Miltonic legacy was more important to the Romantic poets than his image of Innocence. There is of course no room for such a state in Freud, or perhaps in life, which makes its presence in poetry (especially in Milton, Blake, and Keats) especially relevant for the moralist. Paradise is the ultimate symbol of the family romance, the concentrated place of the may-be and the might-have-been which the romance is committed to elaborate.

The "cest of amplest power" appears to be an emblem of the power of Innocence with magical properties (as in Spenser) to sustain the state it signifies. Whatever its genesis, Collins is inventive to the point of extravagance in working out its symbolic potentialities in the mesode:

> The band, as fairy legends say,
> Was wove on that creating day
> When He, who called with thought to birth
> Yon tented sky, this laughing earth,
> And dressed with springs and forests tall,
> And poured the main engirting all,
> Long by the loved Enthusiast wooed,
> Himself in some diviner mood,
> Retiring, sat with her alone,
> And placed her on his sapphire throne,
> The whiles, the vaulted shrine around,

> Seraphic wires were heard to sound,
> Now sublimest triumph swelling,
> Now on love and mercy dwelling;
> And she, from out the veiling cloud,
> Breathed her magic notes aloud:
> And thou, thou rich-haired youth of morn,
> And all thy subject life was born!
> The dangerous Passions kept aloof,
> Far from the sainted growing woof;
> But near it sat ecstatic Wonder,
> Listening the deep applauding thunder;
> And Truth, in sunny vest arrayed,
> By whose the tarsel's eyes were made;
> All the shadowy tribes of Mind
> In braided dance their murmurs joined.
>
>   (23–48)

Let us ignore for a moment the divine primal scene imagined of God and Fancy in favor of a simple connection. The magic girdle or band is woven coincidentally with God's creation, which suggests at least an analogy between the two events. Spenser's account, "as Faeries wont report," has the "pretious ornament" wrought by Venus' husband Vulcan "with unquenched fire" (4.5.4). Collins's girdle is also an *ornament*, a perfect instance of what Angus Fletcher calls the "cosmic image." Fletcher has studied ancient and derived ideas of *kosmos* (Latin *ornament*) and isolated the features of the cosmic image central to allegory. *Kosmos* denotes both order on a universal scale and microcosmic signs of that order, particularly the dress or costume which certifies one's position in the general hierarchy. The cosmic image is synecdochical and, properly read points to the intimate connection or analogy between the small-scale sign—say the sartorial emblem—and the creation itself, conceived as God's ornamenting of chaos. This is precisely the connection implied in Collins's mesode, where God's creation is figured cosmetically, as a dressing of the earth.

Once we are alert to the resonance of *kosmos*, the imagery of the poem begins to make coherent sense. The pervasive image system concerns clothing. In addition to the girdle (band, cest, zone, woof) and the wearing (girding) appropriate to it, there is God's activity (dressing, engirting) and the generation of the "sainted growing woof" itself with Truth looking on "in sunny vest arrayed" and the "braided dance" of the Mind's murmurs. Even the curtain that drops over the inspiring bowers in the Fall of the poem's last lines may be assimilated to the dominant code. We are not surprised to find in one of Collins's possible sources the phrase "the wat'ry zone / Ingirting Albion," since a glance at the *OED* shows that *band, zone,* and *girdle* have common geographical and cosmological significations.

Where does all this—another context—lead? Clearly, the poet-prophet whose loins are girded with the "godlike gift" is consecrated into a special relation to the prelapsarian natural creation. The Fancy or imagination of the elect poet gives him the natural world as a cosmic garment, a part of what the psychologists call the "body image." The girdle symbolizes this privileged relation whose magic is reflexively dependent upon the poet's inner chastity of mind. He is to the "sainted growing woof" what the sun is to the growing natural world. Collins's writing is here highly condensed and has led to several interpretations:

> And she, from out the veiling cloud,
> Breathed her magic notes aloud:
> And thou, thou rich-haired youth of morn,
> And all thy subject life was born!
> The dangerous Passions kept aloof,
> Far from the sainted growing woof.
>
> (37–42)

The orthodox view that Collins is merely referring to the origin of the sun misses the point of the Romantic commentators who find here an Apollonian poet. The debate hinges on how to read metaphor, not what the lines mean. Of course Collins is referring to the sun, but the interpretation of mythopoeic metaphor is not exhausted by pointing to its naturalistic referent. The youth is at once the sun, Apollo, and the poet—the last surely signaled by his birth at the moment when Fancy, or imagination, finds her voice. Just as the natural world is growing like the "subject life" of the sun, so the magic woof is growing like the body or emanative condition of the poet, and the condensation thus yields the ratios Fancy: sun: nature and Fancy: poet: sainted woof. Psychologically, the ratio suggests mother: son: Innocence—the last magical, a fiction destined for Romance.

The absence of God or the Father from this ratio is only apparent. In the first place, he is pretty clearly the genitor of the rich-haired youth. He loves the Enthusiast Fancy, is wooed by her, retires with her alone, places her on his throne; amidst swelling music Fancy breathes notes aloud and the youth is born. If this doesn't suggest sexual union I don't know what does; somewhat incredibly, it is still being denied, as if a divine primal scene were out of place in cosmogony. (Coleridge says the mesode "inspired & whirled *me* along with greater agitations of enthusiasm than any the most *impassioned* scene in Schiller or Shakespeare," which suggests that a scene from which the dangerous passions are kept aloof in mythopoeia may nevertheless draw deeply on fantasy material.) Secondly, the sainted woof is associated with God's creative activity, not Fancy's. It is "wove on that creating day" and is later called "This hallowed work"; only later, "prepared and bathed in heaven," is it given to Fancy for her to assign to the poet (18–19). Ultimately the cest's "amplest power" derives from God who endows chastity with power. Thus the two essential meanings of Collins's symbol, chastity and spiritual power, correspond exactly to the two relations of the family romance. The cest is a precise representation of the ambivalent, symbolic identification with the Father which normatively resolves the oedipus complex. The poetical character accedes to the divine power of the Father precisely when and insofar as it is chaste. Normatively, the "positive" identification is both a sign that the desires are being successfully repressed and an aid enabling the youth to give them up: hence the talismanic property of the girdle, which is both symbol and cause.

This is Collins's family romance, his myth of origins and authority for the poetical character. Romance, however, is not reality, and Collins's acknowledgment of this situation at the end of the mesode refers significantly to the historical moment. Of the sacred girdle he asks:

> Where is the bard, whose soul can now
> Its high presuming hopes avow?
> Where he who thinks, with rapture blind,
> This hallowed work for him designed?
>
> (51–54)

The bards of Collins's day are unworthy in the specific matter of spiritual chastity, for no other capability or principle of election has been suggested. The "I" cannot inhabit the romance elaborated as its ideal compensatory home, because *he* is corrupted by desire and cannot presume to innocence. This is the first stage of disillusionment with the romance, the recognition that one cannot fulfill the ideal role of the youth: to aspire to prophetic innocence is to risk the shame of having one's inner corruption exposed, like the unlucky nymphs.

II

A second disillusionment supervenes in the antistrophe and causes the romance itself to turn against the poetical character as if in conspiracy against its aspiration.

High on some cliff to Heaven up-piled,
Of rude access, of prospect wild,
Where, tangled round the jealous steep,
Strange shades o'erbrow the valleys deep,
And holy genii guard the rock,
Its glooms embrown, its springs unlock,
While on its rich ambitious head,
An Eden, like his own, lies spread;
I view that oak, the fancied glades among,
By which as Milton lay, his evening ear,
From many a cloud that dropped ethereal dew,
Nigh sphered in heaven its native strains could hear:
On which that ancient trump he reached was hung;
   Thither oft his glory greeting,
   From Waller's myrtle shades retreating,
With many a vow from hope's aspiring tongue,
My trembling feet his guiding steps pursue:
   In vain—such bliss to one alone
   Of all the sons of soul was known,
   And Heaven and Fancy, kindred powers,
   Have now o'erturned the inspiring bowers,
Or curtained close such scene from every future view.
                      (55–76)

Collins's Eden is of course an extended allusion to Milton's Eden as seen for the first time by the envious Satan just after he has despairingly confirmed himself in evil on Mount Niphates. It is a brave conceit, and it establishes at once a latent analogy between satanic desperation and the poetical character which has just been confronted with its incapacity for innocence. Collins (or his "I"), it would appear, is to Milton as Satan is to Adam and Eve—but Milton is no longer there. This Eden is postlapsarian; it admits history and is among other things the representation of a historical situation. Milton is dead, but his oak (associated with the penseroso mode and possibly with the druids) and trumpet (public, prophetic poetry) remain as the goal of this quest, which is "retreating" from Augustan poetry. Milton thus becomes for the history of literary consciousness what a lost paradisiacal innocence is for the individual poetic mind. His "evening ear" caught "its native strains"— distinctively English, home-ground strains—directly from heaven; or perhaps the native strains are heaven's, and we are to be reminded of the "Celestial voices to the midnight air" heard by Adam and Eve (*Paradise Lost* 4.680–88).

Milton represents a poetic potentiality prior to the alienation of the divine and the natural, but this possibility is just now closing for the aspiring poet.

Collins's Eden is also psychologically postlapsarian, as a quick look at the Miltonic prototype reveals. Satan approaches

> and to the border comes,
> Of Eden, where delicious Paradise,
> Now nearer, crowns with her enclosure green,
> As with a rural mound the champaign head
> Of a steep wilderness, whose hairy sides
> With thicket overgrown, grotesque and wild,
> Access denied.
>
> (*PL* 4.131–37)

By comparison, the approach to Collins's Eden is somewhat ominously populated. The steep is "jealous"; "Strange shades o'erbrow the valleys deep," as if the approacher were being watched; the rock is guarded by "holy genii." C. S. Lewis, who was not disposed to exaggerate this sort of thing, instructs us not to overlook the "hairy sides" of Milton's description, for "the Freudian idea that the happy garden is an image of the human body would not have frightened Milton in the least," and of course the anatomical significance of mounts within gardens is purely conventional. But Collins's garden, unlike Milton's, is already possessed; its springs have been "unlocked" by the spirits of place who guard it. This landscape is instinct with a sexual possessor who jealously confronts and obstructs the envious aspirant.

Milton, however, of "all the sons of soul," was allowed by the "kindred powers" Heaven and Fancy to lay blissfully in the garden without undergoing the oedipal conflict. The family romance takes a new turn. Milton is a privileged "son of soul," an elder sibling against whom the parents did not combine. He is not himself to blame for obstructing his successors' access to Innocence. Just as Satan envies Adam and Eve but resents God, so the poetical character finds its conditions are imposed by the parent powers. Collins is presenting a literary self-consciousness subtler than mere resentment of the privileged precursor. Somehow the rules—theological, epistemological, and simply moral—have changed for the modern sons of soul. Innocence is no longer possible for the modern—either because the bowers have been destroyed or because they have been hidden. The overturning of the bowers (like Guyon's pitiless wrecking of the Bower of Bliss) suggests suppression (Freud's *Unterdrücking*) under a harsher moral regime, while the alternative "curtained close" suggests the subtler mechanism of repression (*Verdrängung*).

In one sense, the Fall in the last lines of the ode is simply a recognition of what has already occurred in the unhappy progress of consciousness away from the ampler power of Innocence. In another sense, the primary Fall occurs right in the antistrophe as the bowers sought "With many a vow from hope's aspiring tongue" are suddenly ("now") withdrawn "from every future view." The poetical character is thereby poised at the transitional moment when poetic Innocence becomes inaccessible for all time. Event and recognition are always reciprocal aspects in any version of the Fall. Psychologically considered, the Fall represents the passing of the family romance, a reluctant admission of its impossibility. Not only is the contemporary bard unworthy of the role of the blest, prophetic son of soul—that was the first disillusionment—but the role itself has now been rendered inaccessible for any aspirant.

This is where the poem ends and where Collins ends as a poet. It is, I think, a terminus whose significance extends far beyond Collins. He is involuntarily on the verge of a critique of Romance which would, however, be nostalgic and not rebellious. The image of Edenic innocence is a necessary part of the family romance which every ambitious post-Miltonic poet evolves in order to escape (as a poet) his natural condition and validate his intimations of transcendent origin and authority. The protagonist of the romance is the rich-haired youth who, in Coleridge's phrase, hath drunk the milk of paradise. Daemonic Romanticism may be said to commence with the corruption of this youth. In Collins, he is still innocent; at his birth "The dangerous Passions kept aloof." This was not to last and is already giving way in the ode as the inevitable perspective of the poetical character becomes tacitly satanic. We may even descry, though at great remove, the presence of satanic potentiality already in Collins's apostrophe "And thou, thou rich-haired youth of morn, / And all thy subject life was born!" Satan on Mount Niphates had begun his soliliquy of inner torment by likewise addressing the sun—

> O thou that with surpassing glory crowned,
> Look'st from thy sole dominion like the God
> Of this new world;
>
> (*PL* 4.32–34)

and earlier he too had seen a rich-haired angel:

> he soon
> Saw within ken a glorious angel stand,
> The same whom John saw also in the sun:

> His back was turned, but not his brightness hid;
> Of beaming sunny rays, a golden tiar
> Circled his head, nor less his locks behind
> Illustrious on his shoulders fledge with wings
> Lay waving round.
>
> (3.621–28)

To approach this angel (Uriel), Satan turns himself into a rich-haired youth:

> And now a stripling cherub he appears,
> Not of the prime, yet such as in his face
> Youth smiled celestial, and to every limb
> Suitable grace diffused, so well he feigned;
> Under a coronet his flowing hair
> In curls on either cheek played
>
> (3.636–41)

—an appearance that recalls Spenser's young angel, "a faire young man, / Of wondrous beautie, and of freshest yeares" whose "snowy font curled with golden heares, / Like *Phoebus* face adornd with sunny rayes, / Divinely shone." Whatever the provenance of Collins's youth, and this context falls short of allusion, his relation to the poetical character is certainly not a spontaneous, ingenuous identification.

Of course, the satanic undertones of the antistrophe remain latent, unacknowledged, and involuntary. Yet even in a naive reading it is an error to interpret the Fall and expulsion at the end of the ode as Collins's personal self-abnegation—that is, to abandon the myth for an illegitimately intentionalistic referent. Collins says that the "scene," if it is still there at all, will be closed from *every* future view. It is this insistence that places the poetical character not merely in a role *manqué* within the Romance but on the verge of moving beyond Romance. In a speculative spirit we might ask of the poetical character, What next? What are the options open at the end of the poem?

There seem to be two lines of possibility. If the poet is to remain committed to Romance—committed to a transcendent self-justification—he is going to have to assume the daemonic identity which alone remains open, now that Miltonic innocence has been foreclosed. Since direct access to Eden is barred—by oedipal anxiety—he will have to jump over the wall. Among other things, this involves a polemic for a daemonic Milton, a Milton who had all unconsciously played the rebellious, phallic role in his own family romance. Hence, too, the migration of the rich-haired youth from innocence to an alliance with the dangerous passions until he becomes—in Orc; in the poet of whom Coleridge warns "Beware, beware," in Prometheus; in Stevens' arrogant lover—the very figure of desire. Apollo, after all, was the god of sublimated, civilized art; the Romantic Apollo is soon closer to Dionysus. But this figure remains phallic in the precise sense that he can never progress beyond the conflicts, affective and ideological, of the oedipal drama. He becomes entangled in a circuit of desire, frustration, rebellion, and suppression. Eventually he may himself turn into his authoritarian oppressor, in which case the severity of his posture signals a reaction formation: such authority is in the end merely the negative phase of unregenerate desire.

The other possibility at the end of the "Ode on the Poetical Character" has a more liberal aspect. Suppose the poetical character could simply abandon Romance, since the powerful innocence it is intended to secure proves inaccessible. Why play out an expulsion from paradise—still less attempt to usurp it daemonically—when it is a mere fiction of what never was? This means, of course, surrendering the consolations of the family romance, and in particular the poet's claim to divine origin. It would mean a poetry of earth, as if everyday reality were all that is and were enough. Such a poet would have to be on guard lest his experience come to seem extraordinary, himself too favored a being or favored in the archaic way. Should he yield to the blandishments of Romance, he would be swept up into unresolvable conflicts; he would have to insist that his own spirit and nothing else deifies him. Everything in him that seems extraordinary must be ascribable to his natural condition. The chosen few, the blest, prophetic elite, would be discriminated merely by their superior consciousness of what is already the natural birthright of all men. The poet would be a man speaking to men, perhaps a godlike man speaking to godlike men, but never a god speaking to mortals. Such a poetry might, at any rate, be worth a try.

III

We may well wonder whether a poetry totally free from Romance is possible, even in principle. If everyday reality is good enough, what need of poetry? And what is to prevent the naturalistic rejection of Romance from turning into an evasion of the phallic conflicts the Romance is designed to assuage? In principle at least, a poetic identity which declines transcendence—or subdues it to an undifferentiated immanence—is regressing to a prephallic stage of desire, a version of narcissism. Romance or fantasy with its burden of oedipal conflict will remain latent in such an identity, and its eruption will threaten precisely at the moment when desire becomes too intense and too pointed—becomes, in short, phallic, as in Wordsworth's "Nutting" or the Stolen Boat episode.

It would be fatuous to suppose that the possibilities here speculatively advanced are really in question at the end of Collins's progress. "The Ode on the Poetical Character" does seem to me to be without serious rival as a representation of the poet's difficult situation in the middle of the eighteenth century; Gray's ambitious odes seem superficial by comparison, though I may have a blind spot with Gray. But no one would claim major status for Collins, even in the excess of rescuing him from his antiquating critics. What he can teach us is the relation between Romance and the psychology of the negative sublime. In the bulk of doctrine on the sublime, the "secret Terrours and Apprehensions" of the supernatural are associated with the terrifying appearances of the natural sublime. Ultimately, the path of the negative or transcendent sublime leads through the phase of daemonic Romance, with its oedipal anxieties, to a symbolic identification with the father. But poetry itself may be a deviation from this normative path in quest of mistaken beauties. We might at least suspect that in a transcendence fully achieved there is no need or opportunity for poetry, just as Kant's theory of the sublime ultimately dispenses with an empirical ground. It may be that poetry turns means into an end.

PAUL S. SHERWIN

Collins's "Ode to Evening"

Collins's triumph as the poet of Evening is the "Ode to Evening," probably his finest poem. It is also the most profoundly Miltonic of his exercises in the Evening mode. Just how extensive is Collins's absorption in Milton awaits clarification; it is enough at present to observe the most obvious features of indebtedness. First, the unrhymed stanza Collins employs is taken from Milton's translation of Horace's "Ad Pyrrham." More important, because it enables Collins to shape his poem in the absence of rhyme, is the ode's heavily Miltonic diction, which is for the most part a tissue of direct reminiscences and linguistic maneuvers learned from the minor poems and the lyrical interludes of *Paradise Lost*. These verbal affinities, moreover, point to a fundamental likeness between the ambience of the worlds both writers construct. Collins's region of the Evening ear stems from that spirit-haunted world of Miltonic lyricism in which all is distanced by reflection, by a resonant and teasingly indeterminate language that constantly intervenes between reader and setting.

The ode's massive indebtedness to Milton does not, for once, impoverish Collins. If in the "Thomson Elegy" he accepts a secondary, diminished status because of his refusal to sustain the severity of "Lycidas," the "Ode to Evening" does not appear to be shaped from without, converting the alien Miltonic presence to its own substance. A likely explanation is that Collins has captured what is most free-ranging in Milton: the meander, fluidity, and expansiveness of the octosyllabics and the similes of *Paradise Lost*. So long as

From *Precious Bane: Collins and the Miltonic Legacy*. © 1977 by the University of Texas Press. Originally entitled "The 'Ode to Evening.' "

he adheres to this spirit of redemptive gentleness Collins experiences a true
dialectical relation to Milton, at once accepting and rejecting the father,
appeasing and separating the dead. Although Milton is continually called
upon, presumably to confer a certain measure of authority and authenticity,
the voice one hears in the ode, at least in its masterful initial forty lines, is
not an actual but a potential Miltonic voice released through the mediumship
of his descendant. What saves Collins is that the difference between actual
and potential is great enough to preserve his integrity: for example, Milton
would be temperamentally unsuited to undertake the prolonged empathic
labor in the ode which yields a world of ghostlier demarcations, keener
sounds. Writing within Milton's shadow, Collins here realizes his unique
gift more fully than in any other poem, claiming an important element in
Milton as his own in order that he may explore and define the temper of his
own mind.

   The poem begins in typical odic fashion as Collins apostrophizes and
petitions his goddess, the long first sentence concluding with an apparent
epiphanic salute:

            If aught of oaten stop or pastoral song
            May hope, chaste Eve, to soothe thy modest ear,
               Like thy own solemn springs,
               Thy springs and dying gales,
            O nymph reserved, while now the bright-haired sun
            Sits in yon western tent, whose cloudy skirts,
               With brede ethereal wove,
               O'erhang his wavy bed;
            Now air is hushed, save where the weak-eyed bat
            With short shrill shriek flits by on leathern wing,
               Or where the beetle winds
               His small but sullen horn,
            As oft he rises midst the twilight path
            Against the pilgrim borne in heedless hum:
               Now teach me, maid composed,
               To breathe some softened strain,
            Whose numbers stealing through thy darkening vale
            May not unseemly with its stillness suit,
               As musing slow, I hail
               Thy genial loved return!

However, despite appearances—the exclamatory hailing of a divine presence at the climax of a twenty-line sentence—Hartman rightly asserts that the one feature of the Sublime ode "conspicuously absent is the epiphany proper." The passage is, in fact, quasi-epiphanic. The traditional "hail" of line 19 does not betoken a sudden manifestation of the goddess; Collins hails her *while* "musing slow," which is precisely what he has been doing from the outset, and so his greeting is a sustained rhetorical gesture coinciding with the gradual insinuation of twilight. A further indication of this shying away from epiphany is that instead of hailing the goddess by name, as Milton does in "Il Penseroso," Collins hails her "genial loved return." Such indirection prevents Evening from emerging as a discrete figure; rather, she is imagined as a being—more a felt presence than a divine apparition—who merges imperceptibly with the landscape over which she presides.

The Progress theme undergoes a similar modification. With the sun at rest, the continuance of progress is entrusted to Evening. Yet although her chariot is prepared by her attendants in the second movement of the ode, no pageant ensues; there is only the faintest suggestion of the traditional procession, as Evening is asked to lead the poet in his country ramblings. The ode's verbal movement has often been described as processional, but its ceremonious pace is hardly progressive at all, respecting instead the unhurried, desultory rhythms of the natural process it celebrates. The primary impression is one of gradualism, of gradual expansions and blendings, as in lines 3–4, or the lines "The fragrant Hours, and elves / Who slept in flowers the day" (23–24), where "flowers" and "day" emerge elegantly from "fragrant Hours." Such reiterative patterning enforces a distinct sense of continuity, but the periodic flow of the verse remains unpropulsive due to Collins's various delaying devices.

The most prominent of these is the use of loosely connected subordinate clauses in the first sentence to retard, drastically, the poet's simple appeal to his goddess: if any song of mine can soothe you, now teach it to me. Yet this in and of itself is not sufficient to explain the effect Collins achieves, for Milton's implementation of virtually the same technique at the opening of *Paradise Lost* actually enhances the climactic force of his address. Collins removes any possibility of gathering momentum chiefly through the surging-and-ebbing rhythms of the Pyrrha stanza but also through the interweaving of assonantal and consonantal patterns, the most pronounced involving the alternation between sibilants and the *w-b* pairing throughout the first sentence. The preponderance of open and back vowels, moreover, so diminishes the natural forward thrust of the verse that an intensified slow-motion effect, verging upon stasis, results. In the first line, for instance, there is an invitation to pause (note the positioning of "stop" before the initial caesura) and linger over this long-drawn-out protraction of the voice. Arresting tactics of this kind are not calculated to leave the reader in breathless expectancy but to evoke a sense of continuous, steady breathing. We are kept suspended between verticality and horizontal motion, attention centering upon the moment-to-moment extension of Collins's "softened strain," as both reader and writer become absorbed by the tentatively advancing movement of twilight and the twilight consciousness.

Both in its pacing and in its sustained evocation of a continuous present the ode resembles "Il Penseroso." Tracing the peripatetic movements of his Melancholy Man in the middle section of the poem, Milton presents him in a series of exemplary situations and attitudes. Despite the poem's overall progressive design, the structure of the narrative is not genuinely progressive; each frame of the series is a discrete unit, and the movement from frame to frame is highly contingent. Independence from logical sequence enables Milton to avert a spasmodic, halting gait and establish an exceptionally fluid rhythm. The continuum is maintained by a string of casual connectives: "and," "or," "oft," "sometime." The narrator might go here or there, do this or that, do it now or at some other time. What is important is the multiplicity of options available to him and the pleasure each, in its turn, is able to afford.

True to the spirit of Milton's poem, Collins aims for a widening and intensification of consciousness. As in "Il Penseroso," there is no inevitable sequential development. In enumerating the properties of Evening, Collins shifts perspective freely, smoothing over potential discontinuities with the connectives "or," "as," "for," "while," "now," "when," and "then," which tend to obscure causal, modal, and temporal relations. The indeterminacy of the verse is emphasized by the prevailing grammatical mood—which, as in "Il Penseroso," is more or less subjunctive, perhaps optative—and by Collins's peculiarly errant syntax. At line 21, for example, he begins "For when," but it is only after a tenuously related passage on Evening's attendants and a period break that the construction is resolved by "Then lead" at line 29. Collins also loses sight of grammatical structure in the first sentence, where the clause beginning "now air is hushed" (9) is an anacoluthon that results from the poet being distracted by an arresting chorus of sounds. This wandering language, so often a disturbing feature in Collins, is here admirably suited to the mood of abstracted wonder-wandering he has picked up from "Il Penseroso." Collins's avoidance of obtrusive end-rhymes makes his poem even more beautifully uncertain than Milton's, more resistant to closure.

That terminal point he resists may be viewed as the point at which the deferral of time is arrested and pensive reflection becomes self-conscious. Arnold disapprovingly compares the ode to "a river which loses itself in the sand." Yet Collins wishes to be lost, to be led by the hypnotic, weaving rhythms of his style rather than to strive for architectonic rigor. Like Milton in "Il Penseroso," he needs to purge that species of brooding, self-centered melancholy which prompts the poet's ramblings. Regarded in this light, the programmatic intent of his excursive poetics is to keep the mind continually in motion, to keep its options open, so as to preclude fixation upon the self. Significantly, no doctrinal issues intrude, as in the majority of the 1746 *Odes*, and instead of alternating between description and reflection, like Gray in the "Elegy," he consummates their union. He remains remarkably unassertive, not eager for a punctual revelation; he is content to announce a presence whose meaning does not need to be interpreted.

In "Il Penseroso" there is a superb rendition of the dreamy, wandering spirit I have been describing:

> And missing thee, I walk unseen
> On the dry smooth-shaven Green,
> To behold the wand'ring Moon,
> Riding near her highest noon,
> Like one that had been led astray
> Through the Heav'n's wide pathless way;
> And oft, as if her head she bow'd,
> Stooping through a fleecy cloud.
> Oft on a Plat of rising ground,
> I hear the far-off Curfew sound,
> Over some wide-water'd shore,
> Swinging slow with sullen roar.
>
> (65–76)

In addition to motion and stillness, moon and wandering poet converge in these lines, the two subtly meeting through the juxtaposition of the moon *stooping* and the poet listening on *rising* ground. There is a comparable passage in the ode, the one dealing with the pilgrim and beetle:

> Now air is hushed save . . .
>   .   .   .   .
>   . . . where the beetle winds
>   His small but sullen horn,

> As oft he rises midst the twilight path
> Against the pilgrim borne in heedless hum.

Borne along "in heedless hum" as he "winds / His small but sullen horn," Collins's beetle seems to have been trained at a Miltonic music school; not only is he a descendant of the grayfly in "Lycidas" but his drowsy song echoes the cadences of Milton's far-off curfew "Swinging slow with sullen roar." As Merle Brown remarks in her excellent reading of the passage, the phrase "borne in heedless hum" is equally applicable to the pilgrim. Indeed, the pilgrim could be borne along in the heedless hum of the beetle, or be humming to himself as he is borne along in reverie, or now be making a country pilgrimage away from the heedless hum of the town in which he was "born" (the original spelling). The ambiguity is telling because both beetle and pilgrim are subsumed by the larger rhythm of the twilight spirit. Both are heedless: careless or abstracted. The beetle is an active creature, yet its monotonous drone implies aimlessness, and the fact that it rises "oft" indicates random movement. And the pilgrim, though a traveler along the twilight path, is a man absorbed by solitary musing, a leisurely quester unmindful (heedless) of a goal.

One wonders, however, about the beetle's rising "against" the pilgrim: will he be awakened from his reverie? The issue is unexplored, but there is an indication that Collins is bestirred, since at this point he finally introduces the main clause of his sentence with "Now teach me," the only imperative to be found in his circuitous appeal to Evening. The mood of unanxious reverie is nevertheless quickly reinstated, as the poet-quester resumes his petition in which asking and having are perfectly synchronized.

Collins's petition is self-fulfilling because he has accommodated his style to Evening's gradual advent. While Evening's shadows swell through the landscape the numbers of the poet's song fill up the same space, steal*ing* through her darken*ing* vale. Landscape and soundscape become indistinguishable: objects are distanced, the despotic eye is quieted, and aural receptivity is heightened. At the same time language becomes, as it were, "weak-eyed," its iconicity subordinated to more elusive tonal effects. There is an extroversion of language as it seeks, through onomatopoeia and suggestive nuance, to be the proper harmonic echo of the twilight spirit; but since its subject is so tenuous it is continually deflected, casting a translucent word-screen between reader and phenomenon. Milton engages in similar verbal mimicry in those lines in "Il Penseroso" where the speaker retreats from "Day's garish eye" to the semidarkness of a woodland stream:

There in close covert by some Brook,
Where no profaner eye may look,
Hide me from Day's garish eye,
While the Bee with Honied thigh,
That at her flow'ry work doth sing,
And the Waters murmuring
With such consort as they keep,
Entice the dewy-feather'd Sleep;
And let some strange mysterious dream
Wave at his Wings in Airy stream,
Of lively portraiture display'd,
Softly on my eyelids laid.

(139–50)

A wide range of musical and synesthetic effects are drawn upon in the passage to trace the metamorphosis of profane sight into a vision softened through the treble mediation of shadow, sleep, and dream. Here, as Thomas Warton says, the language "would insensibly lull us asleep, did not the imagery keep us awake." The genius of this style resides in its power to entice us to hunt out direct *denotative* meanings (does "they" in line 145 refer to waters or the consorted murmur of waters and bees; is the dream, like sleep, a birdlike creature, or is it the "Airy stream"; is the waving movement to be associated with the fluttering of the eyelids during dream-filled sleep or the motions of a watery stream?) even as it compels us to surrender to a general impression—a deep, imageless feeling—conveyed by a gestural meaning immanent in the discourse.

Turning to Collins's ode, one may adduce several instances of such dreamy confusion, but there is one passage which, although not so rich or sensuous as Milton's, is comparably suggestive:

Then lead, calm vot'ress, where some sheety lake
Cheers the lone heath, or some time-hallowed pile,
   Or upland fallows grey,
   Reflect its last cool gleam.

(29–32)

This is the revised version of a stanza originally appearing the 1746 edition as:

Then let me rove some wild and heathy Scene,
Or find some Ruin 'midst its dreary Dells,
   Whose Walls more awful nod
   By thy religious Gleams.

Martin Price's commentary on the alteration is instructive: "The light is no longer Evening's; it is mediated through reflection. . . . Evening is absorbed into the placid lake, and the lake in turn casts its reflected light over heath, ruin, and fallows; the diffused light is part of the softer, more gently melancholy scene." The success of Collins's revision can be traced to the introduction of a mediator of Evening's light, the lake—which can be viewed as an emblem of another mediator of Evening, the reflective poet. The passage, however, is more indeterminate than Price indicates. For instance, he does not note the puzzling use of "reflect," a grammatical lapse that is a blemish even if it is an intriguing one. There is some question as to whether the lake alone or the complex of lake, heath, pile, and fallows reflects "its last cool gleam." And what is the referent of "its": Evening, the lake, the "shadowy car" of line 28, the evening star? As in the "Il Penseroso" passage, meaning is inseparable from the style which is its vehicle; it is delineated via a conspiracy of image, sound, rhythm, and feeling ("cool gleam" is a fine synesthetic touch), which strongly perplexes the interpretative faculties it genially entertains.

The Evening style of *différance*, in the combined sense of temporal detour and spatial interval, is intrinsically related to the natural phenomenon it represents. While Evening reigns Collins inhabits a "married land" in which both perception and the material of common perception are transfigured. With the ebbing out of light and consequent softening of the eye, cooperation of the senses is established. Although Evening's darkening vale, or veiling, is a token of the estrangement of things, it is the only element in which Collins can approach the heart of things. Enveloping the entire landscape in the same ambience, twilight serves as a conductive medium that permits interaction and interfusion of ordinarily disparate entities: pilgrim and beetle; light, pool, heath, ruin, and fallows. This medium has a counterpart in Collins's delicately woven verse which draws together, through assonance and consonance, such extremes as weak-eyed bat and winding beetle, or sun and ocean:

> while now the bright-haired sun
> Sits in yon western tent, whose cloudy skirts,
> With brede ethereal wove,
> O'erhang his wavy bed.
>
> (5–8)

By opting for suspension rather than climactic effect, he minimizes these contrasts and suggests their equilibrium. In lines 3–4, for example, there is a marked contrast between the somber or heavy and lively or light, but owing to redundancy and retardation they converge unobtrusively in the adjective-noun pairings "solemn springs" and "dying gales." The Evening style depicts a various world of contrary qualities and forces which are revealed to be not so much antitheses as alternate modulations of the same rhythmic counterpoint of surging and ebbing, motion and stasis, energy and repose.

The ode's harmonization or even-ing out of extremes is as much dependent on Evening herself as the medium of twilight she embodies. She is a personification ideally suited to preside over this most successful of Collins's hymns of reconciliation: not only is she the regent of a medial time of day, but she is an intermediate being ontologically—at once natural, human, and divine. That she is a divinity belonging to a privileged mythic order of existence is variously evidenced: by her train, which is comprised of Hours, elves, nymphs, and "Pensive Pleasures sweet"; by her involvement in the seasonal cycle portrayed in lines 41–48; and by the cultic distance separating her from her supplicant in the opening petition.

She is, however, an unusual sort of divine personage. As has often been observed, the presence Collins conjures up is less a spirit *in* the landscape than a spirit *of* the landscape. There is no fixed beholding of Evening. Indeed, our only glimpse of her in the first forty lines is the reference to her "dewy fingers" drawing "the gradual dusky veil." This consistent evasion of blunt determinateness represents a refinement of Milton's technique in "Il Penseroso," where Melancholy appears, albeit briefly, as a picturable presence (33–40) before receding into the background. Collins follows Milton in adopting a predominately adjectival rather than nominal approach to his subject; as in "Il Penseroso," the goddess is evoked through an enumeration of her attributes (Evening is said to be chaste, modest, reserved, and so forth), attendants, and favorite haunts.

The difference resides in the fact that Collins's goddess is the incarnation of a natural process in addition to a state of mind. Nowhere in Milton's poem is there an interpenetration of personification and natural element such as one discovers in the ode. This is most evident in the seasonal section:

> While Spring shall pour his showers, as oft he wont,
> And bathe thy breathing tresses, meekest Eve!
>   While Summer loves to sport
>   Beneath thy lingering light;
> While sallow Autumn fills thy lap with leaves,
> Or Winter, yelling through the troublous air,
>   Affrights thy shrinking train,
>   And rudely rends thy robes.
>
>   (41–48)

Here, as Collins has begun to generalize and thus lose, to a certain extent, his intimacy with Evening, she is no longer presented as a diffusive force animating her sphere of influence but emerges as a giant form. Yet, despite its relative directness, the passage is consonant with the ode's prevailing strategy of balancing numinous and perceivable, transcendent and immanent. Evening remains an elusive nature-spirit, blending into the landscape even more completely than Autumn in the second stanza of Keats's ode: her "breathing tresses" *are* either trees or grain, her lap *is* the lap of earth, and her robes *are* the shades of twilight. We are suspended in the precarious visionary dimension of Milton's belated peasant, unable to tell whether we see or dream we see what we think we see.

Still to be considered is another unifying factor, the perceiving and recording agent. Where does the poet stand in relation to the world of the poem? Like Evening, as Brown argues, he is to be located both inside and outside the scene: "He must be in it when he hails her 'genial lov'd return,' and he may be there too as the 'Pilgrim born in heedless Hum.' But he is absent during the first thirteen lines and during the eight which follow his greeting Eve. . . . He then tells Eve to lead him to a sheety lake, but we do not see him follow." His most direct entry into the scene occurs in the lines:

> But when chill blustering winds or driving rain
> Forbid my willing feet, be mine the hut
>   That from the mountain's side
>   Views wilds and swelling floods,
> And hamlets brown, and dim-discovered spires,
> And hears their simple bell, and marks o'er all
>   Thy dewy fingers draw
>   The gradual dusky veil,
>
>   (33–40)

where, as Brown goes on to observe, "we see not him, but merely his view of the valley below."

What is truly startling here is that it is the *hut* which views, hears, and marks—a radical elision of the perceiving subject, which is the most revealing instance of the ode's practice of eroding the outlines of discrete, localized entities. The above passage is comparable in effect to the tower section of "Il Penseroso," where the poet is discovered looking inward upon an imagined version of himself ("Let my Lamp . . . *be seen* in some high lonely Tow'r"), who is at the same time gazing outward upon an imagined setting. In both poems there is a volatilization of the isolate ego, the rigid authorial mask of the persona, until a condition of virtual invisibility is attained. In both we follow the progress of an invisible poet, accompanied by an invisible goddess, as he wanders through an anonymous landscape which, as Hartman suggests in another context, is not so much one specific place as a generalized English place.

Collins's purgation of the selfhood is founded upon his realization of a larger process in which the individual participates. This, in turn, is dependent on the dual mediation of twilight and its spiritual incarnation, the goddess Evening. While twilight functions as a sustaining perceptual ground that fosters the coalescence of subject and object, Evening's role is to solidify that ground by rendering the scene imagination's landscape, "spreading the tone, and the *atmosphere*, and with it the depth and height of the ideal world around forms, incidents, and situations." Evening spiritualizes nature, and in so doing naturalizes the imagination. One reason she can perform this mediatory service is that, as in the "Ode to Fear," persona and personification are attuned to the same rhythm: all the epithets applied to Evening are implicitly transferable to the poet: she steals over the landscape gradually while he muses slowly; she is "composed" and he is a composer. However, again as in the "Ode to Fear," it is a mistake to identify I and Thou. To collapse the distance separating them is to violate the mystery of goddess and poet alike, to ignore the unappeasable longing for identification which keeps the poet questing. As a being from the "other world," Evening satisfied Collins's love of romance. She is an oracular figure who leads deep within so that the poet can make contact with his own greater-than-rational powers, and she is a muse leading from the present into the rich imaginative past of pastoral (past oral) poetry.

That imaginative past, it should be clear by now, is principally Miltonic. Evening is most obviously a reincarnation of the goddess of "Il Penseroso." Though Collins's diffidence is to be contrasted with Milton's self-confidence, the speaker's relationship to the goddess in both poems is analogous. She is a spirit to be wooed and won, sparking an outwardgoing impulse of love that carries over into his excursion through a landscape which, owing to her guardianship, is perceived as an animate, answerable world. Moreover, the mood or modality of consciousness she represents is essentially the same in both. The goddess is an embodiment of what I have termed the "twilight consciousness" : a mood of pensive reverie poising midway between receptivity and active creation, perception and vision. Where she presides the extremes of "Day's garish eye" and "blackest midnight" are refined away; the poet, in a state of semiwakefulness, inhabits an environment of semidarkness that at once shields him from direct contact with the world and yet, investing it with the charm of aesthetic distance, leads him closer to it.

In Collins the goddess is, by definition, compounded of darkness and light. She draws about the landscape a "dusky veil," which is probably to be identified with her robes of state. Milton's Melancholy is "O'erlaid with black, staid Wisdom's hue" (16), a veil which hides her excessive brightness. In both poems darkness and light combine to shed a "dim religious light," an appropriate medium for the sainted goddess: in Milton she is called "pensive Nun" (31) and "sad Virgin" (103), in Collins "chaste Eve" (2) and "calm vot'ress" (29). The asexuality of the goddess reminds us that the twilight consciousness is a private consciousness, a heightened condition of solitude that occasions the poet's deepened musings.

Another Miltonic virgin goddess that may have influenced Collins's conception of Evening is Sabrina, the protector of chastity in *Comus*. Both are addressed as nymphs. Like Evening, Sabrina is an ontologically amorphous being: originally human, she "underwent a quick immortal change" and was appointed goddess of the river Severn. A true *genius loci*, she is indistinguishable from the natural element she governs:

> By the rushy-fringed bank,
> Where grows the Willow and the Osier dank,
>   My sliding Chariot stays,
> Thick set with Agate and azurn sheen
> Of Turquoise blue and Em'rald green
>   That in the channel strays,
> Whilst form off the waters fleet
> Thus I set my printless feet
> O'er the Cowslip's Velvet head,
>   That bends not as I tread.
>
> (890–99)

As Evening's "shadowy car" is evening itself, Sabrina's "sliding Chariot" is the stream she personifies, its gems the variegated colors of the water. The exquisitely evanescent Sabrina is likewise a spirit of twilight: "oft at Eve" she "Visits the herds along the twilight meadows, / Helping all urchin blasts, and ill-luck signs" (843–45). "If she be right invok't" (855), she will dispense her healing liquor in the service of the ensnared Lady, whose perfected Echo Sabrina is. Is it too extravagant to propose that Collins also requires supernatural intercession, invoking his goddess by her favorite name in order that she may rouse his dormant energies and renew his sorely needed contact with the natural world?

Collins directs us to Evening's most revealing Miltonic analogue by naming his goddess "Eve." While it is true that Collins's Eve is more sober than Milton's, Evening has much in common with Eve, the chaste, unfallen Eve who epitomizes Eden's delights and whose innocence protects her "as a veil" (IX.1054). As Kurt Schlüter observes, Evening "bringt den Menschen das Paradies!" For in that temporal pause when Evening rules the earth Collins recaptures the unitary vision of an unfallen world that Milton projects in the octosyllabics and the Edenic sections of *Paradise Lost*. The human counterpart of this married land is the sexual union of lover and beloved, the chaste "wedded Love" Milton celebrates in Book IV of *Paradise Lost* before leaving Adam and Eve to their spousal rites.

The fact that Collins's "calm vot'ress" is a being outside the line of procreation does not refute an interpretation of him as a new Adam courting his Eve, or interior paramour, the granter of those imaginative pleasures "by him best receiv'd (*PL* IV.309). After all, there is in English poetry, especially pastoral poetry, frequently a close—perhaps perverse—alliance between innocence and eroticism. *Comus*, for example, is at one and the same time a defense of virginity and the most sensuous of Milton's poems. The "Ode to Evening" is a similar fusion of the chaste and erotic, in terms of style as well as sentiment. Its form partakes of that chaste Hellenic simplicity Collins was so fond of, yet its meandering language betrays the luxuriance of a romantic imagination. Hailing Evening's "genial loved return," he offers a prothalamic greeting to a goddess who yields to him as Eve does to Adam, "with coy submission, modest pride, / And sweet reluctant amorous delay" (IV.310–11). This submerged sexual element, though surfacing completely only in the seasonal stanzas, comes very near the surface when Hesperus, termed a "warning lamp" (22), beckons Evening's attendants to prepare her shadowy car. According to Hartman, Collins traces "a ritual . . . progress which draws (like a marriage procession) a 'gradual dusky veil' around the scene. The poem's probable source in conventional odes to an evening star, which guides lover to beloved in the dangerous dark, may also help to induce this prothalamic effect." The Miltonic source is the account in *Paradise Lost* of the nightingale bidding "haste the Ev'ning Star / On his Hill top, to light the bridal Lamp" (VIII.519–20) directly after Eve's creation.

The only problem is that instead of leading to consummation the drawing of Evening's veil results in the separation of lover and beloved. At nightfall the bride departs. One thinks of the conclusion of the "Ode on the Poetical Character" in which the inspiring bowers of Milton's paradise are "curtained close . . . from every future view." Again the poet is a belated quester whose

muse will not, cannot yield herself utterly to him. While Collins's precarious
relation to his muse is not necessarily the consequence of her being already
married to Milton, there can be little doubt that the shadow cast by Milton's
presence imparts a sober coloring to his descendant's vision of a latter-day
Eve. The ode is a good deal more somber and plangent than its primary
source, "Il Penseroso," Collins's pondering considerably more ponderous
than Milton's. Evening is a "pensive Eve" (the original version of "chaste
Eve") who yields her votary a paradise that is not wholly paradisical, one
which bears traces of the original Eden but which also retains the memory
of its loss.

At best Collins's Evening realm is a momentary paradise. Flanked by
daylight and nighttime, Evening is essentially a transitional or transitory
moment, the ultimate Collinsian threshold of experiential betweenness and
bewilderment. The insistence of *"Now* teach me" in the initial petition and
the reference to the evening star as a *warning* lamp imply that despite his
erotic slowing of time Collins is aware of how little time he has to spend
with his goddess. Though her departure is signaled by the drawing of the
veil in line 40, his severance from Evening begins to take effect earlier. At
line 33 he begins to consider not a single evening but several kinds of evenings,
now entering that curiously sentient hut in which he presumably remains
until the conclusion. He is driven there by rough weather, the alteration in
tone marked by the shift from "last cool gleam" to "chill blustering winds."
There is, of course, no possibility of such elemental disturbance in Milton's
Paradise, but with the Fall there is a drastic change in clime:

> At that tasted Fruit
> The Sun, as from *Thyéstean* Banquet, turn'd
> His course intended, else how had the World
> Inhabited, though sinless, more than now,
> Avoided pinching cold and scorching heat?
> These changes in the Heav'ns, though slow, produc'd
> Like changes on Sea and Land, sideral blast,
> Vapor, and Mist, and Exhalation hot,
> Corrupt and Pestilent.
>   (X.687–95)

Universal Discord initiates the pageant of the Seasons. The sequence in the
ode is from storm to seasonal cycle, culminating in a terrific demonic
epiphany:

> Or Winter, yelling through the troublous air,
>   Affrights thy shrinking train
>   And rudely rends thy robes.

No wonder Evening needs to be "soothed." And no wonder that Collins cleaves to that sylvan shed dedicated to the perpetuation of Evening when the approaching night will not arrive as in Paradise, where brightness is succeeded by "grateful Twilight (for Night comes not there / In darker veil) and roseate Dews" (V.645–46).

The pattern is typical: threatened by violence and discontinuity, Collins would secure himself from the variableness of day and night and of weathers, seeking the temperate climate of imaginative repose. The onset of winter and night is a disenchanting reminder that his benign fictional arrest of time cannot charm away the arrest of death, or the death that is self-consciousness. Collins is driven into his sylvan shed—shrine or urn or womb—by the emergent possibility of real solitude, the horror of a direct assault. This helps to explain his earlier delaying tactics, his avoidance of coming to a point. There is in Collins a persistent dread of what is to come: the setting of the virile sun, the northering of the poetical spirit, the veiling of the sources of inspiration. Within his retreat he would extend his Evening musings and so "forget all time" (*PL* IV.639). He is uncomfortable in his situation as a boundary being even though the boundaries of his perfected art extend into eternity, not content with the permanence of an artifact which commemorates the temporary. He wants instead real continuity, a permanent indwelling of the spirit of Evening and her "Pensive Pleasures sweet."

Yet his continuity with Evening, initially violated by nature, is subsequently violated by Collins himself, who in the final stanza betrays his own imagination:

> So long, sure-found beneath the sylvan shed,
> Shall Fancy, Friendship, Science, rose-lipped Health,
>   Thy gentlest influence own,
>   And hymn thy favourite name!

Collins's intentions are clear enough: he wishes, as Hartman states, to wed "the archaic *numen* of nature poetry" to "the ideals of polite society." For once, however, his genius for reconciliation fails him. His earlier vision of Evening, a splendid purgation of ideas of order, is displaced by the bluntly abstract discourse of an adjudicative persona. Miltonic solitude gives way to Horatian retirement, as Collins offers a portrait of a Thomsonian social

Beulah of the "enlightened few" who ward off the terror of the elements with sweet reasonableness.

Collins's anxiety to recapitulate Milton's experience in "Il Penseroso" may have caused him to overextend his poem. He seeks out the peaceful hermitage of his precursor's weary age in which vision will have become habitual. Most significant, however, is what he does not repeat in Milton's experience. There is no ordeal of solitude within his hut. His refusal to venture beyond pastoral innocence, the domain of Evening, dooms him to an abortive rite of passage which signals imagination's defeat. Thus, in the "Ode to Evening," as in the majority of his poems, Collins at once becomes and ceases to be a poet. He knows that paradise is lost. But he cannot sufficiently acknowledge the fact that it must be lost, that any spiritual ideal worth preserving must remain vulnerable. More vulnerable than the great Romantics, Collins cannot freely offer up his spirit to a transforming visionary blindness. Unwilling to remain unconsummated, he does not undertake their dubious explorations of the shadowy ground of human consciousness. He nevertheless heralds their labors of reparation. Enduring the burden of the past, Collins achieves some marvelous breakthroughs which lead him, and English poetry, into the equally exhausting burdens of the present.

HAROLD BLOOM

From Topos to Trope:
Collins's "Ode to Fear"

Doubtless there are many perspectives that could reveal to us the essential continuities between four apparently disjunctive entities: the topics of classical rhetoric, the ideas of Associationist psychology, the tropes of High Romantic poetry, the mechanisms of defense named by Sigmund Freud and eventually codified by his daughter Anna. But I have only my own perspective to offer, and I seek here to develop certain critical notions that have obsessed me in a series of works, culminating in an essay called "Poetic Crossing," to be found as a coda to my book on Stevens. Much that I have to say will be rather technical, but at least it will not be dry. I propose to take William Collins's "Ode to Fear" and to read it rhetorically and psychologically, so as to contrast within it the representations of two related but distinct poetic modes, Sensibility (as Northrop Frye suggested we call it) and Romanticism.

The "Ode to Fear," a remarkable poem by any standards, is perhaps too Spenserian in its diction, and too Miltonic in its procedures, to sustain its own implicit prayer for originality, its own yearnings for strength. Collins was a very learned young poet of real genius, and he seems to have intuited how few years of sanity and control would be available to him. His "Ode to Fear" is a daemonic exercise, a desperate gamble with his poetic limits that rightly reminds us how attractive he was to Coleridge and to Hart Crane, poets who shared his temperament and his ambitions. The modern critical

From *Studies in 18th-Century British Art and Aesthetics.* © 1983 by Harold Bloom. University of California Press, 1985. Originally entitled "From Topos to Trope, From Sensibility to Romanticism: Collins's 'Ode to Fear.' "

theorist who best illuminates daemonic or Sublime poetry is Angus Fletcher, both in his remarkable early book, *Allegory* (1964), and in his more recent essays on threshold rhetoric and personification. But before I expound Fletcher's liminal visions, I need to say something about the puzzling gap between the poets, in their advanced conceptions of rhetoric and psychology, and the critics of later eighteenth- and early nineteenth-century Britain.

We are currently in a literary situation where much critical theory and *praxis* is more on the frontier than most of our best poetry tends to be, a situation infrequent though hardly unique in the history of culture. The criticism and formal psychology of the Age of Sensibility and of Romantic times lagged considerably behind the experiments of Collins and of Shelley. When I began to write criticism, in the mid-1950s, it seemed to me that Wallace Stevens was well out in front of available criticism, though not of the speculations of Freud. We are catching up to Stevens, and perhaps we begin to see precisely what Freud was *not* doing, anyway. Collins implicitly had a Miltonic theory of imagination, as presumably the commentaries on Aristotle that he wished to write would have shown. But what marks both British psychology and literary theory from the mid–1740s down to (and beyond) the time of Coleridge is its conservatism. Hazlitt is a formidable exception, and his theories helped to free Keats from some of the inadequacies of British intellectual tradition, but the main story is elsewhere, with Wordsworth and Coleridge, where the puzzles of the relation between thought and art are still just beyond the analytical range of our critical scholarship.

Dr. Johnson, who wrote of Collins with personal warmth but lack of critical discernment (rather like Allen Tate on Hart Crane) was of course the strong critic contemporary with Collins's experiments in the ode. With his Neoclassic bias, Johnson was critically just not what Collins needed, though humanly the compassionate and sensible Johnson did Collins much good. Poetically, I would say, Collins needed a vital critic to tell him that the trope for time, particularly *literary* time, could be only irony or else metalepsis (also called transumption) and Collins was deliberately one of the least ironic of all gifted poets. He needed a critic rather like Angus Fletcher, who is discussing Coleridge in the passages I am about to quote, but who might as well be describing Collins:

> Coleridge, whose heart is so full, if sometimes only of its own emptiness, its desire to be filled, seems fully aware that the betweenness of time-as-moment, pure thresholdness, barren liminality, at least in what Einstein would call a "space-like" way, must be a nothingness. Between the temple and labyrinth there

must be a crossing which, viewed from the perspective of time, does not stand, stay, hold or persist. Yet the poet craves persistence and duration. . . .

A new or renewed Renaissance mode of personification would seem to be the main yield of the poetry of threshold. . . .

Formally, we can say that personification is the figurative emergent of the liminal scene. . . . Personifications come alive the moment there is psychological breakthrough, with an accompanying liberation of utterance, which in its radical form is a first deep breath.

A Sublime or Longinian critic this acute would have strengthened Collins where he needed it most, in his own sense of poetic election. The "Ode to Fear" could have been called "Ode to Poetic Election," and its opening invocation makes us wonder just what the personification Fear can mean:

> Thou, to whom the world unknown
> With all its shadowy shapes is shown;
> Who see'st appalled the unreal scene,
> While Fancy lifts the veil between:
>   Ah Fear! Ah frantic Fear!
>   I see, I see thee near.

Why name one's own daemon or genius as Fear? Indeed as "frantic Fear"? Is this a free choice among available personifications, a kind of Aristotelian "fear" to be dispelled by an aesthetic catharsis, or is it an overdetermined fear, belonging more to Freud's cosmos than Aristotle's? Perhaps these questions reduce to: is there not a sexual, perhaps a sadomasochistic element, in what Collins calls Fear? The "mad Nymph," Fear, is nothing less than Collins's Muse, rather in the sense that Lacan called Freud's earliest patients, those gifted and charming hysterical young women of Jewish Vienna, Freud's Muses.

The most illuminating reading of the "Ode to Fear" that I know is by Paul Sherwin in his superb book, *Precious Bane: Collins and the Miltonic Legacy* (Austin, 1977). Sherwin rightly emphasizes Collins's teasing technique; we never do see anything of the presumably attractive mad Nymph beyond her "hurried step" and "haggard eye." I agree with Sherwin that there is an affinity here between Collins and Burke. Collins too favors sympathy over imitation, the effects of things on the mind over a clear idea of the things themselves. Milton's "judicious obscurity," as Burke admiringly called it, is followed by Collins, who also rejects mere mimesis. Sherwin approvingly quotes Mrs. Barbauld, that Mrs. Alfred Uruguay of her age, as remarking that Collins's Fear is at once the inspirer of passion and its victim. And so, in Sherwin's reading, is Collins:

> If, on the one hand, his sympathy is drawn out by Fear's all-too-human vulnerability, it is perplexed by her apparent divinity; and whereas the former aspect of the personification establishes the possibility of intimacy, it is the latter aspect, enticing the speaker with the dangerous allure of numinous experience and heightening his sense of self, that provokes him to seek out this precarious communion.

I don't wish to be accused of assimilating William Collins to Ernest Dowson, but I am going to urge a reading rather less ontological and more sexual even than Sherwin's. How after all, experientially speaking, does one go about renewing the link between rhetorical personification and daemonic possession? There is religion of course, presumably more in its esoteric than in its normative aspects. There is intoxication, by drink and by drug, and there is, yet more poetically, the always beckoning abyss of sexuality as taken to its outer limits, where pleasure and pain cease to be antithetical entities. I am not going to give us a William Collins as heroic precursor of the Grand Marquis, or a critical vision of the "Ode to Fear" as a grace note preceding *The Hundred and Twenty Days of Sodom and Gomorrah*. But the pleasures of the "Ode to Fear" are uneasily allied to its torments, and there is an element of sexual bondage in those torments. That even this element should be, ultimately, a trope for influence-anxieties is hardly a revelation, since I know no ampler field for the study of belatedness than is constituted by the sado-masochistic elements in our psyches.

Is it too much to say that Collins, throughout his Ode, attempts to work himself up into a frenzy of fearful apprehension, in the hope that such frenzy will grant him the powers of the tragic poet, of Aeschylus, Sophocles, but above all of Shakespeare? Yes, that is to say too much, because we then underestimate what Freud would have called Collins's overvaluation of the object, when his Fear is that object. Fear indeed is Collins's wounded Narcissism, and so becomes the entire basis for the aggressivity of his poetic drive. But that requires us to name more clearly the Nymph or daemon, since Aristotle's tragic fear hardly seems an apt name for the Sublime hysteria that Collins confronts and desires.

Shall we not call her the Muse of repression, and so of the Counter-Sublime? Perhaps, in Freudian terms, we could call her the Counter-Transference, the analyst's totemic and repressed apprehension that he is in psychic danger of being, as it were, murdered and devoured by his devoted patient. Fear, as Fletcher and Sherwin tell us, is Collins's *own* daemon, his indwelling Urania. Our twentieth-century Collins was Hart Crane, and I turn to Crane for his versions of Collins's Nymph. In a late, unfinished lyric, "The Phantom Bark," Crane rather strangely alludes to Collins, and evidently not to any actual poem Collins wrote:

> So dream thy sails, O phantom bark
> That I thy drownèd man may speak again
> Perhaps as once Will Collins spoke the lark,
> And leave me half adream upon the main.

The reference is purely visionary, as though Collins came back from the dead, say, in Shelley's "Skylark." In some truer sense Collins speaks to his Nymph Fear again when Crane addresses his nymph Helen in *For the Marriage of Faustus and Helen*. Crane too cries out: "Let us unbind our throats of fear and pity," while he goes on to give us his version of "*Vengeance*, in the lurid Air, / Lifts her red Arm, espos'd and bare" as "the ominous lifted arm /That lowers down the arc of Helen's brow / To saturate with blessing and dismay." Crane's later versions of this antithetical Muse include the Paterian Venus of *Voyages* VI, who "rose / Conceding dialogue with eyes / That smile unsearchable repose—," and the woman of "The Broken Tower," a Collinsian poem where the Muse's "sweet mortality stirs latent power" in her poet. A late fragment by Collins actually prophesies Crane's death lyric: "Whatever dark aerial power, / Commission'd, haunts the gloomy tower." Like Collins, Crane invokes the Evening Star as the gentlest form of his Daemon, though Crane's invocation necessarily is more desperate: "O cruelly to inoculate the brinking dawn / With antennae toward worlds that glow and sink;—"

What Crane helps us see is that Collins's Fear is a Muse not so much called on to help the poet remember, as one invoked to help the poet forget. A Muse who forgets, or who needs to forget, is en route to Moneta in *The Fall of Hyperion*, but Collins is rather more Coleridge's precursor than he is Keats's. Except for Scripture and Milton, and perhaps Shakespeare, what passage in poetry haunted Coleridge more productively than this:

> Through glades and glooms the mingled measure stole,
> Or o'er some haunted stream with fond delay,
>   Round an holy calm diffusing,

> Love of peace and lonely musing,
> In hollow murmurs dies away.

From "The Passions" to "Kubla Khan" is a movement from one threshold
to another, and liminal poets have a particularly intense way of recognizing
their family romance and its nuances. Fletcher, the theoretician of thresholds,
reminds us that etymologically the *daemon* is the spirit of division, a reminder
that I remember using as a starting point in working out the revisionary ratio
of *daemonization* or the Counter-Sublime. The Sublime trope for such dividing
tends to be breaking, a making by breaking, or catastrophe creation. I return
to the "Ode to Fear" to trace just such a breaking.

How specific ought we to be in finding an identity for Collins's "world
unknown" and "unreal scene"? The late Thomas Weiskel brilliantly argued
for something like Freud's Primal Scene Fantasy, but here as elsewhere I
would prefer some version of what I have theorized as the Scene of Instruction. Not that the two fantasies are wholly exclusive, since what passes
between the Poetic Father and the Muse has its sexual overtones in the
evening ear of the belated ephebe. Yet Collins's scene can be called more
Yeatsian than Freudian, more at home in the world of *Per Amica Silentia
Lunae* than in that of *Totem and Taboo*. This may be simply because Collins's
"sources" are mostly Spenserian (Masque of Cupid, Temple of Venus), but
I suspect a more crucial reason also; Fear is indeed Collins's own Daemon,
but he has not yet possessed her or been possessed by her. The scene she
partly inhabits by seeing is populated by the fathers, by Spenser, Shakespeare
and Milton, but not by Collins himself. As the Ode begins, Fear sees the
visionary world, but all that Collins sees is Fear. We are in the ancient topos
of Contraries and Contradictories but not yet in the trope of Romantic Irony.
And there I touch at last upon my first theoretical speculation in this essay;
Sublime Personification seems to me an uneasy transitional phase or crossing
between Associationist topos and Romantic trope. Collins's Fear is a commonplace burgeoning but not yet burgeoned into an irony, or as Freud called
it, a reaction-formation. Fear *sees* and is frantic; Collins sees *her*, and becomes
rather less persuasively frantic:

> Ah Fear! Ah frantic Fear!
> I see, I see thee near.
> I know thy hurried step, thy haggard eye!
> Like thee I start, like thee disordered fly.

That repetition of "I see, I see" is already quite Coleridgean, so that we
almost expect Collins to burst forth with "And still I gaze—and with how

blank an eye!" What restrains Collins is an awareness still just short of irony, certainly short of Spenserian irony, regardless of all the Spenserian diction. The contraries of seeing and not-seeing the visionary scene yield to the topoi of definition and division in the remainder of the strophe, as Collins enumerates the monsters appearing in Fear's train. Division is properly daemonic here, with one giant form, a Spenserian Danger, thousands of phantoms: "Who prompt to deeds accursed the mind," as well as an indefinite number of fiends who: "O'er natures wounds and wrecks preside." All these lead up to a highly sadistic Vengeance, who requires considerable scrutiny. But even Danger has his peculiarities:

> Danger, whose limbs of giant mould
> What mortal eye can fixed behold?
> Who stalks his round, an hideous form,
> Howling amidst the midnight storm,
> Or throws him on the ridgy steep
> Of some loose hanging rock to sleep;

The sources here—in Spenser and Pope—are not developed with any particular zest or inventiveness on Collins's part. But we should note the obsessive emphasis again upon the eye of the beholder, the horrified fixation that is one of the stigmata of repression. Spenser's Daunger, that hideous Giant, was associated with hatred, murder, and treason, which may have been daily intimations for Spenser to dread, whether in Ireland or at court, but cannot have had much reality for Collins in the years when he still was sane. His Danger "stalks his round" amid more commonplace sublimities, storm and impending rock fall. These represent surely the psyche's potential for violence, whether aggressivity is to be turned against others or against the self:

> And with him thousand phantoms joined,
> Who prompt to deeds accursed the mind;
> And those, the fiends who, near allied,
> O'er nature's wounds and wrecks preside;

Those wounds and wrecks of nature include internalized disorders, which is what prompts the vision of a ferociously personified feminine superego, as it were, an image of sadomasochistic Vengeance:

> Whilst Vengeance in the lurid air
> Lifts her red arm, exposed and bare,

> On whom that ravening brood of fate,
> Who lap the blood of sorrow, wait;

Again the sources (Milton, Dryden, Pope) are of little consequence except for Collins's own noted reference to the hounds of vengeance in Sophocles' *Electra*. The curious doubling, almost redundant, of Vengeance's lifted arm as both "exposed and bare" enforces how lurid Collins's scopic drive dares to become. There is a troubling ambiguity in the image, as Weiskel noted. Vengeance is a kind of phallic woman, appropriate to a masochistic fantasy, and in some curious way Collins blends her into an Artemis figure, waited upon by destined hounds. There is thus a hint of an Actaeon identity for poor Collins himself, a hint taken up in the couplet closing the strophe:

> Who, Fear, this ghastly train can see,
> And look not madly wild like thee?

Like his daemonic Muse, Collins really does expect to be hunted down and torn apart by the Furies, for his tone lacks any playful element. That he more than half desires his fate is clear enough also. What is beautifully not clear is just who is seeing what in this rather confused scene of sado-masochistic instruction. Fear sees it all, yet Collins is by no means as yet fully one with his own Fear. She sees and yet does not wish to see; Collins sees only in and by visionary fits, yet he does want to see, whatever the cost. Lacan's grim jest about the scopic drive comes to mind: that which we are fixated upon, obsessively stare upon, is precisely what cannot be seen. Only the creativity of Fear can impel Collins beyond this daemonic threshold.

Of course, like Weiskel or to some extent also Sherwin, or Paul Fry in his fine reading of this Ode, I am giving a kind of Freudian reading (broadly speaking) and Collins's own overt psychology was Associationist. But the line between Associationism and Freud is a blurred one, for a number of reasons. One is merely genetic, despite all Freudian denials. Freud's theory of language essentially came from John Stuart Mill (whom Freud had translated) and so was essentially a late version of Associationism. But far more crucially, both the Associationist categories and the Freudian mechanisms or fantasies of defense rely implicitly on rhetorical models, these being the topoi or commonplaces for Associationism and the prime tropes or figures for Freud. Romanticism is of course the connecting link here between topos and trope, association and defense, or to phrase this more saliently, Collins's "Ode to Fear," though a monument of and to Sensibility, is itself a version of that connecting link, a poem verging on High Romanticism and kept back from it mostly by two barriers. Call one of these decorum or diction, and the other Collins's own anxieties, human and creative, and you may be calling a single entity by two misleadingly different names.

I am aware that I am telling what is hardly a new story, scholarly or critical, but this twice-told tale always does need to be told again. The story's troublesome phantom is what we go on calling personification, an old term I have no desire to protest provided we keep remembering that primarily it means not humanization but masking, or as Fletcher has taught us, masking at the threshold, at the crossing between labyrinth and temple, or as I want to say, between limitation and a presentation that is a restitution. Such masking, in Associationist terms, is a movement through categorical places. In Romantic or Freudian terms, it is a movement between tropological or defensive configurations, marked always by ambivalence and duplicity.

The masterpiece of emotive ambivalence, in Freud or in the poets, is called variously the Oedipal conflict, taboo, and transference, and this is where Collins chooses to center his Epode:

> In earliest Greece to thee with partial choice
>   The grief-full Muse addressed her infant tongue;
> The maids and matrons on her awful voice,
>   Silent and pale, in wild amazement hung.
>
> Yet he, the bard who first invoked thy name,
>   Disdained in Marathon its power to feel:
> For not alone he nursed the poet's flame,
>   But reached from Virtue's hand the patriot's steel.
>
> But who is he whom later garlands grace,
>   Who left awhile o'er Hybla's dews to rove,
> With trembling eyes thy dreary steps to trace,
>   Where thou and Furies shared the baleful grove?
>
> Wrapped in thy cloudy veil the incestuous queen
>   Sighed the sad call her son and husband heard,
> When once alone it broke the silent scene,
>   And he, the wretch of Thebes, no more appeared.

Sophocles of course is hardly Collins's poetic father, but the Oedipal scene is very much Collins's own, and the echo of *Comus* in the condition of the maids and matrons has considerable force. Freud has taught us to look for meaningful mistakes, and the learned Collins errs remarkably here. The "sad call" in *Oedipus Colonus* is not sighed once by Jocasta, but frequently by the god, who is summoning Oedipus to join him. I take it that Collins himself is being summoned, not by Apollo but by the Oedipal Muse, for whom another name, we now can see, is Fear:

> O Fear, I know thee by my throbbing heart,
>   Thy withering power inspired each mournful line,
> Though gentle Pity claim her mingled part,
>   Yet all the thunders of the scene are thine!

Pity here is as little Aristotelian as Fear has been. Collins now recognizes Fear as being not only daemon and Muse but as mother, a recognition scene that is the Sublime crisis point of the Ode. In Associationist terms, the Epode has moved from the categories of Contiguity to those of Comparison, from matters of cause and effect to those lying, beyond causation, in the heights and depths of the daemonic Sublime. Collins's heart recognizes what his occluded sight could not, and so he learns, as Stevens phrased it, that the mother's face is the purpose of the poem. But a mother who is more fear than pity, whose power is withering, and who inspires a thunderous Scene of Instruction, is a most extraordinary version of the mother, and suggests an Orphic as well as an Oedipal fate for poor Collins.

But this is of course Collins's own direct suggestion, and the puzzle of the "Ode to Fear" grows ever greater. The Pindaric, from its origins through Collins on to Shelley, courts disaster, as suits the most overtly agonistic of all lyric forms. Paul Fry charmingly suggests that all the "monsters" Collins invokes: "appear to be nothing other than Pindaric odes." I would modify Fry by observing that Collins is a strong enough poet to know that anything he wishes to get into his Pindaric ode must be treated as if it already was a Pindaric ode. A motherly Muse so fearful, indeed so hysterical as to require the analogue of Jocasta, belongs to the same principle of strength and its costs. Collins is frightening himself to some purpose, and I swerve for a brief interval from Collins into Freud not to seek a reductive version of that purpose but rather to show that every strong anxiety is in some sense an *achieved* anxiety, so that Collins mimes a profound constant in the civil wars of the psyche.

Freud, in his later (post-1926) revision of his theory of anxiety, wrote a kind of commentary upon the Sublime ode, not least upon the "Ode to Fear." In Freud's earlier theory, neurotic anxiety and realistic anxiety were rigidly distinguished from one another, since neurotic anxiety was dammed-up libido, caused by unsuccessful repression, while realistic anxiety was caused by real danger. But after 1926, Freud gave up the notion that libido could be transformed into anxiety. Anxiety, Freud came to insist, is prior to repression, and indeed was the motive for repression. The causal distinction between neurotic anxiety and real fear was thus abandoned for good. The doctrine of the priority of anxiety depends on a mapping of the psyche in which the ego itself is viewed as being in large part unconscious, so that we must say we are lived by the id. Oppressed from the other side by the superego, or the ego's own abandoned earlier affections, the poor ego is exposed to the death drive, the final form of sadomasochistic ambivalence aggressively turned in against the self. Real fear and neurotic anxiety alike become interchangeable with the fear of castration, which is to say, the fear of death. But the hapless ego's surrender of its aggressivity, whether against the self or others, does not appease the superego, which progressively grows more murderous toward the ego.

Associationist psychology had no such vision of man, but Collins's "Ode to Fear" does, probably against Collins's own desires and intentions. Weiskel shrewdly observed that Collins had discovered "a fantasy code appropriate to the special crisis of discourse in his day." Freud admitted that the poets had been there before him, and it is uncanny that Collins was more *there* than poets far stronger. We think of Blake in this dark area, but Blake was enough of a heroic vitalist to disengage from his own Spectre of Urthona. Collins, like Cowper, is all but one with that Spectre, with the temporal anxiety that cannot be distinguished from the poetic ambition of the Sensibility poets.

If we glance back at the Strophe of the "Ode to Fear" we can see that its hidden subject is the tormented question: "Am I a poet?" Collins indeed is the Muse's true son, but can the Muse be Fear and nothing more? In the Epode the question is altered, since there the true poet, Aeschylus, is revealed as being fearless. The question therefore becomes "Can I love, or get beyond poetic self-love?" and the answer seems to be highly equivocal, since Oedipal love is narcissistic beyond measure. In the Antistrophe, much the strongest of the poem's three divisions, Collins makes a fierce endeavor to introject poetic immortality, but the Miltonic shadow intervenes, with startling results. The question becomes not what it should be, more life or a wasting death, but the truth and decorum of the romance mode. Collins is, I think, creatively confused throughout the Antistrophe but the confusion, as in so much of Tennyson, becomes an aesthetic gain:

> Thou who such weary lengths hast passed,
> Where wilt thou rest, mad nymph, at last?

> Say, wilt thou shroud in haunted cell,
> Where gloomy Rape and Murder dwell?
> Or in some hollowed seat,
> 'Gainst which the big waves beat,
> Hear drowning seamen's cries in tempests brought!

The sentiment here, though not the mode, suggests Thomas Lovell Beddoes and George Darley, a good three generations later. The "mad nymph" desperately requires rest, but the Miltonic verb "shroud" for "shelter" suggests that no rest is possible for this personification of the poetic. A rested Fear would cease to fear, and so the poem would have to close prematurely. But the transmogrification of personification into phantasmagoria moves Fear from visual to auditory hallucination, which increases psychic disorder, both in the Muse and in her poet. What seem to me the poem's most effective lines mark Collins's crisis of identification, as he seeks to internalize Miltonic power while continuing his avoidance of naming that source of paternal strength:

> Dark power, with shuddering meek submitted thought
> Be mine to read the visions old,
> Which thy awakening bards have told:
> And, lest thou meet my blasted view,
> Hold each strange tale devoutly true;

The Archangel Michael, instructing Adam just before the expulsion from Eden, says it is time to wake up Eve, who has been calmed with gentle dreams: "and all her spirits compos'd / To meek submission." Collins here takes up that feminine and passive stance imposed on Eve by angelic power, and so I think that his union with his Muse Fear now has become a very radical interpenetration. In this progressive internalization, the topos of Resemblance engenders characteristic metaphor, in which nature and consciousness bewilderingly perspectivize one another. Weiskel, acutely aware of this progress from Sensibility to Romanticism, caught it up in an eloquent formulation:

> The "reader's" mind is deeply divided between the powerful and
> dark appeal the fantasies are making and his conscious renuncia-
> tion of the desires they excite. An attitude of meek submission
> holds off his recognition of these desires, but it also prevents his
> Longinian appropriation of the precursor's power as his own. The
> power remains dark, instinct with danger; the liberating power
> of a symbolic identification with the bards is just what is missing.

Sherwin emphasizes "the radical bivalence of the daemon" here, saying of Collins that:

> He has so thoroughly absorbed the rage of his dark angel that the daemon, no longer threatening the poet with engulfment, is viewed as a guide leading beyond itself to the special prerogatives of the prophetic seer.

Both these critics of Collins's Sublime help us to see that Collins is on the verge of strength, yet hesitant to cross over into it, though Sherwin's tone is more positive than Weiskel's. I would add that Collins's baffled version of the Longinian or reader's Sublime is very difficult indeed to interpret. Unlike the idealized Eve's, Collins's meek submission is a "shuddering" one, and that modifier "shuddering" is his ironic response to Milton as an "awakening" bard, that is, a bard who imposed upon the reader a very intense affective burden. So empathic is this response, however ironic, that Collins's eyes are threatened with being blasted, darkened by shock, unless he assents to the Miltonic fable, however strange. If the precise tale here be the expulsion from Eden, then one sees why Collins's subsequent passage returns to the Milton of "L'Allegro" and "Il Penseroso," and of *Comus*, and perhaps to the Shakespeare of *A Midsummer Night's Dream*:

> Ne'er be I found, by thee o'erawed,
> In that thrice-hallowed eve abroad,
> When ghosts, as cottage-maids believe,
> Their pebbled beds permitted leave,
> And goblins haunt, from fire or fen
> Or mine or flood, the walks of men!

That an urbane tone has entered cannot be questioned, but what has departed is the voice of William Collins. We hear the octosyllabic Milton, and not his venturesome and daring ephebe. Had Collins dared further, he would have found the Miltonic rhetoric of transumption or metalepsis for a triumphant closure, but instead he ends quite elegantly but weakly, in an interplay of the topoi of Antecedents and Consequences:

> O thou whose spirit most possessed
> The sacred seat of Shakespeare's breast!
> By all that from thy prophet broke,
> In thy divine emotions spoke,

> Hither again thy fury deal,
> Teach me but once like him to feel:
> His cypress wreath my meed decree,
> And I, O Fear, will dwell with thee!

Collins was capable of strong closure, as the "Ode on the Poetical Character" demonstrates. What defeated him here? Paradoxically, I would assert that the relative failure is in the generation of sufficient anxiety. What fails in Collins is his own capacity for an infinite Fear. Not that courage becomes the issue, but trauma. Apathy dreadly beckons, and Collins prays for the power *to feel*. Yet I do not think he means affect. His knowing failure is in cognition, and I want to look closely at Dr. Johnson's moving dispraise of his learned and gifted young friend in order to see if we can recover a clue to Collins's self-sabotage:

> He had employed his mind chiefly upon works of fiction, and subjects of fancy; and, by indulging some peculiar habits of thought, was eminently delighted with those flights of imagination which pass the bounds of nature. . . .
> This was however the character rather of his inclination than his genius; the grandeur of wildness, and the novelty of extravagance, were always desired by him, but were not always attained. . . . His poems are the productions of a mind not deficient in fire . . . but somewhat obstructed in its progress by deviation in quest of mistaken beauties.

To pass natural bounds, to wander beyond limits, *extra vagans*, that surely was Collins's poetic will, his intended revenge against time's: "It was." Johnson is shrewd, as always, in saying that Collins not only desired too much, but beyond the range of his genius. The fault was not ambition, but rather that Collins had to ask his inventive powers to give him what neither contemporary criticism nor contemporary psychology afforded. Milton stands on the verge of the European Enlightenment, but when it begins to reach him it breaks over him, confirming only his recalcitrant furies. Collins puzzles us because he is spiritually close enough to Milton to acquire more of the Miltonic power than actually came to him. Geoffrey Hartman's sad summary is just, noble, and restrained, and joins Johnson as the classical verdict upon Collins:

> Collins rarely breaks through to the new poetry. . . .
> Collins does teach us, however, that the generic subject of the sublime ode (as distinct from that of individual poems) is the

poetical character: its fate in an Age of Reason. The odes are generally addressed to invited powers and, like the gothic novel, raise the ghosts they shudder at. Their histrionic, sometimes hysterical, character stems from the fact that they are indeed theatrical machines, evoking a power of vision that they fear to use. Collins, like a sorcerer's apprentice, is close to being overpowered by the spirit he summons.

My friend's simile of the sorcerer's apprentice is particularly effective if associated with the version of Dukas in Disney's *Fantasia*. The vision of William Collins as Mickey Mouse overcome by a host of mops is more than any poet's reputation could sustain. Poor Collins indeed! I would prefer another vision of Collins's limitations, one that emphasizes the odd splendor, or splendid oddness, of his liminal achievements. Daemonic poetry is a strange mode, whether in Collins, Coleridge, Shelley, Beddoes, or Hart Crane. When Collins gets it exactly right, then he has the uncanniness of an original, as this cento intends to illustrate:

> And she, from out the veiling Cloud,
> Breath'd her magic Notes aloud:
> And Thou, Thou rich-hair'd Youth of Morn,
> And all thy subject Life was born!

> To the blown *Baltic* then, they say
> The wild Waves found another way,
> Where *Orcas* howls, his wolfish Mountains rounding;
>   Till all the banded West at once 'gan rise,
> A wide wild Storm ev'n Nature's self confounding,
>   With'ring her Giant Sons with strange uncouth Surprise.

> Now Air is hush'd, save where the weak-ey'd Bat,
> With short shrill Shriek flits by on leathern Wing,
>   Or where the Beetle winds
>   His small but sullen Horn,
> As oft he rises 'midst the twilight Path,
> Against the Pilgrim born in heedless Hum.

> What though far off, from some dark dell espied
>   His glimm'ring mazes cheer th'excursive sight,
> Yet turn, ye wand'rers, turn your steps aside,
>   Nor trust the guidance of that faithless light;
> For watchful, lurking 'mid th'unrustling reed,

> At those mirk hours the wily monster lies,
> And listens oft to hear the passing steed,
>   And frequent round him rolls his sullen eyes,
> If chance his savage wrath may some weak wretch surprise.

These are among the breakthroughs from Sensibility into Romanticism, though never into the Wordsworthian mode. What Collins could not learn was what Wordsworth had to invent, a transumptive or time-reversing kind of troping as original as Milton's own, yet plainly *not* Miltonic. Collins's stance was neither ironic nor transumptive, and so temporality remained for Collins a choking anxiety. If Collins was no mere sorcerer's apprentice, it must be admitted he was also no sorcerer, as the baffled closure of the "Ode to Fear" renders too obvious. I circle back to the question prevalent in all criticism of Collins: What made him poor? Why was his psychic poverty, his imaginative need, so scandalously great? To have crossed into the Romantic Sublime only a year or two after the death of Pope was hardly the act of a weak poet, yet Collins will never lose the aura that Johnson gave him and that Hartman has confirmed.

I go back to Collins's true spiritual companion among the critics, Fletcher, though Fletcher alas has published only a few remarks about Collins. In his early masterpiece, *Allegory*, Fletcher has a fine observation on the function of the Sublime:

> Graver poems like the sublime odes of Collins and Gray, and
> later of Shelley, have the direct and serious function of destroying
> the slavery of pleasure.

I interpret Fletcher as meaning that Collins, Gray, and Shelley, in their uncanny Pindarics, are bent on persuading the reader to forsake easier in exchange for more difficult pleasures. Paul Fry, acutely but perhaps too severely, says of the School of Collins and Gray: "An ode that remembers the pastness of others and not the otherness of the past can have nothing to say of fallen experience as a distinct phase." I think that Collins met Fry's challenge by refusing to admit that fallen experience *was* a distinct phase. As Coleridge's precursor, Collins pioneered in representing what Thomas McFarland calls the "modalities of fragmentation" or "forms of ruin" in Romantic poetry. As McFarland is showing us, these *are* modalities, these *are* achieved forms, with aesthetic arguments and structured intensities all their own.

Repetition, as Paul Fry has noted in this context, is very much the issue when we bring Collins to an aesthetic judgment:

Repetition is what unlearns the genealogical knowledge of the
ode, which creates a world and a god with every stroke of the
pen, only in the same movement to absent these creations from
the poet's field of vision.

Fry knowingly follows Paul de Man's theory of lyric here, but I would
suggest Kierkegaard's "repetition" rather than de Man's as being closer to
Collins's Sublime project. Kierkegaard's "repetition" literally means in Danish "a taking again," and is described by Mark Taylor as "the willed taking-
again of a transcendental possibility." Collins wills to take again the transcendental possibility of poetry as he knows it in Spenser, Shakespeare and
Milton. Or rather, he wills to will such a taking-again, so as to affirm again
the possibility of poetic strength. But a will two degrees from the possibility
is a troubled will, too troubled to attempt what McFarland, following Plato,
calls "the Place Beyond the Heavens," the "true being, transcendence, and
the symbolic indication of wholeness" that make up the synecdoches of
visionary poetry. Collins's synecdoches are wounded aggressivities, turned
in against themselves, sadomasochistic vicissitudes of the thwarted poetic
drive against time's "It was." Collins cannot say: "I am," in his poems. Instead
of the synecdoches of wholeness, Wordsworthian or Keatsian, he can offer
only the Associationist categories of Definition and Division.

Yet the "Ode to Fear" remains a unique poem, as do three or four other
major performances by Collins, and its deep mutual contamination of drive
and defense is far closer to the psychic cartography of Freud than to Locke.
Collins survives not so much as a voice but as the image of a voice, perhaps
even as the topos of image-of-voice itself. What Collins knows in that daemonic place is the "continuous present" that Northrop Frye said was representative of the mode of Sensibility and of its exercise of repetition. Gray
and Cowper and Smart perhaps were more at home in that "continuous
present" than Collins was, and what we know of his life shows us how little
Collins ever felt at home anywhere. Only the place of the Daemon could
have been home for Collins, and to that occult place I turn for my conclusion.

Collins, as all his critics rightly say, is a poet always engaged at invocation, in calling, until he seems quite giddy with the strain. Recall that our
word "god" goes back to a root meaning "called" or "invoked," and that the
word "giddy," possessed by god, has the same root. Yeats, in his beautiful
daemonic reverie, *Per Amica Silentia Lunae*, gives us the formula for Collins's
sense of place, for the exact topos of Sensibility:

The Daimon, by using his mediatorial shades, brings man again
and again to the place of choice, heightening temptation that the

choice may be as final as possible, imposing his own lucidity upon events, leading his victim to whatever among works not impossible is the most difficult.

Collins's odes enact that drama over and again. That there should have been a religious element in his final mania is not surprising, for he is nothing but a religious poet, as Shelley and Hart Crane are Orphic religionists also. But to be an Orphic prophet in the mode of Sensibility was plainly not possible, and again it was not surprising that Collins and his odes alike were slain upon the stems of Generation, to adapt a Blakean conceptual image. Yeats, so much stronger a poet than Collins ever could be, must have the final words here. The tragedy of Sensibility is that it could suffer but not write this liminal passage of High Romantic self-revelation, which again I quote from *Per Amica Silentia Lunae*:

> when I have closed a book too stirred to go on reading, and in those brief intense visions of sleep, I have something about me that, though it makes me love, is more like innocence. I am in the place where the Daimon is, but I do not think he is with me until I begin to make a new personality, selecting among those images, seeking always to satisfy a hunger grown out of conceit with daily diet; and yet, as I write the words 'I select,' I am full of uncertainty, not knowing when I am the finger, when the clay.

ODE *to* FEAR

Thou, to whom the World unknown
With all its shadowy Shapes is shown;
Who see'st appall'd th' unreal Scene,
While Fancy lifts the Veil between:
    Ah *Fear*! Ah frantic *Fear*!
    I see, I see Thee near.
I know thy hurried Step, thy haggard Eye!
Like Thee I start, like Thee disorder'd fly,
For lo what *Monsters* in thy Train appear!
Danger, whose Limbs of Giant Mold
What mortal Eye can fix'd behold?
Who stalks his Round, an hideous Form,
Howling amidst the Midnight Storm,
Or throws him on the ridgy Steep

Of some loose hanging Rock to sleep:
And with him thousand Phantoms join'd,
Who prompt to Deeds accurs'd the Mind:
And those, the Fiends, who near allied,
O'er Nature's Wounds, and Wrecks preside;
Whilst *Vengeance*, in the lurid Air,
Lifts her red Arm, expos'd and bare;
On whom that rav'ning Brood of Fate,
Who lap the Blood of Sorrow, wait;
Who, *Fear*, this ghastly Train can see,
And look not madly wild, like Thee?

EPODE.

In earliest *Grece* to Thee with partial Choice,
    The Grief-full Muse addrest her infant Tongue;
The Maids and Matrons, on her awful Voice,
    Silent and pale in wild Amazement hung.

Yet He the Bard who first invok'd thy Name,
    Disdain'd in *Marathon* its Pow'r to feel;
For not alone he nurs'd the Poet's flame,
    But reach'd from Virtue's Hand the Patriot's
        Steel.

But who is He whom later Garlands grace,
    Who left a-while o'er *Hybla's* Dews to rove,
With trembling Eyes thy dreary Steps to trace,
    Where Thou and *Furies* shar'd the baleful Grove?

Wrapt in thy cloudy Veil th' *Incestuous Queen*
    Sigh'd the sad Call || her Son and Husband
        hear'd,
When once alone it broke the silent Scene,
    And He the Wretch of *Thebes* no more appear'd.

O *Fear*, I know Thee by my throbbing Heart,
    Thy with'ring Pow'r inspir'd each mournful Line,
Tho' gentle *Pity* claim her mingled Part,
    Yet all the Thunders of the Scene are thine!

ANTISTROPHE.

Thou who such weary Lengths hast past,
Where wilt thou rest, mad Nymph, at last?
Say, wilt thou shroud in haunted Cell,

Where gloomy *Rape* and *Murder* dwell?
Or in some hollow'd Seat,
'Gainst which the big Waves beat,
Hear drowning Sea-men's Cries in Tempests brought!
Dark Pow'r, with shudd'ring meek submitted Thought
Be mine, to read the Visions old,
Which thy awak'ning Bards have told:
And lest thou meet my blasted View,
Hold each strange Tale devoutly true;
Ne'er be I found, by Thee o'eraw'd,
In that thrice-hallow'd Eve abroad,
When Ghosts, as Cottage-Maids believe,
Their pebbled Beds permitted leave,
And *Gobblins* haunt from Fire, or Fen,
Or Mine, or Flood, the Walks of Men!
   O Thou whose Spirit most possest
The sacred Seat of *Shakespear's* Breast!
By all that from thy Prophet broke,
In thy Divine Emotions spoke:
Hither again thy Fury deal,
Teach me but once like Him to feel:
His *Cypress Wreath* my Meed decree,
And I, O *Fear*, will dwell with *Thee*!

GEOFFREY H. HARTMAN

Christopher Smart's "Magnificat"

What is the consummation of perfect freedom? Not to be ashamed of one's self.
—NIETZSCHE

For when men get their horns again, they will delight to go uncovered.
—C. SMART

THEORY AS PROLOGUE

When we present one person to another, a feeling of formality persists. It may be a residual awe, relating to exceptional presentations (of the child to elders in early or ritual circumstances) or it may be a more general sense of the distance between persons. The latter feeling would still have a psychological component, for the distance between persons is like that between self and other.

What if someone cannot be presented? The sense of distance has been thrown out of balance: either the self feels defective vis-à-vis the other, or the other appears magnified, unapproachable. The someone can be a something: certain subjects may not be introduced into discourse, certain taboos restrict or delimit the kinds of words used.

I introduce the example of words early, because words commonly help to present us. Should we feel that words are defective, or else that we are defective vis-à-vis them (words becoming the other, as is not unusual in poets who have a magnified regard for a great precursor or tradition), then a complex psychic situation arises. It is fair to assume, however, that the distance between self and other is always disturbed, or being disturbed; that

From *The Fate of Reading and Other Essays.* © 1975 by The University of Chicago. The University of Chicago Press, 1975.

there is always some difficulty of self-presentation in us; and that, therefore, we are obliged to fall back on a form of "representation."

Representation implies that the subject cannot be adequately "present" in his own person or substance, so that advocacy is called for. The reason for this "absence," compensated for by "representation," can be various. In legal or ritual matters, the subject may not be of age or not be competent. But even when he is competent, of age, fully presentable, situations arise which produce a fiction of his having to be "seconded": in presentation at court (and sometimes in courts of law) he does not appear by himself but needs the support of someone already admitted into the superior presence.

The self does not, of course, disappear into its representative, for then the means would defeat the end, which remains self-presentation. Even in visionary poetry, which so clearly sublimes the self into the other, or exalts the other into quasi-supernatural otherness, the self persists in selfhood. Though Charles Lamb is right in remarking that Coleridge's Ancient Mariner "undergoes such trials as overwhelm and bury all individuality or memory of what he was—like the state of a man in a bad dream, one terrible peculiarity of which is that all consciousness of personality is gone," the spectral happenings in the poem actually doom the Mariner to survival. He is unable to die, or find release from his experience except in the "punctual agony" of storytelling.

Whether or not this doom of deathlessness is preferable to nothingness—"Who would lose," says Milton's Belial, "Though full of pain, this intellectual being, / Those thoughts that wander through Eternity, / To perish rather, swallow'd up and lost / In the wide womb of uncreated night . . . "—the self can never be so sublimated, or so objectified, that only its representative is left. Even granted that self desires an absolute escape from self, what would be satisfied by that escape: indeed would anything of self be left to register the satisfaction? To urge questions of this kind is to approach psychoanalysis, but at the same time to link it with speculations on the sublime going back at least to Edmund Burke. These speculations ponder the vertiginous relation between self-loss and self-aggrandizement.

Let me return briefly to Coleridge's poem. Why does the Mariner kill the albatross? A fascinating question; but even the simplest answer, that it was willfulness, implies a drive on the Mariner's part for self-presence. The killing is a shadow of the Mariner's own casting. What follows his self-determining, self-inaugural act is, paradoxically, the presence of otherness. In seeking to "emerge," the self experiences separation anxieties, and these express themselves in motions akin to the defense mechanism of "beautiful indifference" (noted by Charcot in patients suffering from hysteria) as well as to the terror which may accompany isolation.

At the same time, there is a movement toward atonement (at-one-ment, reconciliation) in Coleridge's poem. "Representation" cannot be divorced from advocacy. You justify either the self or that which stands greatly against it: perhaps both at once. The situation could be likened to a trial, though not to one resulting in a definite verdict. The trouble with this line of inquiry is that too many metaphors come into play until one begins to move within art's own richness of thematic variation. Yet such metaphors as trial, court, theater, debut and so on, converge on the idea of a place of heightened demand and intensified consciousness. "The daemon," says Yeats, " . . . brings man again and again to the place of choice, heightening temptation that the choice may be as final as possible. . . . " Let us consider the nature of this "place," imagined or real.

When Christopher Smart writes in *Jubilate Agno*, "For I pray the Lord Jesus to translate my MAGNIFICAT into verse and represent it," the pun (magnifi-cat) alluding to the "magnification" of the cat Jeoffrey and of the animal kingdom generally, corroborates what Freud says about wit both submitting to and escaping the censor. To compare a hymn (the Magnificat) associated with the Virgin Mary to the gambols of Jeoffrey is blasphemous—except that the pun remains unexplicit and the poet, in any case, "gives the glory" to God by asking Christ to make his verses acceptable. Yet the anxiety, I believe, or the pressure resulting in this kind of wit, goes deeper. It is not one outrageously smart comparison which is at stake, but the legitimacy of artistic representation as a whole. The magnifi-cat theme expresses, in its marvelous mixture of humility and daring, the artist's sense that he is disturbing the "holy Sabbath" of creation by his recreation; that he is trespassing on sacred property or stealing an image of it or even exalting himself as a maker—in short, that he is magnifying mankind instead of "giving the glory" to God. Smart therefore atones the exposed, self-conscious self by "at-one-ing" it with the creature. He shows mankind "presenting" before God the animal creation it has exploited. And, in return, he asks that his verse-representation be "represented" before God by a mediator who enters the first line of his poem as "Lord, and Lamb." The opening of *Jubilate Agno* sets the pattern by compounding man and animal into ritual pairs:

> Let man and beast appear before him, and magnify his name
>   together.
> Let Noah and his company approach the throne of Grace, and
>   do homage to the Ark of their Salvation.
> Let Abraham present a Ram, and worship the God of his
>   Redemption.

> Let Isaac, the Bridegroom, kneel with his Camels, and bless
> the hope of his pilgrimage.
>
> (A, 3–6)

Inspired by *Revelations*, Smart begins with a judgment scene: it envisages an ark that might survive a second flood. We find ourselves in a place of demand where everything must be "presented." The precise nature of the demand is not absolutely clear, and need not be the same in all works of art: perhaps it varies with historical circumstances, and perhaps it is the interpreter's task to make the relation between demand and response (demand and inner capability) perfectly clear. But artistic representation does seem to mediate a demand of this kind: one, moreover, not to be thought of as coming from outside, but rather, or also, from within. Again, whether "within" means the unconscious, or refers to a self-realizing instinct, may not be possible to determine generally but only in each case.

There is no way of being precise about this without engaging in considered acts of textual interpretation. We have to identify the nature of the challenge met by Smart and the "place" or "situation" he is in. It would be inadequate, for instance, to say of his "representation" of the animal creation that it springs from the same anxiety for the survival of the physical species that, according to Gertrude Levy's *The Gate of Horn* (1948), inspired the Cro-Magnon cave paintings at Lascaux. They may have had an apotropaic function, for they gather the essential traits of the hunted species into totemic sketches that intend to placate the Spirit of the hunted creature and so assure its fertile continuance. The creature is graphically "represented" by man to a Spirit in order for both human kind and the creature to survive.

Such recreative or reparative magic *is* relevant to Smart's poem; the analogy is too strong, and the theme of generation haunts too many of his verses. Yet it is only a beginning to specific interpretation. For we must add that in Smart the very *medium* of representation—visionary language itself—has become questionable, or subject to a demand which it cannot meet except by being renewed. His recreation of visionary categories is literally a recreation: the source of vision is not exhausted but still operative through him. That, at least, is the claim he seems to make, or the test he puts himself to. The anxiety for survival has associated itself with an anxiety for language-source, liturgy, and the entire process of representation.

ENTHUSIASM AND ENTROPY

The fear that visionary language has lost its effectiveness may not be very different from the fear that nature grows old. Such "depletion anxieties" are linked to the not unrational feeling in us that our appetites—including that for presence—put a demand on the order of things which that order may not be able to satisfy; which, indeed, it may resent and reject. The "economy" of language use arising from depletion anxiety ranges from such devices of conservation as double-entendre, hermeticism, and classical restraint, to the complementary if opposite ones of revivalist forgery, radical innovation, and homeopathic promiscuity. You can write as sparse a hymn as Addison's famous "The spatious firmament on high" (1712), which, in spite of its source in Psalm 19, reflects Pascal's fright at the silence of the starry spaces; or you can fill the vacuum with the "clang expressions" of *Jubilate Agno*, till "barrenness becomes a thousand things" (Wallace Stevens).

Smart's aberrant verses would have been classified in their time as a product of "enthusiasm"; and this widespread and loosely knit religious movement was also a kind of counter-entropy. Affecting principally Puritans and Dissenters, it claimed to have uncovered a new source of truth, that of the individual in his privacy, who would know from "internal" grounds what revelation there was; but if that was all there was, then we were abandoned to individuality, and prone to the hell of unrelieved, sterile selfhood. The blessing proved to be the curse; the precious was also the accused object. "My selfhood, Satan, arm'd in Gold" (Blake). The danger in enthusiasm, moreover, was its inevitable closeness to fanaticism, for the enthusiast found it difficult not to impose his "internal" evidences on others, not to exhibit his "antitheatrical" truth. He sought out or compelled a like-minded community.

Enthusiasm in literature took many forms: it attacked, for example, the scientific "Religion of Nature" which affirmed the stability of the cosmos (nature would *not* grow old) at the cost of dehumanizing it and "untenanting Creation of its God" (Coleridge); and it overrode the pessimism of the neoclassic artist who felt he had come too late in history. The visionary or even the poet was felt to be superfluous in an Age of Reason; but the wish for originality, which enthusiasm abetted, increased in direct proportion to one's distance from the possibility. Yet the dilemma, even for the enthusiasts, was that originality and Original Sin were hard to tell apart.

Smart had to find, therefore, not only a well of visionary English but also an undefiled well. Every attempt to replenish, or imitate directly, the great source-books of secular and religious culture was open to the charge of false testimony—of giving glory to God as a cover for "representing" one's own passions. Today we have no problem with the first person singular, and fiction is inconceivable without a semblance of self-exposure. Enthusiasm in art has gone public and taken the name of confessionalism. Consequently, it is hard for us to appreciate Pascal's notorious maxim, "Le moi est haïssable," and the fact that he was so sensitive to the liaison between egotism and enthusiasm that he condemned even Montaigne:

> The stupid plan he has to depict himself, and this not incidentally and against his better judgment as it may happen to all us mortals, but by design and as a matter of principle. For to say foolish things by chance or weakness is an ordinary fault; but to say them intentionally, that is not tolerable, and moreover his kind of stuff.

Yet Pascal is protesting too much, for the lines of confession (his *Mémorial*) found hemmed in his garments at his death showed how close he was to what his time, and the next century, castigated as enthusiasm:

> The year of grace 1654. Monday 23rd November. Feast of St. Clement, Pope and Martyr, and of others in the martyrology. Eve of Chrysogonous. Martyr and others. From about half past 10 in the evening until half past midnight. Fire. God of Abraham, God of Isaac, God of Jacob, not of philosophers and scholars. Certainty, certainty, heart-felt, joy, peace. God of Jesus Christ. God of Jesus Christ. *My God and your God.* Thy God shall be my God. The world forgotten and everything except God . . . Joy, joy, joy, tears of joy.

Apocalyptic visions, trances, egomania, or what Dr. Johnson was to call, memorably, the "hunger" and "dangerous prevalence" of imagination, were the diseases of enthusiasm against which Pascal and others erected their ideal of the "honnête homme," with his good sense, moderation, reasonable language. England, after the Puritan Revolution, imported this neoclassical ideal of correcting and improving not only the understanding but also speech itself, since an erroneous or corrupt language encourages intellectual and religious error. Swift's *Proposal for Correcting, Improving and Ascertaining the English Tongue* (1712) denounced the "Enthusiastick Jargon" of "Fanatick Times" (the Puritan Revolution and its epigones); and as Professor Wimsatt has noted in a remarkable essay on the "laughter" of the Augustans, behind all these calls for decorum there lurked a heightened sense of unreality, which was not dissimilar, perhaps, to experiences of spiritual vastation. The nearness of *flatus* and *afflatus*, of wind and inspiration, the manic-depressive cycle which all these doctors were seeking to cure, kept reasserting itself in epidemics of wit and farfetched conceits, in the incurable prevalence of the mock-heroic mode, in the hysterical style of the sublime ode, and the laughing, biting speech that joins Swift to a late Augustan poet called William Blake.

The wars of religion against enthusiasm are an old story. But why should so irreligious a poet as Keats complain of Wordsworth's *egotistical sublime?* Why is he so defensive with Moneta, denouncing to her "all mock lyrists, large self-worshipers, / And careless Hectorers in proud bad verse" (*The Fall of Hyperion*, I, 207–8)? The reason is that he could not give up the sublime. He feared that poetry without enthusiasm was no longer poetry; and he was all the more sensitive to the charge of self-inflation because he knew that to create a sublime mode not based on personal experience was to revert to a vacuous archaism, to that impersonation of impersonality which MacPherson and Chatterton succumbed to. The sublime had to be associated with personal experience: there was no other way. Something drives fiction to that recognition in the two hundred years which comprise *Paradise Lost*, the neoclassical reaction, the emergence of Romanticism, and that renewed valediction to the sublime which fails so gloriously in Browning's "Childe Roland" and Tennyson's "Morte D'Artur."

Let me add, before returning to Smart, that Freud also treats enthusiasm. He is our latest "doctor of the sublime," the twentieth century facing the gods or the pathology of ecstasy. A modern analytics of the sublime must begin with Boileau's remarks on Longinus, study Vico on the way to Burke, Kant, and Schopenhauer, and then admit that Freud is the inheritor of all these in his canny knowledge of the fortress against enthusiasm which polite society, or the soul itself, builds in the soul. Defense mechanisms cannot blossom when there is nothing—no fire or flood—to defend against.

Smart's poetic career is emblematic of the fate of enthusiasm. It divides neatly into two parts. Before 1756 he was "the ingenious Mr. Smart," a facile and brilliant practitioner of neoclassic modes of verse. But recovering from a serious fever he began "confessing God openly" by praying aloud whenever the impulse came. "I blessed God in St James's Part till I routed all the company" (B 1, 89). He was confined for insanity in 1757–58 and again from 1759–63. During his "illness" he produced two long poems as daring and personal as any the Romantics were to write. The *Song to David* (1763) was dismissed in its time as a "fine piece of ruins," while the *Jubilate Agno* was not published till 1939. Smart's contemporaries saw him as an excellent versifier misled by religious mania, and though he reverted to such modest tasks as translating Horace and composing hymns for children, he never reestablished himself in their eyes.

What is one to do, even today, with verses like "Let Lapidoth with Percnos the Lord is the builder of the wall of CHINA—REJOICE" (B 1, 97)? The marvelous thing here is not, despite appearances, "Enthusiasm, Spiritual Operations, and pretences to the Gifts of the Spirit, with the whole train of New Lights, Raptures, Experiences, and the like." It is the poet's total, consistent, critical rather than crazy, attack on the attenuated religious language of his day. "Percnos" is a bird of prey, like the Persian "Roc," punningly associated with the "Rock of Israel" in a previous line (B 1, 94), while "Lapidoth" (Judges 4:4) is linked to "Percnos-Roc" by an etymological pun which gives the Hebrew name a Latin root that means "stone" (*lapis, lapidis*). Add the "Wall of China" as the greatest stonework in the world, and the line as a whole is seen to "give the glory to the Lord." It says, in effect, "Let Rock with Rock, the Lord is the Rock of Rocks, rejoice."

"In this plenty," to quote Stevens once more, "the poem makes meanings of the rock." Visionary language knows itself as superfluous, redundant; yet its very breaking against the rock reveals a more than gratuitous splendor. The disparity between the sustained base (the unvarying ROCK or RE-JOICE) and Smart's ever-shifting, eclectic play of fancy, discloses a twofold problem of representation: the traditional one of ineffability, related to the belief that God is "dark with excessive bright," or not attainable through mortal speech; and the somewhat rarer view, that the fault lies with language, which has lost yet may regain its representational power. To the crisis which stresses the inattainability of the signified, Smart adds the impressively impotent splendor of the signifier.

This is too cold a description, however, of the agony of the signifier. The question is less whether language can represent than whether by doing so it seconds or comforts the creature. Representation, I have argued, contains the idea of advocacy; and in Christian theology it is Christ who preeminently acts as comforter and advocate. To rejoice in the "Lord, and the Lamb" is to rejoice in the hope that the Judge (Lord) will turn out to be the Comforter (Lamb).

Yet the premise of that comfort, hidden away for the most part in the "Songs of Innocence" of Smart's time—in children's poetry or catechistical emblem books—was that the creation (*res creatae*, Romans 1:20 and 8:19) would help the tormented or doubting spirit to be instructed. By a proliferation of types, emblems, analogies, and the like, the Christian was encouraged to "suck Divinity from the flowers of Nature," in Sir Thomas Browne's words. As long as instruction could be drawn from flower or beast, then "Man and Earth suffer together" (C, 155) while waiting to be redeemed. Smart's poetry serves to strengthen their bond, even if it is one of suffering. But in doing so, in seeking to "represent" the creature, the poet discovers that language too is a creature in need of reparation.

For Smart's animated diction is the other side of his feeling for the lost animal spirits of a language "amerced" of its "horn" (C, 118–62). His poem, therefore, blends theriomorphic and theomorphic as the animals named by Adam in the first act of divinely instituted speech are now named again, restitutively. Language is the rib taken from Adam's tongue to "helpmate" his solitude before Eve. And it is interesting that in *Jubilate Agno* Eve does not formally appear. Even Mary's "Magnificat," when mentioned in B 1, 43, exalts not the woman and mother but rather language in its creature-naming and creature-presenting function. So close is the bondage of language and the bondage of the creature that both are one for a poet who is their male comforter, their *logos*. His Magnificat consoles what originally was to console Adam, by "translating" and "representing" it.

CAT AND BAT

By magnifying Jeoffrey, Smart is training the telescope of wit on an ordinary creature instead of on the heavens or a certifiably divine subject. The meditation on the creature (that is, on anything created, which included the heavens) was not uncommon; and a contemporary of Smart's, James Hervey, Methodist Rector of Weston-Favell, had popularized the genre by his *Meditations Among the Tombs* and *Contemplations of the Starry Heavens* (1746–47). Hervey provides his readers with a flattering humiliation of the spirit, a Urizenic (so Blake will call it) calculus of apparent human power and actual limitation. Hervey, in short, is second-rate Sir Thomas Browne and third-rate Book of Job. "I have often been charmed and awed," he writes, "at the sight of the nocturnal Heavens; even before I knew how to consider them in their proper circumstances of majesty and beauty. Something like magic, has struck my mind, on a transient and unthinking survey of the aethereal vault, tinged throughout with the purest azure, and decorated with innumerable starry lamps. I have felt, I know not what powerful and aggrandizing impulse; which seemed to snatch me from the low entanglements of vanity, and prompted an ardent sigh for sublimer objects. Methought I heard, even from the silent spheres, a commanding call, to spurn the abject earth, and pant after unseen delights.—Henceforward, I hope to imbibe more copiously this moral emanation of the skies, when, in some such manner as the preceding, they are rationally seen, and the sight is duly improved. The stars, I trust, will teach me as well as shine; and help to dispel, both Nature's gloom, and my intellectual darkness. . . .

"I gaze, I ponder. I ponder, I gaze; and think ineffable things.—I roll an eye of awe and admiration. Again and again I repeat my ravished views, and can never satiate my immense field, till even Fancy tires upon her wing. I find wonders ever new; wonders more and more amazing.—Yet, after all my present inquiries, what a mere nothing do I know; by all my future searches, how little shall I be able to learn, of those vastly distant suns, and their circling retinue of worlds! Could I pry with Newton's piercing sagacity, or launch into his extensive surveys; even then my apprehensions would be little better, than those dim and scanty images, which the mole, just emerged from her cavern, receives on her feeble optic. . . . To fathom the depths of the Divine Essence, or to scan universal Nature with a critical exactness, is an attempt which sets the acutest philosopher very nearly on a level with the ideot."

This is also the period of Robert Blair's *The Grave* (1743) and Edward Young's *Night Thoughts* (1742–45). Smart's meditation on Jeoffrey is surely a criticism of such effusions. It replaces their self-regarding, didactic gloom with real observation, empathy, and a spirit as playful as that of the creature portrayed. The cat is the style; and the style, as a sustained song of innocence, is totally unchary. It leaps; it is prankish; not only in its "mixture of gravity and waggery," as when Smart avers "For the Lord commanded Moses concerning the cats at the departure of the Children of Israel from Egypt," but also in its semblance of plot.

The opening of the passage shows Jeoffrey at his "exercises." These ordinary gambols turn into a ritual calisthenics curiously like the "Spiritual Exercises" of Ignatius of Loyola. When the poet "considers" his cat, the word "considers," which seems to have the Latin root for "star" in it, is a technical term from the tradition of the Spiritual Exercises (Compare "I have often been charmed and awed at the sight of the nocturnal Heavens; even before I knew how to consider them in their proper circumstances," and so forth). Here the term is applied *à rebours* to an uncelestial object; yet Jeoffrey *is* a solar creature, worshipping at "the first glance of the glory of God in the East" and counteracting the powers of darkness "by his electrical skin and glaring eyes." The poet's consideration of Jeoffrey is reinforced when Jeoffrey "begins to consider himself" (B 2, 703) "in ten degrees"—"degrees" are also a term common to the genre of the Spiritual Exercises. In the argument prefaced to Smart's *A Song to David*, stanzas 65–71 constitute "An exercise upon the senses, and how to subdue them. . . . [with] An amplification in five degrees."

It is not my intent to turn Jeoffrey the cat into a Christian soldier marching with Loyola. What the poem conveys is a spreading *consideration* from which nothing will eventually be excluded: Smart opens the covenant so that every creature—"The cat does not appear in the Bible," W. F. Stead, Smart's editor, notes drily—or at least the *names* of all created things may enter. "Let the Levites of the Lord take the Beavers of ye Brook alive into the Ark of the Testimony" (A, 16): the Beavers do not appear in the Bible either, but here they enter alive into an Ark which could have proved as deadly as in Exodus 25:9.

At this moment in time the covenant is merely the rainbow language before us, revived by Smart. But perhaps language is the only covenant. Smart renews the responsive prayer of the psalms and of the liturgy as if to provide the Church with a Book of Common Prayer genuinely "common." More and more of creation enters the Ark of Testimony as not only the verses pair ("Let . . . For") but also different orders of creation; and it becomes vain to distinguish in Smart responsive poetry and resurrected wit. Both deal with strange conjunctions, hidden echoes, powerful yokings together, the "grappling of the words upon one another" (B 2, 632). This principle of "clapperclaw," with its residual sexuality, sometimes extends itself into the phonation of single verses, which then seem built, like "clapperclaw" itself, out of the competing responsiveness of mutual parts. "Let Ross, house of Ross rejoice with the Great Flabber Dabber Flat Clapping Fish with hands" (D, 11).

Imagine the House of Ahab rejoicing with Moby Dick. . . . We hear the voice of the hands, in this applause; indeed the animal body itself grows to be all voice and enters the language. "For the power of some animal is predominant in every language" (B 2, 627), writes Smart; and he exemplifies this by an outrageous onomatopoeic punning. "For the pleasantry of a cat at pranks is in the language ten thousand times over. / For JACK UPON PRANCK is in the performance of *peri* together or separate" (B 2, 630–31). (Read *purr* for *pr* or *per*.) This covenant-language is quite literally the Ark where man and animal pair in amity, and the "Cherub Cat is a term of the Angel Tiger" (B 2, 725).

All creatures in Smart become flaming creatures, and the Great Chain of Being a Great Chain of Language. To characterize Smart as a late or parodic meditationist is not adequate, therefore. It does not clarify the nature of the demand on him or the burden of his response. "Gird up thy loins now, like a man, I will demand of thee and answer thou me," God thunders at Job. And Job is finally persuaded to put his finger on his mouth. James Hervey, and other pseudo-enthusiast worshippers of the whirlwind, put their deflating finger of inflated moralistic prose on our mouths. They make us kiss the rod. But Smart is not put out by Newton, Nature, or Nature's God. He escapes the stupor induced by Natural Religion—by the contemplation of Leviathan, Tiger, or the System of the World. And he does so by by answering its "cunning alphabet" with his own force of language. I will demand of thee and answer thou me, means for Smart, girding up the loins of language and meeting the challenge of a divine text. The Bible is less a proof text than a shame text; and to escape this shame which affects, preeminently, the tongue, he must become David again and restore the Chain of Inspiration. "Rejoice in God, O ye tongues. . . . " The Great Chain of Being is honored not on account of order and hierarchy but only as it continues to electrify the tongue and represent the creature. In Smart's "consideration" everything stars; and the elation, or jubilation, of speech seems to sustain a demand put on it by the Book of God or the "cunning alphabet" of the Book of Nature.

Yet Bethlehem is not far from Bedlam. The madhouses of Smart's time had more than one King David in them, not to mention King Solomons and Queens of Sheba. The pressure on Smart of the divine text or of the need to respond to it by the creation of a New Song, that is, by a language covenant embracing the creature which had fallen with and away from man, heaps this Christopher as thoroughly as Melville's white whale "heaped" Ahab. When we read Smart's boast, "I am the Reviver of Adoration amongst English Men," we do not feel the tension of a pun that mounts up in stanzas 50 and following of the *Song to David*:

> Praise above all—for praise prevails,
> Heap up the measure, load the scales . . .

This is followed by twenty stanzas centering on the repeated word "adoration." The method is indeed accumulative, additive, rather than calculating and accounting. Double the "d" in "adoration" and the pun becomes visible.

A "Song to David" means dedicated to, or spoken toward, David, but also *add*ing itself by *ad*oration until measure and scale break and the account is closed. Smart's ad libitum at once acknowledges and destroys the Johnsonian morality of style; the Doctor's reservation, for instance, that "Sublimity is by aggregation" yet that it is impossible to add to the divine glory:

> The ideas of Christian theology are too simple for eloquence, too
> sacred for fiction, and too majestick for ornament. To recommend
> them by tropes and figures is to magnify by a concave mirror the
> sidereal universe.

Omnipotence cannot be exalted; infinity cannot be amplified; perfection cannot be improved.

Smart might have enjoyed William Blake's joshing of Dr. Johnson in *An Island in the Moon*:

> I say this evening we'll all get drunk. I say dash, an Anthem, an
> Anthem, said Suction

> Lo the Bat with Leathern Wing
> Winking & blinking
> Winking & blinking
> Winking & blinking
> Like Doctor Johnson

I quote only the more decent part. Compare cat and bat.

A SPECKLED LANGUAGE

Our delight in Smart is not a constant thing. Even in controlled sequences, like that on Jeoffrey, where the catalogue (no pun intended) is less chaotic than usual, the poet's exuberance may fall into a near-infantile strain:

> For he rolls upon prank to work it in.
> For having done duty and received blessing he begins to
>   consider himself.
>
> (B 1, 702–3)

"Having done duty" may refer to Jeoffrey's sunrise worship, but it could also be a euphemism, especially when followed by a lengthy description of a cat cleaning itself.

> For first he looks upon his fore-paws to see if they are clean.
> For secondly he kicks up behind to clear away there.
> For thirdly he works it upon stretch with fore paws extended.
>
> (B 2, 705–7)

As every child knows, cleanliness is next to godliness, and Jeoffrey provides an emblematic and charming illustration. Yet since Smart seems more wary of mentioning excrement than of mentioning the devil (B 2, 720ff.), and Jeoffrey's ritual exorcism of dirt is continuous with his "dutiful" worship of God, the thought may arise as to what is being euphemistically "pranked" or "worked in" at the higher level of godliness, benevolence, or jubilant verse-making.

One could try to find that "foundation on slander" (or "on the devil") which Smart mentions in B 1, 170. "The furnace itself shall come up at the last" (B 1, 293) he also writes, alluding to Abraham's fearful vision. Whether at the bottom of it all is a lie or evil or detritus, a redemptive poet like Smart has to extend his *contrafactum* to embrace even the excrementitious. The "soil" needed to fertilize the soil works on language too. Yet Smart's consciousness that when the deep opens, or the foundation rises up, it is the

"Adversary" who may appear—indeed the shadow-thought, perhaps there from the beginning, that the tongues invoked in the very first line of the poem might be used for the opposite of glorification—for slander or blasphemy or accusation—could help explain the *Jubilate's* ritual or litany-like character, that apotropaic iteration which limits an otherwise emancipated verse line. Smart's verses are, as he implies, a "conjecture" (B 1, 173), a "cast" of the line or tongue whose outcome is uncertain enough to be the object of a wager like that between God and the Accuser (Satan) in the Book of Job.

The nature of Smart's anxiety about "slander" may never be clear to us. It may not have been clear to himself. It is an anxiety about the foundation, about origins, about genealogy; and so about the truth issuing from his own tongue:

> Let Ziba rejoice with Glottis whose tongue is wreathed in his
>   throat.
> For I am the seed of the WELCH WOMAN and speak the
>   truth from my heart.
> Let Micah rejoice with the spotted Spider, who counterfeits
>   death to effect his purposes.
> For they lay wagers touching my life.—God be gracious to the
>   winners.
>
>   (B 1, 91–92)

Yet Smart's anxiety about "tongues" may have produced too good a poetic defense mechanism. It is not immediately obvious that the animals here are cited for *their* defense mechanisms. "Let Abiezer, the Anethothite, rejoice with Phrynos who is the scaled frog. For I am like a frog in the brambles, but the Lord hath put his whole armour upon me" (B 1, 95). Euphemism and benediction feed the perpetual motion machine of Smart's poetry. "Let" and "For," and such punnable morphemes as "cat" and "ble" (bull), are linguistic simples, easily combined into phrases and sentences. They support the poet's run-on, combinatory technique, his compulsion to perpetual benevolence.

This may turn, also, by a momentum of its own, into a cat-and-mouse game with language, to see how much life can be eked out before the spirit fails and an adversary consciousness, or melancholia, penetrates:

> For the power of some animal is predominant in every
>   language.
> For the power and spirit of a CAT is in the Greek.

For the sound of a cat is in the most useful preposition κατ'
εὐχήν
For the pleasantry of a cat at pranks is in the language ten
thousand times over.
For JACK UPON PRANCK is in the performance of περί
together or seperate.
For Clapperclaw is in the grappling of the words upon one
another in all the modes of versification.
For the sleekness of a Cat is in his ἀγλαίηφι.
For the Greek is thrown from heaven and falls upon its feet.
For the Greek when distracted from the line is sooner restored
to rank & rallied into some form than any other.
For the purring of a Cat is his own τρύζει.
For his cry is in οὐαί which I am sorry for.
For the Mouse (Mus) prevails in the Latin.
For Edi-mus, bibi-mus, vivi-mus—ore-mus.

(B 2, 627–39)

In brief, the overdetermination of simples like "cat" or "mus" keeps us within a sphere of childlike instruction. Smart's poem, at these points, is not so much a renovated liturgy as a marvelously inflated hornbook: a spiritual grammar rock ("Conjunction Junction, What's your function?") which averts discontinuity or catastrophic thoughts. However serious the content, the form remains propaedeutic; however dangerous Smart's insight, the verse recovers into business ("benevolence") as usual.

Despite Smart's delightful and outrageous wordplay, then, his resourcefulness may be a testing of the source, and his witty, promiscuous conjunctions may point to the fear of being cut off, by his family, or eternally by Satanic accusation. How else are we to understand that long fragment which is but a variation of "Let X, house of X, rejoice with creature Y"?

Let Westbrooke, house of Westbrooke rejoice with the Quail of
Bengal. God be gracious to the people of Maidstone.
Let Allcock, house of Allcock rejoice with The King of the
Wavows a strange fowl. I pray for the whole University
of Cambridge especially Jesus College this blessed day.
Let Audley, house of Audley rejoice with The Green Crown
Bird. The Lord help on with the hymns.
Let Bloom, house of Bloom rejoice with Hecatompus a fish
with an hundred feet.

> Let Beacon, house of Beacon rejoice with Amadavad a fine
>   bird in the East Indies.
> Let Blomer, house of Blomer rejoice with Halimus a Shrub to
>   hedge with. Lord have mercy upon poor labourers this
>   bitter frost Decr. 29 N.S. 1762.
>
> (D, 197–202)

Here the themes of house, foundation, fertility and rejoicing are inter-laced with cries for help and mercy. The contiguity of "Maidstone" and "Allcock" is a parallel puzzle. "Without contraries," Blake wrote, "no progression," but what is progressive here except a verse that somehow keeps renewing itself?

I want to explore further the "wreathed" way in which Smart builds his verse. Take his basic words "Let" and "For." Though they "generate" sentences, they are really a *stutterance*: a verbal compromise-formation which at once "lets" (hinders) and forwards his song ("Let Forward, house of Forward rejoice with Immussulus a kind of bird the Lord forward my translation of the psalms this year" D, 220). "Let" is close to being a primal word with antithetical meanings; and the tension between these meanings—whether identified as control and permissiveness or contraction and expansiveness or chastity and promiscuity—can give an extraordinary twist effect to the verse. Sometimes the contraries are almost too close to be spotted (*Let For*ward . . . "); sometimes they seem apposites rather than opposites because of their position in the paired pattern of the verse ("Let . . . For . . . "); and sometimes they form a crisscross pattern varying in distance (how far is it from "Maidstone" to "Allcock"?).

Smart has left us hints of a poetics of pairing, opposition and distancing:

> For the relations of words are in pairs first.
> For the relations of words are sometimes in oppositions.
> For the relations of words are according to their distances from
>   the pair.
>
> (B 2, 600–602)

It could roughly summarize the actual unfolding of verse sentences in Smart: words are in pairs first, "Let Jubal rejoice with Caecilia"; this pairing may also introduce a contrast, "the woman and the slow-worm" (B 1, 43). The contrast may be more pathetic as when "Let jorim rejoice with the Roach" is followed by "God bless my throat & keep me from things stranggled" (B 1, 179). The oppositions Smart mentions can also be that of the "Let" verse

and the "For" response. Relations of distance, finally, are clearest in a group
of iterative or antiphonal verses. In

> Let Jubal rejoice with Caecilia, the woman and the slow-worm
>   praise the name of the Lord.
> For I pray the Lord Jesus to translate my MAGNIFICAT into
>   verse and represent it.
>
> (B 1, 43)

the first, relatively easy relation of words (Jubal and Caecilia being well-
known patrons of music) becomes progressively more allusive and distant.
Caecilia and the worm are linked by an etymological play on the Latin for
the slow- or blind-worm (Caecilian, from *caecus*), but it needs more than
curious learning to connect woman and worm with Mary's Magnificat
through (1) the identification of Jesus as the seed of the woman who bruised
the serpent's head (slow-worm/ Caecilia; serpent/ Eve); (2) the idea of "translation," that is, transformation, as from low to high, or from one species to
another; and (3) the pun on Magnificat which turns the word into a compound
(Magnifi-cat) and so establishes fully the relation between the "Let" and "For"
verses through the paired opposition of lowly worm and magnified creature.

To refine this kind of analysis is to come ultimately on the *hendiadys* in
covert or open form. Puns are condensed or covert two-in-one structures,
while Smart's synthetic "compounding" of nouns or nounlike words provides
a more open form of the hendiadys. Allcock and Maidstone, when interpreted
as two-folds, are simply hendiadys; Magnificat is a somewhat more complex
instance; Jorim seems atomic until we notice its Hebrew plural ending (creating, once again, uncertainty as to whether a creature is to be thought of
as one or more than one); and "the woman and the slow-worm," as it emerges
from the name "Caecilia," is an especially characteristic hendiadys. One
begins to suspect every name, in this name-freighted poetry, of being po-
tentially emanative: other parts of speech too seem often like the attributes
or derived sounds of some magical noun. Smart composes as if he had a
choice between analytic and synthetic language formation, as if he were
writing a Hebrew-English or Hebrew-Greek-Latin-English. Something of
this is certainly in his mind, since he shares in the pentecostal aim to reconcile
Babel into a universal code of worship. But whatever it is he wishes to achieve,
the hendiadys is indispensable. There are remarkable moments in which his
verses "reproduce" or "replicate" by drawing two or even three words out
of one, yet remain one-ly:

> Let Jorim rejoice with the Roach-God bless my throat &
>   keep me from things stranggled.

> Let Addi rejoice with the Dace—It is good to angle with
> meditation.
> Let Luke rejoice with the Trout—Blessed be Jesus in Aa, in
> Dee and in Isis.
>
> (B 1, 179–81)

In the first verse above, Roach, a monosyllable, if read on the analogy of Jorim, becomes disyllabic, with an aspirated ending (Ro-ach), so that the "stranggled" is not only thematically sustained by the image of the caught fish but equally by the throaty sound. In the following verses we see a proper noun, Addi, breaking up into three components that are sounds or rivers or both: Aa, Dee, Isis (A-D-I). Strictly speaking, we need only the "i" of Isis to complete Addi (itself a pun on the additive process?). But even the -sis may be accounted for if we read Isis as I-c's, and by a bit of scrabbling involve the second proper noun, Dace, also composed of the letter-sounds, A, D, and— this time—C. One name is A,D, plus I; the other A,D, plus C; so that Jesus (that famous fish, almost rhyming here with Isis, considering the closeness of I and J) comprehends both names, being blessed in A, in D, and in I, C's.

It is almost impossible to summarize Smart's poetic method. It is not, or not only, a "mad, philological vision of reality." It does not, or not merely, subvert the referential aspect of words like Isis by deconstructing them as acoustic images or magical sounds. It is best seen as a sacred poetics driving to astonishing extremes the principle of antiphony or "parallelism of members" (Is-is!) discovered by Bishop Lowth in the Psalms. So, Jorim goes with the Roach and is paralleled by Addi with the Dace, and even by angle "with" meditation; while Addi and Dace and Isis can be shown to be "members" of Jesus. But how do you fit in Hecatompus with an hundred feet? "Why, then, I'le fit you!" And, indeed, there is a mad attempt to speak with tongues and write with all those feet, to re-member or re-present every last creature by a "pairing" that will exclude nothing from the "Ark" of testimony.

In society the simplest form of representation (in the sense of a normative presentation of the self) is by one's personal name. Names are a compromise, of course; for no name is unique; and Smart's use of single names (Abraham, Jorim, Dace, Hecatompus) makes them ambiguously individual and generic. Names, moreover, like all proper nouns, are curiously split in their semantic character. They tend to be both subsemantic (so conventional as to be meaningless, semantically neutral) and supersemantic (they can be analyzed or pseudoanalyzed into richly meaningful parts). The idea of naming, therefore, recapitulates the drama played out in Smart's verse. Names individualize and socialize: they are always a kind of two-in-one. "Christopher Smart" names a single person whose Christ-bearing (Christopher) wit and wound (Smart) are one like the "Lord, and the Lamb" (A, 1) are one.

Every individual is *impair*. He sticks out or should stick out. Yet selfhood is both a demand to be met and subject to accusation. Analysis could go from here in many directions: religious, sociological, or what I have called psychoesthetic. Smart invariably connects representability of the self (*by* language, *with* the creature, and *to* God) and the treatment of the impair (also the impaired). He first reduces the impair to an infantile charm or a linguistic simple (cat, mus, the opaque proper noun, and so forth). By this method he both acknowledges and comforts the isolation of each creature. The linguistic simple, at the same time, is given the chance to multiply or replicate, but the match that results also escapes divine assessment. It cannot be judged. Will you frown at "Rehob" because he "rejoices with Caucalis Bastard Parsley"? Or at the Wild Cucumber with which "Nebai" is asked to rejoice (C, 152, 160)? Such matchmakings are beyond good and evil.

It may be useful to summarize the ways of Smart with language because his comforting of creatureliness extends to language—to sounds and words, large and small. He delights in (1) morphemes which can be individualized as words (cat, Dee); (2) words that are reduplicative in structure and remain simples because quasi-reversible (Aa, David, Amadavad, Wavow, Immussulus); (3) self-replicating or redundant phrases which can expand into a whole verse, as in the following (D, 175) inspired by the very idea of "re": "Let Ready, house of Ready" (redundancy) "rejoice" (Re . . . Re . . . re . . .) "with Junco The Reed Sparrow" (Ready . . . Reed); (4) the categorical hendiadys, which brings together, not as in the story of Noah, pairs of the same species but unmatable *res creatae*.

If the ark into which these pairs enter cannot be that of generation, it must be that of regeneration. But does regeneration involve or exclude generation? The new order here invoked, at once linguistic and ontic, coexists ambivalently with an older order which it neither subsumes nor yet suppresses. Smart's poetics of relation never quite turns into a poetics of translation. The name "Jesus" embraces the name "Isis" and the result is a speckled language. In the opening scene of the *Jubilate*, when Abraham presents a ram and Jacob his speckled drove, we cannot tell whether sexual generation is being sacrificed or consecrated.

THEORY AS EPILOGUE

A swallow is an emancipated owl,
and a glorified bat . . . an owl

*that has been trained by the
Graces ... a bat that loves the
morning light.*
—J. RUSKIN, Love's Meinie

*Let Shephatiah rejoice with the
little Owl, which is the wingged
Cat.*
—C. SMART

The newest movement in philosophy, which extends into literary studies, questions the idea of presence. It is said to be an illusion fostered by our tendency to privilege voice over the written word. Voice, for Jacques Derrida, is the egotistical sublime, and our desire for the proper name (*mot propre, nom unique*) a metaphysical comfort. The best voice can do is to become literature; that is, to subvert its referential or representational function by bruising itself on the limits of language.

Derrida moves within a philosophical context of his own, and it is confusing to juxtapose his theory and Smart's poetics. I apologize for this "perspective by incongruity," as Kenneth Burke would call it, but I see no better way of suggesting how complex yet empty the concept of representation may become. Even if one acknowledges that Derrida's very aim is to empty this concept, at least of its psychologistic and metaphysical pathos, the "nature" of representation remains a puzzle.

I have argued that representation supports the ideal of self-presence in its psychic and social aspects. "Vilest things become themselves in her," Shakespeare's Enobarbus says of Cleopatra. She is "beautiful in corruption," like Smart's "Eyed Moth" (B 1, 93); and Enobarbus may indeed be playing on the idea of life engendered by Nilotic slime. Yet toward this "becoming," this triumph over the shame of creaturely origin, artistic representation also aspires. It may turn out, of course, that representation is all there is, and that we will never experience a self-presence in which we see—and are seen—not as in a glass darkly but face to face. Yet who can decide how ultimate the category of substitution is, and in particular the substitution of representation for presence?

The tropes of literature, or similar kinds of imaginative substitution, could as easily be said to pursue that "presence" which "identifies" all creatures, as to defer it. Perhaps it does not matter which, since both pursuit and deferment are endless. That the identifying moment, like a snapshot, is too deathlike or ecstatic; that movement or troping must begin again; that the acute self-consciousness must be transcended by an act of what is commonly called imagination—all this is part of the psychopathology of ordinary life, or of that principle of "clapperclaw" which "joyces" language in Shakespeare, Smart, and even in Derrida.

It may be that the theory of representation finds a less problematic exponent in an intermediate figure, more congruous with Smart, and exerting through Proust some influence on French thought. Let me conclude, then, with a note on John Ruskin. His prose may be the best nature poetry in the language. Ruskin also "represents" the creature, though to his fellow-man rather than God. How sane he appears when placed beside Smart, even if touched by a madness and childishness similar to Smart's. There is probably no better antidote to the *Jubilate Agno* than Ruskin's celebration of robin and swallow in *Love's Meinie*.

These lectures, given by him as Slade Professor of Fine Art before the University of Oxford, are clearly acts of reparation toward robin and swallow and, indeed, all "lower classes" exploited by the Victorian combination of Wealth and Science. "That, then, is the utmost which the lords of land, and masters of science, do for us in their watch upon our feathered suppliants. One kills them, the other writes classifying epitaphs." The painters and monks, lumped together by Ruskin, do us no good either. "They have plucked the wings from birds, to make angels of men, and the claws from birds, to make devils of men." The emphasis on genetic development in Darwinian science seems equally pernicious to Ruskin, who fears that all such speculation on origins will distract us from the present, from the endangered beauty and aptness of the *living* creature.

But it is not the common creatures alone, the swallows, fissirostres, or split-beaks, which must be saved. The common words too must be "represented": English names in their vernacular being, winged expressions which lead Ruskin to reflect on the troubadours, Chaucer and the *Romance of the Rose*. The habitat of the creature is in literature and art as well as in wood and field. Nature and art are both endangered by the deadly Latin of modern anatomical analysis. We should not see the things of this world under the species of a false objectivity, or of its killing nomenclature, but through the medium of their own natures and the *lingua franca et jocundissima* of vernacular perception. Reading *Love's Meinie* I repent me for not being able to "translate" such words as "representation." "All of you who care for life as well as literature," Ruskin advises, "and for spirit,—even the poor souls of birds,— as well as lettering of their classes in books,—you, with all care, should cherish the old Saxon, English and Norman-French names of birds, and ascertain them with the most affectionate research."

PATRICIA MEYER SPACKS

William Cowper:
The Heightened Perception

As a writer of hymns, William Cowper is more renowned than Smart; his contributions to the *Olney Hymns* have been admired and sung for almost two centuries. If Smart's hymns gain much of their power from a vision turned freshly outward, Cowper's (to which Smart was a subscriber) depend as heavily on the quality of perception directed within. Several commentators have observed that a personal record of psychological distress and recovery is perceptible in his sequence of hymns. The hymns, says Lodwick Hartley, "represent various stages and aspects of the poet's struggle for faith: an ebb and a flow, but withal a progression, in this one respect not unlike the struggle for faith found in a more elaborate but not more poignant manner in *In Memoriam*." Kenneth MacLean suggests that the unique quality of Cowper's hymns depends on the fact that they "are poems in religious, in primitive fear," an emotion "little considered by poets of Cowper's time." And Maurice Quinlan observes that, in Cowper's poetic production as a whole, "even a brief consideration of [his] imagery reveals that he was one of the most subjective of English poets."

What is particularly striking about Cowper's hymns as compared with his other work is their essentially slight dependence on imagery: their strength derives almost entirely from the quality of their psychological insight, and their attempts to translate that insight into images are rarely and incompletely successful. Key images identified by critics include the worm, the thorn, the tempest, the fig tree, and fetters. To this we may add imagery of light, of battle, and of streams or fountains. All are commonplaces of Evangelical

From *The Poetry of Vision*. © 1967 by The President and Fellows of Harvard College. Harvard University Press, 1967.

discourse; most are common to religious language in general. And, upon examination, few seem truly essential to Cowper's record of religious agony occasionally modified by the faint hope of salvation.

One of the most moving of the *Olney Hymns* is number IX, "The Contrite Heart."

> The Lord will happiness divine
>   On contrite hearts bestow:
> Then tell me, gracious God, is mine
>   A contrite heart, or no?
>
> I hear, but seem to hear in vain,
>   Insensible as steel;
> If ought is felt, 'tis only pain,
>   To find I cannot feel.
>
> I sometimes think myself inclin'd
>   To love thee, if I could;
> But often feel another mind,
>   Averse to all that's good.
>
> My best desires are faint and few,
>   I fain would strive for more;
> But when I cry, "My strength renew,"
>   Seem weaker than before.
>
> Thy saints are comforted I know,
>   And love thy house of pray'r;
> I therefore go where others go,
>   But find no comfort there.
>
> Oh make this heart rejoice, or ache;
>   Decide this doubt for me;
> And if it be not broken, break,
>   And heal it, if it be.

This is almost bare of figurative language; the only clear metaphor is "Insensible as steel"—the broken heart of the final stanza seems not metaphorical but literal. The hymn's power derives largely from its very bareness, and from the conviction with which the poet describes and analyzes his own emotional tension. Conflict is the essence of the poem. Initially, there seems to be a clash between the conventional—the automatic, easy assurance of the first two lines—and the personal: the bewilderment expressed in the succeeding two lines, underlined by the fact that they address a conventionally "gracious" God. Then Cowper redefines the opposition between conventional and personal as one between the expected (the speaker should "hear" the word of God) and the actual (he hears in vain). He is literally "of two minds": one weakly "inclin'd" toward God; the other, more forceful, "Averse to all that's good." Willing to go through the prescribed motions, the sufferer is constantly brought up short by awareness of his own feelings: he *thinks* himself inclined to love God, but *feels* averse to good; he cries, conventionally, "My strength renew," only to *feel* his own weakness; he *knows* that "saints" love church, does what they do, but *feels* the lack of resultant comfort.

The Donnean appeal of the final stanza is fully justified by the exposition that precedes it. It is an appeal that emotion resolve conflict—not knowledge or even faith: God can "decide" the speaker's doubt only by making him *feel* intensely and unambiguously. The extreme economy of the final two lines helps to make them climactically moving. The poet's heart is unavoidably passive: it either is or is not broken; the stress on passive verb forms (increased by the use of *be* as the final rhyme word) emphasizes the human helplessness which is so often Cowper's theme. In contrast, only God is capable of meaningful action: He can "break" (the strong physical connotations of the word increase its power, suggesting the possibility that the will of God could shatter the whole personality) or "heal" all breaks, all human maladies; and breaking as well as healing may be a mode of salvation—through the restoration of feeling.

This evocation of God as all-powerful, but apparently strangely unwilling to use His power, and of man as forced by his own divided state into a condition of helpless passivity, is central to Cowper's thought. The same ideas emerge frequently in his other hymns, but rarely with as much energy and conviction as in "The Contrite Heart." Here is another presentation of the same problem:

> My God, how perfect are thy ways!
>   But mine polluted are;
> Sin twines itself about my praise,
>   And slides into my pray'r.
>
> When I would speak what thou hast done
>   To save me from my sin,
> I cannot make thy mercies known
>   But self-applause creeps in.

> Divine desire, that holy flame
>   Thy grace creates in me;
> Alas! impatience is its name,
>   When it returns to thee.
>
> This heart, a fountain of vile thoughts,
>   How does it overflow?
> While self upon the surface floats
>   Still bubbling from below.
>
> Let others in the gaudy dress
>   Of fancied merit shine;
> The Lord shall be my righteousness;
>   The Lord for ever mine.
>   (No. XI, "Jehovah Our
>   Righteousness")

Once more, the hymn's theme is the nature and destructiveness of the divided human spirit. This time Cowper concentrates on how good impulses can turn into their opposites: prayer into sin, praise into "self-applause," "Divine desire" into impatience; the heart, traditionally the repository of gentle feelings, is actually "a fountain of vile thoughts." Yet the final stanza somewhat smugly asserts the poet's superiority to others because he recognizes his own inability to achieve virtue and therefore relies solely on the goodness of God.

This conclusion is logical enough: the rational content of the poem consists of an elaboration of the opening two lines, and the concluding stanza defines an attitude toward the facts the poem has described. But that attitude, although logically plausible, contradicts the emotional emphasis of the stanzas that precede its statement. One may object to the imagery of serpent and fountain, but its emotional purport is clear: it insists upon self-disgust as the necessary consequence of man's awareness of his sinful nature. To deny that self-disgust in the conclusion exemplifies the very weakness pointed to in the second stanza: "I cannot make thy mercies known / But self-applause creeps in." Although self-awareness is the subject of the hymn, there is none in the resolution. The disdain for less knowledgeable "others" implied by *gaudy*, the easy assurance of the pronouncement, "The Lord for ever mine"—these are far from the sense of doubt and questioning earlier conveyed.

The most moving stanzas are the second and third, most specifically concerned with the nature of inward contradiction, most direct in their statement of the problem. Their paucity of imagery also distinguishes them: "that holy flame" is the only clear metaphor. ("Creeps in," in the preceding stanza, has undeveloped metaphoric implications.) This rather commonplace image exists in dramatic conjunction with expression of a very different sort: the holy flame of divine desire reveals itself to be simply impatience, and one perceives the relative pretentiousness of the metaphor when the quality it refers to receives a different "name." The problem of using language properly is implicit in all but the final stanzas of this hymn: the sinner's self-examination is largely examination of the difficulty of expressing in words any inner integrity he may have. Sin contaminates the words of prayer; the effort to "speak" God's praises turns to self-applause; the name of divine desire becomes the name *impatience*.

Partly because the poem's concerns are mental (or spiritual) and verbal problems, the concreteness of sin conceived as serpent is disturbing: twining and sliding are motions too physical for the context. On the other hand, when Cowper treats sin simply as spiritual fact, in the second stanza, its force is considerably greater. The heart as "fountain of vile thoughts" is momentarily impressive, but as the image is elaborated its details become so concrete and specific as to remove stress from the main point. We may even find ourselves lost in contemplation of how and why the "self" manages to float on the surface of its own heart. The image is vivid, but its meaning becomes shadowy; the relation between the self and the heart is both obscure and grotesque.

The danger of grotesquerie is often imminent for Cowper because of his singular lack of tact in converting his ideas to images. Norman Nicholson may argue that "Praise for the Fountain Opened" ("There is a fountain fill'd with blood") makes us "aware of rituals even older than the Old Testament: of the dying god of the fertility cults and of primitive symbols that probe deeply into the subconscious mind," but the argument seems singularly irrelevant to the immediate effect of the hymn, which, on non-evangelical readers, is likely to be shocking but not illuminating.

> There is a fountain fill'd with blood
>   Drawn from Emmanuel's veins;
> And sinners, plung'd beneath that flood,
>   Lose all their guilty stains.
>
>   .   .   .   .
> E'er since, by faith, I saw the stream
>   Thy flowing wounds supply;
> Redeeming love has been my theme,
>   And shall be till I die.

The effort at fruitful paradox is unsuccessful because the sheer physical specificity of the image, with its insistence on the source of the blood in *veins* (and later *wounds*) is so intense as to overpower its meaning in Christian tradition. Cowper's frequent references to the blood of Christ make it clear that he conceives it not as an image but as a symbol: what it stands for is of course immeasurably more important than what it *is*. Yet since the poet insists on reminding us in some detail of what precisely it *is*, readers less tradition-steeped than he are likely to have difficulty making the transition from image to meaning. "Comfortable thoughts arise / From the bleeding sacrifice," observes another hymn (number VIII, "O Lord, I Will Praise Thee"); it is difficult to imagine anyone but Cowper composing such a couplet. The adjective *bleeding* presumably reminds him of the symbolic import of Christ's sacrifice; for the reader, it turns a relatively abstract noun into a sharp and perhaps unpleasant image. The attempt to evoke a Christian paradox by speaking of *comfortable* thoughts fails; the paradox is too easy to be convincing.

The most vivid single example of Cowper's lack of control of his images is the final hymn of his Olney series, which systematically turns the natural world into a series of emblems for Christ. This can hardly be what Hugh Fausset meant when he maintained that "of all the hymns which Cowper wrote, . . . those come nearest to pure poetry in which God is invoked through Nature." The final stanzas are typical:

> What! has autumn left to say
> Nothing of a Saviour's grace?
> Yes, the beams of milder day
> Tell me of his smiling face.
>
> Light appears with early dawn,
> While the sun makes haste to rise,
> See his bleeding beauties, drawn
> On the blushes of the skies.
>
> Ev'ning, with a silent pace,
> Slowly moving in the west,
> Show an emblem of his grace,
> Points to an eternal rest.
>> (no. LXVII, "I Will Praise the Lord
>> at All Times")

The grotesque conjunction of "the blushes of the skies" and "his bleeding beauties" is the most startling element in these stanzas, but the flatness of the first one quoted, the padding of its opening lines, the anticlimax of its conclusion, are also characteristic of Cowper the hymn-writer at his worst. Although the implied personification of this stanza is thematically appropriate, in the second stanza the personification emphasizes the awkwardness of the emblematic treatment, and in the final stanza it is simply irrelevant: how does evening conceived as a person "point to an eternal rest" in any way importantly different from that of evening as a physical phenomenon? This is poetry *voulue* with a vengeance, justifiable only by reference to its purpose, not to its effects. One recalls Dr. Johnson's strictures on metaphysical imagery: "the force of metaphors is lost when the mind by the mention of particulars is turned more upon the original than the secondary sense, more upon that from which the illustration is drawn than that to which it is applied." Cowper's images, in his hymns, frequently seem to have a sort of fatality, to call one's attention inexorably to the "original" rather than the "secondary sense." And his imagery is often "metaphysical" in two ways: its references, although they may purport to deal with the realm of concrete actuality, really concern only the realm beyond the physical; and the images often embody "the most heterogeneous ideas . . . yoked by violence together." Unfortunately Cowper at his most "metaphysical" resembles John Cleveland ("my pen's the spout/ Where the rain-water of mine eyes runs out") more than John Donne; his extravagances, traditional though they often are, are imperfectly controlled, and likely to alienate rather than to attract the reader.

Yet the imagery of these hymns, when it is less extreme, is strangely revealing. Most deeply-felt of Cowper's images of the sinner's state seem to be those of storm and of battle. God may be a pilot in the storm (Hymn XXXVIII), or He may actually calm the storm (Hymn XLI); He may control the course of battle and supply the weapons (IV, V), or guard the city against besiegers (XIV), or brighten the Christian's armor in answer to prayer (XXIX); when the satanic "foe" takes the guise of bird of prey, God becomes a sheltering bird, protecting His children beneath His wings (XXIV). Only in the last of these functions, though, does god seem vividly present to the poet's imagination. Cowper's reiterated imagery of light (his favorite emblem of God) and of streams and fountains is more convincing. His most typical positive adjectives and nouns (*calm, pleasant, cheerful, peace, comfort*) suggest the state of restored innocence for which he, as a Christian, yearns, a state emblemized by the calm cheer of light, the steady flow of the fountain.

The conjunction of these facts is suggestive; two stanzas from Hymn LVIII, "The New Convert," hint their significance:

> No fears he feels, he sees no foes,
> No conflict yet his faith employs,
> Nor has he learnt to whom he owes
> The strength and peace his soul enjoys.

> But sin soon darts its cruel sting,
> And, comforts sinking day by day,
> What seem'd his own, a self-fed spring,
> Proves but a brook that glides away.

The polarities of Cowper's universe are here suggested and partly described. On the one side is the realm of "conflict." The new convert may postpone awareness of it, but he cannot avoid its actuality; he will ultimately be forced to "see" the foes which have existed all along; his comforts will "sink" as inevitably as the brook glides away. Conflict implies depletion of human resources; it involves a falling away from the state of "strength and peace," of enjoyment, calm, cheer, which is Cowper's most potent vision. He dreams, too, of a never-exhausted fountain of grace, as he dreams of, and believes in, a divine source of spiritual light. But faith and perception seem, in this hymn at least, fundamentally opposed: faith temporarily protects a man from "seeing" what is to be seen; as the power of sin counteracts that of faith, he comes to realize that the inexhaustible spring is only a transient brook. In some of the most convincing hymns Cowper's perceptions of nature support him in his non-rational conviction of the essential hostility of the universe he inhabits. Yet his fundamental effort in all his poetry was to justify, and thus to retain, his dream of idyllic peace, in which he might return to the child-like state of the new convert.

In the hymns, by their very nature, Cowper's religious conviction dominates his poetic gifts. It is not necessary to agree with Hugh Fausset that the poet's life and work demonstrate the unalterable and fundamental opposition between his poetic impulses and his religious bias ("Throughout his life Cowper's allegiance was disastrously divided between poetry and religion."); one may still see that the hymn form emphasizes a dichotomy which may elsewhere disappear. In his most successful poetry, Cowper's concern with art and his preoccupation with morality unite—despite the fact that his own utterances on his poetry occasionally suggest a drastic separation between them, insisting even that all artistic devices must be a means for moral instruction. "My principal purpose," he wrote to the Rev. John Newton, of *The Task*, "is to allure the reader, by character, by scenery, by imagery, and such poetical embellishments, to the reading of what may profit him." Newton was far more interested in Cowper's spiritual development than in his artistic achievement; the poet's statement of his intent may have been colored by his sense of what his mentor expected of him. But his sense of a responsibility to make his poetry "useful" emerges elsewhere as well. "I can write nothing without aiming at least at usefulness," he explained to the Reverend

William Unwin: "it were beneath my years to do it, and still more dishon-
ourable to my religion."

One reason for Cowper's insistence on the didactic function of poetry
seems to have been his conviction that his contemporaries subordinated matter to manner. An important subject of "Table Talk" is the deterioration of
value implicit in the fact that modern standards of poetic excellence stress
technique rather than content: "Manner is all in all, whate'er is writ,/ The
substitute for genius, sense, and wit" (ll. 542–43). Cowper insists that poets
must be judged by their subject matter:

> To dally much with subjects mean and low
> Proves that the mind is weak, or makes it so.
>
> . . . .
>
> The man that means success should soar above
> A soldier's feather, or a lady's glove;
> Else, summoning the muse to such a theme,
> The fruit of all her labour is whipt-cream.
>
>   (544–45, 548–51)

Yet Cowper's notion of the poet's proper subject matter was by no means
limited to the promulgation of religious doctrine; he had also an idea of
imaginative truth. His scorn for "mere matters of fact" is worthy of a nineteenth-century "Romantic": "I do not know," he writes to Newton, "that a
poet is obliged to write with a philosopher at his elbow, prepared always to
bind down his imagination to mere matters of fact." And his concern for the
substance of poetry did not prevent him from being deeply aware of the
demands and resources of technique, considered in isolation from content.
The struggle for technical dexterity offered a sort of salvation for him. In a
touching letter to Newton, Cowper dilates upon his religious despair, describing himself as engaged in "continual listening to the language of a heart
hopeless and deserted" and therefore as unfit for conversation about theological matters. He admits, however, that he is able to write verse about
subjects he cannot discuss in talk or in written prose. The reason is that
"The search after poetical expression, the rhyme, and the numbers, are all
affairs of some difficulty; they amuse, indeed, but are not to be attained
without study, and engross, perhaps, a larger share of the attention than the
subject itself. Persons fond of music will sometimes find pleasure in the tune,
when the words afford them none. Cowper was much concerned with the
"tune" of his poetry in its very specific aspects. "To make verse speak the
language of prose, without being prosaic—to marshal the words of it in such
an order as they might naturally take in falling from the lips of an exemplary

speaker, yet without meanness, harmoniously, elegantly, and without seeming to displace a syllable for the sake of rhyme, is one of the most arduous
tasks a poet can undertake." This is, at least in its opening phrases, such an
ideal as Wordsworth was to enunciate, and Cowper appears to have pursued
it assiduously.

Yet Donald Davie is surely right in maintaining that Cowper's "work
is far more the consummation of one tradition than the prelude to another."
Mr. Davie points out that the Augustans in general, like Wordsworth, insisted
"that the poet had a duty to the spoken language.... But for them this
requirement, this duty laid upon the poet, was one among many, others
being the observance of decorum, the need for compactness, and metrical
felicity." Cowper's adverbs in the passage quoted above (*harmoniously, elegantly*) indicate his concern with decorum and "felicity." The extent to which
his poetic principles corresponded to those of his contemporaries and predecessors emerges even more vividly in his ideal of "perspicuity." "Blank
verse, by the unusual arrangement of the words, and by the frequent infusion
of one line into another, not less than by the style, which requires a kind of
tragical magnificence, cannot be chargeable with much obscurity,—must
rather be singularly perspicuous,—to be so easily comprehended. It is my
labour, and my principal one, to be as clear as possible." Again, six years
later: "Only remember, that in writing, perspicuity is always more than half
the battle: the want of it is the ruin of more than half the poetry that is
published. A meaning that does not stare you in the face is as bad as no
meaning, because nobody will take the pains to poke for it." Years before,
Fénelon had written, "We shou'd use a simple, exact, easy Stile, that lays
every thing open to the Reader, and even prevents his Attention. When an
Author writes for the Publick, he shou'd take all the Pains imaginable to
prevent his Reader's having any." The goal, and the sense of audience which
determines it, remain precisely the same at the century's end as at its beginning. The most authoritative critics of Cowper's own time were unwavering
in their advocacy of perspicuity as a prime—perhaps *the* prime—poetic virtue.
Lord Kames exposes the logic of their view: "communication of thought
being the chief end of language, it is a rule, That perspicuity ought not to
be sacrificed to any other beauty whatever." Blair echoes him with greater
elaboration and even more emphasis: "Perspicuity, it will be readily admitted,
is the fundamental quality of Style; a quality so essential in every kind of
writing, that, for the want of it, nothing can atone.... This, therefore, must
be our first object, to make our meaning clearly and fully understood, and
understood without the least difficulty."

For twentieth-century readers, trained to value complexity as an index to poetic merit, such an ideal may seem to promise a dull and obvious sort of poetry. These adjectives, however, do not describe Cowper's best poetic achievement (any more than they describe much of the other poetry written in the service of the same ideal). One may theorize that Cowper was wiser as a poet than as a commentator on poetry, that he did not actually attempt to achieve the goals to which he pays lip service. But the goal of perspicuity itself implies a more complicated critical perception than one may at first realize, for perspicuity can only be achieved through simultaneous awareness of the demands of form and of content: indeed, it specifically implies a union of these concerns. Style, Hugh Blair pointed out, "is a picture of the ideas which rise in [an author's] mind, and of the manner in which they rise there; and, hence, when we are examining an author's composition, it is, in many cases, extremely difficult to separate the Style from the sentiment. . . . Style is nothing else, than that sort of expression which our thoughts most readily assume."

The style most readily assumed by Cowper's thoughts, in *The Task* for example, is fluent and deceptively simple. "I always write as smoothly as I can," he explained to Joseph Johnson; "but . . . I never did, never will, sacrifice the spirit or sense of a passage to the sound of it." On the other hand, he scorned a poet "Too proud for art, and trusting in mere force" ("Table Talk," 683) and articulated a poetic ideal involving both form and content:

> Fervency, freedom, fluency of thought,
> Harmony, strength, words exquisitely sought;
> Fancy, that from the bow that spans the sky
> Brings colours, dipt in heav'n, that never die;
> A soul exalted above earth, a mind
> Skill'd in the characters that form mankind.
>   ("Table Talk," 700–705)

This passage on the poetic character develops an elaborate simile of the poet as resembling the sun:

> Like his to shed illuminating rays
> On ev'ry scene and subject it surveys.
>   (712-13)

It was not a new comparison: Daniel Webb, for example, had pointed out that "poetry is to the soul, what the sun is to nature; it calls forth, it cherishes, it adorns her beauties." Yet as an instance of Cowper's poetic technique and as a statement of conviction, this description of the poet's gifts is important. Its insistence on metaphors from nature (the rainbow, the sun) is more than accidental: the best examples of Cowper's successful and quite individual fusion of the claims of form and content characteristically develop from his concern with natural imagery. The intellectual progressions recorded in *The Task* depend heavily on the implications of images often presented quite unemphatically.

Cowper's letters sometimes expressed his worry that *The Task* might not immediately reveal its coherence. In a letter to Unwin he supplied his most detailed account of what he considers himself to have achieved in the poem. His defense of his own achievement rests on his expressed belief that his work demonstrates independence of spirit (in its use of his own experience as the sole basis for descriptions both of human and terrestrial nature, and in its "numbers"), authenticity of feeling and, he strongly implies, a rather more "regular" plan than may be immediately apparent. The explanation is worth quoting in full:

> My descriptions are all from nature: not one of them second-handed. My delineations of the heart are from my own experience: not one of them borrowed from books, or in the least degree conjectural. In my numbers, which I have varied as much as I could (for blank verse without variety of numbers is no better than bladder and string), I have imitated nobody, though sometimes perhaps there may be an apparent resemblance; because at the same time that I would not imitate, I have not affectedly differed.
>
> If the work cannot boast a regular plan (in which respect however I do not think it altogether indefensible), it may yet boast, that the reflections are naturally suggested always by the preceding passage, and that except the fifth book, which is rather of a political aspect, the whole has one tendency: to discountenance the modern enthusiasm after a London life, and to recommend rural ease and leisure, as friendly to the cause of piety and virtue.

Cowper here suggests that the unity of *The Task* derives from its consistent recommendation of country over city life, its insistence that "God made the country, and man made the town"; but he explicitly excepts the "political" fifth book from the general unity of the whole. Yet the fifth book, too, fits into a more subtly articulated pattern of unity than Cowper ever explicitly claimed, a unity derived largely from the reiteration and elaboration of certain sorts of imagery and reference. Examination of the first book— which contains Cowper's announcement of his intentions in the poem along

with certain well-known passages of natural description—and the fifth—
largely concerned with political and theological issues—may suggest the nature of that unity.

Book I, entitled "The Sofa," begins with a mock-heroic account of the
evolution of the sofa. With a rather heavy-handed piece of levity Cowper
announces that, having previously sung "Truth, Hope, and Charity," he
now proposes to "seek repose upon an humbler theme" (5). The justification
for such a concern is merely that "the Fair commands the song" (7); in an
accompanying note the author explains the origin of the poem in the arbitrary
and fanciful suggestion of Lady Austen. In the succeeding history of the
sofa's development, occasional references suggest the possibility of some
allegorical connection between the creation of sofas and the creation of poems.
Both may be "employed t'accommodate the fair" (73); both may be based on
plans simple or elaborate; both may use shepherds or flowers as decoration
(see 35–38). And both attain excellence only as a result of slow, hard labor
(83–85). Such connections are merely hinted; their significance emerges
gradually.

The transition from consideration of the sofa to presentation of the poet's
experience of the natural world involves a rejection of the indoor life associated with diseases resulting from "libertine excess" (106). The speaker, who
prefers the outdoors, recounts his memories of the sights and sounds of the
country (109–364); these lead him to reflections on their significance which
occupy most of the rest of the first book. The visual perceptions he offers
are organized in "scenes." The value of these, the real point of their inclusion,
seems to be their effect on the observer rather than any inherent meaning.

> scenes that sooth'd
> Or charm'd me young, no longer young, I find
> Still soothing, and of pow'r to charm me still.
> (141–43)

> Scenes must be beautiful, which, daily view'd,
> Please daily.
> (177–78)

> Now roves the eye;
> And, posted on this speculative height,
> Exults in its command.
> (288–90)

The observer is more important than the phenomena he perceives. In a revealing sequence, Cowper discusses a small cottage which he has named "the peasant's nest" and romantically yearned to inhabit. Considering the possibilities more carefully, he realizes that life in such rural isolation would offer far too many hardships, and concludes

> thou seeming sweet,
> Be still a pleasing object in my view;
> My visit still, but never mine abode.
>   (249–51)

To make external reality into a series of pleasing objects in his view seems to be part of Cowper's goal; a partial justification for this procedure is that it does no harm: "the guiltless eye/ Commits no wrong, nor wastes what it enjoys" (333–34).

The reduction of nature to an object of aesthetic perception implies the possibility of a close relation between nature and art; this relation is a significant part of Cowper's subject, although his concern with it sometimes emerges only through his choice of metaphors. His description of rural scenes frequently insists, explicitly or implicitly, on the fact that nature provides "works of art" for contemplation. Like many eighteenth-century poets, Cowper often perceives landscapes as spatially organized like paintings, but he seems more aware than most of what he is doing. A typical passage is full of indications of spatial relationships: *there, here, there, far beyond*. But it also expresses the perceiver's conscious—or almost conscious—pleasure in having discovered a point of view from which nature and people in the natural world can be considered as purely aesthetic phenomena.

> Thence with what pleasure have we just discern'd
> The distant plough slow moving, and beside
> His lab'ring team, that swerv'd not from the track,
> The sturdy swain diminish'd to a boy!
> Here Ouse, slow-winding through a level plain
> Of spacious meads with cattle sprinkled o'er
> Conducts the eye along its sinuous course
> Delighted. There, fast rooted in their bank,
> Stand, never overlook'd, our fav'rite elms,
> That screen the herdsman's solitary hut;
> While far beyond, and overthwart the stream
> That, as with molten glass, inlays the vale,
> The sloping land recedes into the clouds.
>   (158–71)

The sturdy swain, visually diminished to a boy, therefore need not be considered as a suffering, striving human being. The pleasures of perspective make it unnecessary to contemplate hard realities. (Cowper elsewhere in *The Task* demonstrates some capacity to participate imaginatively in the difficulties of peasant life. He does so clearly from a sense of duty; the pleasure of contemplating peasants depends on thinking of them as children, or as figures in a landscape). Similarly, the cattle, "sprinkled o'er" the spacious meads, are elements of composition, not real animals; even the "lab'ring team" is described with primary emphasis on its participation in a visual pattern ("swerved not from the track"). The Ouse is significant because, like a river in a painting, it can conduct the eye along its sinuous course and thereby "delight" the perceiver. The final metaphor of the stream "inlaying" the vale "as with molten glass" sums up many implications of the passage. The visual joys of nature are thoroughly analogous to those of art; to see the river as resembling a stream of molten glass is to assert its place in an ordered aesthetic whole. This is nature tamed and methodized in a particularly significant way, nature made comprehensible through analogy, subordinated to the aesthetic needs of the observer.

The scenes Cowper describes frequently have this sort of neatness, orderliness—frequently, but by no means always. The first book, however, describes the natural universe almost entirely from the point of view of the connoisseur of art, whose eye orders even the relative confusion of the forest.

> Nor less attractive is the woodland scene,
> Diversified with trees of ev'ry growth,
> Alike, yet various. Here the gray smooth trunks
> Of ash, or lime, or beech, distinctly shine,
> Within the twilight of their distant shades;
> There, lost behind a rising ground.
>
> (300–305)

Once more we have the *here-there* organization; Cowper asserts confidently, "No tree in all the grove but has its charms" (307), and then specifies with sharp visual detail the individual attractions of each, providing a brilliant objectification of that Augustan ideal of "order in variety" hinted by the opening lines of the passage. He can perceive the panorama of hill and valley between wood and water as "a spacious map" (321) with no implied deprecation of its beauty: the fact that it is describable in terms of human achievement suggests its praiseworthy orderliness. The effect of this reference to nature as a map is at the opposite pole from that of Smart's "All scenes of painting crowd the map/ Of nature," which dramatizes the poet's impres-

sion of an overflowingly rich universe, in which the distinction between the
works of God and those of man becomes finally irrelevant. Cowper's metaphor describes a world in which the human need for perceptual order is
dominant.

"The love of Nature, and the scene she draws,/ Is Nature's dictate,"
Cowper observes (412-13) in one of his most explicit uses of the analogy
between nature and art. The purpose of the analogy is to insist on the
superiority of nature to art:

> Strange! there should be found,
>
> . . . .
>
> Who, satisfied with only pencil'd scenes,
> Prefer to the performance of a God
> Th' inferior wonders of an artist's hand!
> Lovely indeed the mimic works of art;
> But Nature's works far lovelier.
>
> (413-21)

Cowper offers a standard argument for the greater loveliness of nature: painting pleases only the eye, "sweet Nature ev'ry sense" (427). But this is only
a superficial justification for a preference which is in fact the key to the
structure and meaning of the first book and in a sense of the poem as a whole.

The more profound significance of the poet's belief in the aesthetic
superiority of nature to art emerges only gradually, although it is implicit
even in the early natural descriptions. Immediately after his direct statement
that nature's works are lovelier than man's—in the same verse paragraph—
Cowper begins exploring the aesthetic principle of contrast which had interested Thomson and Akenside. The prisoner, the invalid, the sailor de-
prived of sight of land: these appreciate the "feast" spread by nature (433)
more than can men to whom that feast is constantly available. (In the case
of the sailor, longing for the beauty of nature brings about his destruction:
looking into the ocean he sees "visions prompted by intense desire" [451],
visions of the fields he has left behind; seeking those fields, he plunges to his
death. The destructive agent is not nature but his own imagination. The
dangers of fancy are an important subordinate theme of *The Task*.) Earlier,
Cowper had pointed out the principle of contrast operating in other areas:
nature herself subsists by constant change (367-84); man gains the greatest
goods through alternation of activity and rest. "Measure life/ By its true
worth, the comforts it affords," the poet commands (396-97); then one perceives that only through contrast can genuine pleasure be achieved.

The greatest pleasure for Cowper is unquestionably aesthetic contemplation, contemplation as an observer. Actual participation in life is dangerous and debilitating; life can become "A peddler's pack, that bows the bearer down" (465); men cling to it although it is essentially meaningless, long for society through mere dread of solitude. Cowper's images of all but peasant life are characteristically images of deprivation and desperation. To the horrors of the urban life which, through its very gaiety, "fills the bones with pain,/ The mouth with blasphemy, the heart with woe" (504–5), the poet opposes, once more, his vision of nature as essentially designed for human contemplation:

> The earth was made so various, that the mind
> Of desultory man, studious of change,
> And pleas'd with novelty, might be indulg'd.
>
> (506–8)

The principle of change and contrast in nature seems now to exist to fulfill man's aesthetic needs: man may become bored with individual "prospects," but other prospects always exist; he may contemplate landscapes interrupted by hedges which provide visual variety; the shapeless gorse offers "ornaments of gold" (529) made more pleasing because opposed to the "deform'd" (527) bush itself.

In the last third of the first book, nature as aesthetic object is not so important. The organization of episodes now begins to seem relatively random; yet subterraneously the same theme remains dominant: the theme of nature's importance as an object of contemplation and a source of the comforts life affords, its superiority in these respects to human art and artifice. We learn about crazy Kate, whose insanity results from an over-active fancy (534–56); then about the gypsies, lazy and immoral, who none the less enjoy "health and gaiety of heart" (587), direct results of their contact with nature. Then comes, rather surprisingly, an extended passage of praise for civilization (592–677), in the course of which Cowper considers the limitations of the "noble savage." Finally the book moves into its lengthy denunciation of cities (a denunciation which, however, painstakingly accords credit to urban achievement) and its ultimate praise of the superiority of country life (678–774).

The need to record the glories of civilization seems to come, in the context, from recognition of the fact that man is, after all, by necessity, a being who must act as well as contemplate. In the first two-thirds of this book, Cowper has insisted upon the value of nature to man, who is the passive recipient of what it has to offer. Partly through reiterated analogies between nature and art, he has stressed the inferiority of art to nature as an object of contemplation, the aesthetic value of nature, the moral innocence of "nature appreciation," the importance of the physical and mental health which nature offers man as recipient. As long as man *sees* rather than *does*, he is secure; he may even be happy, gaining the "comforts" by which the value of life is to be judged. On the other hand, there have also been hints of darker possibility. The sailor is killed, Kate crazed as a result of the operations of fancy. The gypsies steal; as *doers* they are unattractive, though blessed as recipients of nature's power. And we have a somber sketch of those who give their lives to the pursuit of pleasure in a social environment: a pursuit which makes life empty, valueless. On the other hand, Cowper has asserted the value of "strenuous toil"—but only because it provides, by contrast, "sweetest ease" (388).

In the context of the values implied, Cowper faces a dilemma when he begins to consider the possibility of man's acting positively rather than neg-atively. In what context can man act properly; and what, precisely, is the relation between action and contemplation? Does action necessarily result in that "sinking" of comfort which the poet so deeply dreads? Only civilization, Cowper concludes, makes possible true and consistent virtue in action. "Here virtue thrives as in her proper soil" (600): repeated uses of natural analogy insist that the patterns of nature are the models to man. Thus civilized virtue is "By culture tam'd, by liberty refresh'd,/ And all her fruits by radiant truth matur'd" (ll. 606–7). It tends to exist only in temperate climates; the inhabitant of the frozen north feels "severe constraint" (612), and—more interestingly— residents of tropic isles

> Can boast but little virtue; and inert
> Through plenty, lose in morals what they gain
> In manners—victims of luxurious ease.
> These therefore I can pity, plac'd remote
> From all that science traces, art invents,
> Or inspiration teaches.
>
>   (623–28)

The distaste for the inertness of ease and of over-constraint, the admi-ration for the accomplishments of science and art—these are standard eigh-teenth-century attitudes, associated with belief in the doctrine of progress. They are not, however, really compatible with Cowper's more fundamental convictions, and his uneasiness with them soon emerges through his ex-pressed consciousness of the gap between the ideal of progress and the ac-tuality. Ideally, civilized virtue is "gentle, kind" (605). Actually, it is Omai, the South Sea Islander, who is gentle—and he is a "gentle savage" (633). The real result of civilization is

> With what superior skill we can abuse
> The gifts of Providence, and squander life.
>   (637–38)

"Doing good,/ Disinterested good, is not our trade," Cowper explains (673–74); the conflict between commercial and moral values is fundamental and unalterable. Lacking such conflicts, the South Sea Islander, despite his lack also of civilized graces, seems in all his passivity the moral superior of the energetic Englishman. Like Wordsworth, who advocated a "wise passiveness" toward nature, unlike Thomson, who felt obliged to condemn such passivity as "indolence," Cowper seems to feel the passive relation to nature as an ideal state of being. Indeed, in one of his letters he suggests that man can achieve even active virtue only in a state of nature. "I accede most readily to the justice of your remark on the subject of the truly Roman heroism of the Sandwich islanders," he wrote John Newton. "Proofs of such prowess, I believe, are seldom exhibited by a people who have attained to a high degree of civilization. Refinement and profligacy of principle are too nearly allied, to admit of any thing so noble."

Cowper insists on a distinction between the "civilization" of cities—characterized by "refinement"—and that of the country. Virtue thrives "in the mild/ And genial soil of cultivated life" (678–79)—"Yet not in cities oft" (681), to which flow, as to a sewer, "The dregs and feculence of ev'ry land" (683). In one respect alone are cities truly praiseworthy: they are "nurs'ries of the arts" (693). The poet praises Joshua Reynolds—who can turn "a dull blank" into "A lucid mirror, in which Nature sees/ All her reflected features" (700–702)—the sculptor John Bacon, and the powers of sculpture in general. He also appears to admire the achievements of "philosophy" and of commerce—although his comparison of London as the thriving mart of commerce with ancient Babylon, the city of captivity, qualifies the positive implications of his presentation. His damnation of London is far more emphatic than his praise; it centers on the evils of urban activity, the injustice and hypocrisies of a life where "civilized" forms have quite replaced moral content.

The argument of the first book is now complete: Cowper has both asserted and demonstrated the value of aesthetic contemplation of the natural world; he has opposed to his insistence on nature's aesthetic value an equally clear awareness of the dangers of participation in worldly activity. He has suggested repeatedly that art is necessarily inferior to nature, although art provides useful analogies for the understanding of nature—and nature for

the proper appreciation of art. And he has hinted that commitment to the
life of imagination may be dangerous: the perception through which man
sees, the memory with which he recalls satisfying sights, the judgment with
which he guards against moral danger—all these human faculties are more
unambiguously valuable than the fancy. The final lines of the book, beginning, "God made the country, and man made the town," sum up these
implications.

> What wonder then that health and virtue, gifts
> That can alone make sweet the bitter draught
> That life holds out to all, should most abound
> And least be threaten'd in the fields and groves?
>
> (750–53)

Nature's lack of threat to passive man is as significant a value as her more
positive virtues. But the ultimate value is once more aesthetic. Cowper abandons city-dwellers to their own element: they "taste no scenes/ But such as
art contrives" (756–57). Then he returns to the "scenes" which interest him
more, the groves and birds and moonlight of the country, whose aesthetic
appeal is now systematically contrasted with that achieved by human art and
artifice. The conclusion strikes a strong moral note:

> Folly such as your's,
> Grac'd with a sword, and worthier of a fan,
> Has made, what enemies could ne'er have done,
> Our arch of empire, stedfast but for you,
> A mutilated structure, soon to fall.
>
> (770–74)

This final condemnation of those who live in cities is justified by reference
to no sin more serious than their preference of opera singers to birds, lamp-
light to moonlight. In Cowper's ethical system, however, such lapses of
judgment, such willing acceptance of inferior sorts of perception, amount to
genuine moral failing. He has not yet fully revealed the basis for his consistent
association of strong perceptual response to nature with moral uprightness;
it emerges completely in the fifth book, paradoxically one of the sections of
the poem least obviously concerned with nature.

Book V, despite its title ("The Winter Morning Walk"), is a record
primarily of man reflecting rather than man perceiving. It begins with a
hundred and seventy-five lines of description and meditation on nature and
man in nature, but the succeeding seven hundred and thirty lines virtually
abandon nature as subject. Yet the problem of perception is once more central

to the argument of the book, although liberty and permanence are the subjects which most clearly unify the poet's concerns.

The opening lines present a direct record of perception, visual awareness modulating imperceptibly into moral. The sun, at first an image of great power, loses force as it rises. First "with ruddy orb/ Ascending, [it] fires th'horizon" (1–2); the regal associations of *orb* support the sense of potency in the image of the sun "firing" the whole horizon. By line 4, the sun is no longer an orb, but merely a disk. Two lines later, "his slanting ray/ Slides ineffectual down the snowy vale" (6–7); with an increasing sense of the sun's ineffectuality we learn that now its power consists merely in "tinging all with his own rosy hue" (8)—a considerable falling-off, both visually and conceptually, from the energy which fired the horizon. Finally, the sun creates shadows; the observer in the scene is thus united with "ev'ry herb and ev'ry spiry blade" (9), which, like him, cast their shadows. When the human participant in the natural scene reflects on the import of his shadow he announces, with surprising levity, one of the major themes of this book. The relative impermanence of man and his achievements will come to seem more and more important as the book proceeds; here, on the other hand, the poet's verbal attempt to assert his own transience is immediately counteracted by the enduring reality of nature, which seems infinitely more significant. The transience of man is almost a joke; recognition of it coincides with awareness of the visual grotesqueness of the shadow's transformation of well-proportioned limb to lean shank.

> Mine, spindling into longitude immense,
> In spite of gravity and sage remark
> That I myself am but a fleeting shade,
> Provokes me to a smile. With eye askance
> I view the muscular proportion'd limb
> Transform'd to a lean shank.
>
> (11-16)

The observer, perceiving the natural world sharply, feels himself essentially a part of that world; his abstract awareness that he is "but a fleeting shade" is far less compelling than the comic visual reality of distorting shadow, and the pleasure derived from perception of that reality.

The revelatory power of nature is important throughout this description.

> the bents,
> And coarser grass, upspearing o'er the rest,
> Of late unsightly and unseen, now shine

> Conspicuous, and, in bright apparel clad
> And fledg'd with icy feathers, nod superb.
>
> (22–26)

Frost makes the unseen seeable, the unsightly beautiful. This natural power is meaningful not, as in Thomson, primarily for the kind of energy it manifests, but for the transformed world it displays. The display implies the great kinships of nature—weeds metaphorically unite with men by being "clad" in "apparel," with birds by being "fledged with . . . feathers"—but its chief impact is visual. Similarly, as the vignette continues, it directs our attention chiefly to the visual effect of mourning cattle, working man, scampering dog, and only secondarily to the implications of order and permanence in the description of the haystack, for example, or even of the woodman moving "right toward the mark" (53).

Reflection about what happens to various kinds of animals and insects in winter leads Cowper to the two central images of Book V: the frozen surroundings of the waterfall and the ice palace of Empress Anna of Russia. The waterfall itself is too forceful to be "bound" by frost, but the mist it throws off freezes into fantastic and compelling forms. "See," the poet commands, with Thomsonian emphasis,

> where it [the frost] has hung th' embroider'd banks
> With forms so various, that no pow'rs of art,
> The pencil or the pen, may trace the same!
>
> (107–9)

Once more the specific "scene" raises the issue of nature's relation to art; once more Cowper insists that neither the painter nor the poet can capture the beauty of natural reality. Art is clearly inadequate as the "mirror" of nature; if it aspires to mirror, it must fail. (Elsewhere in the poem, Cowper explains that the mind of the artist is a mirror, and that the responsibility of the poet is

> T'arrest the fleeting images that fill
> The mirror of the mind, and hold them fast,
> And force them sit till he has pencil'd off
> A faithful likeness of the forms he views.
>
> [II, 290–93]

Art—specifically poetry—may provide a mirror for nature, but in a moral, not an aesthetic sense; Cowper describes his "stream" of poetry as "reflecting clear,/ If not the virtues, yet the worth, of brutes" [VI, 723–24].) Continuing to describe the wonders of the frozen landscape, Cowper concentrates on suggestion more than precise visual detail: "Here grotto within grotto safe defies/ The sunbeam" (117-18). The reader is invited to consider the significance, the mystery of the frost's achievement as well as to "see" its manifestations. And the poet concludes his treatment of this magical creation with yet another extended and emphatic statement of nature's superiority to art:

> Thus nature works as if to mock at art,
> And in defiance of her rival pow'rs;
> By these fortuitous and random strokes
> Performing such inimitable feats
> As she with all her rules can never reach.
>
> (122–26)

Gone is Pope's sense of the essential, inevitable harmony between art and nature; now the two are "rival powers," with nature clearly the victor. Nature's aesthetic superiority to art is clearly explained:

> The growing wonder takes a thousand shapes
> Capricious, in which fancy seeks in vain
> The likeness of some object seen before.
>
> (119–21)

The fancy, the human creative power which produces art, is limited, Locke had explained, to forming new combinations or interpretations of objects (or parts of objects) previously perceived. It cannot create anything entirely new, completely unrelated to earlier perception. Nature as artist, on the other hand, suffers from no such limitation: its creations bear no likeness to any object seen before. Only nature can provide new material for fancy to work upon. The perceptual grounds for its aesthetic superiority to art are perfectly apparent.

The man-made ice palace contrasted with the nature-created grottoes also offers aesthetic appeals—despite the fact that it is "less worthy of applause, though more admir'd" (126). Its attractiveness, however, derives largely from the illusion it creates of permanence and accordingly of man's dominance over nature.

> though smooth
> And slipp'ry the materials, yet frost-bound
> Firm as a rock. Nor wanted aught within,

> That royal residence might well befit,
> For grandeur or for use.
>
> (154–58)

But it is, after all, a "brittle prodigy" (154); the moral satisfaction of considering its "evanescent glory, once a stream,/ And soon to slide into a stream again" (167–68) counteracts the aesthetic satisfaction of contemplating its apparent permanence and order. "In such a palace Poetry might place/ The armory of Winter" (138–39), Cowper observes; this idea causes him to consider the power of winter, which produces "snow, that often blinds the trav'ler's course,/And wraps him in an unexpected tomb" (142–43). No human structure adequately contains the menace of winter; if the lamps within the palace seem "Another moon new risen, or meteor fall'n/ From heav'n to earth, of lambent flame serene" (152–53), it is only by an illusion of human perception. The apparently successful manipulation of nature by man is temporary, soon to vanish, offering but the pretence of permanence.

The complex combination of immediately perceived solidity with intellectually recognized evanescence makes the ice palace the type of all human achievement; for this reason it provides an underlying metaphor throughout the rest of Book V. Its metaphoric value is underlined at the end of the description:

> Alas; 'twas but a mortifying stroke
> Of undesign'd serenity, that glanc'd
> (Made by a monarch) on her own estate,
> On human grandeur and the courts of kings.
> 'Twas transient in its nature, as in show
> 'Twas durable.
>
> (169–74)

The "mortifying stroke" is the palace's sliding back into a stream. The palace is the emblem of princely endeavor, which may struggle for dominance "by pyramids and mausolean pomp" (182), by building; or by destroying, provoking wars in which kings make "the sorrows of mankind their sport" (186). The desire of kings to assert their power in tangible form causes war, but war originated, Cowper explains, in man's attempt to extend his dominance over nature, when he "had begun to call/ These meadows and that range of hills his own" (222–23). Continuing his discussion of warfare and of the presumption of kings, the poet defines the king's pride: it consists in thinking "the world was made in vain, if not for him" (271). Man persists in believing that he is in some real sense master of the natural world; it is an odd corollary that he should believe that some are fit to be masters of others, even though a king is a man

> Compounded and made up like other men
> Of elements tumultuous, in whom lust
> And folly in as ample measure meet
> As in the bosoms of the slaves he rules.
>
>   (307-10)

So it is that man loses his freedom in his political institutions: through a misinterpretation of his own humble position in the universe which remotely parallels the misinterpretation involved in believing an ice palace to be permanent or its lights to be equivalent to the moon.

We are not directly reminded of the ice palace, however, until the very end of the discussion of political liberty, when Cowper returns to the metaphor of building:

> We turn to dust, and all our mightiest works
> Die too:
>
> .   .   .   .
>
> We build with what we deem eternal rock:
> A distant age asks where the fabric stood.
>
>   (531-32, 534-35)

The state itself can be described as an "old castle" (525); the entire issue of political liberty is evanescent as the ice palace in comparison with the far more fundamental problem of spiritual liberty which Cowper next considers.

The essence of spiritual liberty is its permanence, in comparison with which nature itself seems transient. In His visible works, God,

> finding an interminable space
> Unoccupied, has fill'd the void so well,
> And made so sparkling what was dark before.
> But these are not his glory.
>
>   (556-59)

On aesthetic grounds, man supposes that "so fair a scene" (560) must be eternal—as he supposes the permanence of the ice palace on the basis of visual evidence (the adjective *sparkling*, like *glitter* in the lines quoted below, may remind one of the connection between the two phenomena). Yet nature, considered in terms of the divine plan, is merely another sort of artifice, the product of an "artificer divine" (561) who has Himself "pronounc'd it transient, glorious as it is" (563) because He values spiritual, not physical, permanence. Cowper's values are similar; he elaborates for almost two hundred lines on the value, the essentiality, of spiritual liberty. Yet the resolution of the discussion of spiritual freedom accepts once more the profound aesthetic value of nature, and makes the ability to perceive this value a touchstone of one's spiritual state.

> He is the freeman whom the truth makes free,
> And all are slaves beside.
>
> . . . .
>
> He looks abroad into the varied field
> Of nature, and, though poor perhaps compar'd
> With those whose mansions glitter in his sight,
> Calls the delightful scen'ry all his own.
>
> . . . .
>
> Are they not his by a peculiar right,
> And by an emphasis of int'rest his,
> Whose eye they fill with tears of holy joy,
> Whose heart with praise, and whose exalted mind
> With worthy thoughts of that unwearied love
> That plann'd, and built, and still upholds, a world
> So cloth'd with beauty for rebellious man?
>   (733–34, 738–41, 748–54)

The beauty of the world is God's special gift to man; visual "possession" of "delightful scenery" is more valuable than wealth. Moreover, true aesthetic response to nature depends on a proper relation with God:

> Acquaint thyself with God, if thou would'st taste
> His works. Admitted once to his embrace,
> Thou shalt perceive that thou wast blind before:
> Thine eye shall be instructed; and thine heart,
> Made pure, shall relish, with divine delight
> Till then unfelt, what hands divine have wrought.
>   (779–84)

Understanding of God's dominance over nature (in contrast to the false belief in man's control of nature) produces the perception which distinguishes men from brutes (see 785–90), gives the soul "new faculties" (806) which enable it to discern "in all things, what, with stupid gaze/ Of ignorance, till then she overlook'd" (808–9). When man holds converse with the stars, the special significance of the "shining hosts" (822) is that they "view/ Distinctly scenes invisible to man" (825–26); heightened perception is a metaphysical goal. The "lamp of truth" enables man to "read" nature (845); and liberty itself "like

day,/ Breaks on the soul, and by a flash from heav'n/ Fires all the faculties
with glorious joy" (883–85).

> In that blest moment Nature, throwing wide
> Her veil opaque, discloses with a smile
> The author of her beauties, who, retir'd
> Behind his own creation, works unseen
> By the impure.
>
> (891–95)

If God is the source of proper perception, He is also the *end* of perception:
this is the final word of Book V. The fired faculties which liberty creates
lead man ultimately to God, healing the potential and sometimes actual split
felt between God and nature as objects of contemplation. The poignant story
which Cowper tells in his *Memoir* is well known: how, exalted and soothed
by contemplation of a marine sunset, he was subsequently overwhelmed
with guilt at the realization that he had sinfully attributed to the power of
nature the psychological healing that could only be due to the power of God.
In the logic of Book V of *The Task* such distinctions virtually disappear—
not because nature and God are identical ("Nature is but a name for an
effect,/ Whose cause is God" [VI, 223–24]), but because the ability to perceive
nature is the result of a proper relation with God, and the heightening of
faculties which makes possible an enlightened aesthetic response to nature
also produces an awareness of how God expresses Himself through nature.
The ability to appreciate the "scenes" which nature provides becomes thus
virtually a test of one's spiritual condition; the belief in the aesthetic superiority of nature to art is not a matter merely of personal response, but a
product of the realization that nature has intrinsic significance which no work
of art can achieve. Elsewhere in *The Task*, some of the most compelling
passages of natural description attempt to define and delineate this significance. The substructure which justifies such attempts is probably most apparent in Book V, itself comparatively bare of description.

For Cowper, then, the act of visual perception, which had provided
subject matter and metaphors for poets throughout the eighteenth-century
development of the poetry of image rather than action, finally takes on metaphysical importance. Thomson had attempted to "see" significance as well
as appearance, Collins had "seen" into a realm of fantasy as well as of reality,
Gray had used contrasting "visions" to create a poetry of tension, Smart had
seen the natural world and then gone beyond his own seeing to establish
connections with a realm of transcendental truth. For Cowper the seeing

itself implied the transcendental truth; the physical power of vision became a spiritual reality.

Donald Davie has remarked of Cowper that he is, "after Ben Jonson, . . . the most neglected of our poets." The neglect is of analysis rather than simply of attention: Cowper has been written about voluminously—as a psychological case, as a representative of piety, as a phenomenon of his century. Few critics, however, have made any serious attempt to examine the source or nature of his poetic effects; those who have tried to describe his poetry often take so large a view that all possibility of accuracy vanishes. Thus we are told, for example, that " 'The Task' resembles the conversation of one dowered with no special gifts of intellect; of an interesting quiet man, of humour and austerity with an intensely human hand-grip." Alternately, its form, "remarquable par sa simplicité audacieuse," is that of fragments of a journal. "To Cowper," another critic observes, "nature is simply a background, . . . essentially a *locus in quo*—a space in which the work and mirth of life pass and are performed." Or we are informed that "his intuition was comparatively superficial, if disinterested, because he never strove to discipline ideas to facts or to interpret facts ideally, but only to invest them with sentiment or reflect upon them." All such statements seem plausible when one considers *The Task* casually as a whole; all lost their plausibility if closely examined in relation to specific passages, which reveal at least a potential unity far more rigorous than that of a conversation or a journal, demonstrate the fundamental importance of nature not as a *locus in quo* but as an object of contemplation, and suggest that Cowper at his best characteristically "interpret[s] facts ideally." It is extremely difficult to generalize accurately about *The Task* because although, as I have attempted to show, an underlying structure of ideas does in fact unify many of its apparently disparate concerns, it remains a poem of details, details which depend upon varied techniques and apparent preoccupations. The poem's variety is particularly confusing with regard to its language. The diction of *The Task* ranges from "poetic" to colloquial, from abstract to concrete, apparently depending on many different principles of control. The magnitude of the poet's concerns emerges vividly through examination of his language.

The prevailing critical attitude toward the diction of *The Task* has been that it is remarkable for its "plainness." In Cowper's own time plainness was thought to be one of his chief poetic merits; thus a reviewer of his first volume observes: "Anxious only to give each image its due prominence and relief, he has wasted no unnecessary attention on grace and embellishment; his language, therefore, though neither strikingly harmonious nor elegant, is plain, forcible, and expressive." Specifically with regard to *The Task*, another of Cowper's contemporaries, remarking "the familiarity of the diction," observes, "The language may sometimes appear below the poetical standard; but he was such a foe to affectation in any shape, that he seems to have avoided nothing so much as the stiff pomposity so common to blank verse writers." More modern critics have echoed this view: "the language is of the purest and finest, but it is not strikingly ornamented. It is without anything unusual in poetic diction." And Thomas Quayle singles out "the moral and didactic portions" as characterized by language "as a rule, uniformly simple and direct."

Yet these judgments, too, seem perplexing when one examines specific passages of *The Task* to find Cowper writing, "The verdure of the plain lies buried deep/ Beneath the dazzling deluge" (V, 21–22), or—for a more extended example—

> Now from the roost, or from the neighb'ring pale,
> Where, diligent to catch the first faint gleam
> Of smiling day, the gossip'd side by side,
> Come trooping at the housewife's well-known call
> The feather'd tribes domestic. Half on wing,
> And half on foot, they brush the fleecy flood,
> Conscious, and fearful of too deep a plunge.
> The sparrows peep, and quit the shelt'ring eaves
> To seize the fair occasion. Well they eye
> The scatter'd grain; and, thievishly resolv'd
> T'escape th' impending famine, often scar'd,
> As oft return—a pert voracious kind.
>
> (V, 58–69)

This is part of the opening description of man, animals and vegetation in a winter landscape. It is not, in its diction, fully characteristic of Cowper's technique, but it demonstrates the dexterity with which the poet turns varied conventions to personal use.

In language and in sentence structure, these lines seem to come from the mid, not the late, eighteenth century. The pseudo-Miltonic inversions, such Thomsonian formulations as "the feather'd tribes domestic," the unrealized personification of "smiling day," the automatic phrase, "the fair occasion," the periphrases of "fleecy flood," "feather'd tribes," "pert voracious kind": all these belong to well-established poetic patterns—patterns which we might expect Cowper to avoid. They seem to be used for familiar reasons: to establish metaphoric links between man and lower forms of nature which will reinforce the reader's sense of some vast natural harmony. One may note Cowper's accuracy of perception in such phrases as "Half on wing/ And half on foot," or the vividness of "brush" (in "they brush the fleecy flood"), the figurative appropriateness of "gossip'd"; still, the impression remains that the passage as a whole is almost pure convention, in language and in concept.

To understand its function in *The Task* one must turn to its context, which significantly modifies the effect of the lines considered in isolation. A few lines taken from either side of the description of the birds may suggest the nature of that context. The first of these passages focuses on an individual animal, sharply perceived in his separateness; the second, although it too is rich in specific detail, is more general. The first makes emphatic use of inversion, and offers the Thomsonian "wide-scamp'ring"; the second has no striking structural peculiarities and its diction provides no special associations. Yet these two descriptions resemble one another far more than they resemble the description of domestic fowl. The voice that speaks in them, although it is not emphatically distinctive, is none the less individual in comparison to that which speaks of a "fleecy flood." One sees here the effect of an eye trained steadfastly upon the object, a mind concerned to discriminate and to define not on the basis of relationships or of categories ("kinds") but in terms of specific individual perceptions.

> Shaggy, and lean, and shrewd, with pointed ears
> And tail cropp'd short, half lurcher and half cur—
> His dog attends him. Close behind his heel
> Now creeps he slow; and now, with many a frisk
> Wide-scamp'ring, snatches up the drifted snow
> With iv'ry teeth, or ploughs it with his snout;
> Then shakes his powder'd coat, and barks for joy.
>   (V, 45–51)

> The very rooks and daws forsake the fields,
> Where neither grub, nor root, nor earth-nut, now
> Repays their labour more; and, perch'd aloft
> By the wayside, or stalking in the path,
> Lean pensioners upon the trav'ler's track,
> Pick up their nauseous dole, though sweet to them,
> Of voided pulse or half-digested grain.
> The streams are lost amid the splendid blank,
> O'erwhelming all distinction.
>   (V, 89–97)

The lines beginning with allusion to the rooks and daws deal with transformations effected by winter, and with the resulting paradoxes: birds forsake their "natural" habitat for traveled roads; the "nauseous dole" voided by the travelers is "sweet to them"; winter creates a "splendid blank,/ O'erwhelming all distinction," while the poet insists precisely on the distinctions of the chill landscape. The passage on the dog, with its emphasis on energetic verbs (*snatches, ploughs, shakes, barks*; the noun *frisk* and the participle *widescamp'ring* also suggest the energy of action), dramatizes the way in which the power of winter may inform the animal kingdom: if it immobilizes water, it intensely animates dogs.

Each of the three passages, then, represents a different way, almost a different principle, of "seeing." The eye focuses on an individual phenomenon in the lines about the dog, discriminates the details of the animal's appearance ("Shaggy, and lean, and shrewd, with pointed ears/ And tail cropp'd short"), then moves on to contemplate the exact nature of his activity. The language of the description is "plain," generally direct, heavily Anglo-Saxon. Interpretation is kept to a minimum, suggested only by the adjective *shrewd* and the phrase "barks for joy"; the scene is self-sufficient, containing its meaning in its details. One sentence is simple, one compound; the coordinate conjunction *and*, occurring six times in the seven lines, is vital in establishing relationships.

In the passage about rooks and daws, a single, elaborate complex sentence occupies seven of the nine lines; the increased complexity of structure is paralleled by heightened dignity of tone. Although direct, simple description remains important, with the plain diction appropriate to it, Latinate words now assume a more significant role. They convey the interpretive judgment of the author in such key terms as *labour, pensioners, nauseous, splendid, distinction*. Meaning as well as appearance is important here; this fact accounts for the heightened dignity of language and structure. The central paradox that privation and beauty are by winter mysteriously connected, a paradox embodied in the phrase "splendid blank," is elaborated both through the specificity with which Cowper details the nature of privation and its compensations and through the generality of his final descriptive allusion to the snow which covers everything.

The heavy stress on established poetic diction in the section on domestic fowl does not obscure the clarity of the poet's observation any more than does the complexity of structure or the relative elevation of language in the lines on rooks and daws. Here, though, the principle of "seeing" is to place observed details in the context of a tradition, to remind the reader of eternal rather than immediate patterns, to insist on the fundamental kinships of the

universe. The descriptive emphasis is on characterization, the special personality of these birds. But unlike the dog's "personality," which is conceived
as his specifically animal nature, the character of the birds is at least analog-
ically human: they "gossip," "troop," compose "domestic" tribes, are "conscious, and fearful," sensitive to the "fair occasion," capable of being
"thievish." Winter, which increases the dependency of the animal kingdom
on man, increases as a consequence human awareness of the links that bind
all creation, so that analogies between the look of sheep and of snow, the
nature of chickens and of the housewife who feeds them, or between sparrows
and children (this barely suggested: but children too might under some circumstances be defined as a "pert voracious kind," although this was not the
typical eighteenth-century view of them), take on true significance.

These three modes of "seeing" the panoramas which winter presents,
with the dictions appropriate to each mode, suggest how functional Cowper's
varieties of perspective and technique can prove. In the early descriptive
section of Book V, the poet demonstrates the nature of that true perception
which by the end of the book he will assert to be a product of man's right
relationship with God. True perception does not depend on anything so
simple as constant assertion of the connections between God and His creation,
but it does involve completeness, wholeness of vision. Such wholeness is the
sum of many parts, many incomplete visions; in this long descriptive portion
of his poem, Cowper isolates and emphasizes various ways of seeing in a
fashion that may prepare us to believe in the significance of their combination.
His variations of technique reflect quite precisely the shifts in emphasis of
his subject matter.

One cannot always believe that Cowper's diction conforms exactly to
the meanings it is intended to convey. His verse seems dependably good
when its content is descriptive, its subject that perception which Cowper
found both emotionally and philosophically so important. Larger portions
of *The Task*, however, are moralistic rather than descriptive; nor does the
moralizing always resolve itself, as in Book V, in terms of the poet's commitment to the value of perception. Book II, "The Time-Piece," for example,
contains no extended treatment of the external world; it is entirely reflective.
Although it includes sections of great vigor and poetic skill, it also displays
Cowper at his worst—and his "worst" is characteristically his most rhetorical.

Considering two particularly weak passages, we may find it hard to
understand why either of them should be poetry rather than prose. By
Coleridge's well-known standard ("whatever lines can be translated into other
words of the same language, without diminution of their significance, either
in sense, or association, or in any worthy feeling, are so far vicious in their

diction"), most of these lines are excellent examples of "vicious diction," in spite of the fact that, with some exceptions, the diction does not call special attention to itself. In the first passage, Cowper considers the institution of preaching; the second deals with an individual exemplar of the institution. Both treatments may be the product of deep conviction, but it is not embodied in any way likely to move a reader. "Men love to be moved, much better than to be instructed," Joseph Warton pointed out; Cowper's calculated rhetoric is only "instructive." Here are the passages:

> The pulpit, therefore (and I name it fill'd
> With solemn awe, that bids me well beware
> With what intent I touch that holy thing)—
> The pulpit (when the sat'rist has at last,
> Strutting and vap'ring in an empty school,
> Spent all his force and made no proselyte)—
> I say the pulpit (in the sober use
> Of its legitimate, peculiar pow'rs)
> Must stand acknowledged, while the world shall stand,
> The most important and effectual guard,
> Support, and ornament, of virtue's cause.
>
> (326–36)

The second selection describes the bad pastor,

> Perverting often, by the stress of lewd
> And loose example, whom he should instruct;
> [he] Exposes, and holds up to broad disgrace
> The noblest function, and discredits much
> The brightest truths that man has ever seen.
> For ghostly counsel; if it either fall
> Below the exigence, or be not back'd
> With show of love, at least with hopeful proof
> Of some sincerity on th' giver's part;
> Or be dishonour'd, in th' exterior form
> And mode of its conveyance, by such tricks
> As move derision, or by foppish airs
> And histrionic mumm'ry, that let down
> The pulpit to the level of the stage;
> Drops from the lips a disregarded thing.
>
> (551–65)

The repeated, self-conscious parentheses of the first passage, the artifice of the reiterated phrase "the pulpit," which produces an inadvertent comic effect, the factitious-seeming indignation in the denunciation of the satirist, the padding in such phrases as "solemn awe" and "well beware," even the relatively skillful play on *stand*—all these contribute to one's sense that the poet as contriver has here superseded the poet as expresser of felt, perceived or imagined reality. The passage has almost the effect of parody. One believes in the existence of the felt reality, but not that Cowper is committed to it; his obvious concern with the proper mode of expression seems strangely isolated from what he has to say, seems not a concern for the best way to convey emotion or meaning so much as for the moral posture appropriate to a man of his convictions. In the second passage, the moral posture itself seems suspect: is "*show* of love," with its conceivable implication of hypocrisy, really adequate for the "good" pastor? or is merely "hopeful proof/ Of some sincerity"? The poet concerns himself almost entirely with appearances, with what he himself calls "th' exterior form/ And mode of . . . conveyance" of divine truths; yet he appears to make a distinction between exterior forms and what he evidently considers inner reality—reality demonstrated by "show of love" or "proof/ Of some sincerity." In the actual concerns of the passage, then, form and content blur, and exterior forms assume dispropor-tionate importance—just such importance as they seem to assume in the poetic rendering of the ideas, which itself has some aspect of "histrionic mumm'ry." The language of the passage, with the possible exception of the word *exigence*, is quite ordinary and straightforward; its structure, with its deliberate slowness and suspension, moving with measured pace toward the calculated anticlimax of "disregarded thing," seems anything but straight-forward, and its contrived complexity reflects no corresponding complexity of thought.

One striking fact about the relatively weak moralistic sections of *The Task* is that they are so radically different in technique from the worst of Cowper's hymns. If the special talent manifested in the hymns is the ability to turn the perceptive faculty inward, to define and render directly certain sorts of psychic activity and psychic stasis without significant recourse to visual metaphor, the talent which created *The Task* seems adept at rendering inner states by suggestion, through reference to and reliance on imagery of the external world. Conversely, the hymns at their worst depend most heavily on metaphor; *The Task*, whose central subject is concrete reality in its spiritual context, is at its worst often almost bare of imagery, lapsing into concern only with abstractions. There is a kind of metaphor (although a weak and sketchy one) in "ghostly counsel" dropping, a "disregarded thing"; aside from that, and the vague metaphoric possibilities of *touch* in line 328, *empty school* in line 330, the only metaphor in the two passages is "The brightest truth that man has ever seen," a reference characteristic of Cowper's conventional interest in light as an emblem of spiritual reality, but hardly more than a reference.

But if these passages manifest little distinct visual awareness, they also demonstrate little psychic awareness. What "perception" they display seems theoretical ("philosophical," Cowper might say) rather than direct, the product of what the poet has been told, not what he has himself "seen." Cut off from his deepest sources of feeling, he produces impoverished language; the more barren sections of *The Task*, which by implication deny the validity of that very perception that the poem at its best strongly affirms, are boring. "Where the Idea is accurate, the terms will be so too; and wherever you find the words hobble, you may conclude the notion was lame; otherwise they wou'd both have had an equal and graceful pace." So wrote John Constable, and his terms suggest an appropriate vocabulary to indict Cowper at his worst.

But Cowper also had at his disposal strikingly individual language. Trying to describe the writer characterized by "simplicity" (a term which in his usage as in Collins's has rather complex implications), Hugh Blair observes, "There are no marks of art in his expression; it seems the very language of nature; you see in the Style, not the writer and his labour, but the man, in his own natural character." The distinction he makes is difficult to enforce, but it seems appropriate to one of Cowper's characteristic modes, a mode which defines his most personal ways of perceiving. "All we behold is miracle," Cowper points out, "but, seen/ So duly, all is miracle in vain" (VI, 132–33). The statement might serve as text for *The Task*, which at its best uncovers the miracle of the commonplace, sometimes employing a distinctive rhetoric to emphasize its revelations. Divine power operates "all in sight of inattentive man" (VI, 120); the poet's responsibility is to make man more attentive, so that his "sight" will be more significant. Man sees the dearth of winter; he should be conscious simultaneously of the richness it foretells.

> But let the months go by, a few short months,
> And all shall be restor'd. These naked shoots,
> Barren as lances, among which the wind
> Makes wintry music, sighing as it goes,
> Shall put their graceful foliage on again,
> And, more aspiring, and with ampler spread,
> Shall boast new charms, and more than they have lost.
>
> (VI, 140–46)

Both the lines about miracle and the first line of this description employ rhetorical repetition. Unlike the reiteration of "the pulpit" in the moralizing passage, this duplication is a device of progression rather than of suspension. It intensifies an atmosphere of calm assurance (defined particularly by the grand inclusiveness of "all shall be restor'd") instead of creating, like the other repetitive pattern, merely a sense of dogged determination. Now Cowper relies heavily on metaphoric suggestion, both the conventional associations of *aspiring* and *boast*, and a more complex and personal effect in the description of "naked shoots,/ Barren as lances." The defencelessness implied by *naked* is immediately denied when the nakedness becomes that of an aggressive weapon. But the implications of *lances* are in turn opposed by the further transformation of lances into musical instruments; and the fact that the music derives from the "sighing" of the wind adds a final degree of perceptual and emotional complexity. The beauty of winter is as real as that of spring, although it is beauty of an entirely different order. Nature embodies the Christian sequence of death and resurrection. The poem directs one's attention to the beauties of winter as well as those of spring, to the beauty of apparent death and that of rebirth, reinforcing the aesthetic contrast by the opposition between the conventional language of personalization applied to spring and the more direct, personal language through which winter is evoked.

This passage continues with one of the catalogues so characteristic of Cowper, introduced by a generalization couched entirely in "poetic diction," in a form which reminds one of the associations of that diction with the language of science.

> Then, each in its peculiar honours clad,
> Shall publish, even to the distant eye,
> Its family and tribe. Laburnum, rich
> In streaming gold; syringa, iv'ry pure;
> The scentless and the scented rose; this red
> And of an humbler growth, the other tall,
> And throwing up into the darkest gloom
> Of neighb'ring cypress, or more sable yew,
> Her silver globes, light as the foamy surf
> That the wind severs from the broken wave;
> The lilac, various in array, now white,
> Now sanguine, and her beauteous head now set
> With purple spikes pyramidal, as if,

Studious of ornament, yet unresolv'd
Which hue she most approv'd, she chose them all.
                                    (VI, 147–61)

This is slightly less than half the full catalogue, but it suggests the technique
and quality of the whole. The imagined conjunction of flowers is complexly
perceived, with reference to form (*streaming, globes, pyramidal*), color, balance
and contrast ("The scentless and the scented rose," tall and short, dark and
light, white and purple), and metaphor. Metaphors of richness (*gold, iv'ry,
silver, ornament*) dominate the scene, and two key images insist on relationships among the parts of the created universe: the emphatic association of
the "silver globes" of the rose with the bits of surf "severed" from the wave,
and the description of the lilac as a human belle.

The powerful effect of this catalogue depends heavily on the relationship
between the directness of the diction (only *sable, sanguine,* possibly *beauteous*
and *gloom,* have predominantly poetic associations; the adjectives and nouns
which carry the weight of the description are on the whole precise and limited
in their individual meanings) and the elaboration of the picture and meaning
created by the simple language. As Cowper saw in the naked branches of
winter a rapidly shifting range of meanings, he perceives in a static panorama
of spring and summer flowers so many sorts of meaning and relationship—
visual and "philosophic"—that his presentation of the scene pulses with energy.
The source of that energy, and its significance, become explicit at the end:

From dearth to plenty, and from death to life,
Is Nature's progress when she lectures man
In heav'nly truth; evincing, as she makes
The grand transition, that there lives and works
A soul in all things, and that soul is God.
The beauties of the wilderness are his,
That makes so gay the solitary place
Where no eye sees them.
                                    (VI, 181–88)

The "lecture" nature offers is the revelation that there is no separation,
finally, between the visual glory (or, for that matter, the visual barrenness)
of the natural world and its theological meaning. The vibrant "soul in all
things" need only be recognized; perception of its energy is part of Cowper's
direct relation-seeking poetic perception of the imagined scene itself. The
force of that perception, expressed through unpretentious but intricately

organized language, leads the poet finally to the realization that meaning and beauty are inherent in the natural world independently of the perceiver—"Where no eye sees them." The perceiver, even at the beginning of this passage, is only a "distant eye"; the splendor of the scene does not depend on human perception. In this pageant of inanimate nature, the vegetative world finally embodies full richness, dignity, even hints of eroticism ("her beauteous head"). God's plenty is here; religious, aesthetic, emotional meaning fuse. The greatest achievement of *The Task* (not only here; in other passages as well) is this fusion. In the hymns, Cowper conveyed his fear that man must move inevitably from an infantile state of pure dependence and complete comfort to an anguished awareness of conflict and the loss of peace, comfort. Elsewhere in *The Task*, he reminds us that the eye is "guiltless": no blame can attach to aesthetic contemplation; passivity is associated with lack of vice. In the flower passage, contemplation is not merely guiltless; it becomes essentially an act of worship, of such total worship that it involves the poet's entire sensibility—his desire for peace, for beauty, for piety; his emotional and religious yearnings, his intellectual convictions. The act of visual perception has finally become fully inclusive as it leads Cowper back to his ideal state of faith and ease.

JOHN L. GREENWAY

Macpherson's Ossian
and the Nordic Bard as Myth

Few now tremble at the dauntless heroism of Fingal, and none of us, I fear, are tempted to don Werther's yellow vest and share the misty signs of Temora. Indeed, the noble passions of this Last of the Bards have been treated with a neglect less than benign. Though we no longer read Ossian, we do read writers who, convinced of his authenticity, attempt to recapture what they imagine to be that synthesis of vigor and sentiment possessed by their Northern ancestors. As I have already implied, I propose to take Ossian seriously, and to suggest that he functioned as a mythic narrative for a modern era—"mythic" not in the Enlightenment sense of "falsehood," but in the more recent sense of "symbolic apprehension of reality." But what can Ossian have to do with reality?

Let us consider for a moment the nature and function of mythic narrative. The myths of a culture provide an orientation for man's moral experience in that they bestow an objective status upon values of the present, preserving them from relativism. Myths of gods and heroes show that the paradigms for human action not only exist outside man, but can be a part of genesis itself; that is, present values are legitimized, transferred from the profane world to the sacred by projecting them *in illo tempore* (to use Mircea Eliade's term): a static time of creation when a culture's truths were established. I see Ossian and his imitators as doing essentially the same thing, and on a pre-rational level of cultural consciousness—legitimizing the values

From *Studies in Eighteenth-Century Culture* 4 (1975). © 1975 by the American Society for Eighteenth-Century Studies. Originally entitled "The Gateway to Innocence: Ossian and the Nordic Bard as Myth."

of sentimental primitivism through a mythic narrative (the Ossianic poems) which showed that sentimental views of human nature, virtue, and vice were really present at the dawn of Northern, *non*-classical civilization.

This brings us to a second point about myth, one which in a sense distinguishes modern myths such as Ossian from pre-scientific myths. The anthropologist Malinowski has noted that while we see myth, rite, and ritual as symbolic, the believer does not: to him, the constructs of myth are empirically real. Modern man, however, defines truth in terms of rational thought, and either tends to see myth as falsehood, or as symbolizing an empirical or conceptual content. But, as Cassirer and others have shown, the impulse to myth-making is not negated by reason, for modern myths must maintain their objectivity in *two* realms: first, as narratives expressing spontaneously the world of feeling, and second, as historical, empirical fact. As an illustration of this, the assumed literary merit of Ossian was predicated upon his historicity; indeed, this was the most important single fact about the forgeries, in that Ossian's status as historical document objectified values, much as ritual validates rites by presenting them to a receptive audience as reenactments of sacred paradigms of the *illud tempus*. As a means of organizing values, myth is neither true nor false—it is expressive or inexpressive.

Ossian validated and gave factual status to several primitivist fantasies of the Nordic past. Basically, the Ossianic poems fused in one symbolic universe what had been a paradox since the first humanist attempts to build a national past upon Tacitus' *Germania*, first edited in the fifteenth century. This paradox, simply stated, was that enthusiasts for Germanic valor such as Conrad Celtis could admire our heroic ancestors for their martial vigor and, at the same time, following Tacitus, point to tribes of chaste, democratic, freedom-loving (Humanist) Teutons. Obviously, one part of this mythic construct ran counter to another, older view, which helps to give substance to the paradox; that is, this very martial vigor destroyed classical culture, and brought on what Renaissance scholars called those dark "Ages in the Middle." In the eighteenth century, Shaftesbury was not alone in identifying "Gothic" with "barbaric," and the dual nature of the myth continued even into the next century.

Before Ossian, the "nobler qualities of the mind" necessary to complement the fascinating barbarity of the North in a primitivist myth had to be supplied by conjecture. In 1763, the year of *Temora's* appearance, Bishop Percy complained that "many pieces on the gentler subjects" must exist, but that they simply have not been edited. With the appearance of the Ossianic poems, however, there was no longer need for apologies or conjectures such as the German Humanists of the sixteenth and Swedish historians of the seventeenth-century Great Power Era had had to make, for the mythic imagination had received its document.

As myth, Ossian was more expressive than Homer, his southern counterpart, in that his poems expressed no moral ambivalence. The Humanists had seen history in terms of a struggle between virtue and vice (witness the popularity of Virgil), but this makes a balanced conflict difficult to portray in a moral narrative. In *Temora*, Macpherson is ingenious; in the first book he kills off the villain, whose noble brother Cathmor is obliged by honor to oppose the mighty Fingal. Macpherson was then able to sustain his narrative by more than token opposition to Fingal's moral (hence, martial) invincibility.

Fingal fights only defensive wars (*Fingal*), or he fights the *bellum justum* to further social justice (*Temora*). "My arm was the support of the injured," he says, "but the weak rested behind the lightning of my steel." Fingal thus functioned paradigmatically, in fulfillment of one of the great Enlightenment axioms that emancipated valor must triumph over tyranny and idolatry. This Fingal does, always.

The legacy of barbarism, which was an integral part of the myth of the Nordic past, is also present in the Ossianic poems. Macpherson assigns this role to the Scandinavians; and Starno, in the poem "Cath-Loda," is a repository for all the pejorative connotations of "Gothic." But even though we find that his Scandinavians are barbaric, tyrannous idolaters, Macpherson's "Caledonians" are not, as his notes make clear. And though Ossian believes in spirits, Fingal's defeat of the Scandinavian chimera "Cruth-Loda" indicates that neither Fingal nor Ossian was an idolator nor obnoxiously superstitious.

Within this large universe legitimizing truths that the Enlightenment held to be "self-evident," Ossian also validated several other literary myths, among them that of the spontaneous perception of nature by the primitive poet. W. K. Wimsatt has pointed out that in eighteenth-century literature it was not easy to express a sense of animate or "souled" nature, for the conscious use of mythology was generally restricted to decorative, intellectual allegory. When the setting of the poem was temporalized, however, and the narration placed in the *illud tempus* of the Nordic past, it was possible to create the illusion of the naive experience of Northern nature for the modern reader, by giving him the impression that the poem is being narrated by a naive *Volksdichter* as the reader reads it. Northrop Frye calls this technique that of "poem-as-process," saying that "Where there is a sense of literature as process, pity and fear become states of mind without objects, moods which are common to the work of art and the reader, and which bind them together psychologically instead of separating them aesthetically." Herder used this technique in his *Abhandlung über den Ursprung der Sprache* to recreate for the reader the illusion of the creative process of the primitive mind:

> Since all of nature sounds, nothing is more natural to a sensuous human being than to think that it lives, that it speaks, that it acts. That savage saw the tall tree with its mighty crown and sensed the wonder of it; the crown rustled! There the godhead moves and stirs! The savage falls down in adoration! Behold, that is the story of sensuous man, the dark link by which nouns are fashioned from verbs.

Herder was not the only critic attempting to convey the illusion of process in essays describing the creative process of the primitive, though what others did was sometimes derivative; for example, certain data concerning the "wild" Nordic nature appear to have been taken from *The Castle of Otranto*. But Macpherson employed the illusion in what became mythic narratives. The belief in Ossian's authenticity implied that "poem-as-process" had been an actual technique of the primitive Northern poet.

Macpherson's creation of the illusion of process and his validation of the technique are actually rather sophisticated—sophisticated in that the reader is taken through time by several devices. The first element is his use of the mythic figure of the naive *Volksdichter*, the Bard. Bishop Percy and Thomas Gray had been central in establishing this persona in the 1760's. Here I will mention only briefly Thomas Gray's ode "The Bard" (1757), which was central to the establishing of the *Volksdichter* as a narrative persona in the 1760s. Gray employs the knavish Edward I and the naive national Bard of the Golden Age, and as the last of the bards "plunged to endless night," the Golden Age ended and the modern, fallen world began.

Ossian as Bard was a principal part of Macpherson's mythmaking, establishing a psychological tie from the historical present to the mythic past, and part of the success of the "ancient epics" was owing to Macpherson's structuring of these poems. By means of a fairly complex point of view, he managed to create the illusion that the reader was experiencing directly the "raw nature and noble passion" of his ancestors. Ossian, near death, a death that will mark the end of the Golden Age (it always does, in these cases), is singing to Malvina, the fiancée of his dead son Oscar, "a song of the days of old," in which Fingal, Ossian's father, is the principal character. In all this, the illusion of the spontaneous process is maintained by several devices: Ossian can make himself a character in his own poem and by doing so remind one that there is a narrator ("I walked over the heath"); or he can remind one of the narrator by breaking his own narration ("Malvina! Why that tear?

Oscar is not dead yet"). We participate in the Golden Age through the naive songs of the Bard, yet we are constantly made aware that it is coming to an end, and our own unheroic time is beginning.

Ossian as myth legitimized as being "Nordic" not only the naive Bard and the illusion of process, but a particular kind of imagery used to express this spontaneous relationship to nature. Indeed, one of the merits of Ossian, and one of the inadequacies of his imitators, was just this use of sympathetic imagery (where nature is an extension of character or mood) to integrate landscape into the action. For instance, when things are going badly for the noble Cuchullin, Macpherson's use of sympathetic imagery both amplifies the impending disaster and isolates the warrior by focusing down upon him: "The winds came down on the woods. The torrents rushed from the rocks. Rain gathered round the heads of Cromla. And the red stars trembled between the flying clouds. Sad by the side of a stream whose sound was ecchoed by a tree, sad by the side of a stream the chief of Erin sat." (One of the facts that had filtered out of Antiquarian editing was that Northern poetry was alliterative.)

Macpherson's notes are an integral part of Ossian-as-myth, for they provide a constant empirical commentary, emphasising the historicity and verisimilitude of the poems. They also make of Ossian an epic counterpart to Homer, Virgil, and Milton, showing that though Ossian expressed a superior Northern morality, he obeyed the "general rules" of the epic. A growing accretion of appended commentary elaborated upon this, beginning with Hugh Blair's essay. In Germany, Denis translated the poems into hexameters, adding his own notes and those of Cesarotti to the poems and to Blair's essay as well.

Initially, then, Ossian served to provide an epic Northern counterpart to Homer, unifying the genesis of the primitive Nordic genius in the minds of the primitivists, as Madame de Staël illustrates in *De la littérature*. Secondly, and more importantly, Ossian's mythic function as the objectification of the Northern muse helped break down the stigma of Northern barbarity, in that he either modified the view of the Nordic past or shaped reactions to it. Ossian could animate the nostalgia of Denis for the lost Lieder of Charlemagne, while in Denmark, Blicher saw the same virtues celebrated in Ossian and in the Icelandic sagas. Ossian's main function, however, was as a mythic paradigm, a touchstone for contemporary poets. If we look at the Ossianic poems and those they inspired, we see that Macpherson enjoyed a relationship to the Golden Age unavailable to other moderns. He was actually a kind of modern folk poet, transmitting primal truth in a quasi-oracular form, not creating on his own. In the Swedish poet Thomas Thorild we can see this difference between Macpherson and his imitators. Though Thorild felt himself to be part of Ossian's Golden Age ("You should have seen me . . . when I first saw the sun set in Glysisvall, when with Ossian I can feel [*sic*] the shades of heroes about me"), his creativity was limited to incantation, not recreation of the naive experience:

> Stream exultation! To You, ah, You immortal, gentle, All-ele- vating; you Nature, my trembling harp is tuned. Silently weave about me, spirit of Ossian!

The Ossianic muse came to dubious fruition in Germany with the "Bardic Movement," sustained by a group of mediocre poets who were primed by a bowdlerized version of Herder's concept of *Volkspoesie*, but who were not galvanized into imitation until they encountered the paradigms of Ossian, the Bard, and Germania. Most of these poets exist today only in literary histories and dissertations, for their poetry functioned as myth for only a few years in the 1760's—during the first Ossianic craze—and was particularly vulnerable to the dialectic process that ultimately overtook Ossian himself.

The mythic aspect of the Bardic lyrics was almost immediately inade- quate; as it not only objectified contemporary literary values (Ossian being the paradigm), but also depended upon an assumption of historical objectiv- ity, the Bards' myth was fatally vulnerable in two areas. First, it succumbed to the revolutionary effects of Herder's conjectures concerning the literary imagination; second, to philology.

The idol of the Germanic Bards was Klopstock, who read Ossian before reading about Norse mythology: Klopstock's "Nordic" poems and dramas are predicated upon the superiority of an Ossian-constituted Teutonic muse to that of the artificial South. In "Der Hügel und der Hain" (1767), the Southern poet is defeated in the battle for a modern poet's soul by a Bard who sings of "souled nature," and whose Telyn (a musical instrument) sounds "Fatherland."

Though Klopstock is widely cited as inaugurating a new sensibility of nature into German poetry, it is clear that his poetic convention could not assimilate a subject-matter intrinsically "Teutonic," not even such a Teutonic subject matter as the Golden Age of Ossian's invention. In 1767, for instance, Klopstock "Nordicized" his ode "An des Dichters Freunde" (1747), merely by removing Apollo and plugging in Braga: "Would you be verses, O song? Or, / Unsubmissive, like Pindar's songs, / Like Zeus' noble, intoxicated son,/ Whirl free from the creating soul?" became "Would you be verses, O heroic song? / Would you soar lawless, like Ossian's flight, / Like Uller's dance upon sea-crystal, / Free from the poet's soul?"

But such was the momentary power of this myth to constitute reality that Lessing could praise lines like the following from Klopstock's drama *Hermanns Schlacht* (1769) as being "completely in the ancient German manner" (Hermann speaks): "Noble lady of my youth! Yes, I live, my Thusnelda! Arise, you free princess of Germany! I have not loved you before, as today! Has my Thusnelda brought me flowers?" Klopstock, too, was convinced that this was pretty accurate dialogue, and footnotes the morality of his Teutons. The central role of Ossian in this drama is obvious, except that Klopstock has choruses of Bards chanting "Höret Thaten der vorigen Zeit!" whereas Macpherson had been content with Ossian's beginning "A song of the days of old!"

The most common effect of the Ossianized Nordic muse was what Northrop Frye calls "psychological self-identification." As an example we may consider the otherwise forgettable masterpiece of K. F. Kretschmann, *Gesang Ringulph des Bardens, als Varus geschlagen var* (1768). Again, the mythic world here derives much of its texture from the defeat of Southern tyranny by Northern freedom, thanks both to the hero Hermann and to the Ossianic Bard, Ringulph, who implements the transition to the sacred *illud tempus*. "Ha!" Ringulph begins, giving the sense of process by recalling the scene in present tense, "There they lie, yes! / The legions lie slain!" "Ha's" and "Ach's" dot the narrative to support the illusion of spontaneity. But the fundamental contradiction in the Bardic myth is obvious; that is, despite the ostensible epic purpose of the poem—"Allvater" tells Ringulph to quit singing about his beloved Irmgard and sing about Hermann—only a small part of the fourth *Gesang* (out of five) concerns the battle. The rest is mostly about Ringulph himself.

Central to the "poetics" of the Bards was that their function as poets and their literary products were reincarnations of an actual Teutonic genius, Ossian, of course, being the paradigm. Denis emphasizes in his well-informed essay "Vorbericht von der altern vaterlaendischen Dichtkunst" that the modern Bard must not betray his muse through anachronisms. But it is a singular commentary on the power of this myth to regulate rational inquiry that Denis, the most philologically oriented of any of the Bards, cites the poems of Klopstock and Kretschmann as exemplary for those who wish a "complete transition of oneself into other times." Denis was correct in a sense he did not intend, for the mythic world given symbolic form by Ossian, Klopstock, and Kretschmann was for a time *more real* to the general perception of the age than historical fact.

Even though myth's truths are not primarily validated by reason, a
modern myth must maintain a factual superstructure to complement that
part of it which operates extra-rationally. This requirement implies a separation of Faith and Reason, which in fact worked to render the Bardic myth
inexpressive. And the separation was ultimately to undermine Ossian himself. Concerning Denis, Gleim wrote to Jacobi in 1768, "my Herder, who
has long sighed deeply for such a Bard, will rejoice." But Herder, though
unaware of Ossian's role as myth, sensed the great discrepancy between the
lyrics of the Bards and those of his idol: they are not *Volkspoesie*, but *about
Volkspoesie*, he maintained. His response to lines such as these by Kretschmann
is also telling:

> I crept in the forest
>
> .   .   .   .
>
> In the high peaks roared
> The spirits of airy night;
> Then a chill broke out on my brow,
> And strongly beat my heart.
> And look! It seemed to me
> As though there stood a man . . . Are you a man? An elf
> Of midnight?

Herder sensed the great flaw in Kretschmann's myth: "Where Ringulph, the
Bard, sings well, he sings modern."

If one thinks of them in the context of eighteenth-century primitivism,
Fingal and *Temora* were indeed folk-epics, but because of their pretense to
historicity, both Ossian and the Bardic Movement were vulnerable to the
latent sundering of the temporary accommodation between myth and reason.
In 1800, Kretschmann in effect defended the myth in an article asking "Did
the Germanic Peoples have Bards and Druids or Not?" He supported his
affirmative argument with sources dating from the days of the Humanists.
The next month, H. Anton argued persuasively that "The Germanic Peoples
had no Bards and no Druids," attacking not only Kretschmann's methodology
(argument by analogy), but the veracity of his sources—his "factual" base:
"I assumed," Anton says, "That we in our criticism at the end of the century
must be more advanced that we were at the beginning." His view heralds
the Twilight of the Bards.

Herder and others were able to dispatch the Bardic lyrics by the sheer
force of individual critical acuity. More theoretical criticism of the Bards was
taken up by philologists, who tested the paradigm of the myth with an
informed methodology. That basis was Ossian himself. Earlier assaults on

Ossian, Hume's, for example, had been based upon aesthetic distaste. But these empiricist attacks were philological. In the 1780s, John Pinkerton concentrates on what he terms the "fierce light of Science" upon the vision of the Nordic past and finds error wherever he looks. Conversant with the recent Scandinavian scholarship of Suhm, Schøning, and others, Pinkerton demolishes the Ossianic universe by showing the Norse myths to be "merely" myths, and not real at all. He then attacks Ossian's "costume." Since historicity was an integral part of Ossian's mythic significance, the exposure of anachronism was mortal: "Eternal ladies in mail, where no mail was known," writes Pinkerton, "sicken one at every turn."

In 1817, the Swedish poet and critic Erik Gustaf Geijer could look back upon this period as closed, and describe it as an unsuccessful attempt to "return to ourselves." His comments upon the ineffectiveness of the Klopstock method of studding manuscripts with "By Thor!" are an index to the increased sophistication with which a new generation viewed the Nordic past. Though the figure of the Bard, perched at the end of the sacred Golden Age and at the beginning of profane, historical time, continued (Hugo, Scott, and Geijer himself, among others, used the persona), the assault on Ossian was symptomatic of a larger process, the calling into question of the whole moral universe of sentimental primitivism. Geijer and others saw that the simple structure of good *vs.* evil, virtue *vs.* vice was inadequate to explain the colliding contraries of moral experience. For a later generation Ossian was, in important ways, dead. Yet, in the myth of Ossian's synthetic spontaneity we can see a lasting legacy—the genesis of the contemporary attempt to merchandise both electronic Bards and the sentimental naive.

DONALD S. TAYLOR

Chatterton's Art: Ælla

For all of Chatterton's heroic starts in a variety of formal directions and subjects, no large-scale structures except "Bristowe Tragedie" and "Parlyamente" have as yet been brought to completion [up to the time of his writing *Ælla*]. Furthermore, "Bristowe Tragedie" gained its impact more as a series of scenes than as an interwoven action, and "Parlyamente" was a pageant. His finished successes have been the short celebratory odes—the songs to Werburgh, Baldwin, and Ella. The more ambitious actions—"Ynn auntient Dayes," "The Unknown Knyght," the two Hastings poems, and "Merrie Tricks"—have been consistently abandoned near their beginnings or in mid-action. *Ælla*, then, represents a major step forward. It has the finish and the spirit of the celebratory odes, and it builds on a large-scale structural idea that is effectively worked out in detail. We have already noted evidence of various kinds that both subject and form were long meditated.

Ælla is surrounded by documents that tell us Chatterton knew that he had accomplished something very substantial. He did not at first show the play to his Bristol patrons; he sold Catcott a transcript only in April, 1770, over a year after the play was completed. He had, apparently, larger plans. On 15 February 1769 he offered it to the London publisher James Dodsley, and his letter does not soft-pedal his price in what Rowley has done.

> It is a perfect Tragedy, the Plot, clear, the Language, spirited, and the Songs interspersed in it, are flowing, poetical and Elegantly Simple. The Similes judiciously applied and tho' wrote in

From *Thomas Chatterton's Art: Experiments in Imagined History.* © 1978 by Princeton University Press. Originally entitled "The Rowleyan Works."

the reign of Henry 6th., not inferior to many of the present Age.
. . . the Monks . . . were not such Blockheads, as generally thought
and . . . good Poetry might be wrote, in the dark days of Superstition as well as in these more inlightened Ages.

Once again Rowley is the enlightened, correct, polished Pope of his
century.

His two Popean verse letters to Canynge, both prefatory to *Ælla*—
"Epistle to Mastre Canynge on Ælla" and "Letter to the Dygne Mastre
Canynge"—are, understandably, more modest. The excellences of these two
poems . . . are helpful to our present inquiry because they suggest what Chatterton wants us to see in *Ælla*. From the "Epistle" we learn that we are to
expect truth and morality, not ribaldry, ostentation, or mindless jingling.
The play will be free of pedantry and Latinizing—right English. It will avoid
superstitious legendry catering to the laughter and tears of the tasteless rabble
(of "Plays of Mirracle and Maumerys"). More positively and specifically, it
will be "somme greate storie of a manne," and this is reiterated in the "Letter,"
which promises a boundless, vigorous, noble subject, not ploddingly limited
to fact, but soaring, with Poetry, " 'bove trouthe of historie." The prosody
will be masculine, not overly refined. The final prefatory piece, intended as
a part of the performance itself, is the rime royal "Entroductionne." It echoes
Queen Mab's opening speech in "Parlyamente": usually the faults of heroes
are generously buried with them, but in this play we shall rouse Ælla up
(for the third time) "before the judgment daie" to tell us what he now knows
about "howe hee sojourned in the vale of men." Part of the soaring, then,
will be the revelation of flaws, perhaps a tragic flaw, in the hero.

As a matter of fact, Ælla's story and his very existence are purely the
growths of Chatterton's imagination. The few historical hints from which
he worked and the gradual growth of the legend are given in detail in *Works*,
but Chatterton's major givens for the play are literary. The action is starkly
constructed from conventional situations—nearly every scene could be assigned parallels from earlier drama, and yet the feeling of the whole is fresh
and original. I believe that only *Othello*, Shakespeare's battle scenes, and
William Thompson's *Gondibert and Birtha* (1751) exert major direct influences,
and even here everything is transformed by the shaping idea and by Chatterton's unique treatment.

Works analyzes the prosody at length. Suffice it to say here that though
the Rowleyan stanza is still used for the set, measured effects required in
description, soliloquy, and formal confrontation, Chatterton also demonstrates to the full its possibilities in handling episodes of conflict with their

rapid exchanges of brief, charged statement. The stanza predominates, but variants of it are freely used and a considerable variety of lyric measures have the effect of being inlaid, each for its special purpose, within the predominant texture of the full decasyllabic stanza with alexandrine. The Rowleyan language too is by now the completely responsive medium for whatever effects Chatterton needs; there are no traces of archaism for its own sake.

Ælla is best understood, both in its informing principle and in its consequent artistic problems, as an eighteenth-century response to this question: "Where does one go from *Othello?*" We rightly think of Chatterton as a precursor of the romantic poets, but the extent to which he is at home in eighteenth-century sensibilities has not been sufficiently noted. Chatterton uses *Othello* very much in the spirit in which Restoration and eighteenth-century dramatists adapted Shakespeare, very much in the spirit of heroic plays. Complexities of action, character, and situation are conflated, reduced, or eliminated; individualizing character detail is dropped; symmetries and echoing in plot, character relationships, and scene structure are underlined or emphatically introduced. Perhaps the best way to summarize the direction of change is to say that what in Shakespeare is individual, concrete, and humanly evocative gives way in Chatterton to operatic effects; human tragedy becomes grand—even grandiose—heroic tragedy. Moreover, it is in terms of action and of consequent decisions about character, thought, and diction that Chatterton attempts to move from *Othello* to his own tragic idea.

The shaping idea that governs all subordinate elements in Chatterton's tragedy is that the ideal love between Ælla and Birtha is fated to go unconsummated. What might have been a temporary separation, heightening the joy of their eventual reunion, is brought about, first, by a Danish invasion to which Ælla must respond, even on his wedding night, and, second, by Celmonde, whose hopeless passion for Birtha decides him to renounce loyalty and personal honor and ravish her. Ælla disposes of the first threat by complete victory over the invaders, and the heroic Danish leader Hurra disposes of the second threat by killing Celmonde just as he is about to rape Birtha. At this point, nothing would seem to prevent the joyful reunion of Ælla and Birtha. Yet Ælla's character proves an insurmountable barrier: his groundless jealousy, somehow linked inextricably to his heroism, seals the fate of their love just at the point when all might have been well.

The basic ways in which all of this grows from *Othello* are clear enough. In Shakespeare's play the trust of an ingenuous hero is diabolically played upon; as a result, an ideal yet very human love is destroyed, and the lovers, for whom we have wished everything good, perish. Othello's double weakness is his trusting nature and his contradictory potential for jealousy. It would appear that Chatterton felt that though jealousy was congenial to an heroic nature, the ease with which it was evoked in Othello *by another* detracted from his heroism. A hero, it would seem, should be autonomous, his faults, like his virtues, sovereign and independent. Heroic character must not be the toy of a plotter. Chatterton conceives an action, therefore, in which his hero's love as first presented is as admirable and human as Othello's, in which his valor exceeds Othello's, in which the malignancy of another—though more clearly and singly motivated than Iago's—is finally powerless against him. The tragic jealousy must, in short, be self-engendered—a part of his heroism and inseparable from his character. Also, to take this autonomy one step further, Ælla's jealousy acts only upon himself. Whereas Othello killed himself only when he learned that he had been tragically wrong in killing Desdemona, Ælla, having learned (as he thinks) that Birtha is false, does not once think of killing her. Even his revenge is directed at himself. It is as though he had incorporated Birtha when he married her and so can only destroy himself.

The derivation of the other principals—in essential traits, in role, and in their interrelationships—from the more complex characters of *Othello* is fairly obvious. Birtha is an abstract of Desdemona; no quadrant of her life or character unconnected to Ælla is suggested. Celmonde is Iago with different and clearer motivation (borrowed from Roderigo) and hence lacking Iago's spontaneous malignancy; also, he performs Iago's choral function. Even Egwina, Birtha's maid, has much of Emilia's function, though almost nothing of her individuality. As in the action, so with the characters: the lines are fewer and more heavily drawn; humanizing touches and chiaroscuro effects are largely eliminated. The feeling, again, is operatic.

The uses of *Othello* in the sequence and internal structuring of scenes is equally striking and takes like directions. Although Chatterton does not divide his play by acts, the action falls quite naturally into four parts. He has, on the other hand, indicated scene divisions. Even though these divisions frequently occur within a continuous action, they mark distinct stages of the action and consequent shifts in the focus of our concern and response. To demonstrate the power of Chatterton's art, I shall summarize the action by act and scene, noting the *Othello* borrowings and the changes wrought by Chatterton's own artistic idea.

The first act (ll. 119–547) establishes Celmonde as a serious threat, leads us to full sympathy for the love of Ælla and Birtha, then pulls them physically and emotionally apart by the threat of the Danish invasion. The act concludes with the opening situation completely reversed. Celmonde has come from total despair to fresh hope for a dishonorable enjoyment of Birtha, whereas the lovers, jubilant and expectant at the start, have quarreled and, though reconciled, are driven apart by the sudden change of circumstance. Thus the major lines of action have been set going and the separation on which the whole play rests has taken place. Celmonde's opening soliloquy (I, i) catches our sympathy by collapsing Roderigo's balked passion and Iago's plotting, both from Shakespeare's first scene, into one speech. His despair at Birtha's approaching wedding to Ælla is convincing, and we see that his poisoning threat is not idle. Celmonde is thus established as a complex, believable antagonist. Although the particular plot of poisoning is quickly rendered superfluous by the Danish invasion, Celmonde will eventually accomplish what he proposes here, though through means he cannot now imagine. "Assyst mee, Helle! lett Devylles rounde mee tende, / To slea mieselfe, mie love, and eke mie doughtie friend." He forshadows, then the total action of the play and his passion for Birtha is one of the two causes of the tragedy, both of which are necessary for the separation of the lovers to be irrevocable.

Chatterton drops from the start such complicating lesser roles as those of Brabantio, the Duke, the Senate, and Cassio and any such complicating issue as the propriety of the love of his hero and heroine. Thus, what remains is to convince us that Ælla's and Birtha's love is as substantial and laudable as that to which Othello and Desdemona publicly testify in *Othello* (I, iii). Chatterton convinces us of this effectively and with originality in a sequence of three operatically structured scenes. The love debate of Ælla and Birtha (I, ii) makes us wish them well. He is jubilant; this will be better than beating the Danes, he says in effect. When Birtha modestly promises rewards meet for his devotion and kindness, he jocularly rants of the wonders he must have performed to deserve even a smile. Birtha brings him gently to earth:

> As farr as thys frayle brutylle [brittle] flesch wyll spere [allow],
> Syke [such], and ne fardher I expect of you;
> Be noote toe slacke yn love, ne overdeare;
> A smalle fyre, yan [than] a loude flame, proves more true.

He has the enthusiasm, vigor, and zest of a young bridegroom, and she is warm, loving, and above all full of good sense. She might have been drawn from Pope's characters of perfection in woman—from Clarissa's speech in *The Rape of the Lock* or the conclusion of the second *Moral Essay*; good sense will surely here preserve what beauty has gained. It will be, we see, a good marriage, and the more we wish this young couple well, of course, the greater our anxiety at their separation, the greater our pity at the tragic conclusion of their love. Moreover, Celmonde's opening soliloquy has ensured that anxiety for them will be with us from the start, a somber ground bass to their love duet.

If we need reminding, Celmonde breaks in upon them (I, iii) with minstrels, fulsome well-wishes, and a jocular invitation to drink the (poisoned) ale. Then the minstrels' songs begin. . . . Their function in this scene is both subtle and essential to our sense of what is about to be lost. Prosody and style are in marked contrast to the Rowleyan stanzas of the play proper, which are narrative, declamatory, full of action and impassioned debate. The songs quit this heroic world, serving something of the function of subplot in Elizabethan drama or of chorus in Greek tragedy. Their actions and thoughts lend broader relevance and profounder meaning to the central issue of the play—the love of Birtha and Ælla.

The love debate between Robin and Alice brings love to the pastoral, the simplest human level. Like Ælla, Robin is impetuous—nature courses in him, urging him to immediate consummation. Alice calls on nature too, but she is cautious. They hear opposing lessons in the birds' songs, and Alice makes the necessary distinction between man and the rest of nature. Alice's good sense conquers Robin's impetuosity; they marry and live in love and goodness. The song has the odd effect of taking the heroic love that we have just been witnessing, bringing it to the broadest human level, and suggesting at the same time the teasing courtship and the mock-real struggles that must have preceded our own first glimpse of Birtha and Ælla. Throughout the song, nature—landscape, birds, plants, animals—supports the love that Robin urges and with which Alice happily but judiciously complies.

In the second song, both nature and the appetites and joys of human love are handled on a philosophic level. The first minstrel complains that in spring, with nature at her fairest, he still feels a void. Adam felt this void in the garden, replies the second minstrel: he needed "an help meet" for him. Take a wife into your arms and even winter will have a charm for you. The third minstrel complains that his joy in golden, fruitful autumn is "purpled" (both the autumn color and perplexity are suggested) with care. Here the second minstrel gives a fuller answer. It is desire you feel: only angels are free from it, and it can only be quieted by woman. Woman was made from a part of you—with much water and little fire—and so women too seek man to make themselves complete. Man without woman is savage, but woman is so fed with the spirit of peace that, tempered with this cool, angelic joy, men become angels. So take a wife to your bed. Thus the implicit moral of Robin's and Alice's coming together is given a philosophic dimension, and this is managed, through the first and third minstrels' complaints, without losing the connection with nature and nature's urgings. The effect of the songs so far has been to humanize and then to deepen our sense of the heroic love of Ælla and Birtha.

We are to be brought back from ideas to people, though, and this is done most effectively in the third song—a simpler pastoral in which Elinor celebrates the joys of marriage. She was happy with her father "yn marrie Clowddell," duties there were at her pleasure, but she still wanted something she could not name. Thus the theme of the second song, the emptiness of the heart before love comes, is brought down to the everyday, seen this time from the woman's side. As if to prove Elinor's joy, Lord Thomas returns from the hunt, she puts up her knitting, and "wee leave hem bothe kyndelie embracynge." In view of the previous songs, "*kyndelie*" must here refer, as it so often does in Chatterton, to the impulses and appetites of nature as well as to mutual kindness.

The songs have made a pause—a musical A B A—and that is surely their intent; we are to relish the full implications of the marriage that has just taken place and that ought shortly to be lovingly and "kyndelie" consummated. Yet the separating forces are now introduced at full strength. We are brought back to thoughts of Celmonde's sad scheme when Ælla says, "Come, gentle love, we wyll toe spouse-feaste goe, / And there ynn ale and wynne bee dreyncted [drowned] everych woe." This is only prelude to the entrance of a more pressing reality and its demand for action which shall effectively break up all the joy that has been promising (I, iv). The messenger's announcement of the Danish invasion at Watchet saves the three principals from Celmonde's deadly cups but also introduces the train of events that shall tear Ælla and Birtha apart physically and then, with Celmonde's and Ælla's help, emotionally, and shall insure that they are brought together only in death. We must, therefore, watch closely this separation. The immediate division of minds takes the form of an impassioned, almost formal love vs. honor debate. The apparent postponement of the joys so long anticipated tests them both. Here their relative strengths are reversed. Ælla is stronger, more stable than Birtha; he is angered by the separation but knows what honor demands of him. Birtha tries recriminations, threats, and evasions, but he calls her gradually to sorrowful assent, and he, seeing her once more herself and mistress of her grief, has an even more poignant sense of what he must now lose. This tense scene of cross-purposes, reproaches, and sad reconciliation evokes two responses—a sense of the intensity of their love and of the irresistible pull of Ælla's vocation. She loves the hero in him, and he could not love her half so much, loved he not honor more. As they part Birtha has a premonition of the truth: "He's gon, he's gone, alass! percase [perhaps] he's gone for aie."

As if to underline the difficulty of Ælla's honorable choice, Celmonde's soliloquy (I, v), closing the act as he opened it, reveals his exultation at this sad interruption of Ælla's and Birtha's love: "I see onnombered joies around mee ryse; / Blake [naked] stondethe future doome, and joie doth mee alyse [free, let loose]." For Ælla, honor's call is stronger than his love. This very heroism in Ælla is opportunity for Celmonde, who answers the call to warfare readily enough, but abandons honor, love, and friendship in the face of the even stronger pull of his appetite for Birtha. Again Chatterton has united in him the secret lover and the plotter: what Celmonde says draws from Roderigo and Iago in the final scene of Shakespeare's first act. He will "follow these wars," as Iago counseled Roderigo, but he foresees such new changes at Birtha as Iago promised Roderigo. Iago revealed the direction of his schemes at the close of the first act.:

> The Moor is of a free and open nature
> That thinks men honest that but seem to be so;
> And will as tenderly be led by th' nose
> As asses are.
> I have't! It is engend're! Hell and night
> Must bring this monstrous birth to the world's light.

Celmonde likewise denounces honor and invokes Hell to steel his soul for unspecified strange and doleful deeds.

The second act (II. 548–950) is all battle, a triumph that fully justifies Ælla's heroic reputation. What the storm does to the Turkish fleet between Shakespeare's first two acts is here inflicted upon the Danish invaders by Ælla's valor and leadership. For the most part, the battle is reported, not presented visually as in the two versions of Hastings. Our attention is focused, therefore, on the characters of the warriors and the quality of their heroism. The symmetries and polarities of structure and response are further strengthened. The abrupt transition to the Danish camp is skillfully managed by having the Danish priest invoke his gods in incantatory rhythm, much as Celmonde had just invoked Satan. The core of the first act, the love debate interrupted by the messenger and so shifting to a love-honor debate, is here echoed by the violent flyting of Magnus and Hurra, interrupted in its turn by news of Ælla's approach. The quarrel between the two Danish leaders also offers a telling parallel to Ælla and Celmonde. Ælla, truly heroic, reluctantly turned from love to honor, whereas Celmonde vowed to sacrifice love, honor, and friendship to appetite. Hurra will speak his valor in deeds, whereas Magnus speaks valor but will act cowardice.

The lengthy Magnus-Hurra Flyting (II, i) has other essential functions. The Danes become something more than the enemy—this lesson was learned from Chatterton's mistake in "Battle of Hastynges I." The Danish leaders are two individuals—Magnus boastfully anxious, Hurra scornfully valorous, ready to chance his life in battle—and this distinction is to be used by Chatterton. Magnus's panic about Ælla insures the English victory. Hurra, on the other hand, must be established as a man of heroic deeds if he is to play the generous role allotted to him in the next two acts. Finally, the flyting, in addition to being good, thick rant, establishes the reputation of Ælla in the mouths of his enemies. Since Chatterton has wisely chosen not to show Ælla's slaughters on stage, this reputation is a major help in convincing us of his stature.

The rest of the second act, except for Celmonde's final thirty lines, is all Ælla, and it contains some of the finest poetry Chatterton wrote. We have shifted from personal confrontation bringing out character under stress to the spontaneous rhetoric of individual response. All three remaining scenes in this act intensify our sense of Ælla's instinctive heroism. The troops respond to his dignified, impassioned battle speech as we can imagine ourselves responding. The Danes, flying in terror, gasp out graphic testimonies to his might; and even Celmonde must celebrate him with undisguised enthusiasm. Act two is Ælla's high point in the play, and we rejoice for him. He is Bristol's Henry V. The careful reader may consider lines 706–9, 720–39, 760–69, 770–809, 824–30, and 865–70 if he has any doubts about Chatterton's poetic power. He may then consider how these same passages work toward the establishment of Ælla as hero—in stirring an army to its finest effort, in the terror his strategy has worked in the enemy, and in the spontaneous admiration of the man who is his deadly rival. Chatterton's poetry, admirable in itself, serves the larger purpose of building a poem.

How ominous, then, is the plot we see forming in Celmonde's mind as his soliloquy again closes an act (II, iv). His intensely debating honor vs. gratification and again invoking Hell give us a sense of the strength and deviousness that oppose Ælla's and Birtha's happiness (ll. 941–950). Thus the act leaves us with simultaneous joy over Ælla's triumph, anticipation over the lovers' reunion, and anxiety over Celmonde's threat. Here Chatterton has turned once more to the thought and diction of Iago. Celmonde concludes, "Nowe, Ælla, nowe Ime plantynge of a thorne, / Bie whyche thie peace, thie love, and glorie shall be torne." This cannot but recall Iago's setting in motion (II, i), through Roderigo, of his plan concerning Cassio and his subsequent soliloquy concerning Othello's nobility, his own qualified lust for Desdemona, and his determination to "Make the Moor thank me, love me, and reward me / For making him egregiously an ass / And practicing upon his peace and quiet / Even to madness."

The third act (ll. 951–1253) takes us from general apprehension to surges of quite specific suspense. It is a series of rather short scenes at Bristol Castle, Watchet, and the night forest between. The action is taking its by-now independent course: Chatterton calls for help from Shakespeare only in the first scene. Here, as Birtha languishes for news of Ælla, Egwina calls for the lovely minstrel's song "O! Synge untoe Mie Roundelaie" to divert her. The scene and its ironies are sharply reminiscent of the chamber scenes between Emilia and Desdemona. The minstrel's song foretells Birtha's fate, bringing her tragedy once more to the broader human scale of a shepherdess recalling her dead swain and dying at his grave. To underline the irony, it is made clear that Birtha does not catch the thrust of the song, so anxious is she about her swain. "Thys syngeyng haveth whatte could make ytte please; / Butte mie uncourtlie shappe [destiny] benymmes [bereaves] mee of all ease." We know that Celmonde is on his way, and this doubles our apprehension for Birtha. Though the roundelay borrows primarily from Ophelia's song, Desdemona's lines about Barbary's song might serve as epigraph for what this song forebodes for Birtha, just as "Willow" is so sadly portentous for Desdemona:

> She was in love; and he she lov'd prov'd mad
> And did forsake her. She had a song of "Willow."
> And old thing 'twas, but it express'd her fortune,
> And she died singing it.

We move momentarily to Watchet to hear Ælla, as if in echo of Birtha's grief, fretting at his wound, finding no satisfaction in victory, and determining to ride to Birtha immediately (III, ii). However, Celmonde is already with her (III, iii). He skillfully plays on Birtha's love for Ælla and her bravery to entice her away, ostensibly to Watchet so that she can restore Ælla. Meanwhile Hurra and the Danish remnant lurk in the forest between, planning rapine on villages and travelers (III, iv).

The next scene of act three (III, v) brings suspense to its painful height as Celmonde's cruel intent gradually dawns on Birtha's terrified mind. She, like Ælla in the final act, prefers death to dishonor, but the threat to her is real. Hurra hears her cries, kills Celmonde, and rescues her (III, vi). When he learns that she is Ælla's wife he is tempted to kill her. Yet he recalls Ælla's generosity to the Danish captives and a responding magnanimity, well prepared for in the first scene of the second act, moves him: he will conduct

Birtha to Bristol Castle and Ælla. This is again an echo of an earlier action. In the first act a love duet was interrupted, in the second the hate duet between Magnus and Hurra. Here Hurra providentially breaks in upon the lust-terror duet of Celmonde and Birtha. All now could be well. We sense the state of Ælla's mind, but we can hope that Birtha and Hurra will reach the castle in time. Our apprehensions about Ælla are vague, but it would be difficult to imagine a calm, wait-and-see attitude in the impatient hero who rode wounded from Watchet.

The tempi and motifs of the first three acts have been set and constructed with musical acumen. The first began with Celmonde's frantic despair, explored the love scene joyfully and, in the three songs, deeply, building to the impassioned debate, increasing in tempo as passions struggled with each other, and climaxing in Celmonde's dark jubilation. In the second act, the measured anger between the Danish chiefs was displaced by the rapid surge of battle and Ælla's triumph, concluding with more specific haste and frightening jubilation as Celmonde sets his treacherous scheme in motion. In the third act, the shifts from place to place and the sudden changes of fortune further speed up the tempo, with the undersong of Celmonde's intent running throughout. Each new thrust of will and decision arouses fresh possibilities for good or ill. From the fourth scene to the sixth scene of act three, each new crossing of the contradictory purposiveness of the principals is an effective physical embodiment of our uncertainty—our hope and anxiety. All is moving toward the climactic return to the scene of the jubilant young love we first saw threatened, and in both tempo and feeling the fourth act is frantic and thick with revelations of the movements of hearts.

The fourth act (ll. 1254–1365) also brings Chatterton to the crucial artistic problem of his play, and he turns to *Othello* for his most extensive borrowings. Ælla must be brought to suicide because Birtha's absence convinces him that she is unfaithful. His mind leaps to conclusions from singularly scanty evidence. He arrives at the castle, reads the anxiety in Egwina's face, and when Egwina says Birtha is gone, he swoons away, then revives to say that he is no longer Ælla. He threatens Egwina in his rage for fuller information. When she tells him that last night she left Birtha pining for love, he leaps to suspicion: "Her love! to whom?" Nothing has prepared us for this in Ælla. He gives Egwina's assurances the lie, momentarily doubts his fears, then is more certain—though with no further evidence—as he precipitately fills in the details of his jealous fantasy. A servant now gives an inaccurate account of a stranger's appearance and Birtha's departure, and this brings on Ælla's strange speech before he stabs himself, a speech whose implications must be considered in some detail.

At this point Birtha and Hurra arrive (IV, ii), she passionately inquiring for Ælla. He coldly tells her that her foulness urged his death wound and she faints. Hurra now tells the story of Celmonde's attempt, and Ælla embraces the news. He has become himself again, but it is too late. Birtha revives, forgives his fear, and begins to fill in details of Celmonde's treachery and Hurra's magnanimity, at which Ælla exclaims, "Oh, I die content." When Birtha sees him dead, she says, echoing the minstrel's song, that his grave shall be her bridebed and faints upon his body. Coernicus, left to sum up the tragedy, asks who can fathom the workings of Heaven and fate and delivers Ælla's epitaph. "Ælla, thie rennome was thie onlie gayne; / For yatte, thie pleasaunce, and thie joie was loste."

We are left, then, with a serious artistic problem. Ælla had no sufficient grounds for his almost immediate suspicion, his jealousy, and his suicide. To put the situation at its full irrationality, when the entire issue of the play is consummation, Ælla, unconsummated, dies "content." That Birtha was not another's is more essential to him than that she was never fully his. The reason for this folly would seem, strangely enough, to be Chatterton's admiration of and his consequent wish to compete with *Othello*, which he now turns to for help with the artistic problems that his operative extrapolations from *Othello* have led him into. He must make the suicide believable without an Iago to engender and foster Ælla's jealousy. Chatterton attempts to make Ælla's spontaneous psychological combustion convincing by his heaviest borrowings thus far.

Before considering these borrowings in detail, let us consider the conceptual development to this point of the idea of heroism in the play. Heroism has been defined by the actions of the hero, by the nobility of the rescuing Dane Hurra, and negatively, by the actions and thoughts of Celmonde, who is valorous in deed but base in mind. The sympathy between the heroic and the more broadly human has been explored in the four pastoral songs. The essense of the heroic has been displayed in Ælla's speech before the battle and by the accounts from both his military and personal enemies of his actions there. In addition to all of this, the concept of heroism has been constantly on the tongues of all principals, arising whenever the words *rennome, honnoure*, or *myndbruch* [injured honor] are used and whenever, as is very frequent, questions of identity arise. Ælla's obsession with honor, reknown, reputation, identity, the whole code by which he lives, engenders the folly of his groundless jealousy, or so Chatterton would wish us to believe. Yet we must ask how such a hero can be so fearful of Birtha's love. This argues a serious defect in his character, and we can only agree when Ælla says of his feelings about Birtha, "This only was unarmed of all my sprite."

Chatterton seems to have sensed, in fact, that "this only was unarmed of all" his play. We can argue that a jealousy that has even less motive than Iago's malignancy has support in _Othello_, for Emilia holds (and Freud with her) that jealousy is indeed self-engendered:

> But jealous souls will not be answer'd so;
> They are not ever jealous for the cause,
> But jealous for they're jealous. It is a monster
> Begot upon itself, born on itself.

Jealousy, indeed, needs neither grounds nor an Iago. It can create its own conspiratorial world out of whatever evidence presents; all is evidence. Yet Emilia and this point of view generally can only be ironic commentators upon heroism; Chatterton stumbles when he incorporates Emilia's choral wisdom into the conception of his protagonist. Also, Chatterton seems to sense that an empirical view of jealousy sorts ill with the convention of a believable hero. Lacking an Iago to engine the mind of his hero, he turns to various expressions of violent states of mind in _Othello_ to give convincing texture to _his_ hero's violent folly.

Line by line in the crucial last act he rings the changes on states of mind expressed by Othello, Iago, even Cassio, hoping thereby to lead us to belief. He must work the changes in Ælla in forty-nine lines of his fourth act that Shakespeare worked, with Iago, through most of his play, but particularly in the 476 lines of the third scene of act three. Chatterton fails, I believe, to convince us that a hero must or even could be believably jealous without either grounds or malignantly worked trustfulness. Ælla's tragedy (and Birtha's) is caused finally by a jarring flaw in his heroism, a flaw from which we cannot reason back to humanly admirable causes. The detailed borrowings in this last act and especially in the forty-nine lines in which jealousy seizes Ælla should be examined in detail. It is abundantly clear that Chatterton has trusted primarily to the power of Shakespeare's diction to establish in a moment what required in _Othello_ the long and complex machinations of an Iago.

The argument thus far has been that, in shaping concept, major characters and their relationships, the development of much of the action, the internal structuring of several scenes, and finally the very language of his antagonist in soliloquy and his protagonist in extremity, Chatterton's tragedy has been an extrapolation from Shakespeare's. It is of interest that Chatterton's borrowings are of two quite distinct kinds. The borrowings in concept and character structure provide a starting point for what is essentially a rival work. _Ælla_ will "improve" _Othello_ according to the lights of a sensibility that

I have called operatic. The borrowings in scene structure and language, on the other hand, while not clashing with this sensibility, are devices for solving artistic problems raised in the working out of Chatterton's derivative overall concepts. We might schematize the two sorts of borrowing and their relationship thus:

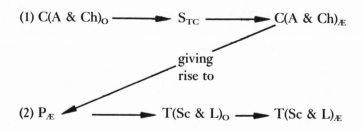

$$(1)\ C(A\ \&\ Ch)_O \longrightarrow S_{TC} \longrightarrow C(A\ \&\ Ch)_{\cancel{E}}$$

giving
rise to

$$(2)\ P_{\cancel{E}} \longleftarrow \qquad \longrightarrow T(Sc\ \&\ L)_O \longrightarrow T(Sc\ \&\ L)_{\cancel{E}}$$

[C Concept, A Action, Ch Characters, O *Othello*, S Sensibility, TC Chatterton, Æ Ælla, P Artistic Problems, T Treatment, Sc Scenes, L Language]

The first borrowing is competitive, the second collaborative. The influencing work is first catalytic; then the artistic carrying-out of the derived concepts raises problems that return the borrowing artist to admired techniques of arrangement and language in the source. Probably each instance of artistic borrowing will have its unique characteristics, but the emergence here of two quite distinct sorts of borrowing (or influence) ought to be distinguished.

The mediating condition in both sorts of borrowing, but especially in the first, is Chatterton's "operatic" sensibility, which . . . groups him with his Restoration and eighteenth-century predecessors at least as closely as with such later travelers in this path as Rossini and Verdi. We ought here to summarize briefly the operatic qualities other than the abstracted action, the simplified character structures, and the starker scene outlines already noted. The emotional sequence of the tragedy is strikingly symmetrical. In the first act, both the songs with their pastoral echoes of heroic love and the complete reversal of expectation between Celmonde and the two lovers underline this symmetry. The act ends with Celmonde invoking Hell in incantatory rhythms, and act two opens with the incantations of the Danish priest. The core of the first act—the love debate interrupted and transformed by news of attacking Danes—was echoed in the interruption of act two's hate debate (the Danish flyting) and (after the minstrel's song's foreboding) in the interruption of the third act's lust-terror debate. The skillfully building, interrelated and contrasting emotional tempi of the scenic progression have also been noted. There is symmetry also in the irony of the total action. The friend of act one proves an enemy, the enemy a friend. The love that was about to be joyfully consummated in act one is finally consummated in double death. Protagonist and antagonist are heroic in all but love, and their profound flaws in love—lack of trust and cruel lust, respectively—show almost equal failure to understand the heroine. As in *Othello* one is tempted to feel the final tragedy as the heroine's, and both heroines die forgiving the folly that has destroyed them. Birtha's steady human sense and warmth have no room for operation in a world of violent, unthinking heroes. Perhaps the crowning ironic symmetry, though, is that of all the principals only Celmonde has achieved what he threatened at the beginning of the play. At the end of his opening soliloquy, planning the poisoning, he commanded, "Assyst me, Helle! lett Devylles rounde mee tende, / To slea mieselfe, mie love, and eke mie doughtie friend." Perhaps a composer with a feeling for these operatic qualities could best bring out the strengths of Chatterton's tragedy and lend musical support to the weak element in its conception.

Identifications and definitions of such sensibilities as the operatic are most valuable as literary-historical instruments when they locate gaps in our own capacity to respond to modes that once had the power to move. We find in ourselves now just such a resistance to the sensibility invoked in *opera seria*, heroic plays, Ossianics, and great odes (to name a few of what seem to me to be its eighteenth-century manifestations). Our disinclination toward the grand and the sublime would seem to block our artistic understanding of such works for the time being. Yet in the past the identification of sensibilities unsympathetic to our own has been a first step in coming to terms with them. At this point in our state of knowledge, the operatic sensibility represents an area of imperfect sympathy and, hence, of literary-historical ignorance. Shakespeare's way rings truer for us—not just because he is a greater poet, but because he is actually closer to our way of looking at things.

This difficulty aside, *Ælla* can, I believe, stand confidently with Restoration heroic plays and head and shoulders above most of the tragedies of Chatterton's own century. Yet after *Ælla* Chatterton does nothing very good in the Rowleyan drama. The last two Rowleyan plays—"The Tournament" and "Goddwyn"—neither illustrate further developments in a theory of stanzaic drama nor embody any compelling problems or experiments in subject, treatment, or form. . . . We might appropriately ask ourselves here why Chatterton should apparently have lost interest in drama after the close approach to greatness in *Ælla*. "The Tournament" is only perfunctorily completed and "Goddwyn" is scarcely begun. It seems to me quite possible that Chatterton's inability to publish *Ælla* may have been a major discouragement: if he could interest no one in something so good and so difficult to write, why bother?

Why work his way through the hundreds of lines that effective completion of "Goddwyn" would have entailed? Artists who build from past achievements have, typically, attentive audiences; Chatterton, we must remember, had none.

In his letter of 15 February 1769 offering *Ælla* to James Dodsley, Chatterton, after appending lines 730–39 of Ælla's battle speech as a sample, writes, "If it should not Suit you, I should be oblig'd to you if you would calculate the Expences of printing it, as I will endeavor to publish it by Subscription on my own Account—" This is sad. It is doubtful, considering the modest circumstances of Chatterton's acquaintances, that he could have found enough subscribers to cover such costs. We do not know whether Dodsley answered this letter, though Chatterton's boastful letter to Stephens of 20 July 1769 ("My next Correspondent of note is Dodsley") and his first letter from London ("called upon Mr. Edmunds, Mr. Fell, Mr. Hamilton and Mr. Dodsley. Great encouragement from them; all approved of my design") have been taken to mean that Dodsley gave some sort of encouragement. Yet the sample lines seem not to have captured Dodsley's fancy; if they had, we might have very different histories of Chatterton and of his poetry.

William Blake's Poetical Sketches

*P*oetical Sketches was printed (1783) but not published, as no copies were ever offered for sale. Blake seems not to have given away many copies, and presumably the choice not to publish was his own. *Poetical Sketches* manifests many influences, but these are homogeneous, and show Blake to be in the direct line of the poets of the Age of Sensibility, particularly Collins. Had we only these youthful poems of Blake (written between his twelfth and twentieth years), it is likely we would place him as a second and greater Collins. As with Collins, his early poems are haunted by the pastoral elements in the King James Bible, Spenser, Shakespeare, and Milton. Coming later than Collins, Blake shows the full effect of the Gothic Revival—of Percy's *Reliques*, Chatterton, Ossian, and the Old Norse poetry, probably this last through the medium of the poetry of Gray. The movement from personification to mythical confrontation, evidenced in the Revival, is nowhere clearer than in Blake's four poems on the seasons, which open *Poetical Sketches*.

In *To Spring* the tone of the Song of Songs is heard. The lovesick Earth has bound up her modest tresses in mourning for her absent lover, Spring. He returns to deck her forth with his fair fingers, and to put the crown of new growth upon her head. In this poem personification clearly still prevails.

To Summer is an address from the landscape to an Apollo figure who resembles the Poetical Character of Collins's *Ode*:

From *The Visionary Company*. © 1961 by Harold Bloom. Cornell University Press, 1971. Originally entitled "William Blake."

> thou, O Summer,
> Oft pitched'st here thy golden tent, and oft
> Beneath our oaks hast slept, while we beheld
> With joy thy ruddy limbs and flourishing hair.

Here the abstraction and the figure are too fused for separate consideration; neither the season nor the god takes priority. In *To Autumn* the humanization of landscape and season is complete, as Earth and Autumn carry on a dialogue. Earth speaks:

> O Autumn, laden with fruit, and stained
> With the blood of the grape, pass not, but sit
> Beneath my shady roof; there thou may'st rest,
> And tune thy jolly voice to my fresh pipe;
> And all the daughters of the year shall dance!
> Sing now the lusty song of fruits and flowers.

It takes an effort to remember that "my shady roof" refers to foliage, and that the jolly singer who replies is a season. In *To Winter* the transition to myth-making is complete. Urizen, the withered limiter of desire, makes a premonitory appearance as the devouring season:

> Lo! now the direful monster, whose skin clings
> To his strong bones, strides o'er the groaning rocks:
> He withers all in silence, and his hand
> Unclothes the earth, and freezes up frail life.

The groaning rocks are nearly those of the barren realm of Ulro, where the self-absorbed consciousness will dwell in holy communion with itself. These hints of incipient myth are subtler elsewhere in *Poetical Sketches*. *To Morning*, a Spenserian lyric echoing the *Epithalamion*, salutes Morning as a "holy virgin" who unlocks the "golden gates" of heaven, and then hunts with the sun across the sky:

> O radiant morning, salute the sun,
> Rouz'd like a huntsman to the chace, and, with
> Thy buskin'd feet, appear upon our hills.

The "buskin'd feet" identify Morning as a huntress, and as she is a "holy virgin," a Diana association is inevitable. In Psalm 19, also echoed by Blake, the sun is described "as a bridegroom coming out of his chamber, and rejoiceth as a strong man to run a race." Blake makes the race into a hunt, and the light ambiguous touches ("golden gates" is equivocal, and so are "purest white" and a reference to Eos or Aurora as a "holy virgin") reinforce the Diana image to give the little poem a faintly sinister quality. The exquisite *To the Evening Star* is the finest result in *Poetical Sketches* of Blake's animating vision. The Spenserian coloring is again present, but a new movement enters into the marriage imagery:

> Let thy west wind sleep on
> The lake; speak silence with thy glimmering eyes,
> And wash the dusk with silver.

Blake was always capable of putting sensuous apprehension into euphonious form, but when mature he generally avoided it except for special purposes, as in his Beulah imagery. Blake is one of the technical masters of English poetry; whatever he wanted to do he could do. The odd but popular notion that he wrote more harshly as he grew older because he had lost his lyrical gifts is nonsense.

The poems so far described are in the tradition of landscape verse. A larger group in *Poetical Sketches* are songs in the Elizabethan manner. The most beautiful of them is also the most profoundly deceptive. Perhaps inspired by a line from the Elizabethan Davies, "Wives are as birds in golden cages kept," Blake writes a song mingling Innocence and Experience:

> How sweet I roam'd from field to field,
>   And tasted all the summer's pride,
> 'Till I the prince of love beheld,
>   Who in the sunny beams did glide!
>
> He shew'd me lilies for my hair,
>   And blushing roses for my brow;
> He led me through his gardens fair,
>   Where all his golden pleasures grow.
>
> With sweet May dews my wings were wet,
>   And Phoebus fir'd my vocal rage;
> He caught me in his silken net,
>   And shut me in his golden cage.
>
> He loves to sit and hear me sing,
>   Then, laughing, sports and plays with me;
> Then stretches out my golden wing,
>   And mocks my loss of liberty.

Eros, Prince of Love, is here also Helios or Apollo, Prince of Light, and a male equivalent of Keats's Belle Dame. The silken net of courtship and the golden cage of sexual capture are related to Petrarchan convention, but by association with the sun they become nature's entrapments also. The gardens fair that grow the golden pleasures of sexuality grow also the fruits of deceit and sadism, jealous possessiveness, and the depravity of a natural heart. Apollo kindles the bird into song, and also shuts her in the cage that will mock the earlier sweetness of free roaming. The poem's last ironic touch is the gilding of the trapped bird's outstretched but ineffectual wing. Gold is becoming Blake's prime emblem of the tyranny of nature.

The *Mad Song* is the furthest reach of the *Poetical Sketches* toward the *Songs of Experience*. The tradition of mad songs goes from the Elizabethans to the Romantics, and thence to Yeats in his last phase. Blake is unique in evading both the line of pathos (Ophelia's songs, Madge Wildfire's in Scott, the afflicted mothers of Wordsworth and Tennyson) and that of wisdom (the Fool in *Lear*, the great *Tom-O-Bedlam's Song* "From the hag and hungry goblin," and the Crazy Jane of Yeats). Blake's *Mad Song* is a satire upon its singing protagonist, and through him upon all who choose to narrow their perceptions to a chink in the cavern of nature. The poem's madman welcomes sleep as an unfolder of griefs and is so attached to night that he crowds after it as it goes, and so is sleepless because of his own fear of half of the natural cycle. The grim humor of the poem is that he is not as mad as he wishes to be, but presumably will attain the state through perseverance. He accepts outer realities only insofar as they accord with his preferred inner state (wild winds, cold night) and turns his back on light and warmth, though he can still recognize them as comforts. His ideal is to be:

> Like a fiend in a cloud,
> With howling woe.

Thus amorphous, he could escape the consequences of shape even as he seeks to escape those of duration. For even his heaven is a paved vault, and therefore an image of the bounded. He is a potential visionary gone wrong by an inadequate because simplistic metaphysic. Oppressed by space and time he does not see through those conventions but merely flees them into the evasions of a willful madness. The poem may well be Blake's ironic commentary on the escape into melancholia and despair of the poets of the Age of Sensibility—Smart, Cowper, Chatterton, Macpherson, and Collins. Blake's sardonic reaction to being accused of madness was to read and annotate at least part of a work on insanity. He comments there on the relation between religious enthusiasm and madness: "Cowper came to me and said: 'O that I were insane always. I will never rest. Can you not make me truly insane? I will never rest till I am so.' "

This has in it a touch of the *Mad Song*, and the gallows humor is parallel, for Cowper goes on to say: "You retain health and yet are as mad as any of us all—over us all—mad as a refuge from unbelief—from Bacon, Newton and Locke."

The gathering ironies of *Poetical Sketches* culminate in *To the Muses*, Blake's charming mockery of the state of eighteenth-century poetry, in what had become its own frozen diction. Wherever the "fair Nine" are, they are not on the English earth, and have forsaken poetry:

> How have you left the antient love
> That bards of old enjoy'd in you!
> The languid strings do scarcely move!
> The sound is forc'd, the notes are few!

As Frye observes, this is the germ of Blake's myth which separates the "Daughters of Beulah," human inspiration, from the "Daughters of Memory," the Nine Muses, natural inspiration from the generative world. To understand this distinction, we need to leave *Poetical Sketches* and begin to explore Blake's somewhat technical concept of Beulah.

CAROL McGUIRK

Robert Burns as Bard: The Songs

Of Burns's 330 songs, some are wholly original and others almost wholly traditional. Like the ratio of vernacular Scots to standard English in Burns's poetic language, the ratio of traditional to new material in Burns's songs varies considerably. The task of determining the extent of Burns's contributions is, however, simplified by the existence of an "interleaved" copy of Johnson's *Scots Musical Museum* that Burns annotated, often recording the traditional stanzas he had worked from and discussing his reasons for altering them. Most of the songs discussed in this [essay] received this special attention from Burns, or are texts for which the extent of Burns's contribution has been otherwise determined.

There are other unusual problems posed by Burns's songs. Some lyrics that work beautifully on the page are ill-matched to their tunes and cannot be regarded as great if strictly considered as songs (for example, "Mary Morison"). Other songs that may seem on the page to verge on doggerel rhythm are set to intricate tunes and are brilliantly fluid in performance. . . . Songs that may seem rather slight on the page achieve an exquisite simplicity when heard with their perfectly matched melodies; "The bonny wee thing" is one such song. Finally, many of Burns's finest songs are set to dance and fiddle music (instrumental "reels," "jigs," and such that Burns slowed to adapt them to lyric stanzas): it is a matter of interpretation just how slowly Burns intended his songs to be performed. Thus, not only Burns's words but also the "airs" to which he set the words offer a spectrum of interpretative

From *Robert Burns and the Sentimental Era.* © 1985 by the University of Georgia Press. Originally entitled "The Songs."

possibilities. For some sense of how broad that spectrum is, the spare, powerful recordings of Burns's songs made by Ewan MacColl may be compared to the more elaborate arrangements of Jean Redpath (whose more studied versions are, incidentally, probably closer to what Burns intended when he set out to provide "drawing room" verses for the old airs of Scottish bawdry).

The most comprehensive treatment of Burns as a lyric writer is Thomas Crawford's *Society and the Lyric*; and the best discussion of the musical quality of the songs is Cedric Thorpe-Davie's "Robert Burns, Writer of Songs." The discussion that follows will, by contrast, be selective rather than exhaustive. I will focus on a wide range of songs, of high literary quality, that we know Burns revised. The consistency and coherence of Burns's mature aesthetic can only be understood fully in terms of how and why he changed traditional folk material.

In one of his annotations to Johnson's *Scots Musical Museum*, Burns said of the air "Corn rigs are bonie" that "there must have been an old song under this title, the chorus of it is all that remains":

> O corn rigs and rye rigs,
> O corn rigs are bonie;
> And whene'er ye meet a bonie lass,
> Preen up her cockernony.

In Stenhouse's commentary to James Johnson, another version of "Corn rigs" current in Burns's day is cited, Allan Ramsay's conclusion to *The Gentle Shepherd*:

> Let maidens of a silly mind
> Refuse what maist they're wanting;
> Since we for yielding are design'd,
> We chastely should be granting;
> Then I'll comply, and marry Pate,
> And syne my cockernony,
> He's free to touzle, air or late,
> Where corn-riggs are bonny.

One would never know from Ramsay's rhetorical version that he was not one of Edinburgh's literary lawyers. His shepherdess, with her syllogistic assent to Pate, is wholly unlike Burns's heroine in his version. Burns wrote the following stanzas in the earliest stage of his career, between 1774 and 1784:

It was upon a Lammas night,
  When corn rigs are bonie,
Beneath the moon's unclouded light,
  I held awa to Annie:
The time flew by, wi' tentless heed,
  Till 'tween the late and early;
Wi' sma' persuasion she agreed,
  To see me thro' the barley.

. . . .

I hae been blythe wi' Comrades dear;
  I hae been merry drinking;
I hae been joyfu' gath'rin gear;
  I hae been happy thinking:
But a' the pleasures e'er I saw,
  Tho' three times doubl'd fairly,
That happy night was worth them a',
  Amang the rigs o' barley.

Chorus
Corn rigs, an' barley rigs,
  An' corn rigs are bonie:
I'll ne'er forget that happy night,
  Amang the rigs wi' Annie.

This very early song shows an already mature lyric ability. Like most of Burns's early work, "Corn rigs are bonie" sounds autobiographical, but except for this self-reference, it can be compared to his later revisions. Notable throughout Burns's songs, early and late, is the absence of a double standard for sexuality. Annie agrees "wi' sma' persuasion"—Burns does not present the "happy night" so much as a seduction as an episode involving mutual agreement. The fragment of the folk stanza quoted above is impersonal and anecdotal, as the old fragments often are. "Whene'er ye meet a bonie lass/ Preen (pin) up her cockernony (hair)" is a rather crude parody of a proverb. Burns's "I held awa' to Annie," on the other hand, introduces two individuals into the setting of the harvest fields and makes a story out of a piece of gnomic advice. Allan Ramsay took from the old fragment only the harvest setting and the idea of tousling the girl's hair (he applied the image more literally than in the folk chorus, where double entendre was intended).

In the second and third stanzas of his version, Burns develops the harvest theme simultaneously with the theme of mutual pleasure by alternating his rhymes: the fruition of the environment is juxtaposed to the fulfillment of the lovers' feelings:

> The sky was blue, the wind was still,
>   The moon was shining clearly;
> I set her down, wi' right good will,
>   Amang the rigs o' barley:
> I ken't her heart was a' my ain;
>   I lov'd her most sincerely;
> I kiss'd her owre and owre again,
>   Amang the rigs o' barley.
>
> I lock'd her in my fond embrace;
>   Her heart was beating rarely:
> My blessings on that happy place,
>   Amang the rigs o' barley!
> But by the moon and stars so bright,
>   That shone that hour so clearly!
> She ay shall bless that happy night,
>   Amang the rigs o' barley.

The first stanza concentrates on the speaker's feelings, describing them in concert with the blue sky, still wind, and clear moon of the environment; the second describes Annie's, again in harmony with the natural setting. The speaker blesses "that happy place" while avowing that Annie herself will always bless that "happy night." Happiness links the characters to their environment and to each other. Burns's version of "Corn rigs" is designed to convey a totality of happy emotions; it blends description and appraisal, avoiding both the baldness of the folk source and the rhetorical excesses (emotional falseness) of Ramsay's version.

In a letter of April 1793 to George Thomson, Burns tried to persuade the editor to insert his version of "Corn rigs are bonie" into the *Select Collection* in preference to Ramsay's: "[His version] is surely far unworthy of Ramsay, or your book.—My Song, 'Rigs of barley,' to the same air, does not altogether please me; but if I can mend it, & thresh a few loose sentiments out of it, I shall submit it to your consideration." Thomson, however, continued to prefer Ramsay's song (in a typical demonstration of his tastelessness), and Burns's version went to Thomson's rival editor, James Johnson. (It had appeared, without musical notation, in the Kilmarnock edition of his *Poems*.) Burns's statement that "Corn rigs" was not yet pulled together to his satisfaction (some "loose sentiments" remained to be "threshed out") indicates the high standard to which he submitted his work.

This standard was a matter of delicate balance between the natural and the artificial, and Burns's view of the dynamic requirements of good lyric writing seems to have been shaped to some extent by the work of John Aikin (1747–1822), a man he admired as "a great Critic . . . on songs." In his *Essays on Song Writing* (1772), Aikin—a physician and brother of Mrs. Barbauld— had separated songs into several types:

> The rude original pastoral poetry of our country . . . [is] ballads. These consist of the village tale, the dialogue of rustic courtship, the description of natural objects, and the incidents of a rural life. . . . Nature, further refined, but still nature, gives the second class of pieces containing the sentimental part of the former, abstracted from the tale and rural landscape, and improved by a more studied observation of the internal feelings of passion and their external symptoms. It is the natural philosophy of the mind, and the description of sensations.

Aikin's first and most primitive song type, the ballad, primarily tells a story. His second, the sentimental song, primarily conveys a feeling. Both song types confine themselves to a rustic subject matter; what separates the two is the level of emotional integration. Aikin's sentimental song is in fact an internalized "refinement" and "improvement" on the ballad: the ballad's emphasis on narrative has become subordinated to the expression of some powerful feeling.

It was, of course, Aikin's sentimental song that corresponded to Burns's own revisions, virtually all of which are "abstracted" from tales of "rural life" but "improved by a more studied observation of . . . feelings." Burns loved the old Scots airs exactly as they were, but he considered the fragmentary existing verses fair game for refinement and improvement. Like Aikin, Burns distinguished between ancientness and authenticity as lyric effects and aimed his own revisions toward the latter. There is every evidence that Burns, like Aikin, without actually wishing to suppress older verses, considered many of them too "rude" to deserve preservation. In one letter, for instance, he dismissed the traditional stanzas to "The posie": "it is well known in the West country, but the old words are trash."

In his introduction to *Notes on Scottish Song*, J. C. Dick cites Joseph Ritson's "Historical Essay," prefixed to the collection *Scotish Songs* (1794), as the first real history of Scots lyric writing ever to appear. Dick does not also mention Burns's dislike of some of Ritson's ideas. Burns's resistance has its bearing, however, on his support of Aikin's theories and his attitude toward song revising. Ritson (1752–1803) was a folklorist, vegetarian, and polemicist who had written on English lyric tradition before turning to Scottish song. What immediately struck Ritson was the prevalence of revisionism among the Scottish bards. Ritson was annoyed at the "impunity" with which such poets as Ramsay had rewritten old song fragments. Ritson's view was that "modern taste" was inimical to the pith of realism that animates old texts; and his annoyance is expressed in the introduction to *Scotish Songs* in highly sarcastic passages: "Why the Scotish literati should be more particularly addicted to literary imposition than those of any other country, might be a curious subject of investigation for their new Royal Society. . . . The history of Scotish poetry exhibits a series of fraud, forgery and imposture, practiced with impunity and success."

Ritson included two songs by Burns in his collection: "When *Guilford* good our Pilot stood" and "Willie brew'd a peck o' maut." Neither is an especially lyrical lyric: Ritson's selections show his antiquarian and anthropological orientation. A pioneer collector of Robin Hood legends and English fairy tales, Ritson seems to have been rather insensitive to lyric poetry, judging by his verdicts both on Robert Fergusson and Robert Burns: "Robert Fergusson . . . is the author of two tolerably pretty love-songs. . . . Robert Burns, a natural poet of the first eminence, does not, perhaps, appear to his usual advantage in song: *non omnia possumus*." A man who could miss Fergusson's comic genius and print "two tolerably pretty" love songs and then question Burns's talent for lyric composition was bound to irritate Burns. Most interesting is Burns's accusation in a letter to George Thomson that Ritson sent his unretouched songs "naked into the world": "A lady of my acquaintance, a noted performer, plays, 'Nae luck about the house,' & sings it at the same time so charmingly, that I shall never bear to see any of her songs sent into the world as naked as Mr. What-d-ye-call-um has done in his London Collection." Burns is criticizing Ritson's omission of music from his English songbook; but both the lack of musical accompaniment and the purist approach to the old song fragments signified to Burns a museum-piece attitude toward what Burns liked to regard as a malleable living tradition. Indeed, as a folklorist, Ritson's chief interest necessarily was in Aikin's primitive first category of song—the rude ballad. And though Burns thought Ritson's critical approach in the English songbook "interesting," he resented Ritson's apparent view in the Scottish collection that Robert Burns should be grouped with the primitives: "The legion of Scotish Poetasters of the day, whom your brother Editor, Mr Ritson, ranks with me as my coevals, have always mistaken vulgarity for simplicity; whereas Simplicity is as much eloignée from vulgarity, on the one hand, as from affected point & puerile conceit, on the other." "Vulgarity" on the one hand and "puerile conceit" on the other were the two extremes between which the lyric writer of Aikin's "natural" but refined second category had to steer his songs; and Burns could be a harsh judge if he perceived too much of either quality in a composition. One of his own revisions, "The last time I came o'er the moors," was ultimately rejected on the grounds of "affected point": "On reading over this song, I see it is but a cold, inanimate composition." He criticized vulgarity elsewhere, criticizing Thomson's selection of one popular old text, for instance, as "foolish": "I am out of temper that you should set so sweet, so tender an air, as 'Deil tak the war,' to the foolish old verses."

Burns's concept of lyric simplicity is, then, Horatian: a bard mediates between the two undesirable extremes of "vulgarity" on the one hand and frigid "affected point" on the other. To Burns, a bard's relationship to tradition was properly self-conscious, not naive: the texts to songs, old or new, should measure up to a high standard of emotional coherence and expressiveness. Thus, Burns greatly differs from Ritson (and the folkloric or anthropological approach to song collecting) and corresponds closely to Aikin.

Both Burns and Aikin valued what they called a realistic effect, yet both saw realism to result from an emphasis on feelings. Ritson and other antiquarians, on the other hand, perceived "realism" to be that shaggy, brusque effect often created by the interplay of different "voices" within the collective repository of the folk text. To Ritson, whatever parts of songs showed integration of personal statement were immediately to be suspected as forgeries. To Aikin and Burns, however, integration of emotion within a single speaker was the sole purpose of that second, sentimental category of lyric writing. As Aikin writes:

> The lover . . . must seek. . . . to express the emotions of his mind.
> He must *burn* with desire, and *freeze* with disdain; rage with the
> *ocean*, and sigh with the *zephir*. . . . The effects which the passions
> produce upon the body . . . also prove a happy source of the de-
> scription of emotions. Thus the fluttering pulse, the changing
> colour, the feverish glow, the failing heart and the confused
> senses, being natural and invariable symptoms of the passion of
> love . . . successfully heighten his description. Hitherto all is sim-
> ple and natural, and poetry so far from being the art of fiction,
> is the faithful copyist of external objects and real emotion.

Aikin's requirement that his second category of songs be "simple and natural" is actually rigorous, because in his view this naturalness was a result of the adept recreation of "real emotions." And as his own cliché-ridden list of possible tropes indicates, "real" emotion is not that easy to express in words. Burns, a poet rather than a doctor, avoided Aikin's clinical approach to describing the "symptoms" of passion; and even in his adaptation of one set of old verses in which the speaker is experiencing something like Aikin's "freezing disdain," Burns is able to authenticate the commonplace:

> Oh, open the door, some pity to shew,
>   If love it may na be, Oh;
> Tho' thou hast been false, I'll ever prove true,
>   Oh, open the door to me, Oh.
>
> Cauld is the blast upon my pale cheek,
>   But caulder thy love for me, Oh:
> The frost that freezes the life at my heart,
>   Is nought to my pains frae thee, Oh.
>
> The wan moon sets behind the white wave,
>   And time is setting with me, Oh:
> False friends, false love, farewell! for mair
>   I'll ne'er trouble them, nor thee, Oh.

Burns's original touches to this old Irish song constitute the finest lines: the last two of the second stanza and the first two of the third, for instance, are by Burns. W. B. Yeats singled out the beginning of stanza three in a discussion of poetic diction:

> There are no lines with more melancholy beauty than these by Burns—
>
> > The white [sic] moon is setting behind the white wave,
> > And time is setting with me, O!
>
> and these lines are perfectly symbolical. Take from them the whiteness of the moon and of the wave, whose relationship to . . . time is too subtle for the intellect, and you take from them . . . their beauty. . . . All sounds, all colours, all forms, either because of their preordained energies or because of long association, evoke indefinable and yet precise emotions, or, as I prefer to think, call down among us certain disembodied powers, whose footprints over our hearts we call emotions.

Like Burns and Aikin, Yeats saw reality in poems to be a matter of the emotional intensity conveyed. What Yeats called "symbolism," Burns, following Aikin, called "simplicity." When Burns praised an old Scots air, it was often in terms highly similar to Yeats's praise above of Burns's lines. In one letter to Frances Dunlop, for instance, he defined a song's symbolic power: "Notwithstanding its rude simplicity [it] speaks feelingly to the heart." And when Burns sought to expand the emotional significance of conventional figures or old texts, he tended, like Yeats, to stress "colors," "forms," "precise yet indefinable" feelings. As other critics have observed, one of his most famous songs, "A red red Rose," is distinguished largely by the inspired repetition of "red" in the first line, which encourages the reader or listener to see the rose—reanimating a too-familiar image.

Even in his comic songs or densely vernacular lyrics, Burns's chief concern was to use his folk models expansively—to show characters who embody certain emotions. Modern critics writing on Burns have tended to overstress the songs' "realism"; actually, Burns's song revisions are both more and less than "real." Burns's sturdy and impulsive heroines, for instance, though thoroughly appealing, do not sustain the claims of several critics that Burns was a "master of feminine psychology." His women speakers are indeed, as Thomas Crawford calls them, "the feminine equivalent of the 'man o' independent mind' " that Burns saw as the masculine ideal. But the wholly positive attitude of his heroines to sexual experience is essentially supported by their complacent attitude toward unwanted or unwed pregnancy; and this had more to do with the wishes of Burns than with the psychology of women. To be candid, even feckless, in one's emotional responses was central to Burns's idea of being heroically human (as later discussion of "Tam o' Shanter" will show). But no real woman has ever combined an independent mind with the total lack of rancor shown by the abandoned narrator of "Here's his health in water":

> Although my back be at the wa',
>   And though he be the fautor,
> Although my back be at the wa',
>   Yet here's his health in water.—
>
> O wae gae by his wanton sides,
>   Sae brawly's he could flatter;
> Till for his sake I'm slighted sair,
>   And dree the kintra clatter:
> But though my back be at the wa',
>   Yet here's his health in water.—

Burns had a prototype for a tolerant female temperament in his own wife, Jean Armour—by all accounts a paragon either of magnanimity or passiv-

ity. But Jean lacked the spirit of Burns's song heroines: she had forbear-
ance but was easily bullied, or so it appears from Burns's descriptions of
her in letters to friends around the time of their marriage. Burns's heroines, like his songs themselves, were symbolic more than descriptive—
they were collages of traits he liked in different women. Much like his male
characters, they seem simultaneously lifelike and larger than life. All
Burns's speakers display an unclouded vehemence of opinion and heroic
consistency of attitude: even his bawdry emphasizes the dominant person-
alities of his characters—the power of their feelings—rather than just their
biological destinies.

Indeed, though the Scottish folk tradition has a reputation for cheerful
sensuality largely because of Burns's dominance of it, the sexual attitudes
conveyed by old bawdry often seem more ambivalent than those in Burns's
genial adaptations:

> The modiewark has done me ill,
> And below my apron has biggit a hill;
> I maun consult some learned clark
> About this wanton modiewark.
>
> (*Merry Muses*)

In this old stanza, with which Burns was familiar, the attitude toward sex
is more ironic than that to which the reader of Burns is accustomed. Moles
and molehills are the metaphors, and the four stanzas dwell on this equivocal
image, with its connotations of blindness, creeping, and darkness. When
Burns took up the "modiewark" metaphor (Kinsley, at any rate, endorses
this as Burns's work; the authorship of many pieces in *The Merry Muses of
Caledonia* [a collection of bawdry collected and partially written by Burns] is
difficult to determine), he used it briefly, and only to highlight his speaker's
frank enthusiasm for sex:

> The Mouse is a merry wee beast,
>   The Moudiewart wants the een;
> And O' for a touch o' the thing
>   I had in my nieve yestreen.
>
> (*The Poems and Songs*)

Even in bawdry, Burns orchestrated his materials for expressive rather than
purely graphic ends: characters and what they stand for dominate and integrate the descriptions.

Burns's set of "polite" verses to the tune "Moudiewort" is a courtship
rather than an erotic song, but its speaker demonstrates the forcefulness
typical of all Burns's characters:

And O, for ane and twenty Tam!
　　An hey, sweet ane and twenty, Tam!
I'll learn my kin a rattlin sang,
　　An I saw ane and twenty, Tam.

. . . .

A gleib o'lan', a claut o' gear,
　　Was left me by my Auntie, Tam;
At kith or kin I need na spier,
　　An I saw ane and twenty, Tam.
　　　An O, for etc.
They'll hae me wed a wealthy coof,
　　Tho' I mysel' hae plenty, Tam;
But hearst thou, laddie, there's my loof,
　　I'm thine at ane and twenty, Tam!
　　　An O, for etc.

Burns's speaker seems positively to enjoy the prospect of fighting with her family for the three years that remain until she can claim her inheritance and marry penniless Tam. It is not surprising that a poet whose heroines declare sentiments like "I'll learn my kin a rattling sang" was unmoved by Richardson's *Clarissa*, a novel Burns dismissed in a letter to Dr. John Moore as an entertainment suitable only to "captivate the unexperienced, romantic fancy of a boy or a girl."

One of Burns's most famous character sketches is his portrait of an old Scots woman in his "polite" version of "John Anderson my Jo." The oldest verses to this tune had appeared in Percy's *Reliques*:

> *Woman.*
> John Anderson my jo, cum in as ze gae bye,
> And ze sall get a sheip's heid well baken in a pye;
> Weel baken in a pye, and the haggis in a pat;
> John Anderson my jo, cum in, and ze's get that.

Kinsley's note to Burns's version indicates that the text Burns worked with was probably not the Percy fragment, but a later and less elliptical set of erotic stanzas to the tune. Legman's note to this bawdy version in *The Merry Muses* indicates that Burns's source is still popular in Scotland:

> John Anderson, my jo, John,
> 　　I wonder what ye mean,
> To lie sae lang i' the mornin',
> 　　And sit sae late at een?
> Ye'll bleer a' your een, John,

> And why do ye so?
> Come sooner to your bed at een,
>   John Anderson, my jo.
>
> . . . .
>
> I'm backit like a salmon,
>   I'm breastit like a swan;
> My wame it is a down-cod,
>   My middle ye may span:
> Frae my tap-knot to my tae, John,
> I'm like the new-fa'n snow;
> And its a' for your convenience
>   John Anderson, my jo.

In this version the neglected wife progresses through a succession of moods: loneliness, reminiscence, desire, and finally a threat of infidelity. Unlike most of the songs in *Merry Muses*, this is not bawdry dependent on punch lines; it is a dramatic monologue with some good poetry in it. (The imagery of the second stanza above is similar to images occurring in the well-known song "Annie Laurie.") When Burns worked up "drawing room" stanzas for "John Anderson my Jo," he kept its monologue form and the reflective mood of its speaker (reverie is in any case well-suited to the slow sadness of the tune). He changed the topic from sex specifically to marriage generally, and he equalized the ages of John Anderson and his wife. Burns adapted the "plot" so that the speaker can describe John Anderson's decline from youth but share in it. Complaint is changed to tolerance:

> John Anderson my jo, John,
>   When we were first acquent;
> Your locks were like the raven,
>   Your bony brow was brent;
> But now your brow is beld, John,
>   Your locks are like the snaw;
> But blessings on your frosty pow,
>   John Anderson my Jo.
>
> John Anderson my jo, John,
>   We clamb the hill the gither;
> And mony a canty day, John,
>   We've had wi' ane anither:

Now we maun totter down,
    John,
And hand in hand we'll go;
And sleep the gither at the foot,
    John Anderson my Jo.

In the bawdy source the endearment "jo" is applied sarcastically. Burns's speaker uses it unironically, to affirm her affection despite John's age and their mutual decline. Burns took several images from the older version but changed their import by applying them commonly to the couple rather than invidiously only to John. "We clamb the hill the gither" is a different application of a climbing metaphor than "I've twa gae ups for ae gae-down, / John Anderson my jo," which is an accusation, not a reminiscence. In the bawdy version, too, physical description of John is negative while the speaker insists on her own beauty. In Burns's version, the speaker concludes her description of John with a benediction intended to compensate for her insistence on John's decline; and the second stanza emphasizes what the couple has done and will do together.

"John Anderson my Jo" bears an interesting relationship to Burns's other revisions of bawdry—it is one of few cases where his effort does not work so well as the original. It is a matter of the reader's mood whether the last three lines of Burns's version—as expressive and economical a conclusion as he ever wrote—redeem earlier lines that border on mawkishness. "Totter down," for instance, seems too self-consciously pathetic for it to accord well with the speaker's otherwise consistent mood of practical sturdiness; and the character who would begin her reminiscence with the reticent "when we were first acquent" would probably not indulge in a sudden effusion like "But blessings on your frosty pow." Burns's song is largely successful, but there are inconsistencies within it; and the bawdy source remains the more integrated lyric. This is not the case with other revisions, such as the transformation of the bawdy stanzas of "Duncan Davison" into Burns's lovely early song "Mary Morison," written to the same tune.

Although there was a Mary Morison living in Mauchline during Burns's residence at nearby Mossgiel, most scholars agree that Burns's choice of her name had more to do with its euphonious sound and compatibility with his air than his feelings for her (he was in love at that time with a girl of invincibly prosaic surname: Begbie):

Yestreen when to the trembling string
    The dance gaed through the lighted ha',

To thee my fancy took its wing,
   I sat, but neither heard, nor saw:

Though this was fair, and that was braw,
   And yon the toast of a' the town,
I sigh'd, and said amang them a',
   "Ye are na Mary Morison."

Hugh MacDiarmid called that last line, "Ye are na Mary Morison," the "most powerful" that Burns ever wrote. The way Burns works up to the line is just as impressive. Having assigned to nameless females the usually desirable attributes of beauty, fashion, and popularity, the speaker simply rejects these qualities as having any part in Mary Morison's appeal. The conventional adjectives of love lyrics, then, are introduced not to explain Mary Morison's attractiveness but to affirm her transcendence of merely conventional standards. She is the center of specific gravity in the song: Mary Morison is the only proper noun in it, and reference to other girls is not even expressed in common nouns but in impersonal pronouns—"this," "that," and "yon." Yet Mary Morison remains partly unknown. The speaker can only be sure of what she is not: not subject to the usual standards of female excellence, not in love with him, but—he hopes—not capable of outright cruelty:

If love for love thou wilt na gie,
   At least be pity to me shown;
A thought ungentle canna be
   The thought o' Mary Morison.

"Mary Morison" is one of Burns's best evocations of tenderness as an adjunct to sexual attraction, and the tenderness is entirely Burns's contribution to the text. Unlike "John Anderson my Jo," which owes its reflective mood to its bawdy source, his "Mary Morison" owes none of its tender inflections to "Duncan Davidson," which is crude and jocular:

There was a lass, they ca'd her Meg,
   An' she gaed o'er the muir to spin;
She feed a lad to lift her leg,
   They ca'd him Duncan Davidson.
     Fal, lal, etc.

Meg had a muff and it was rough,
   Twas black without and red within;
An' Duncan, case he got the cauld,

He stole his Highland p—e in.
   Fal, lal, etc.

Meg had a muff, and it was rough,
And Duncan strak tway handfu' in
She clasp'd her heels about his waist,
   "I thank you Duncan! Yerk it in!!!"
   Fal, lal, etc.

Duncan made her hurdies dreep,
   In Highland wrath, then Meg did
     say;
O gang he east, or gang he west,
   His ba's will no be dry to day.
              (Merry Muses)

The distance between Burns's version and its folk-collected source was often similarly astronomical.

David Herd's *Ancient and Modern Scots Songs* (1769) was headed by a brief preface, in which Herd called the characteristic effect of Scottish song "a forcible and pathetic simplicity, which at once lays strong hold upon the affections: so that the heart may be considered as an *instrument*, which the bard or minstrel harmonizes" (Herd's italics). Herd's view of the bard or minstrel as an orchestrator of emotions is similar to Aikin's view of refined lyric and corresponds closely to Burns's attitude toward his sources. Burns in theory revered them and relied on the tunes and traditional metaphors of the folk tradition, but when he worked with them it was usually to introduce more expressiveness into them—to enlarge their evocative possibilities.

In his notes to Johnson's *Scots Musical Museum* Burns recorded political stanzas to an old version of "To daunton me" that he thought had "some merit":

To daunton me, to daunton me,
O ken ye what it is that'll daunton me?
There's eighty eight and eighty nine,
And a' that I have borne synsyne,
There's cess and press and Presbytrie,
I think it will do meikle for to daunton me.
But to wanton me, to wanton me,
O ken ye what it is that wad wanton me,
To see gude corn upon the rigs,

> And banishment amang the Whigs,
> And right restor'd where right sud be,
> I think wad to meikle for to wanton me.
> *(Notes on Scottish Song)*

When Burns worked his own version of "To daunton me," he expanded the emotional power of the melody's defiant self-assertion by changing the text from politics to courtship. In Burns's version a young girl is declaring herself unmoved by the proposal of an older man:

> The blude-red rose at Yule may blaw,
> The simmer lilies bloom in snaw,
> The frost may freeze the deepest sea,
> But an auld man shall never daunton me.—
> *(The Poems and Songs)*

Kinsley's note to Burns's version states that other courtship stanzas had been fitted to the tune, but that no parallel exists for Burns's first stanza quoted above. The significant and characteristic trait of this stanza is the way it states the girl's defiance in terms at once metaphorical yet unequivocal. "Precise yet indefinable emotion," Yeats's notion of the stuff of poetry, is at the center of the young girl's speech. Her pride suffuses the song. She does not specifically call herself a rose, a lily, or a sea—yet in declaring she is even less likely to betray her own nature than these other beautiful phenomena, she symbolically asserts the resemblance.

A similar instance of Burns's use of first stanzas to enlarge the emotional expressiveness of his source occurs in "Ay waukin O." Herd's collection of manuscripts preserves the old text from which Burns probably worked:

> O wat, wat—O wat and weary!
> Sleep I can get nane
> For thinking on my deary.
> A' the night I wak,
> A' the day I weary,
> Sleep I can get nane
> For thinking on my dearie.

The fragment, like the dramatic tune to which it is set, is expressive as it stands. When Burns adapted it, however, he intensified the mood by deferring the specific complaint of the lover until the second stanza. As is characteristic of Burns's songs of lamentation, a context stanza is provided to extend into Nature the echoes of the narrator's melancholy:

Simmer's a pleasant time,
  Flowers of every colour;
The water rins o'er the heugh,
  And I long for my true lover!

Chorus
Ay waukin, Oh,
  Waukin still and weary:
Sleep I can get nane,
  For thinking on my Dearie.—

When I sleep I dream,
  When I wauk I'm irie;
Sleep I can get nane,
  For thinking on my Dearie.—

Burns's economy of expression (what he called "simplicity") creates an effect of conclusive alienation between the "pleasant" season and the weariness of the speaker and does it with a masterful reticence.

"O saw ye bonie Lesley" was written in 1792 for an acquaintance of Burns, Miss Lesley Baillie of Mayfield:

O saw ye bonie Lesley,
  As she gaed o'er the Border?
She's gane, like Alexander,
  To spread her conquests farther.

To see her is to love her,
  And love but her for ever;
For Nature made her what she is
  And never made anither.

. . . .

The deil he could na scaith thee,
  Or aught that wad belang thee:
He'd look into thy bonie face,
  And say, "I canna wrang thee!"

Burns exploits the implicit irony of hyperbole in the first and third stanzas quoted. In stanza 1, Lesley is a female conqueror, Alexander the Great on the march; then, in a reversal, she is seen as charmingly helpless—the disarming potential victim of the "deil" (devil) himself. Lesley's beauty is celebrated both in the reference to classical Alexander and and folk-mediated "deil": she is made relevant to both worlds, to all worlds. The irony inherent in Burns's gentle exaggerations does not undercut, but rather heightens, our sense of Lesley's all-encompassing charm. Irony's edge, however, touches the speaker himself. He is clearly among her already conquered victims, sharing the "deil's" attraction to her with all its diabolical potential (the "wrang" he cannot do her). Irony seems to be a vehicle for distancing the poet away from the direct expression of his feelings. In their indirect (ironic) presentation, the attraction of one man for one woman (and a woman inaccessible because of a disparity in their social classes) becomes an expression of wonder at the chastening power of beauty. The song, then, expands a restricted and exclusive subject (pretty Lesley) into an expression of illimitable feeling (the power of beauty). As Thomas Crawford notes in writing of this song, "In the early poems . . . positive value had resided in strong drink, or comradeship, or "generous love"; now, it is inherent in Beauty" (*Burns: A Study of the Poems and Songs*). As has been mentioned, the later songs characteristically reject the sentimental preoccupation with eccentricity, turning instead to the expansive evocation of commonly felt emotions. Even songs addressed to women Burns knew personally follow "bonie Lesley's" pattern of universalization.

"The bonie wee thing," praised both by Thomas Crawford and Cedric Thorpe-Davie as one of Burns's finest songs, was inspired by Miss Deborah Duff-Davies—like Lesley Baillie, a young acquaintance of Burns:

Chorus
Bonie wee thing, canie wee thing,
    Lovely wee thing, was thou mine;
I wad wear thee in my bosom,
    Least my Jewel I should tine.—

Wishfully I look and languish
    In that bonie face o' thine;
And my heart it stounds wi' anguish,
    Lease my wee thing be na mine.—
        Bonie wee etc.

Wit, and Grace, and Love, and Beauty,
    In ae constellation shine;
To adore thee is my duty,
    Goddess o' this soul o' mine!

Attraction to Miss Davies, as in the "deil" stanza of "bonie Lesley," becomes subsumed in a mood of protectiveness. The song turns a limitation and potential flaw—the girl's tiny stature—into the basis of her claim to tender protection. By the concluding stanza, she has become a fixed "constellation" of lovely qualities, a paradigm. As in "bonie Lesley," then, a finite (in this case, literally tiny) heroine becomes the basis for an idealized projection of feeling.

The later songs are not always tender, of course: some of the best focus on other feelings. The Jacobite songs often rearrange traditional material to create powerful expressions of anger and despair. "Here's a Health to them that's awa" is one example of brilliant generalization based on the amplification of an older source. Kinsley quotes the old song from which Burns may have worked:

> Here's a health to them that's away,
> Here's a health to them that's away,
> Here's a health to him that was here yestreen,
> But durstna bide till day.
> O wha winna drink it dry?
> O wha winna drink it dry?
> Wha winna drink to the lad that's gane,
> Is nane o' our company.

This stanza, with its anticlimactic final line, stands in marked contrast to Burns's revision, in which every stanza builds to a crescendo of defiance:

> Here's a health to them that's awa,
> Here's a health to them that's awa;
> Here's a health to Charlie, the chief o' the clan,
> Altho' that his band be sma'.
> May Liberty meet wi' success!
> May Prudence protect her frae evil!
> May Tyrants and Tyranny tine i' the mist,
> And wander their way to the devil!
>
> Here's a health to them that's awa,
> Here's a health to them that's awa;
> Here's a health to Tammie, the Norland laddie,
> That lives at the lug o' the law!
> Here's freedom to him that wad read,
> Here's freedom to him that wad write!
> There's nane ever fear'd that the Truth should be heard,
> But they whom the Truth wad indite.

The song's specific subject—Jacobite rebellion and allegiance to the Stuart kings—expands outward into a protest against all political oppression. The traditional source makes no effort to draw in the unconverted; rather, it specifically excludes from the company all who reject the Stuart kings. Burns's version, on the other hand, retains the peculiar vehemence of partisan expression but attaches that vehemence to values (for freedom, for the brave defiance of tyranny) that anyone not utterly insensible would instinctively embrace. Through Burns's amplification of his source, the partisan feeling becomes an emotional universal.

In "I hae a wife o' my ain," a song written in 1792, pride is the feeling Burns amplifies. Quoting Stenhouse, Kinsley cites the "trifling verses" that probably were Burns's source:

> I hae a wife o' my awn,
> I'll be haddin to naebody;
> I hae a pat and a pan,
> I'll borrow frae naebody.

Burns's adaptation brings the traditional speaker's self-sufficiency to the edge of misanthropy, an effect heightened in performance by the somewhat rigid and implacable tune to which it is set:

> I hae a wife o' my ain,
>   I'll partake wi' naebody;
> I'll tak Cuckold frae nane,
>   I'll gie Cuckhold to naebody.—
>
> I hae a penny to spend,
>   There, thanks to naebody;
> I hae naething to lend,
>   I'll borrow frae naebody.—
>
> I am naebody's lord,
>   I'll be slave to naebody;
> I hae a gude braid sword,
>   I'll tak dunts frae naebody.—
>
> I'll be merry and free,
>   I'll be sad for naebody;
> Naebody cares for me,
>   I care for naebody.—

Crawford, following his theory that Burns is generally autobiographical, discusses this song as a humorous self-portrait:

Now, Burns is the independent small farmer *par excellence*, be-
holden to no feudal superior or bureaucratic caste, and resentful
of supervision and control, however paternally exercised; he is
the small owner in love. Nowhere in literature, perhaps, is there
a more succinct, more engaging, more sympathetically humorous
presentation of a *petit bourgeois* attitude. . . . By thus giving expression to what millions of lower-middle-class people have known,
he makes us feel for and with them as *people*, so that we glory in
their essential humanity.

While the song does embody a doughty middle-class independence, it does
not seem to me to do so with humor. Crawford's interpretation fails to
acknowledge the hostility that is surely the primary feeling conveyed by the
song. Suspicious alienation, an emotional reality for more than just members
of the "lower middle class," is the amplified extreme of the independence
expressed by Burns's source. However negative, this feeling nonetheless is
felt occasionally by everyone. The song, then, like many of Burns's most
powerful, addresses itself to reawakening feelings already in the emotional
repertoire of the listener. Its effect is more immediate and powerful than the
effect of material primarily biographical or autobiographical, in which the
listener feels the emotions as those of another person. Self-sufficiency—and
misanthropy—are human universals; and the powerful resonance of such
universals seems to me to be the primary focus of Burns's later songs.

One of Burns's most simple and powerful lyrics was written about a
month before he died. He was being nursed by Jessie Lewars, the young
sister of a friend who worked with him at the Excise; and Burns's gratitude
for the girl's help to his family (his wife Jean was experiencing a difficult
pregnancy, and Jessie was tending the children as well as Burns) was expressed in "Oh wert thou in the cauld blast," an exceptionally fine song. He
asked the girl to play her favorite tune for him and then worked new stanzas
to it in her honor. The consensus of biographers has been that Jessie chose
"The robin came to the wren's nest" set to the air "Lenox love to Blantyre"
(see Snyder, *The Life of Robert Burns*). Ironically, "The Wren's Nest" had
already been refurbished by Burns himself in the *Scots Musical Museum* volume
for 1796:

> The Robin cam to the wren's nest
>   And keekit in and keekit in,
> O weel's me on your auld pow,
>   Wad ye be in, wad ye be in.

> Ye'se ne'er get leave to lie
>   without,
>   And I within, and I within,
> As lang's I hae an auld clout
>   To row you in, to row you in.

Allan Cunningham's *Songs of Scotland* (1825) presents as "early" two additional stanzas to the song which, if authentic, bear an interesting relationship to the symbols used in Burns's version. Before quoting these stanzas, however, I should mention that Cunningham is notorious for inventing many of his "ancient" texts:

> The robin came to the wren's nest,
>   And gae a peep and gae a peep—
> Now weels me on thee, cuttie quean,
>   Are ye asleep, are ye asleep?
> The sparrow-hawk is in the air,
>   The corbie-craw is on the sweep;
> An' ye be wise, ye'll bide at hame,
>   And never cheep, and never cheep.
>
> The robin came to the wren's nest,
>   And keekit in, and keekit in—
> I saw ye thick wi' wee Tam-tit,
>   Ye cuttie quean, ye cuttie quean,
> The ruddy feathers frae my breast
>   Thy nest hae lined, thy nest hae lined;
> Now wha will keep ye frae the blast,
>   And winter wind, and winter wind?

Cunningham's note to "The Wren's Nest" calls it "so simple and absurd, so foolish and yet so natural, that I know not whether to reject or retain it," a cool appraisal it seems unlikely he would have applied to an interpolation of his own. In any case, when Burns worked from the old texts he abandoned their central feature, the use of the robin and wren. Speaker and addressee become "I" and "thee" and the whimsy of the original vanishes. Burns retained and expanded, however, the mood of endearment and protectiveness:

> Oh wert thou in the cauld blast,
>   On yonder lea, on yonder lea;
> My plaidie to the angry airt,
>   I'd shelter thee, I'd shelter thee:

Or did misfortune's bitter storms
  Around thee blaw, around thee blaw,
Thy bield should be my bosom,
  To share it a', to share it a'.
Or were I in the wildest waste,
  Sae black and bare, sae black and bare,
The desart were a paradise,
  If thou wert there, if thou wert there.
Or were I monarch o' the globe,
  Wi' thee to reign, wi' thee to reign;
The brightest jewel in my crown,
  Wad be my queen, wad be my queen.

This song shows the features typical of Burns's best revisions from folk sources. He simplified the "plot" by substituting people for talking birds; yet he retained and exploited figurative connotations from the old sources: the offer of shelter and sacrifice, for instance, and the wistful status of "robin" (Burns's nickname) as an outsider. Burns's song is in the subjunctive throughout; not an indication of merely rhetorical emotion but rather the sign of reticence that generally characterized his songs to very young women. Most interesting of all, though the song sounds "real," the situation it describes was exactly opposite to the relationship that inspired it. The song offers the speaker's protection to Jessie in various threatening situations; when he wrote it, however, it was he who was receiving the help his song hypothetically showers on Jessie. Burns probably transferred his own jeopardized situation to her in order to imagine a reciprocity in their friendship: he offers an equal support throughout vicissitude and in the final quatrain extends his pledge to assert that the girl would be prized above all even were he "monarch o' the globe." "Oh wert thou in the cauld blast" is characteristic of Burns as a bard in the way it abstracts from a painful situation and a fragmentary old text a powerful, transcendent feeling. The concluding line, however, implies reality in its stress on the subjunctive "wad" (would). Jessie "wad be" his queen if life worked like lyric poetry. The moving connotation—and the plain fact—is that life does not.

James Beattie's *The Minstrel; or, The Progress of Genius* (1771–74) offers some fascinating parallels to Burns's career as a bard. Beattie's poem, for one thing, furnished Mackenzie with the fatal epithet "heaven-taught," which occurs in stanza 7; and *The Minstrel* provided Burns himself with some of his favorite all-purpose quotations. (His early letters frequently refer to the "malignant star" that dogged his life—that phrase occurs in Beattie's first stanza, though it is also congruent with Tristram's sense of fated failure in *Tristram Shandy*.) More important, *The Minstrel* shows that, although Burns's final project of song revising did evoke some of his best poetry, it also corresponded to contemporary notions about all bards and how they worked their lyric magic. Beattie's injunction to other minstrels was that they should broaden and substantiate their instincts in their lyrics, and this was Burns's enterprise. Beattie assigned to minstrels the role of spokesmen for freedom and assigned them, too, an inevitable though righteous poverty. Stanza 7 is especially interesting in relationship to Burns:

> Then grieve not, thou, to whom th' indulgent Muse
> Vouchsafes a portion of celestial fire;
> Nor blame the partial Fates, if they refuse
> The imperial banquet, and the rich attire:
> Know thine own worth, and reverence the lyre.
> Wilt though debase the heart which God refined?
> No; let thy heaven-taught soul to heaven aspire,
> To fancy, freedom, harmony, resigned;
> Ambition's grovelling crew for ever left behind.

Bombast aside, Beattie's sentiments do apply to Burns as a bard. Burns reworked traditional sources precisely to expand their potential for expressing "fancy, freedom, harmony." And Burns's "reverence" for song did go along with his rejection of a grand public destiny as a poet and his "resignation" to an obscure role—often an anonymous one—as a bard. Both his "reverence" for song and his "resignation" to its transcending qualities were, as in Beattie's poem, more or less consciously undertaken as compensation for a life Burns did perceive as materially unlucky. Compensation accounts for why Burns's songs—the most serene and benign portion of his creative work—were his major interest after leaving Edinburgh, a time when his life was difficult and his mood often bitter. The dying bard who presented young Jessie Lewars with the self-effacing lyric discussed above seems a different character altogether from the embittered man who—that same month in 1796—greeted Maria Riddell at their last meeting with the guilt-inducing pleasantry, "Well, Madam, have you any messages for the other world?"

Mackenzie had applied the epithet "heaven-taught" to Burns as though it simply meant unlettered. Beattie, however, intended the expression to signify the idealizing impulse of the true bard. The heaven-taught minstrel "left behind" the crass material world to seek "celestial fire." In Burns's songs, of course, the daily world was not thus rejected; but it was also not accepted without alteration. Burns simplified the circumstantial details in his folk sources and in that way amplified their significance: the effect is transcendence through description. "Oh wert thou in the cauld blast" synthesizes depressing autobiographical circumstances with mitigating fantasy; it draws on a folk text for its protective mood, yet Burns's treatment of the source has broadened the whimsy of the original into a comprehensive tenderness.

In *The Minstrel*, Beattie condemns a "witty" approach to life, which subjects everything to microscopic dissection by one critical mind:

> dark, cold-hearted skeptics, creeping, pore
> Through microscope of metaphysic lore:
> And much they grope for Truth, but never hit.
> For why? Their powers, inadequate before,
> This idle art makes more and more unfit;
> Yet they deem darkness light, and their vain blunders wit.

Beattie's minstrel is rather a telescopic interpreter; his hero is an "enlarged" soul, whose view of life is suitably magnanimous and comprehensive: "For Nature gave him strength, and Fire, to soar / On Fancy's wing above this vale of tears." Here Beattie may be drawing on sentiments expressed by Thomas Gray in a Pindaric imitation, "The Progress of Poesy," where Gray claims total independence from circumstance:

> Oh! Lyre divine, what daring Spirit
> Wakes thee now? Tho' he inherit
> Nor the pride, nor ample pinion,
> That the Theban Eagle bear
> Sailing with supreme dominion
> Thro' the azure deep of air:
> Yet oft before his infant eyes would run
> Such forms, as glitter in the Muse's ray
> With orient hues, unborrow'd of the Sun:
> Yet shall he mount, and keep his distant way
> Beyond the limits of a vulgar fate,
> Beneath the Good how far—but far above the Great.
>
> (112–23)

[Elsewhere] I discussed some tendencies Burns shared with other mid and late eighteenth-century poets. A distinction of Burns's songs is that, while as linked to an established convention as Gray's Pindaric odes, they do not disdain "the limits of a vulgar fate" as do so many poems of the day. In his songs Burns moves beyond the sentimental heroics of his early poems; he incorporates the magnanimous, bardic perspective on life with the detailed circumstantial spirit of his folk sources. Burns's songs demonstrate a profound respect for people as they really are; but at the same time they also manage to convey the ideal capacities of human nature and the infinite dimensions of such commonly experiences feelings as pity, rebellion, tenderness, anger, and love. In his songs, then, Burns projects a sensibility simultaneously definitive and expansive.

When Christopher Smart produced his version of Scripture, he was working—as Gray was from Pindar—from a sublime model down to his personal message. The descent is sometimes from the biblically sublime ("Blessed be the meek") down to the biographically quaint ("For I bless God for the immortal soul of Mr. Pigg of in DOWNHAM in NORFOLK"). Burns's relationship to folk song is as revisionary as Smart's to Scripture. Yet in adapting "John Anderson my Jo," Burns revised not the paradoxes of Matthew or Job but the caustic reverie of a bored farm wife. Often, his sources were just an aggregate of vivid incongruities loosely coordinated within a tune. (He very seldom tampered with already transcendent material, such as the ballads.) Such emphatic details as the sheep's head well-baked in a pie which the woman in Percy's version of "John Anderson my Jo" offers as an enticement into her house are characteristic of the popular folk tradition; folk song as a model is fundamentally circumstantial. Burns, a bard trained in the eighteenth-century mode, generalizes from and in that way radically changes his sources.

Thus, Burns's revisions usually synthesize two quite different elements: the collective folk tradition and the eighteenth-century cult of heroic bards. These two elements—the one anonymous, the other conspicuously self-conscious—combine to create Burns's inimitable lyric effect: a radical, meaningful simplicity. In the best of Burns's revisions, a self-conscious artistry enlarges and intensifies the symbols implicit in the source, usually by appropriating them to the clarification of the feelings of a central speaker. At the same time, the vividly circumstantial spirit of the folk source enters into and substantiates the bard's self-conscious idealism.

My sense of Burns's transcendence of folk models is supported in an odd way by the hostility with which antiquarians have always treated his songs. From Ritson to Legman to MacDiarmid, a chorus of objection has accused Burns of unwittingly killing the Scots vernacular tradition by the very success of his own free adaptations. The folklorists understandably wish that Burns's idealizaton of realistic folk models were not so commonly confused with folk realism as it is expressed in the authentic (genuinely collective) folk tradition. While even the folklorists do not wish Burns's revisions away, they see him essentially as a forger—a vernacular Chatterton claiming to discover texts that were actually shaped by his own complex vision.

Chronology

1700   James Thomson born at Ednam, Roxburghshire, September 11 (old style).

1716   Thomas Gray born December 26 in Cornhill.

1720   Thomson contributes his first poems to the *Edinburgh Miscellany*.

1721   William Collins born about Christmas, at Chichester.

1722   Christopher Smart born April 11 in Shipbourne, Kent.

1726   Thomson publishes *Winter*.

1727   Thomson publishes *Summer* and *A Poem Sacred to the Memory of Sir Isaac Newton*.

1728   Thomson publishes *Spring*.

1729   Thomson publishes *Britannia* anonymously.

1730   Thomson publishes *Sophonisba*. Finishes *The Seasons*.

1731   William Cowper born November 15 in Hertfordshire.

1736   James Macpherson born October 27 at Ruthven, Inverness. Thomson finishes *Liberty*.

1738   Thomson's *Agamemnon* performed at Drury Lane. Collins's first published verse, "On Hercules," appears in *Gentleman's Magazine*.

1739   Thomson's *Edward and Eleanora* banned from performance for political reasons.

1740   Thomson and Mallet's *Alfred: A Masque* privately produced at Clivedon.

1742   Collins publishes *Persian Eclogues*.

1743   Collins publishes *Verses Humbly Addres'd to Sir Thomas Hanmer*, anonymously.

1744   Collins publishes *An Epistle: Addrest to Sir Thomas Hanmer* and *A Song from the "Cymbelyne."*
        Revised and expanded version of Thomson's *The Seasons* appears.

1745   Thomson's *Tancred and Sigismunda* performed at Drury Lane.

1746   Collins publishes *Odes on Several Descriptive and Allegoric Subjects*.

1747   Gray's Eton Ode published.

1748   Thomson's *The Castle of Indolence* published. Thomson dies August 27.
        Gray publishes Eton Ode and "Ode on the Death of a Favorite Cat" in R. Dodsley's *Collection of Poems*.

1749   Thomson's *Coriolanus* performed at Covent Garden.
        Collins publishes *Ode Occasioned by the Death of Mr. Thomson*.

1751   Gray publishes "Elegy Written in a Country Churchyard."

1752   Thomas Chatterton born November 20 in Bristol, Gloucestershire.
        Smart's *Poems on Several Occasions*, his first verse, published by Newbery.

1753   Gray's *Six Poems* appears shortly after his mother's death.
        Smart publishes *The Hilliad*, a satire.

1756   Cowper contributes five papers to *Connoisseur*.

1757   William Blake born November 28 in London.
        Gray's *Odes* published, including "The Progress of Poesy" and "The Bard."
        Collins's *Persian Eclogues* altered and reissued as *Oriental Eclogues*.

1758   Macpherson publishes his first volume of poems, *The Highlander*.
        Cowper translates Voltaire's *Henriade*.

1759   Robert Burns born at Alloway, Ayrshire, on January 25.
        William Collins dies June 12.
        Smart is committed to Bethnel Green, a home for the insane, where he remains until 1763, writing and translating. His extraordinary work of this period, *Jubilate Agno*, did not appear until 1939, when W. F. Stead edited and published it as *Rejoice in the Lamb: A Song from Bedlam*.

1760   Macpherson publishes *Fragments of Ancient Poetry Translated from the Original Gallic or Erse Language*.

1762   Macpherson publishes *Fingal*, a volume of poetry in the ancient Gaelic epic style, claiming that it is based on the 3rd-century poet Ossian (no known Gaelic manuscripts date before the 10th century). Chatterton, age 10, writes his first known poem, "On the Last Epiphany."

1763   Smart leaves Bethnel Green and publishes *A Song to David*. Chatterton writes first of the "Rowleyan" poems, ascribed to a fifteenth-century monk of Bristol named Thomas Rowley (a fictitious character). Macpherson publishes *Temora*, another Ossianic epic.

1768   Gray's *Poems* published by Dodsley.

1769   Chatterton's "Elinoure and Juga" published. Gray's "Ode for Music" performed at installation of the Duke of Grafton as Chancellor of Cambridge University.

1770   Chatterton writes "An Excelente Balade of Charitie," the most pathetic of the Rowleyan poems. Finally having failed to win the sponsorship of Dodsley or Walpole, and in financial straits, Chatterton takes arsenic and dies August 24.

1771   Christopher Smart dies May 21. His *Hymns for the Amusement of Children* is published posthumously in 1775. Thomas Gray dies July 30.

1781   Cowper, after several bouts with mental illness, publishes *Anti-Thelyphthora*, anonymously.

1782   Cowper publishes *Poems of William Cowper of the Inner Temple, Esq.*

1783   Blake's *Poetical Sketches* published, containing poems written 1769–78. Burns writes his first poems.

1785   Cowper's second volume of poetry appears, includes *The Task*. Burns publishes *Poems, Chiefly in the Scottish Dialect*, including "To a Mouse." Burns begins contributing songs to James Johnson's *Scots Musical Museum*.

1789   Blake completes engraving of *Songs of Innocence* and *The Book of Thel*.

1790   Blake writes *The Marriage of Heaven and Hell* at the Christological age of thirty-three.

1791   Blake's *The French Revolution* printed by left-wing publisher Joseph Johnson, but the poem is abandoned in proof sheets.

1793   Blake finishes the engravings of *America* and *Visions of the Daughters of Albion*.
        Burns begins contributing songs to George Thomson's *Select Collection of Original Scottish Airs for the Voice*, including "Green Grow the Rushes O," "Auld Lang Syne," and "Comin' Thro' the Rye."

1794   Blake finishes engravings of *Songs of Experience*, *Europe*, and *The Book of Urizen*.

1795   Blake finishes *The Book of Los*, *The Song of Los*, and *The Book of Ahania*.

1796   James Macpherson dies February 17 in Bellville, Inverness. A committee appointed to investigate the authenticity of his poems finds that Macpherson liberally edited Gaelic poems and inserted verses of his own.
        Robert Burns dies July 21.

1797   Blake begins to write *Vala*, or *The Four Zoas*.

1799   Cowper writes *Montes Glaciales* and *The Castaway*, his last poems.

1800   William Cowper dies April 25.

1804   Blake dates the composition of *Milton* and *Jerusalem* from this year, but they are believed to have been finished later.

1809   Blake writes *A Descriptive Catalogue* to accompany an exhibition of his paintings, containing his remarkable criticism of Chaucer.

1820   Blake completes woodcuts to Virgil's *Pastorals*.

1825   Blake completes engravings for *The Book of Job*.

1826   Blake completes illustrations to Dante.

1827   William Blake dies August 12.

Contributors

HAROLD BLOOM, Sterling Professor of the Humanities at Yale University, is the author of *The Anxiety of Influence*, *Poetry and Repression*, and many other volumes of literary criticism. His forthcoming study, *Freud: Transference and Authority*, attempts a full-scale reading of all of Freud's major writings. A MacArthur Prize Fellow, he is general editor of five series of literary criticism published by Chelsea House.

NORTHROP FRYE is University Professor Emeritus at the University of Toronto. He is the principal literary theorist of our century. His major works include *Fearful Symmetry*, *Anatomy of Criticism*, and *The Great Code: The Bible and Literature*.

GEOFFREY H. HARTMAN is Karl Young Professor of English and Comparative Literature at Yale University. Besides his writings on Wordsworth, his books include *Beyond Formalism* and *Saving the Text*.

MARTIN PRICE is Sterling Professor of English at Yale University. His books include *Swift's Rhetorical Art*, *To the Palace of Wisdom*, and *Forms of Life*.

STEVEN KNAPP teaches English literature at the University of California, Berkeley. He is the author of *Personification and the Sublime: Milton to Coleridge*.

KEN FRIEDEN is Assistant Professor in the Department of Modern Languages and Classics at Emory University. He is the author of *Genius and Monologue* and *The Dream of Interpretation*.

PAUL H. FRY is Associate Professor of English at Yale University. He is the author of *The Poet's Calling in the English Ode* and *The Reach of Criticism*.

PETER M. SACKS teaches in the Writing Seminars at The Johns Hopkins University. He is the author of *The English Elegy* and of *In These Mountains*, a book of poems.

JEAN-PIERRE MILEUR teaches English at the University of California, Riverside. He is the author of *Vision and Revision: Coleridge's Art of Immanence* and *Literary Revisionism and the Burden of Modernity*.

THOMAS WEISKEL taught at Yale University until his tragic accidental death. His masterly book, *The Romantic Sublime*, appeared first in 1976, and is currently being reissued.

PAUL S. SHERWIN is Dean of Humanities at the City College of New York. He is the author of *Precious Bane*, and of essays on Keats and Mary Shelley.

PATRICIA MEYER SPACKS is Professor of English and head of the department at Yale University. Her books include *The Poetry of Vision*, *The Female Imagination*, and *Gossip*.

JOHN L. GREENWAY teaches in the Department of Literature at the University of Kentucky. He has written *The Golden Horns: Mythic Imagination in the Nordic Past*.

DONALD S. TAYLOR teaches in the Department of English at the University of Oregon. He is the author of *Thomas Chatterton's Art: Experiments in Imagined History*.

CAROL McGUIRK is Associate Professor of English at Florida Atlantic University. She has written *Robert Burns and the Sentimental Era*.

Bibliography

Abrams, M. H. *The Mirror and the Lamp*. New York: Oxford University Press, 1953.

Davie, Donald. *Purity of Diction in English Verse*. New York: Oxford University Press, 1953.

Hilles, Frederick W., and Harold Bloom, eds. *From Sensibility to Romanticism*. New York: Oxford University Press, 1965.

Monk, Samuel H. *The Sublime: A Study of Critical Theories in Eighteenth-Century England*. New York: Modern Language Association of America, 1935.

Price, Martin. *To the Palace of Wisdom: Studies in Order and Energy from Dryden to Blake*. Garden City, N.Y.: Doubleday and Company, 1964.

Spacks, Patricia Meyer. *The Poetry of Vision*. Cambridge: Harvard University Press, 1967.

Wasserman, Earl R. *The Subtler Language: Critical Readings of Neoclassic and Romantic Poems*. Baltimore: The Johns Hopkins University Press, 1959.

JAMES THOMSON

Campbell, Hilbert H. *James Thomson*. Boston: G. K. Hall, 1979.

Cohen, Ralph. *The Art of Discrimination: Thomson's* The Seasons *and the Language of Criticism*. Berkeley: University of California Press, 1964.

Grant, Douglas. *James Thomson: Poet of the Seasons*. London: Cresset Press, 1951.

Jones, William Powell. *The Rhetoric of Science: A Study of Scientific Ideas and Imagery in Eighteenth-Century English Poetry*. Berkeley: University of California Press, 1966.

Tillotson, Geoffrey. *Augustan Poetic Diction*. London: Athlone Press, 1964.

Wasserman, Earl R. *Elizabethan Poetry in the Eighteenth Century*, 110–22. Urbana: University of Illinois Press, 1947.

THOMAS GRAY

Brooks, Cleanth. *The Well-Wrought Urn: Studies in the Structure of Poetry*. New York: Reynal and Hitchcock, 1947.

Cecil, David. *Two Quiet Lives*. London: Constable, 1948.

Empson, William. *Some Versions of the Pastoral*. London: Chatto and Windus, 1935.

Golden, Morris. *Thomas Gray*. New York: Twayne Publishers, 1964.

Hagstrum, Jean H. *The Sister Arts: The Tradition of Literary Pictorialism and English Poetry from Dryden to Gray*. Chicago: The University of Chicago Press, 1958.

Jones, William Powell. *Thomas Gray, Scholar: The True Tragedy of an Eighteenth-Century Gentleman*. Cambridge: Harvard University Press, 1937.

Ketton-Cremer, R. W. *Thomas Gray*. Cambridge: Cambridge University Press, 1955.

Maclean, Norman. "From Action to Image: Theories of the Lyric in the Eighteenth Century." In *Critics and Criticism*, edited by R. S. Crane, 408–60. Chicago: The University of Chicago Press, 1952.

Reed, Amy Louise. *The Background of Gray's Elegy: A Study in the Taste for Melancholy Poetry 1700–1751*. New York: Columbia University Press, 1924.

Sells, Arthur Lytton. *Thomas Gray: His Life and Works*. Boston: George Allen & Unwin, 1980.

WILLIAM COLLINS

Ainsworth, Edward Gay, Jr. *Poor Collins*. Ithaca, N.Y.: Cornell University Press, 1937.

Brown, Merle E. "On William Collins's 'Ode to Evening.' " *Essays in Criticism* 11 (April 1961): 136–53.

Carver, P. L. *The Life of a Poet*. London: Sidgewick & Jackson, 1967.

Doughty, Oswald. *William Collins*. London: Longmans Green, 1964.

Garrod, H. W. *Collins*. Oxford: Oxford University Press, 1928.

New, Melvyn. "Surviving the Seventies: Sterne, Collins, and Their Recent Critics." *The Eighteenth Century* 25, no. 1 (1984): 3–24.

Sherwin, Paul S. *Precious Bane: Collins and the Miltonic Legacy*. Austin: University of Texas Press, 1977.

Sigworth, Oliver F. *William Collins*. New York: Twayne Publishers, 1965.

Wendorf, Richard. *William Collins and Eighteenth-Century English Poetry*. Minneapolis: University of Minnesota Press, 1981.

CHRISTOPHER SMART

Ainsworth, Edward Gay. *Christopher Smart*. Columbia: University of Missouri Press, 1943.

Blaydes, Sophia B. *Christopher Smart as Poet of His Time*. The Hague: Mouton, 1966.

Dearnley, Moira. *The Poetry of Christopher Smart*. London: Routledge & Kegan Paul, 1968.

Devlin, Christopher. *Poor Kit Smart*. London: Rupert Hart-Davis, 1961.

Friedman, John Block. "The Cosmology of Praise: Smart's *Jubilate Agno*." *PMLA* 82 (1967): 250–56.

Sherbo, Arthur. *Christopher Smart: Scholar of the University*. East Lansing, Mich.: Michigan State University Press, 1967.

WILLIAM COWPER

Cecil, Lord David. *The Stricken Deer, or, The Life of Cowper*. Indianapolis: The Bobbs-Merrill Company, 1930.

Free, William N. *William Cowper*. New York: Twayne Publishers, 1970.

Golden, Morris. *In Search of Stability: The Poetry of William Cowper*. New York: Brookman Associates, 1960.

Hartley, Lodwick Charles. *William Cowper: The Continuing Revelation*. Chapel Hill: University of North Carolina Press, 1960.

Hutchings, Bill. *The Poetry of William Cowper*. London: Croom Helm, 1983.

Memes, John Smythe. *The Life of William Cowper*. Port Washington, N.Y.: The Kennikat Press, 1972.

Newey, Vincent. *Cowper's Poetry: A Critical Study and Reassessment*. Liverpool: Liverpool University Press, 1982.

Nicholson, Norman. *William Cowper*. London: J. Lehmann, 1951.

Priestman, Martin. *Cowper's Task: Structure and Influence*. New York: Cambridge University Press, 1983.

Quinlan, Maurice James. *William Cowper: A Critical Life*. Minneapolis: University of Minnesota Press, 1953.

JAMES MACPHERSON

Nutt, Alfred Trubner. *Ossian and the Ossianic Literature*. New York: AMS Press, 1972.

Smart, John Semple. *James Macpherson*. New York: AMS Press, 1973.

Stewart, Larry L. "Ossian, Burke, and the 'Joy of Grief.'" *English Language Notes* 15, no. 1 (September 1977): 29–32.

THOMAS CHATTERTON

Kelly, Linda. *The Marvelous Boy: The Life and Myth of Thomas Chatterton*. London: Weidenfeld and Nicolson, 1971.

Meyerstein, E. W. H. *A Life of Thomas Chatterton*. New York: Charles Scribner's Sons, 1930.

Nevill, John Cranston. *Thomas Chatterton*. London: F. Muller, 1948.

Taylor, Donald S. *Thomas Chatterton's Art: Experiments in Imagined History*. Princeton: Princeton University Press, 1978.

WILLIAM BLAKE

Adams, Hazard. *Blake and Yeats: The Contrary Vision*. New York: Russell and Russell, 1968.

Ault, Donald. *Visionary Physics: Blake's Response to Newton*. Chicago: The University of Chicago Press, 1974.

Beer, John. *Blake's Humanism*. Manchester: Manchester University Press, 1968.

Behrendt, Stephen C. *The Moment of Explosion: Blake and the Illustration of Milton*. Lincoln: University of Nebraska Press, 1983.

Bloom, Harold. *Blake's Apocalypse: A Study in Poetic Argument*. Ithaca, N.Y.: Cornell University Press, 1970.

Bronowski, Jacob. *William Blake and the Age of Revolution*. London: Routledge & Kegan Paul, 1972.

Curran, Stuart, and Joseph Wittreich, Jr., eds. *Blake's Sublime Allegory: Essays on* The Four Zoas, Milton, Jerusalem. Madison: University of Wisconsin Press, 1973.

Damon, Samuel Foster. *William Blake: His Philosophy and Symbols*. Gloucester, Mass.: P. Smith, 1978.

Damrosch, Leopold. *Symbol and Truth in Blake's Myth*. Princeton: Princeton University Press, 1980.

Erdman, David V. *Blake: Prophet against Empire*. Princeton: Princeton University Press, 1969.

Essick, Robert N. *The Visionary Hand: Essays for the Study of William Blake's Art and Aesthetics*. Los Angeles: Hennesy and Ingalls, 1973.

Fisher, Peter F. *The Valley of Vision*, edited by Northrop Frye. Toronto: University of Toronto Press, 1961.

Fox, Susan. *Poetic Form in Blake's* Milton. Princeton: Princeton University Press, 1976.

Frosch, Thomas R. *The Awakening of Albion: The Renovation of the Body in the Poetry of William Blake*. Ithaca, N.Y.: Cornell University Press, 1974.

Frye, Northrop. *Fearful Symmetry: A Study of William Blake*. Princeton: Princeton University Press, 1947, 1974.

Gallant, Christine. *Blake and the Assimilation of Chaos*. Princeton: Princeton University Press, 1978.

George, Diana Hume. *Blake and Freud*. Ithaca, N.Y.: Cornell University Press, 1980.

Gillham, D. G. *William Blake*. London: Cambridge University Press, 1973.

Glechner, Robert F. *The Piper and the Bard: A Study of William Blake*. Detroit: Wayne State University Press, 1959.

Hagstrom, Jean H. *William Blake: Poet and Painter, an Introduction to the Illuminated Verse*. Chicago: The University of Chicago Press, 1964.

Harper, George Mills. *The Neoplatonism of William Blake*. Chapel Hill: The University of North Carolina Press, 1961.

Hilton, Nelson. *Literal Imagination: Blake's Vision of Words*. Berkeley: University of California Press, 1983.

Howard, John. *Blake's* Milton: *A Study of the Selfhood*. Rutherford, N.J.: Fairleigh Dickinson University Press, 1976.

Jackson, Wallace. *The Probable and the Marvelous: Blake, Wordsworth and the 18th-Century Critical Tradition*. Athens: University of Georgia Press, 1978.

James, David E. "Blake's 'Laocoon': A Degree Zero of Literary Production." *PMLA* 98, no. 3 (March 1983): 226–36.

Keynes, Geoffrey. *Blake Studies: Essays on His Life and Work*. 2nd ed. New York: Oxford University Press, 1971.

Klonsky, Milton. *William Blake: The Seer and His Visions*. New York: Harmony Books, 1977.

Mellor, Anne Kostelanetz. *Blake's Human Form Divine*. Berkeley: University of California Press, 1974.

Mitchell, W. J. T. *Blake's Composite Art: A Study of the Illuminated Poetry*. Princeton: Princeton University Press, 1978.

Nurmi, Martin K. *William Blake*. Kent: Ohio State University Press, 1976.

O'Neill, Judith, ed. *Critics on Blake*. Coral Gables, Fla.: University of Miami Press, 1970.

Paley, Morton D. *Energy and Imagination: A Study of the Development of Blake's Thought*. Oxford: Clarendon Press, 1970.

Raine, Kathleen Jessie. *William Blake*. London: Thames and Hudson, 1970.

————. *Blake and the New Age*. Boston: George Allen and Unwin, 1979.

Sabri-Tabrizi, G. F. *The "Heaven" and "Hell" of William Blake*. London: Lawrence and Wishart, 1975.

Schorer, Mark. *William Blake: The Politics of Vision*. New York: Vintage Books, 1959.

Van Sinderen, Adrian. *Blake and the Mystic Genius*. Syracuse, N.Y.: Syracuse University Press, 1949.

Vogler, Thomas A. *Preludes to Vision: The Epic Venture in Blake, Wordsworth, Keats and Hart Crane*. Berkeley: University of California Press, 1971.

Wagenknecht, David. *Blake's Night: William Blake and the Idea of the Pastoral*. Cambridge, Mass.: The Belknap Press, 1973.

Witcutt, William Purcell. *Blake: A Psychological Study*. Folcroft, Pa.: Folcroft Library Editions, 1974.

ROBERT BURNS

Crawford, Thomas. *Burns: A Study of the Poems and Songs*. Palo Alto, Calif.: Stanford University Press, 1960.

Daiches, David. *Robert Burns*. New York: Macmillan, 1967.

————. *Robert Burns and His World*. London: Thames and Hudson, 1971.

Jack, R. D. S., and Andrew Noble, eds. *The Art of Robert Burns*. London: Vision Press, 1982.

Low, Donald A. *Critical Essays on Robert Burns*. Boston: Routledge & Kegan Paul, 1975.

Acknowledgments

"Towards Defining an Age of Sensibility" by Northrop Frye from *Fables of Identity* by Northrop Frye, © 1963 by Harcourt Brace Jovanovich, Inc. Reprinted by permission of the publisher.

"False Themes and Gentle Minds" by Geoffrey H. Hartman from *Beyond Formalism* by Geoffrey H. Hartman, © 1970 by Yale University. Reprinted by permission of Yale University Press.

"The Sublime Poem: Pictures and Powers" by Martin Price from *The Yale Review* 58, no. 2 (Winter 1969), © 1969 by Yale University. Reprinted by permission.

"Sublime Personification: Implications for Poetic Practice" by Steven Knapp from *Personification and the Sublime: Milton to Coleridge* by Steven Knapp, © 1985 by The President and Fellows of Harvard College. Reprinted by permission of Harvard University Press.

"The Eighteenth-Century Introjection of Genius" by Ken Frieden from *Genius and Monologue* by Ken Frieden, © 1985 by Cornell University. Reprinted by permission of Cornell University Press.

"The Theatre of Mind: Edward Young and James Thomson" (originally entitled "The Theatre of Mind") by Martin Price from *To the Palace of Wisdom* by Martin Price, © 1964 by Martin Price. Reprinted by permission of Doubleday & Company, Inc. and the author.

"Thomas Gray's Feather'd Cincture: The Odes" (originally entitled "Thomas Gray's Feather'd Cincture") by Paul H. Fry from *The Poet's Calling in the English Ode* by Paul H. Fry, © 1980 by Yale University. Reprinted by permission of Yale University Press.

"Gray's 'Elegy' " (originally entitled "Johnson, Dryden, and Gray") by Peter M. Sacks from *The English Elegy: Studies in the Genre from Spenser to Yeats* by Peter M. Sacks, © 1985 by The Johns Hopkins University Press, Baltimore/London. Reprinted by permission.

"Thomas Gray" by Jean-Pierre Mileur from *Literary Revisionism and the Burden of Modernity* by Jean-Pierre Mileur, © 1985 by The Regents of the University of California. Reprinted by permission of the University of California Press.

"William Collins's 'Ode on the Poetical Character' " (originally entitled "The Sublime as Romance: Two Texts from Collins") by Thomas Weiskel from *The Romantic Sublime: Studies in the Structure and Psychology of Transcendence* by Thomas Weiskel, © 1976 by The Johns Hopkins University Press, Baltimore/London. Reprinted by permission.

"Collins's 'Ode to Evening' " (originally entitled "The 'Ode to Evening' ") by Paul S. Sherwin from *Precious Bane: Collins and the Miltonic Legacy* by Paul S. Sherwin, © 1977 by the University of Texas Press, Austin. Reprinted by permission of the author and the publisher.

"From Topos to Trope: Collins's 'Ode to Fear' " (originally entitled "From Topos to Trope, From Sensibility to Romanticism: Collins's 'Ode to Fear' ") by Harold Bloom from *Studies in 18th-Century British Art and Aesthetics*, edited by Ralph Cohen, © 1983 by Harold Bloom. Reprinted by permission.

"Christopher Smart's 'Magnificat' " by Geoffrey H. Hartman from *The Fate of Reading and Other Essays* by Geoffrey H. Hartman, © 1975 by The University of Chicago. Reprinted by permission of The University of Chicago Press.

"William Cowper: The Heightened Perception" by Patricia Meyer Spacks from *The Poetry of Vision* by Patricia Meyer Spacks, © 1967 by The President and Fellows of Harvard College. Reprinted by permission of Harvard University Press.

"Macpherson's Ossian and the Nordic Bard as Myth" (originally entitled "The Gateway to Innocence: Ossian and the Nordic Bard as Myth") by John L. Greenway from *Studies in Eighteenth-Century Culture* 4 (1975) edited by Harold E. Pagliaro, © 1975 by the American Society for Eighteenth-Century Studies. Reprinted by permission.

"Chatterton's Art: *Ælla*" (originally entitled "The Rowleyan Works") by Donald S. Taylor from *Thomas Chatterton's Art: Experiments in Imagined History* by Donald S. Taylor, © 1978 by Princeton University Press. Reprinted by permission.

"William Blake's *Poetical Sketches*" (originally entitled "William Blake") by Harold Bloom from *The Visionary Company* by Harold Bloom, © 1961 by Harold Bloom. Reprinted by permission of the publisher, Cornell University Press.

"Robert Burns as Bard: The Songs" (originally entitled "The Songs") by Carol McGuirk from *Robert Burns and the Sentimental Era* by Carol McGuirk, © 1985 by the University of Georgia Press. Reprinted by permission of the publisher.

Index